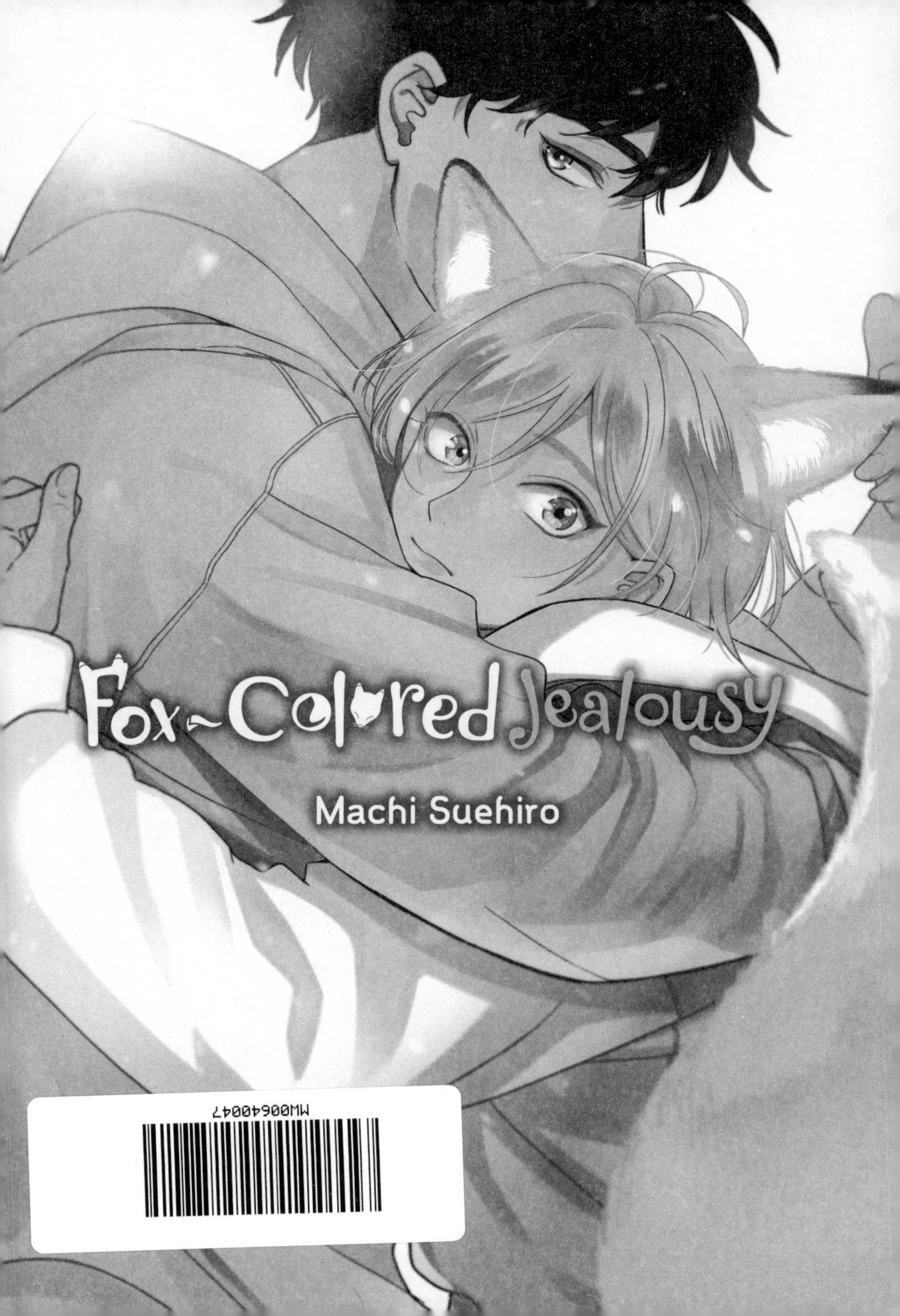
Fox-Colored Jealousy
Machi Suehiro

Fox~Colored Jealousy

CONTENTS

Chapter 1

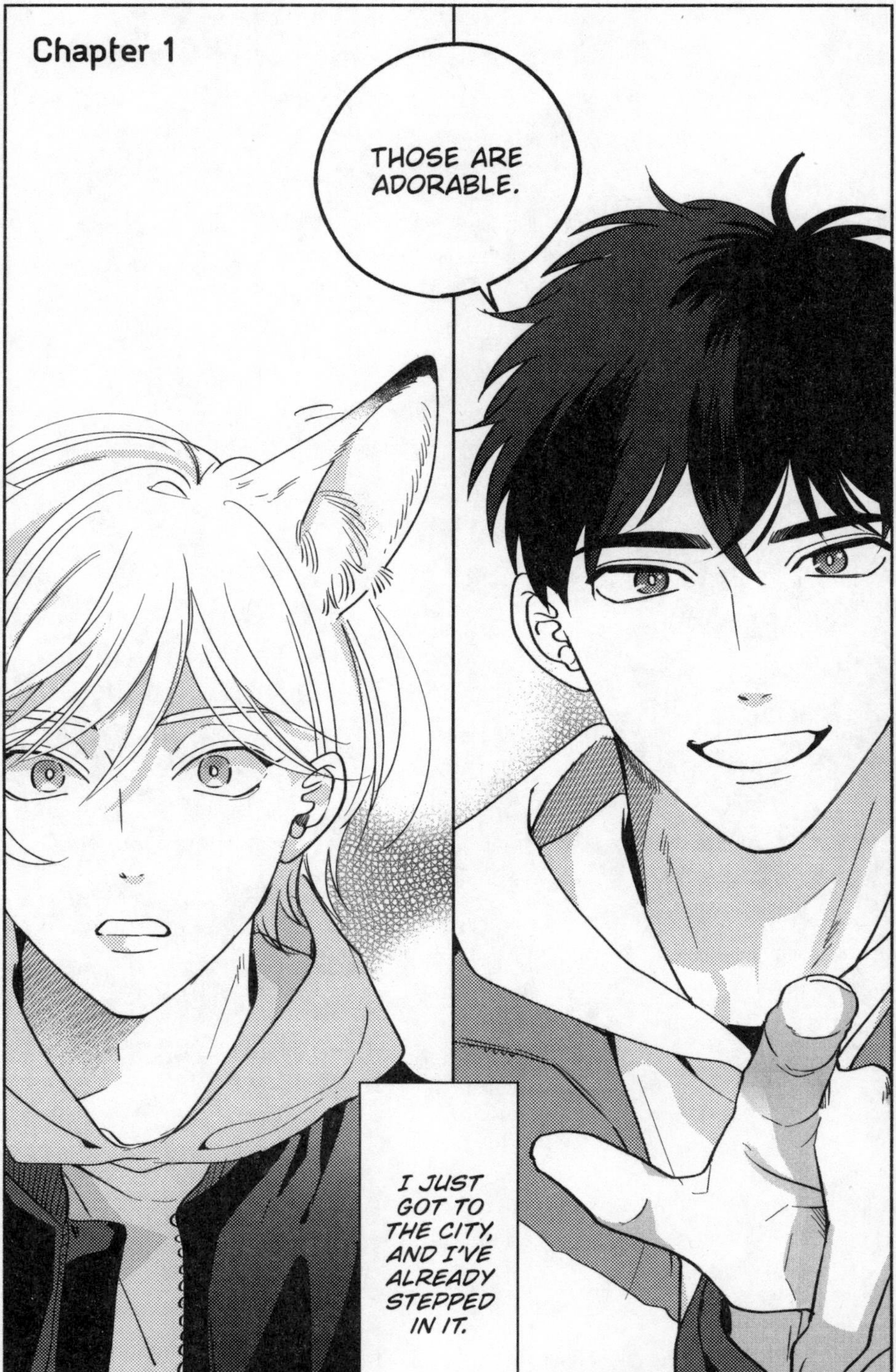
THOSE ARE ADORABLE.
I JUST GOT TO THE CITY, AND I'VE ALREADY STEPPED IN IT.

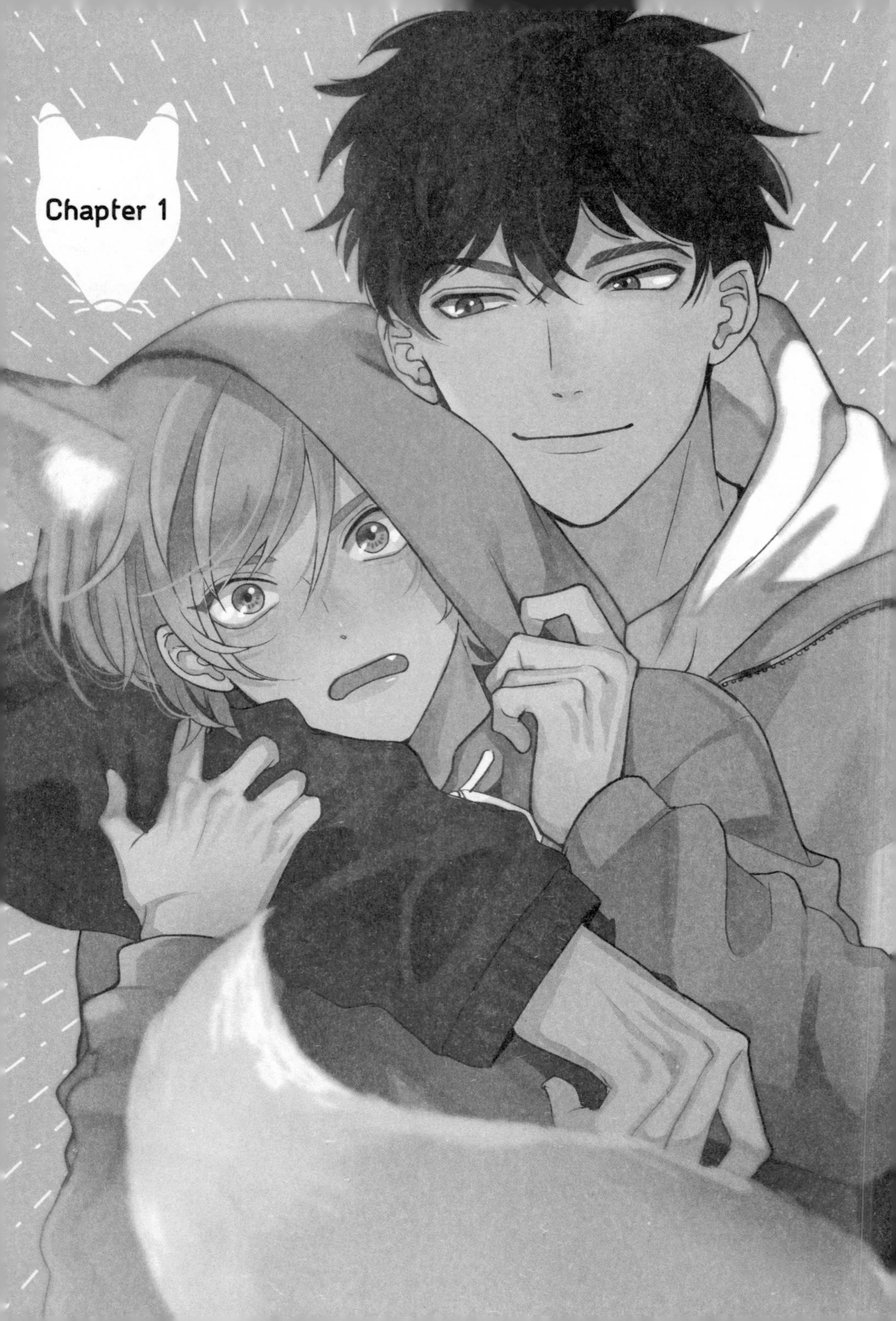
Chapter 1

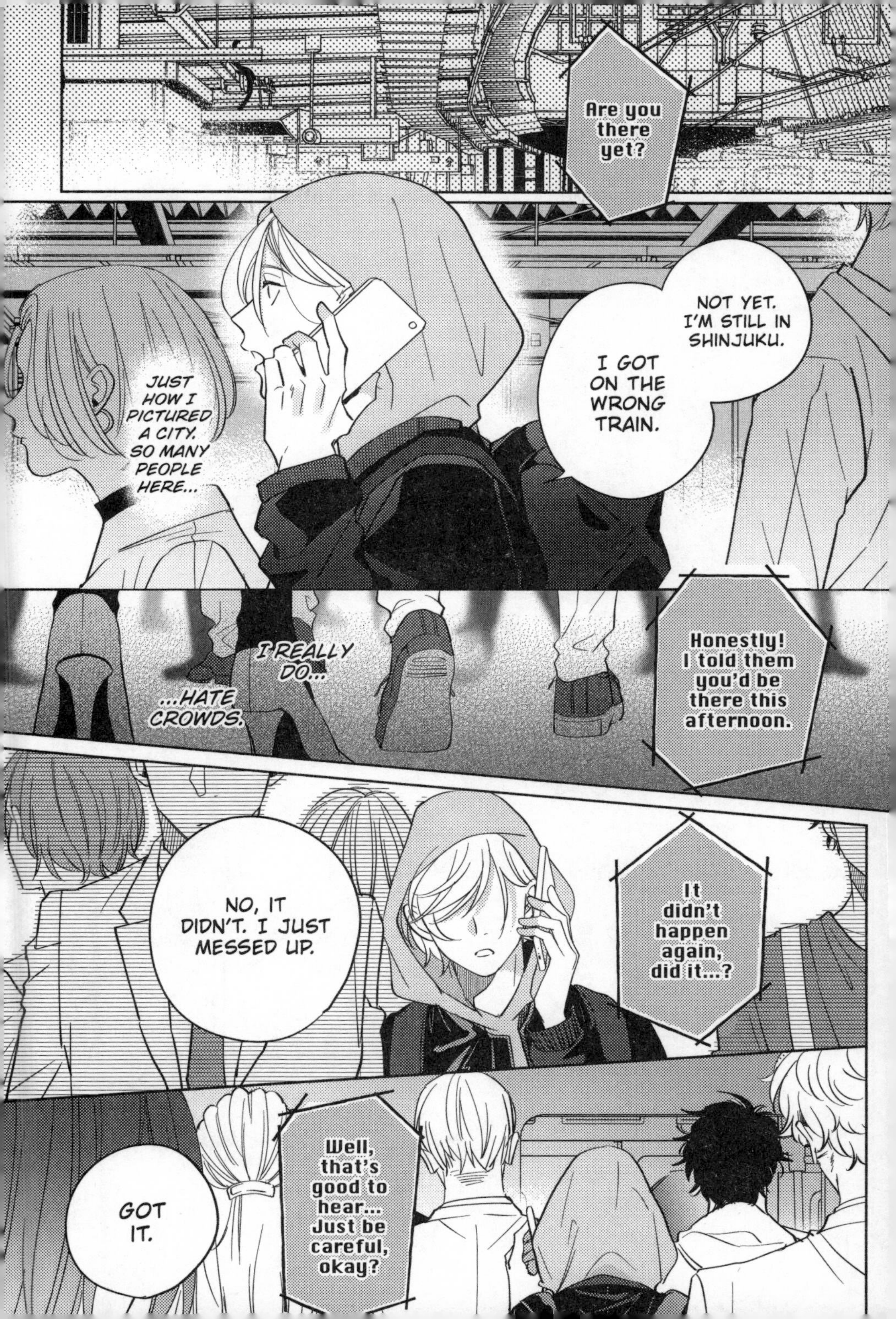

Are you there yet?
NOT YET. I'M STILL IN SHINJUKU.
I GOT ON THE WRONG TRAIN.
JUST HOW I PICTURED A CITY. SO MANY PEOPLE HERE...
Honestly! I told them you'd be there this afternoon.
I REALLY DO...
...HATE CROWDS.
It didn't happen again, did it...?
NO, IT DIDN'T. I JUST MESSED UP.
Well, that's good to hear... Just be careful, okay?
GOT IT.

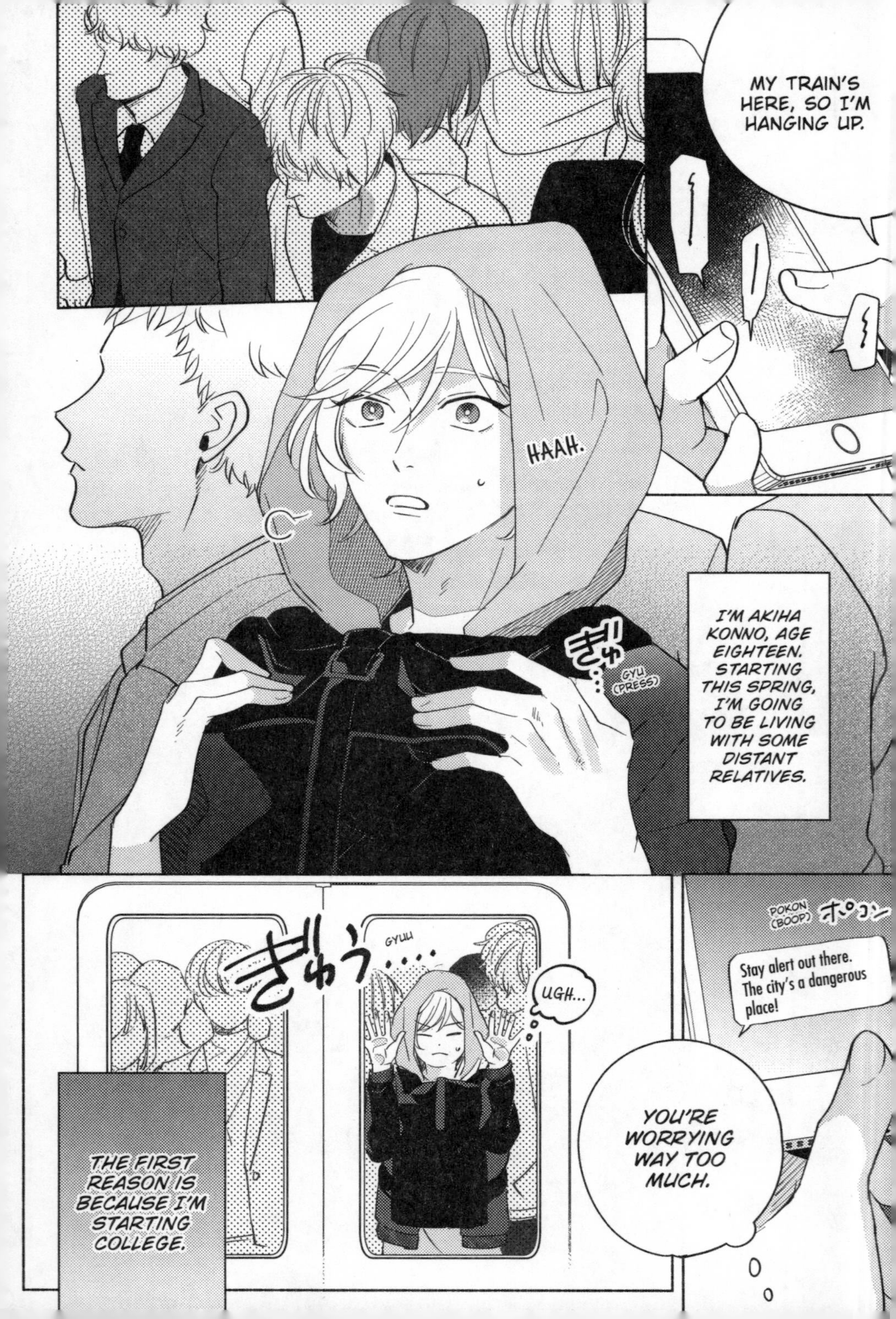
MY TRAIN'S HERE, SO I'M HANGING UP.
HAAH.
ぎゅ…
GYU (PRESS)
I'M AKIHA KONNO, AGE EIGHTEEN. STARTING THIS SPRING, I'M GOING TO BE LIVING WITH SOME DISTANT RELATIVES.
POKON (BOOP) ポコン
Stay alert out there. The city's a dangerous place!
YOU'RE WORRYING WAY TOO MUCH.
ぎゅう….
GYUU
UGH...
THE FIRST REASON IS BECAUSE I'M STARTING COLLEGE.

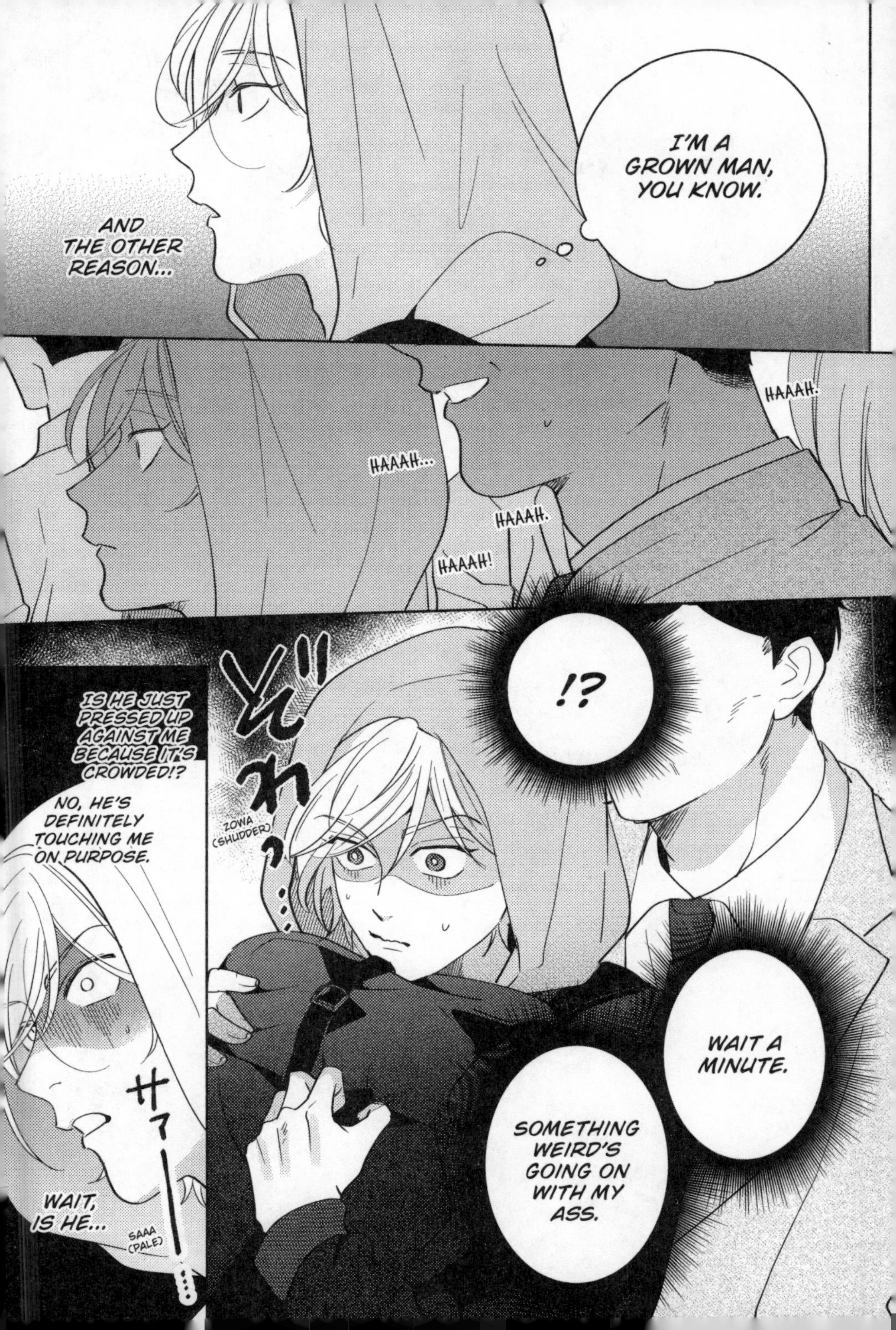
I'M A GROWN MAN, YOU KNOW.
AND THE OTHER REASON...
HAAAH.
HAAAH...
HAAAH.
HAAAH!
!?
ZOWA (SHUDDER)
WAIT A MINUTE.
SOMETHING WEIRD'S GOING ON WITH MY ASS.
IS HE JUST PRESSED UP AGAINST ME BECAUSE IT'S CROWDED!?
NO, HE'S DEFINITELY TOUCHING ME ON PURPOSE.
WAIT, IS HE...
SAAA (PALE)

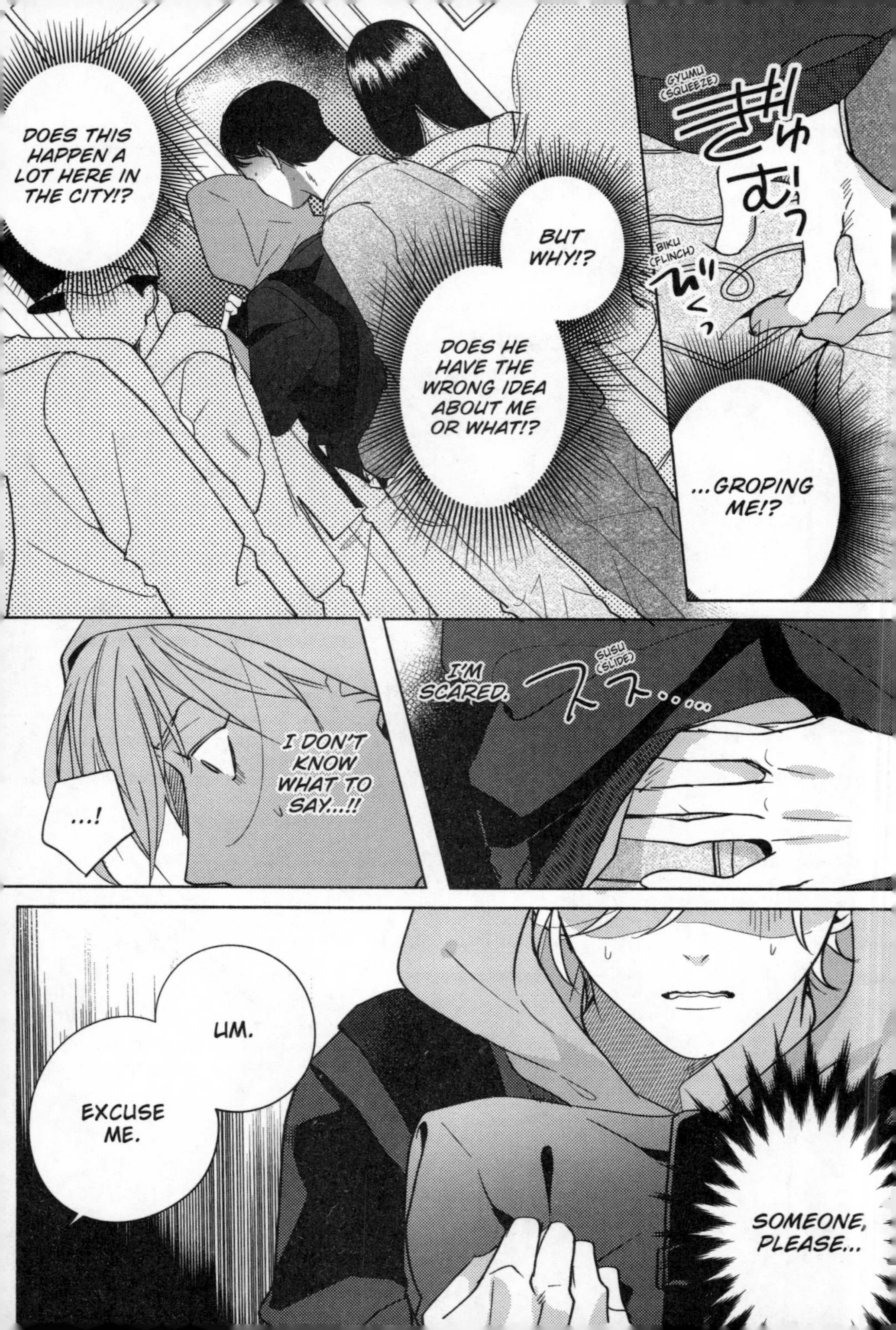
GYUMU (SQUEEZE)
ぎゅむっ
BIKU (FLINCH)
びくっ
...GROPING ME!?
BUT WHY!?
DOES THIS HAPPEN A LOT HERE IN THE CITY!?
DOES HE HAVE THE WRONG IDEA ABOUT ME OR WHAT!?
I'M SCARED.
SUSU (SLIDE)
スス……
I DON'T KNOW WHAT TO SAY...!!
...!
SOMEONE, PLEASE...
UM.
EXCUSE ME.

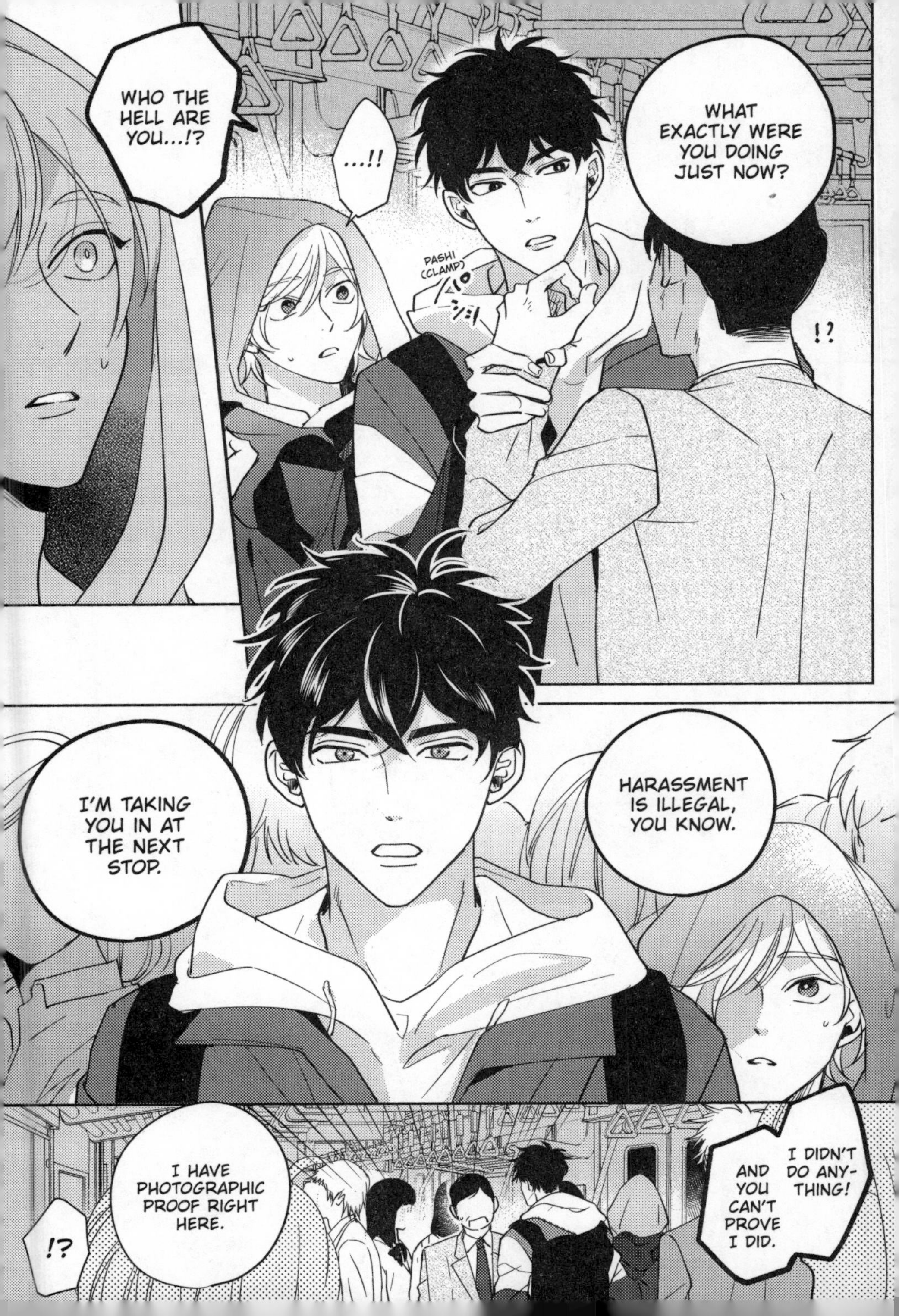
WHAT EXACTLY WERE YOU DOING JUST NOW?
!?
PASHI (CLAMP)
...!!
WHO THE HELL ARE YOU...!?
HARASSMENT IS ILLEGAL, YOU KNOW.
I'M TAKING YOU IN AT THE NEXT STOP.
I DIDN'T DO ANYTHING!
AND YOU CAN'T PROVE I DID.
I HAVE PHOTOGRAPHIC PROOF RIGHT HERE.
!?

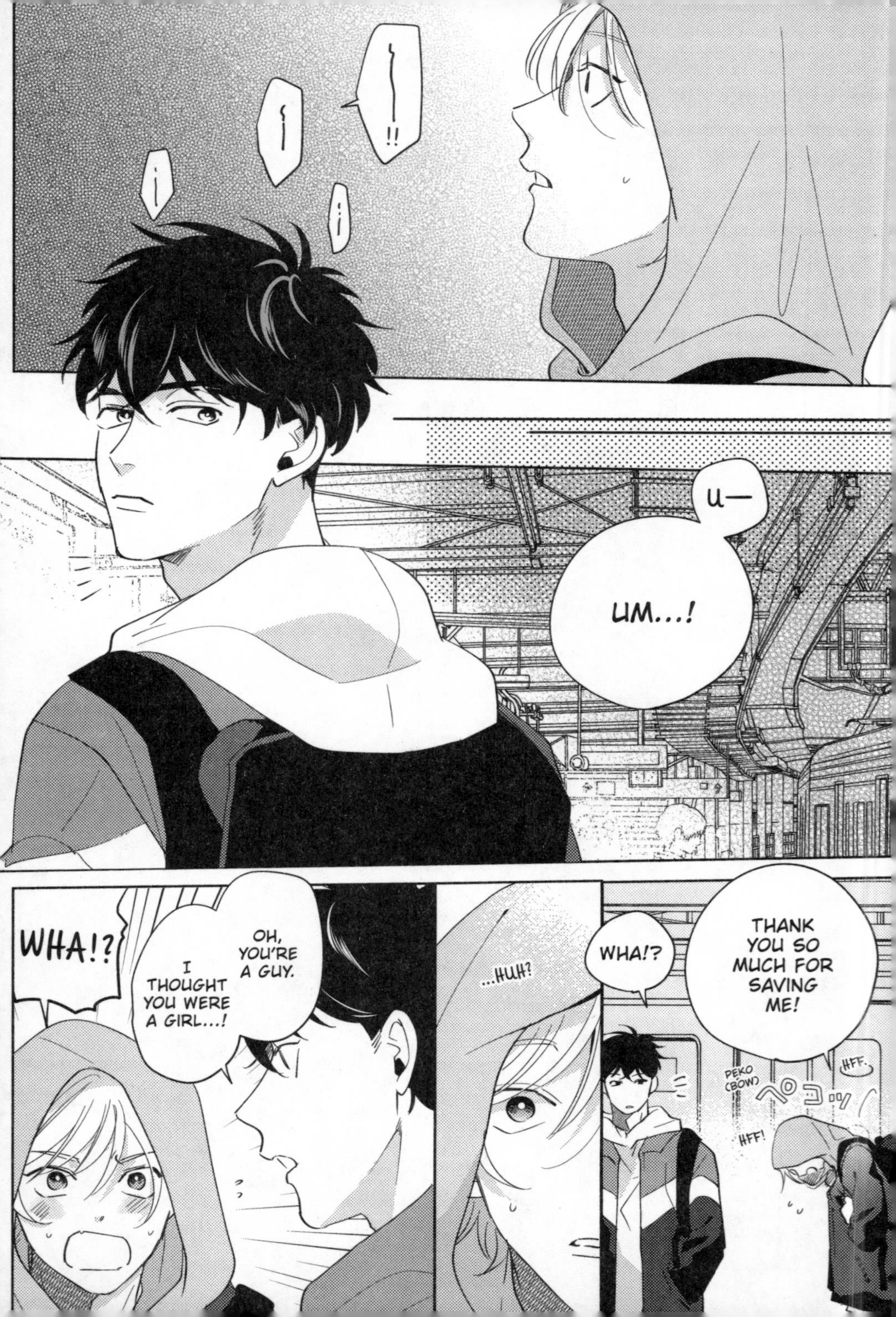
U—
UM...!
THANK YOU SO MUCH FOR SAVING ME!
HFF.
PEKO (BOW)
HFF!
WHA!?
...HUH?
OH, YOU'RE A GUY.
I THOUGHT YOU WERE A GIRL...!
WHA!?

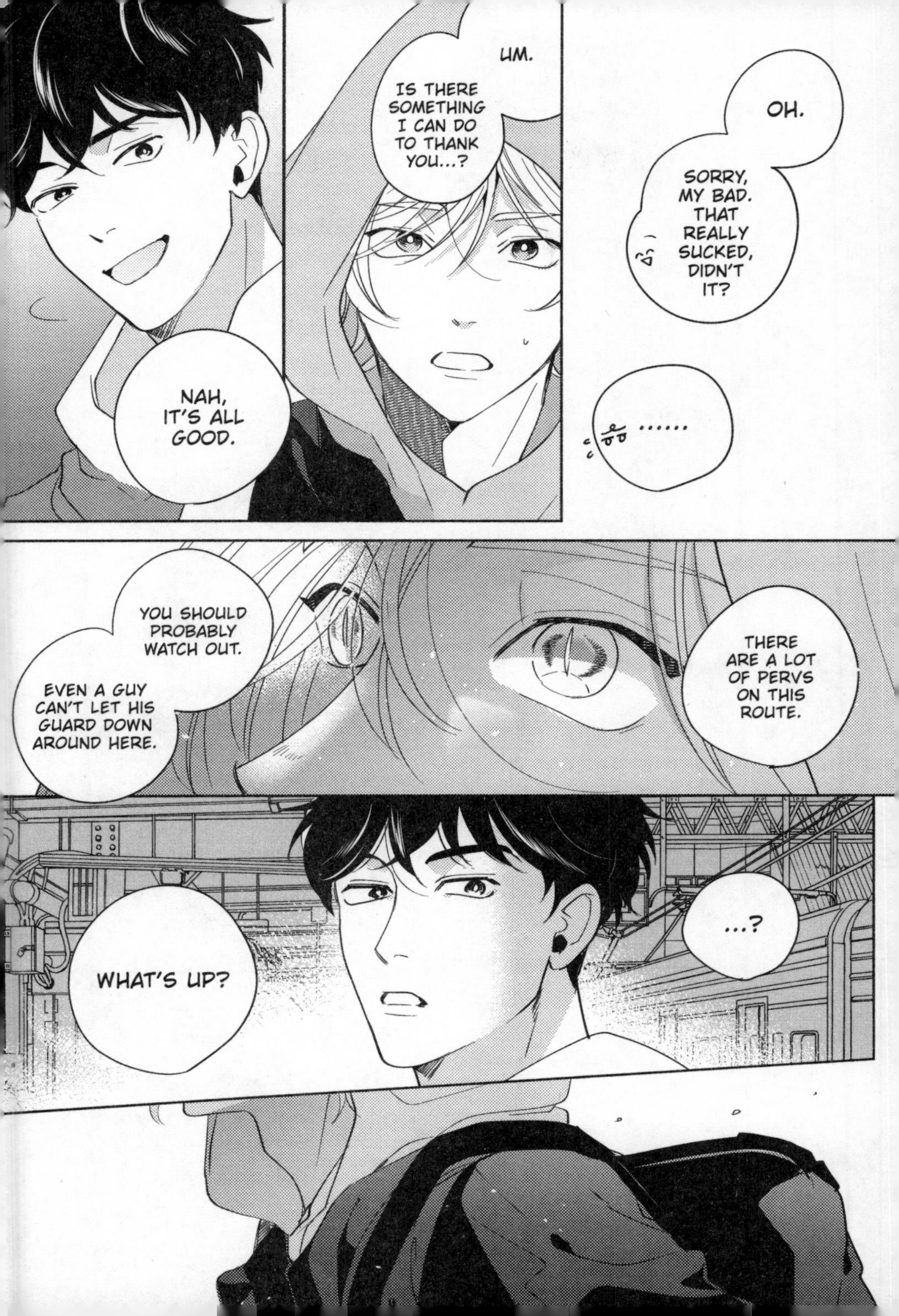
OH.
SORRY, MY BAD. THAT REALLY SUCKED, DIDN'T IT?
......
UM.
IS THERE SOMETHING I CAN DO TO THANK YOU...?
NAH, IT'S ALL GOOD.
THERE ARE A LOT OF PERVS ON THIS ROUTE.
YOU SHOULD PROBABLY WATCH OUT.
EVEN A GUY CAN'T LET HIS GUARD DOWN AROUND HERE.
...?
WHAT'S UP?

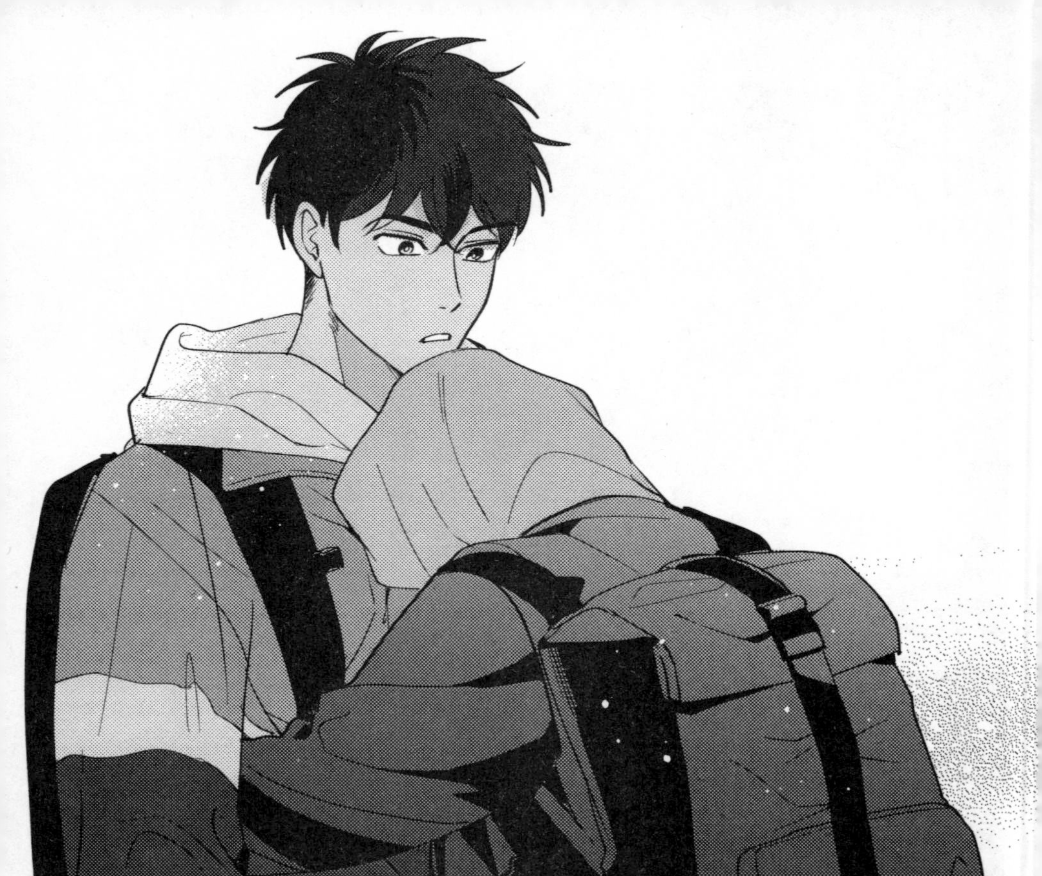

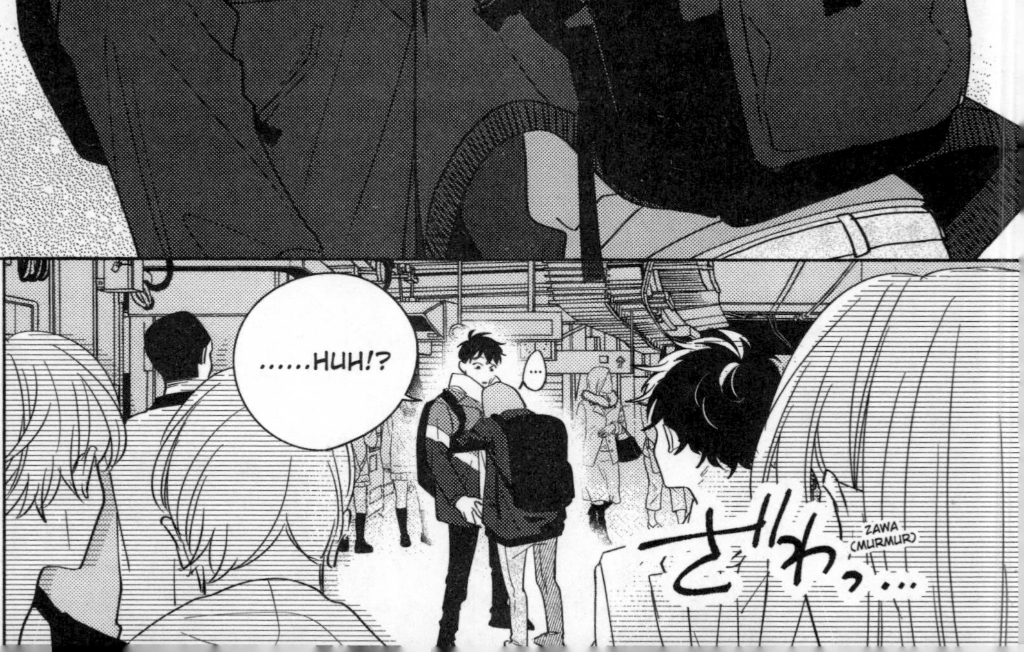
......HUH!?
...
ざわっ...
ZAWA
(MURMUR)

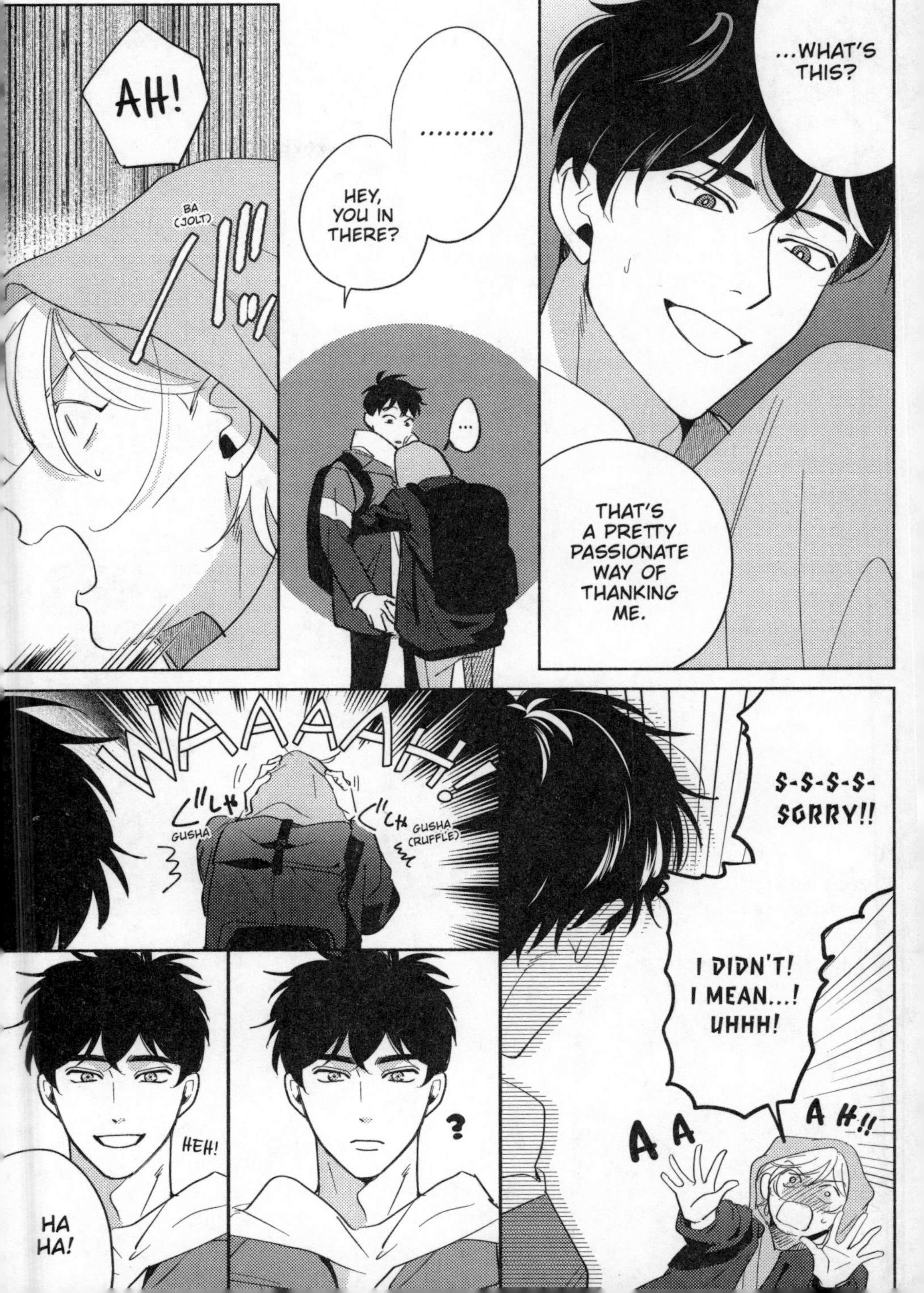
...WHAT'S THIS?
THAT'S A PRETTY PASSIONATE WAY OF THANKING ME.
....
HEY, YOU IN THERE?
...
AH!
BA (JOLT)
S-S-S-S-SORRY!!
I DIDN'T! I MEAN...! UHHH!
A A A H!!
WAAAAH!
ぐしゃ GUSHA (RUFFLE)
ぐしゃ GUSHA
?
HEH!
HA HA!

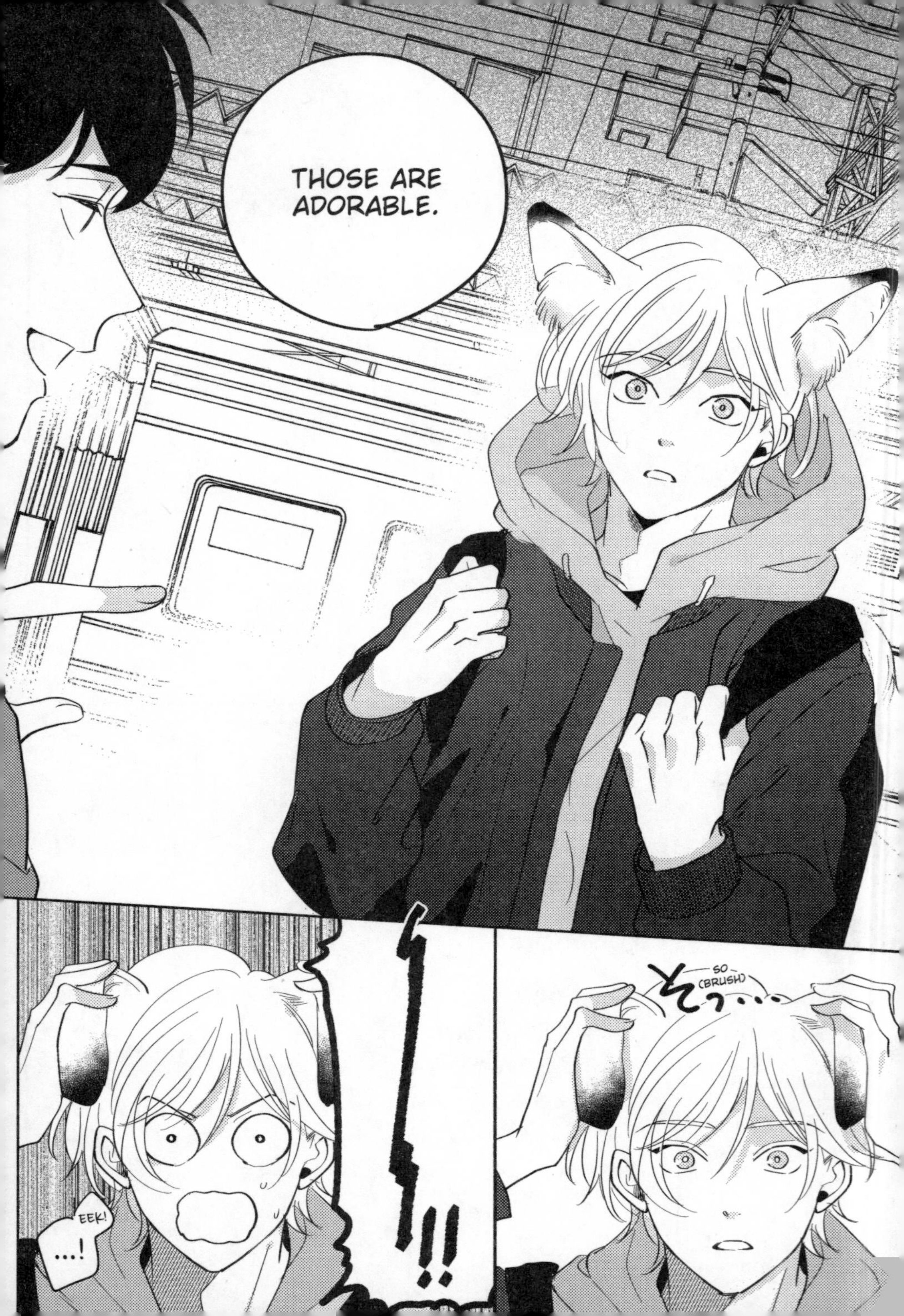
THOSE ARE ADORABLE.
そっ…
SO (BRUSH)
!!
EEK!
...!

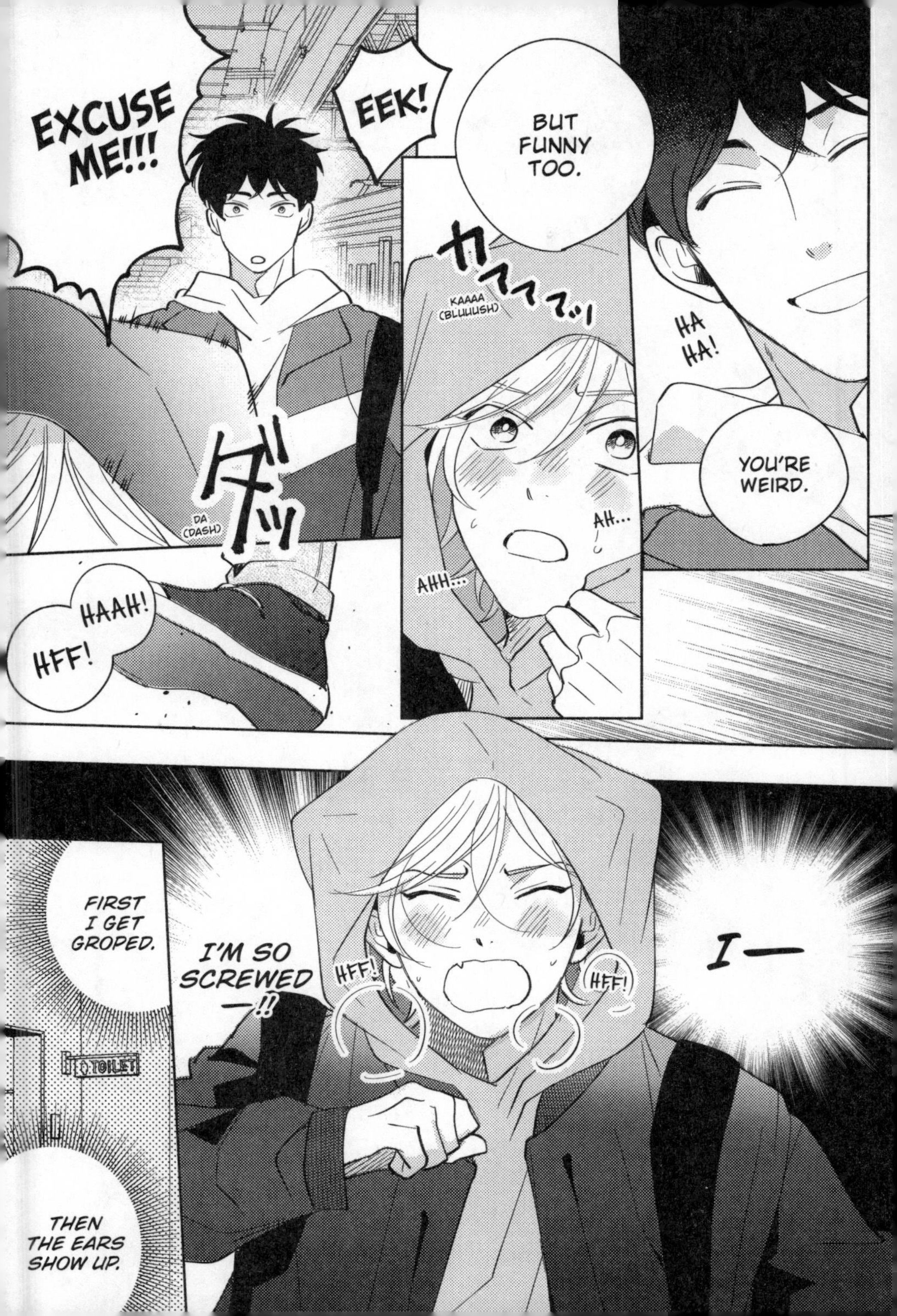
HA HA!
YOU'RE WEIRD.
BUT FUNNY TOO.
カァァァッ
KAAAA (BLUUUSH)
AH...
AHH...
EEK!
EXCUSE ME!!!
ダッ
DA (DASH)
HAAH!
HFF!
I—
HFF!
HFF!
I'M SO SCREWED—!!
FIRST I GET GROPED.
TOILET
THEN THE EARS SHOW UP.

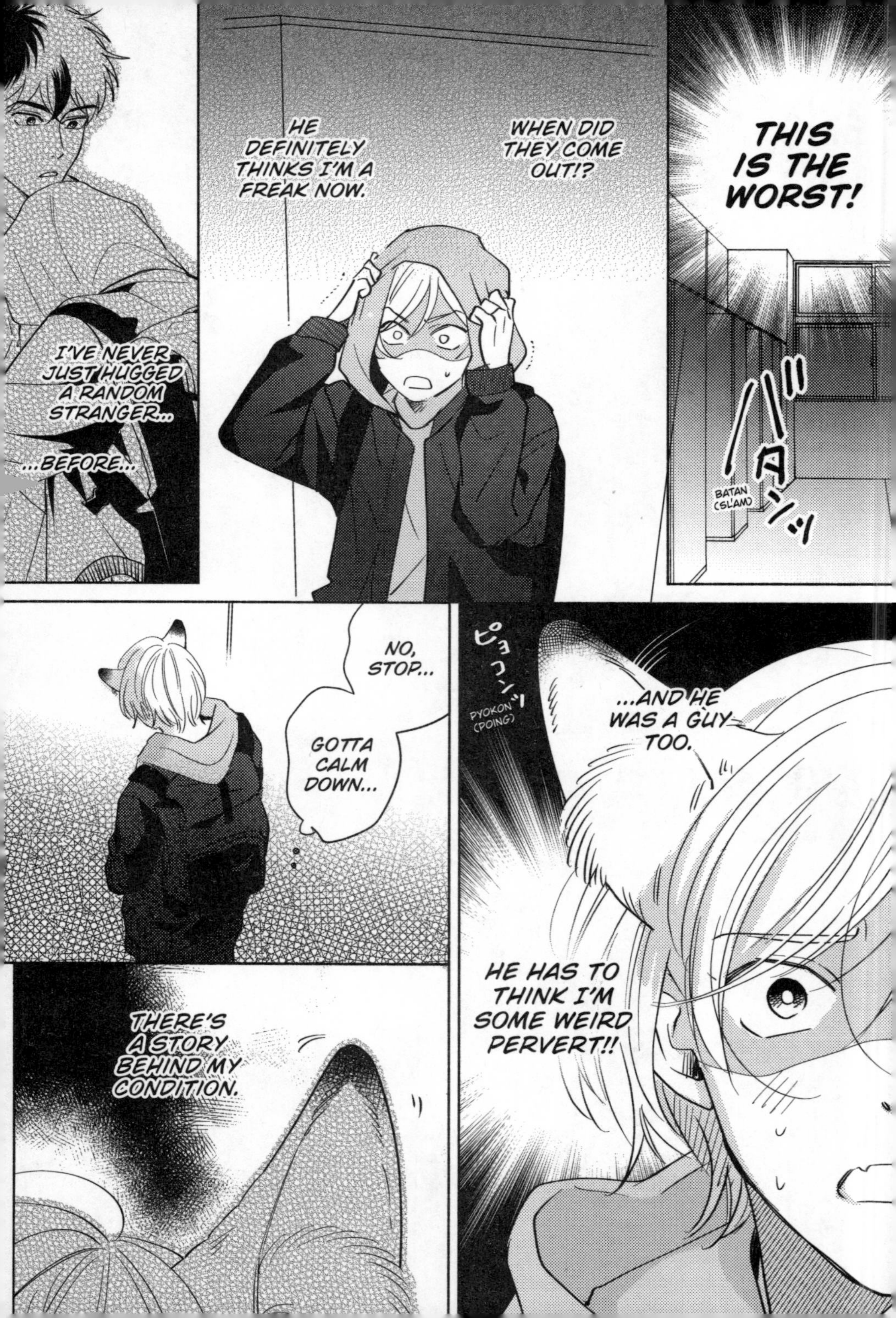
THIS IS THE WORST!
バタンッ
BATAN (SLAM)
WHEN DID THEY COME OUT!?
HE DEFINITELY THINKS I'M A FREAK NOW.
I'VE NEVER JUST HUGGED A RANDOM STRANGER...
...BEFORE...
ピョコンッ
PYOKON (POING)
...AND HE WAS A GUY TOO.
HE HAS TO THINK I'M SOME WEIRD PERVERT!!
NO, STOP...
GOTTA CALM DOWN...
THERE'S A STORY BEHIND MY CONDITION.

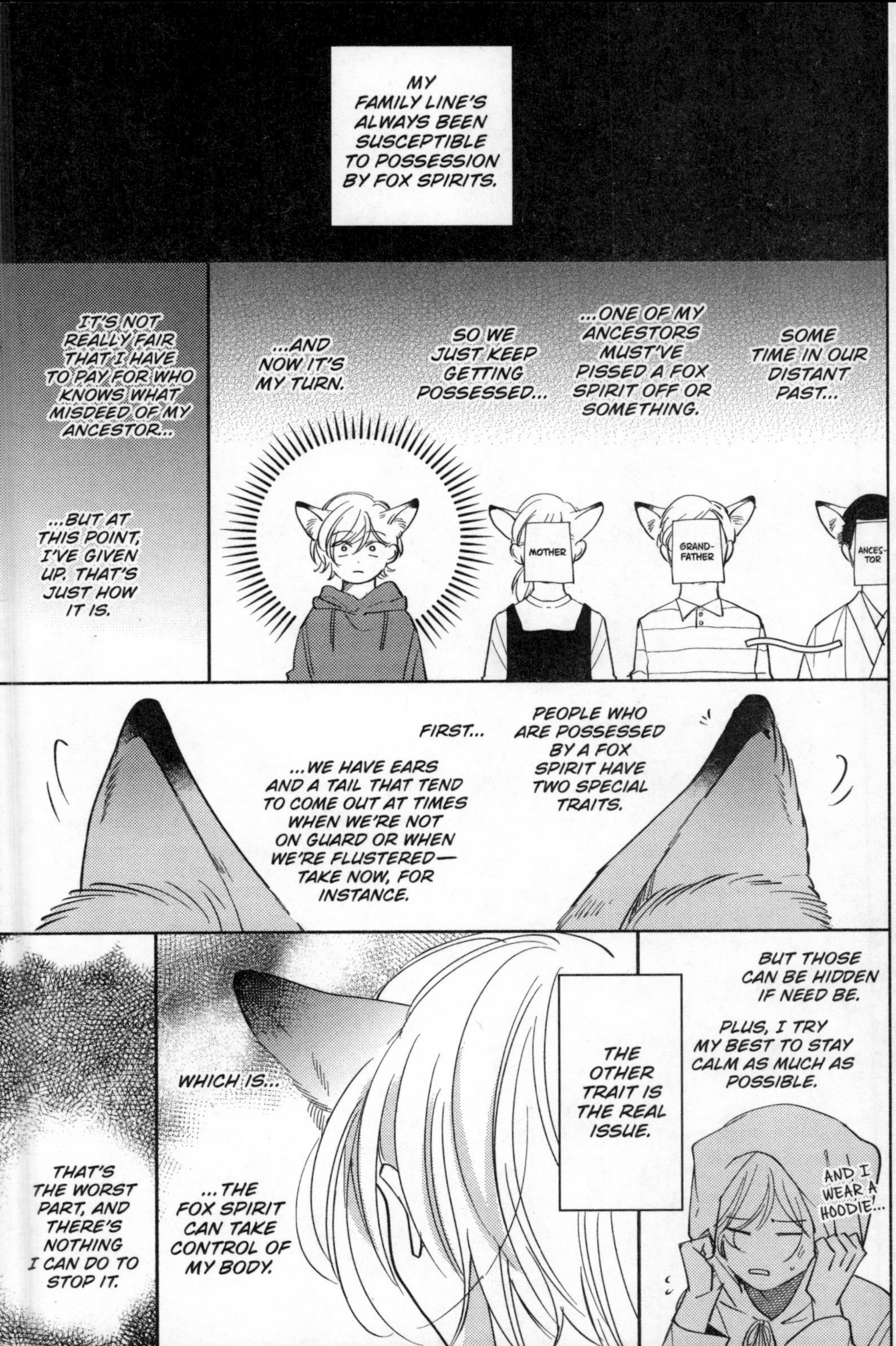
MY FAMILY LINE'S ALWAYS BEEN SUSCEPTIBLE TO POSSESSION BY FOX SPIRITS.
SOME TIME IN OUR DISTANT PAST...
...ONE OF MY ANCESTORS MUST'VE PISSED A FOX SPIRIT OFF OR SOMETHING.
SO WE JUST KEEP GETTING POSSESSED...
...AND NOW IT'S MY TURN.
ANCES-TOR
GRAND-FATHER
MOTHER
IT'S NOT REALLY FAIR THAT I HAVE TO PAY FOR WHO KNOWS WHAT MISDEED OF MY ANCESTOR...
...BUT AT THIS POINT, I'VE GIVEN UP. THAT'S JUST HOW IT IS.
PEOPLE WHO ARE POSSESSED BY A FOX SPIRIT HAVE TWO SPECIAL TRAITS.
FIRST...
...WE HAVE EARS AND A TAIL THAT TEND TO COME OUT AT TIMES WHEN WE'RE NOT ON GUARD OR WHEN WE'RE FLUSTERED—TAKE NOW, FOR INSTANCE.
BUT THOSE CAN BE HIDDEN IF NEED BE.
PLUS, I TRY MY BEST TO STAY CALM AS MUCH AS POSSIBLE.
AND I WEAR A HOODIE...
THE OTHER TRAIT IS THE REAL ISSUE.
WHICH IS...
...THE FOX SPIRIT CAN TAKE CONTROL OF MY BODY.
THAT'S THE WORST PART, AND THERE'S NOTHING I CAN DO TO STOP IT.

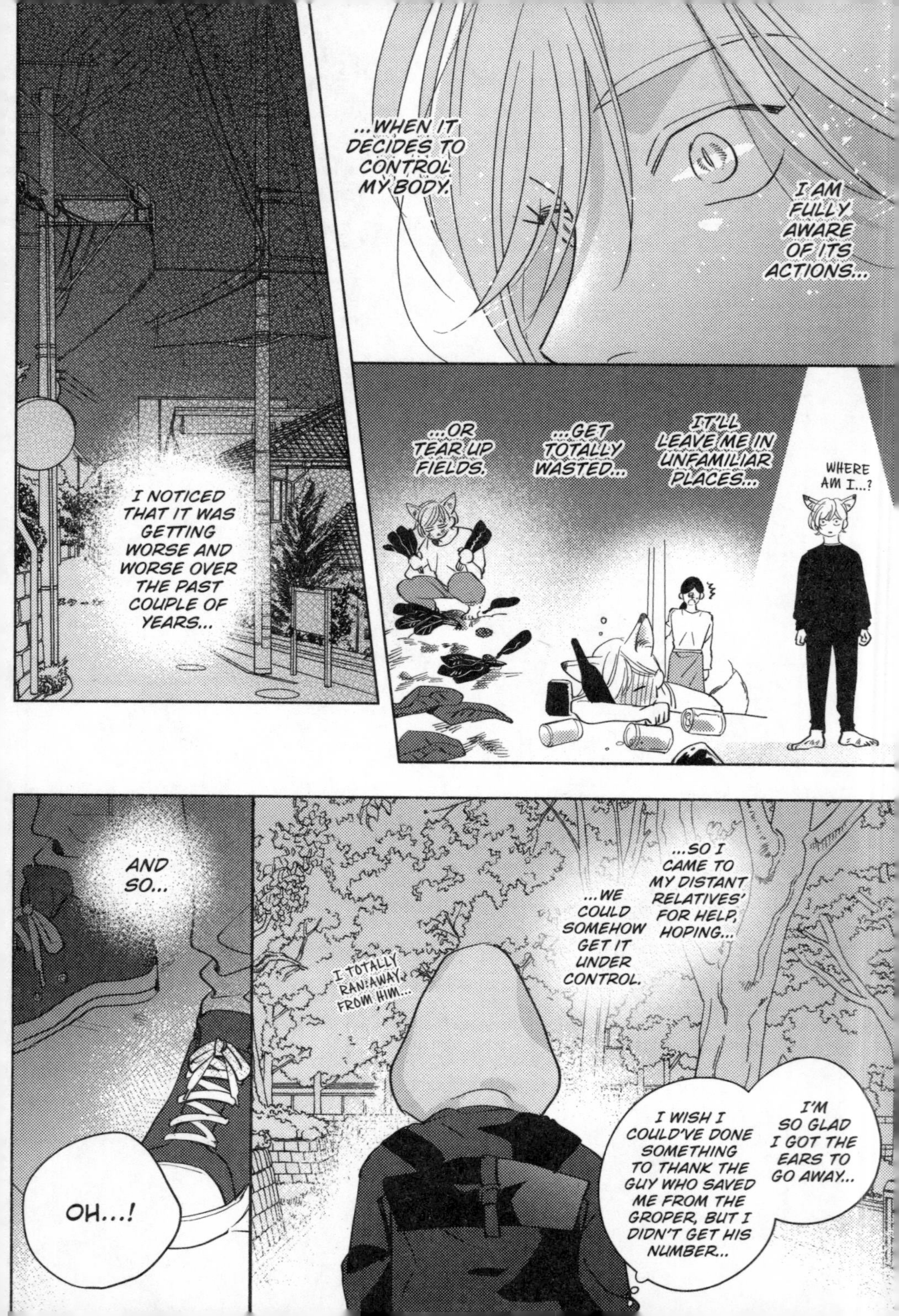
I AM FULLY AWARE OF ITS ACTIONS...
...WHEN IT DECIDES TO CONTROL MY BODY.
WHERE AM I...?
IT'LL LEAVE ME IN UNFAMILIAR PLACES...
...GET TOTALLY WASTED...
...OR TEAR UP FIELDS.
I NOTICED THAT IT WAS GETTING WORSE AND WORSE OVER THE PAST COUPLE OF YEARS...
I'M SO GLAD I GOT THE EARS TO GO AWAY...
I WISH I COULD'VE DONE SOMETHING TO THANK THE GUY WHO SAVED ME FROM THE GROPER, BUT I DIDN'T GET HIS NUMBER...
...SO I CAME TO MY DISTANT RELATIVES' FOR HELP, HOPING...
...WE COULD SOMEHOW GET IT UNDER CONTROL.
I TOTALLY RAN AWAY FROM HIM...
AND SO...
OH...!

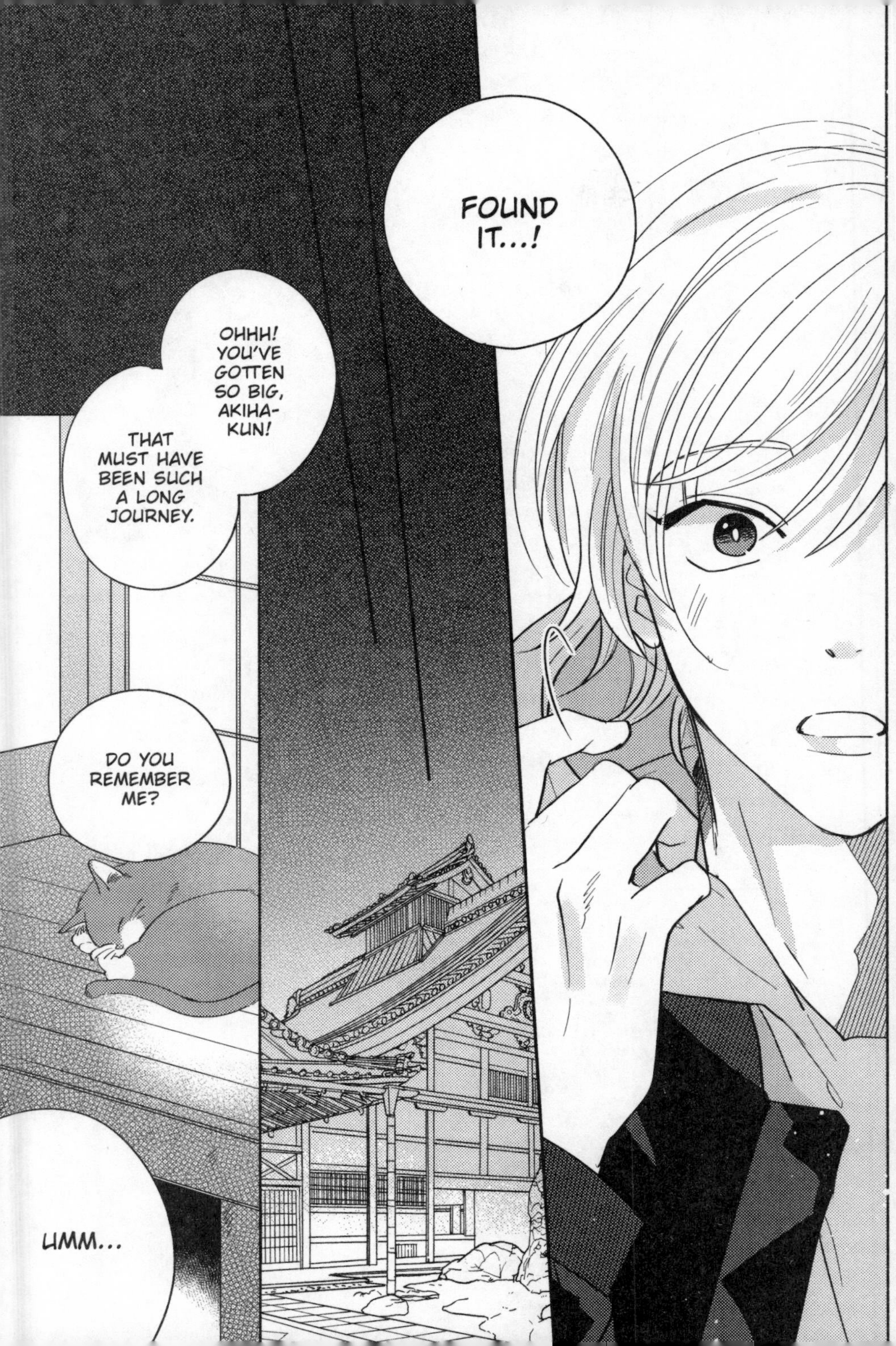
FOUND IT...!
OHHH! YOU'VE GOTTEN SO BIG, AKIHA-KUN!
THAT MUST HAVE BEEN SUCH A LONG JOURNEY.
DO YOU REMEMBER ME?
UMM...

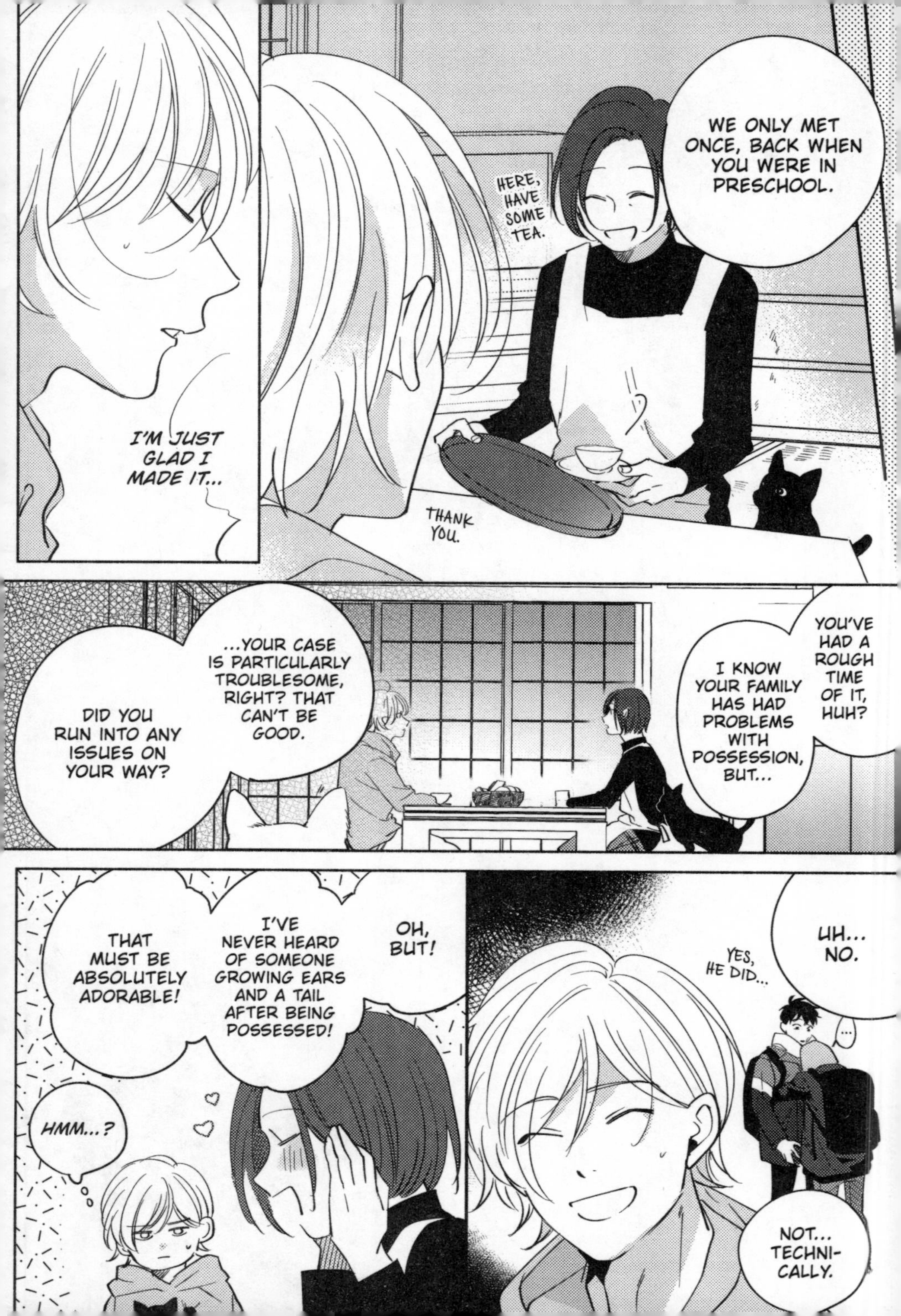
WE ONLY MET ONCE, BACK WHEN YOU WERE IN PRESCHOOL.
HERE, HAVE SOME TEA.
THANK YOU.
I'M JUST GLAD I MADE IT...
YOU'VE HAD A ROUGH TIME OF IT, HUH?
I KNOW YOUR FAMILY HAS HAD PROBLEMS WITH POSSESSION, BUT...
...YOUR CASE IS PARTICULARLY TROUBLESOME, RIGHT? THAT CAN'T BE GOOD.
DID YOU RUN INTO ANY ISSUES ON YOUR WAY?
UH... NO.
YES, HE DID...
...
NOT... TECHNICALLY.
OH, BUT!
I'VE NEVER HEARD OF SOMEONE GROWING EARS AND A TAIL AFTER BEING POSSESSED!
THAT MUST BE ABSOLUTELY ADORABLE!
HMM...?

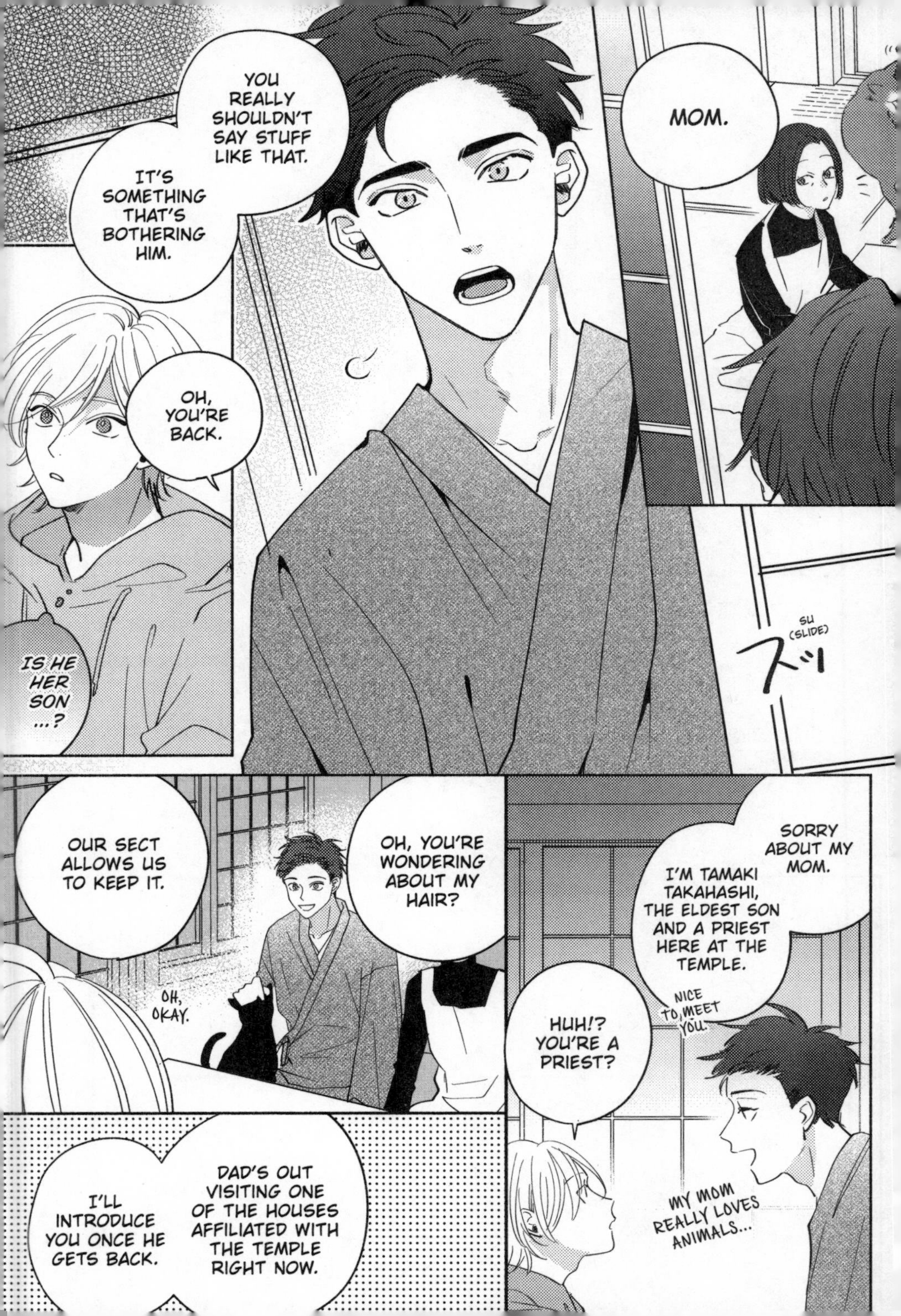
MOM.
SU (SLIDE)
ズッ
YOU REALLY SHOULDN'T SAY STUFF LIKE THAT.
IT'S SOMETHING THAT'S BOTHERING HIM.
OH, YOU'RE BACK.
IS HE HER SON ...?
SORRY ABOUT MY MOM.
I'M TAMAKI TAKAHASHI, THE ELDEST SON AND A PRIEST HERE AT THE TEMPLE.
NICE TO MEET YOU.
HUH!? YOU'RE A PRIEST?
MY MOM REALLY LOVES ANIMALS...
OH, YOU'RE WONDERING ABOUT MY HAIR?
OUR SECT ALLOWS US TO KEEP IT.
OH, OKAY.
DAD'S OUT VISITING ONE OF THE HOUSES AFFILIATED WITH THE TEMPLE RIGHT NOW.
I'LL INTRODUCE YOU ONCE HE GETS BACK.

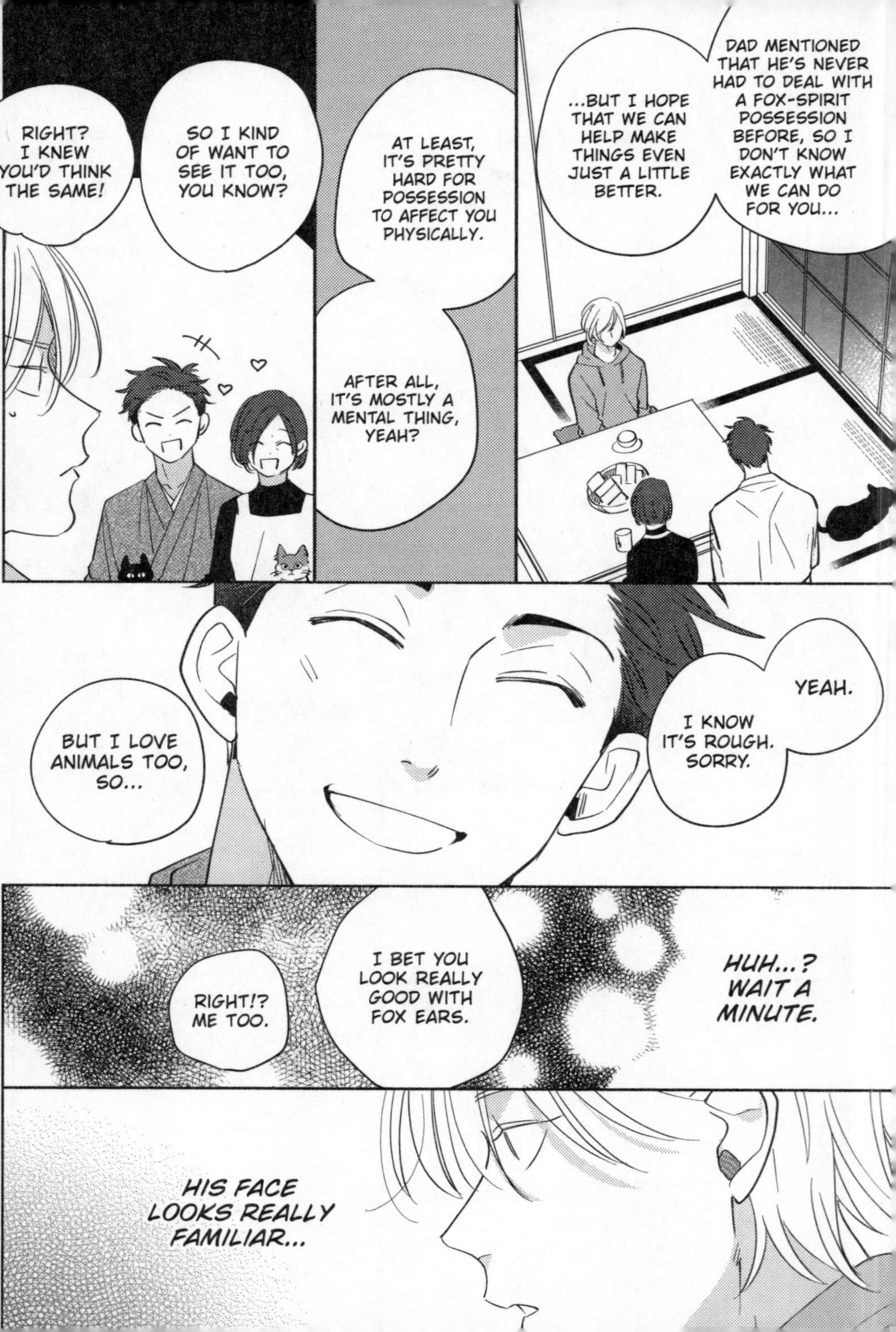
DAD MENTIONED THAT HE'S NEVER HAD TO DEAL WITH A FOX-SPIRIT POSSESSION BEFORE, SO I DON'T KNOW EXACTLY WHAT WE CAN DO FOR YOU...
...BUT I HOPE THAT WE CAN HELP MAKE THINGS EVEN JUST A LITTLE BETTER.
AT LEAST, IT'S PRETTY HARD FOR POSSESSION TO AFFECT YOU PHYSICALLY.
AFTER ALL, IT'S MOSTLY A MENTAL THING, YEAH?
SO I KIND OF WANT TO SEE IT TOO, YOU KNOW?
RIGHT? I KNEW YOU'D THINK THE SAME!
YEAH.
I KNOW IT'S ROUGH. SORRY.
BUT I LOVE ANIMALS TOO, SO...
HUH...? WAIT A MINUTE.
I BET YOU LOOK REALLY GOOD WITH FOX EARS.
RIGHT!? ME TOO.
HIS FACE LOOKS REALLY FAMILIAR...

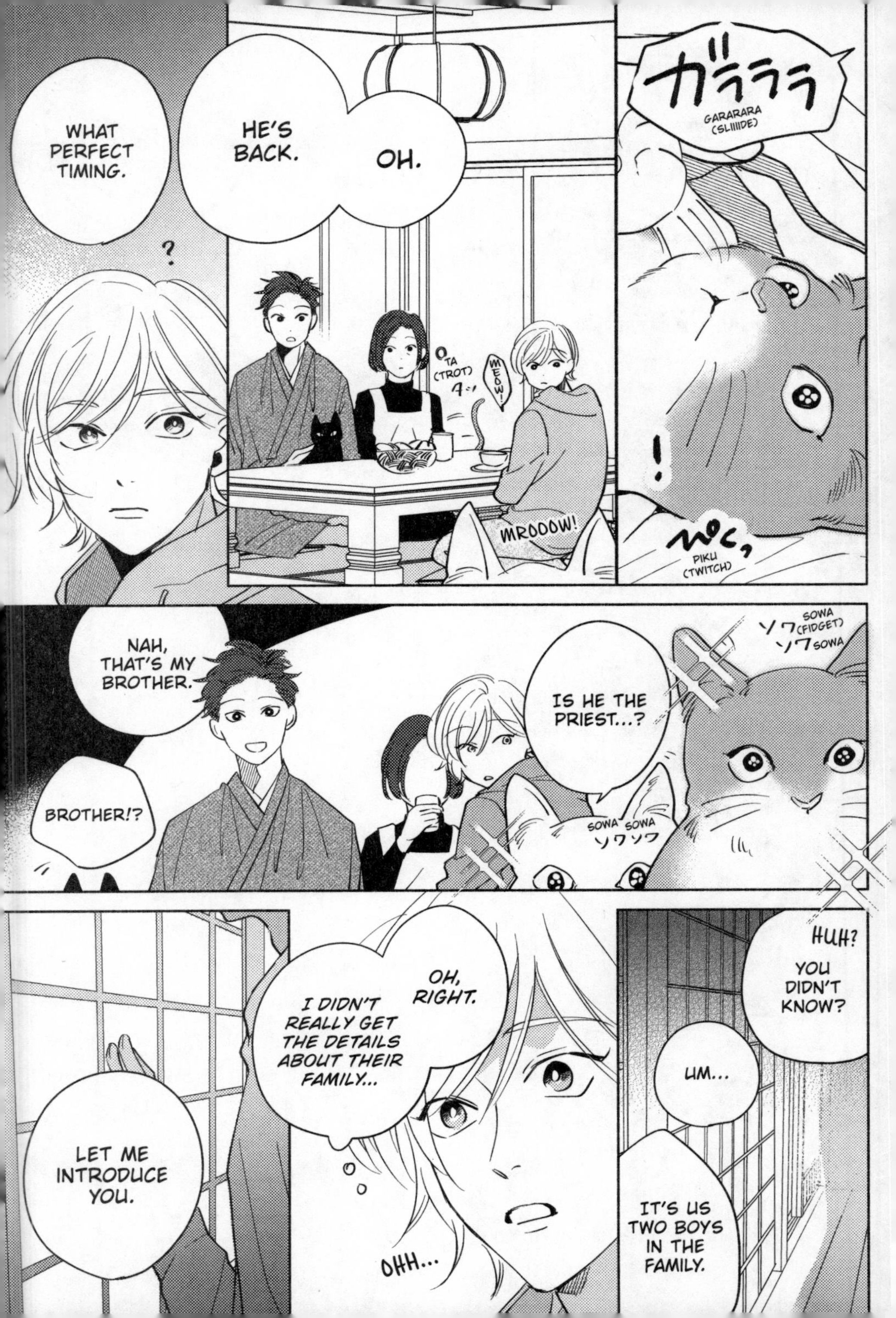
ガラララ
GARARARA (SLIIIIDE)
!
ぴくっ
PIKU (TWITCH)
OH.
HE'S BACK.
TA (TROT)
タッ
MEOW!
MROOOW!
WHAT PERFECT TIMING.
?
ソワソワ
SOWA (FIDGET) SOWA
IS HE THE PRIEST...?
SOWA SOWA
ソワソワ
NAH, THAT'S MY BROTHER.
BROTHER!?
HUH?
YOU DIDN'T KNOW?
UM...
IT'S US TWO BOYS IN THE FAMILY.
OH, RIGHT.
I DIDN'T REALLY GET THE DETAILS ABOUT THEIR FAMILY...
OHH...
LET ME INTRODUCE YOU.

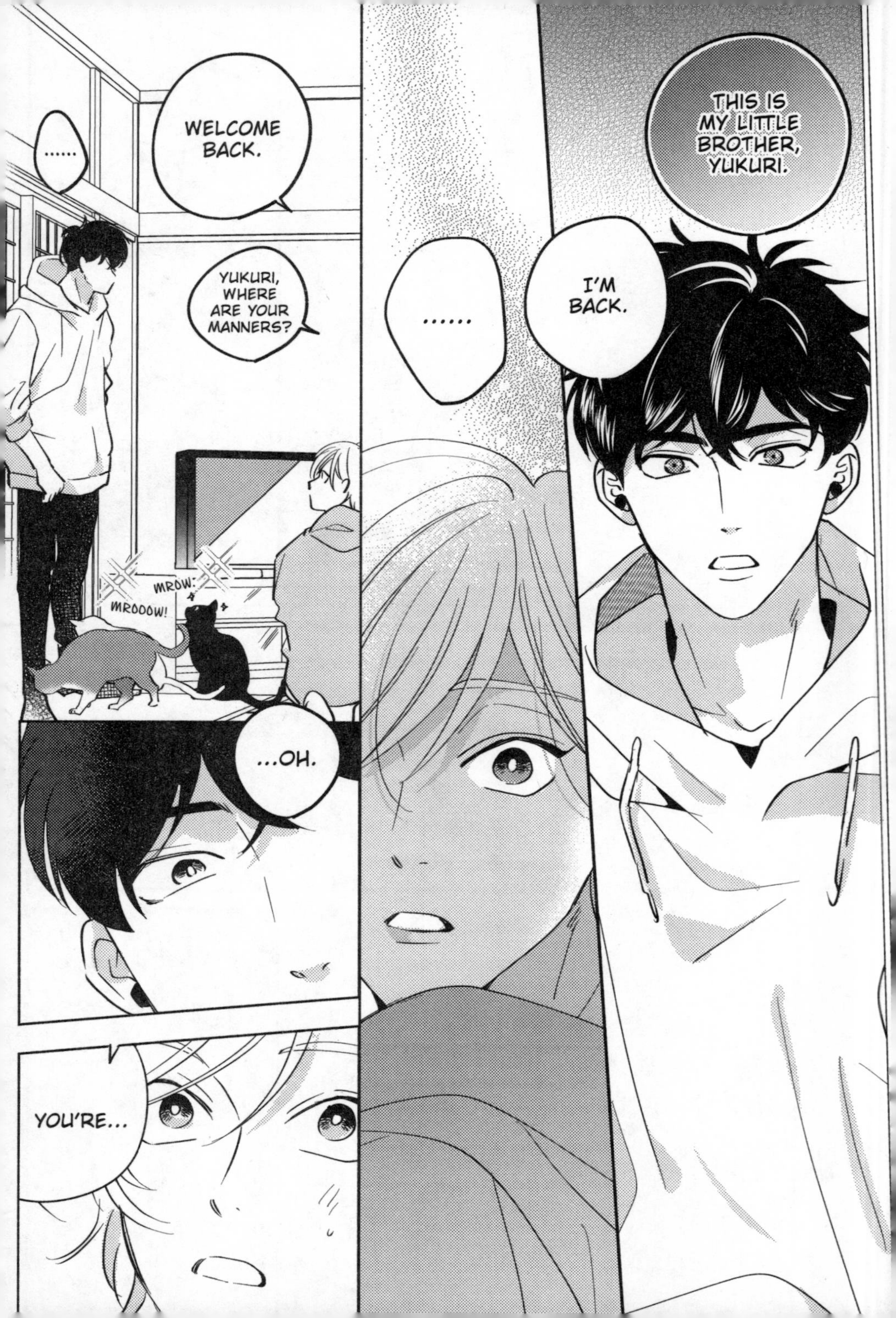
THIS IS MY LITTLE BROTHER, YUKURI.
I'M BACK.
......
WELCOME BACK.
......
YUKURI, WHERE ARE YOUR MANNERS?
MROW
MROOOW!
...OH.
YOU'RE...

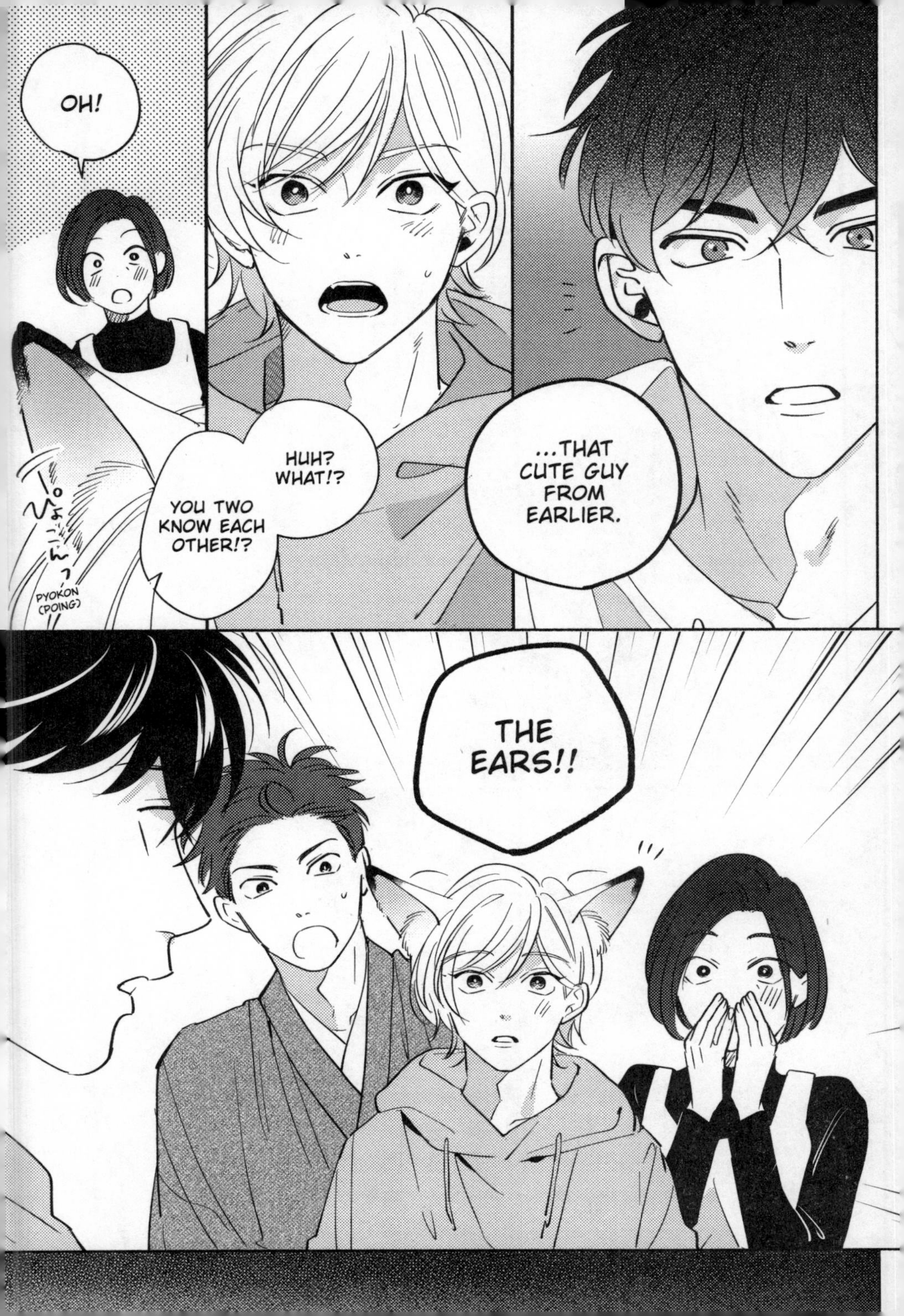
...THAT CUTE GUY FROM EARLIER.
OH!
HUH? WHAT!?
YOU TWO KNOW EACH OTHER!?
ぴょこんっ
PYOKON (POING)
THE EARS!!

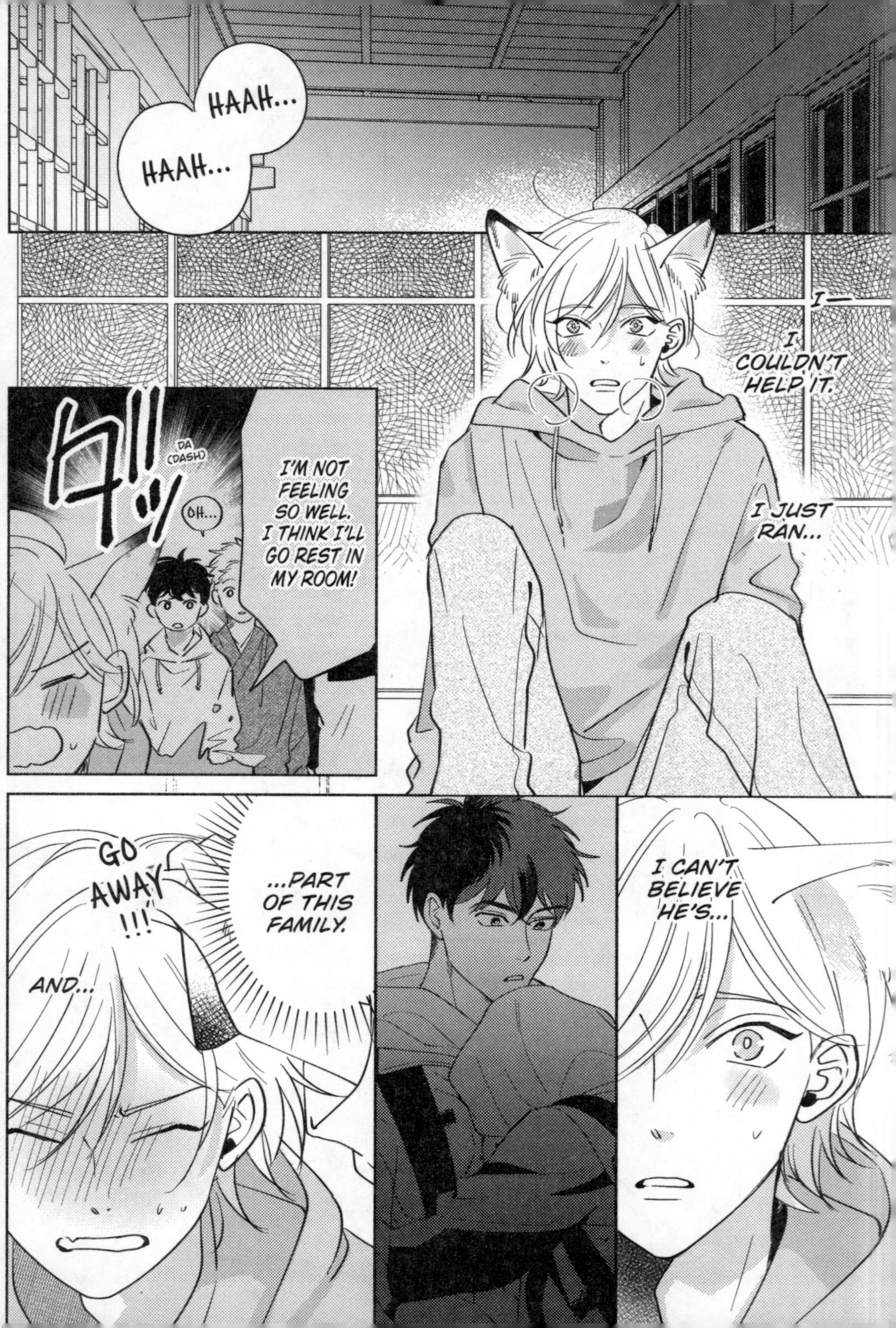
HAAH...
HAAH...
I— I COULDN'T HELP IT.
I JUST RAN...
I'M NOT FEELING SO WELL. I THINK I'LL GO REST IN MY ROOM!
ダッ
DA (DASH)
OH...
I CAN'T BELIEVE HE'S...
...PART OF THIS FAMILY.
GO AWAY!!!
AND...

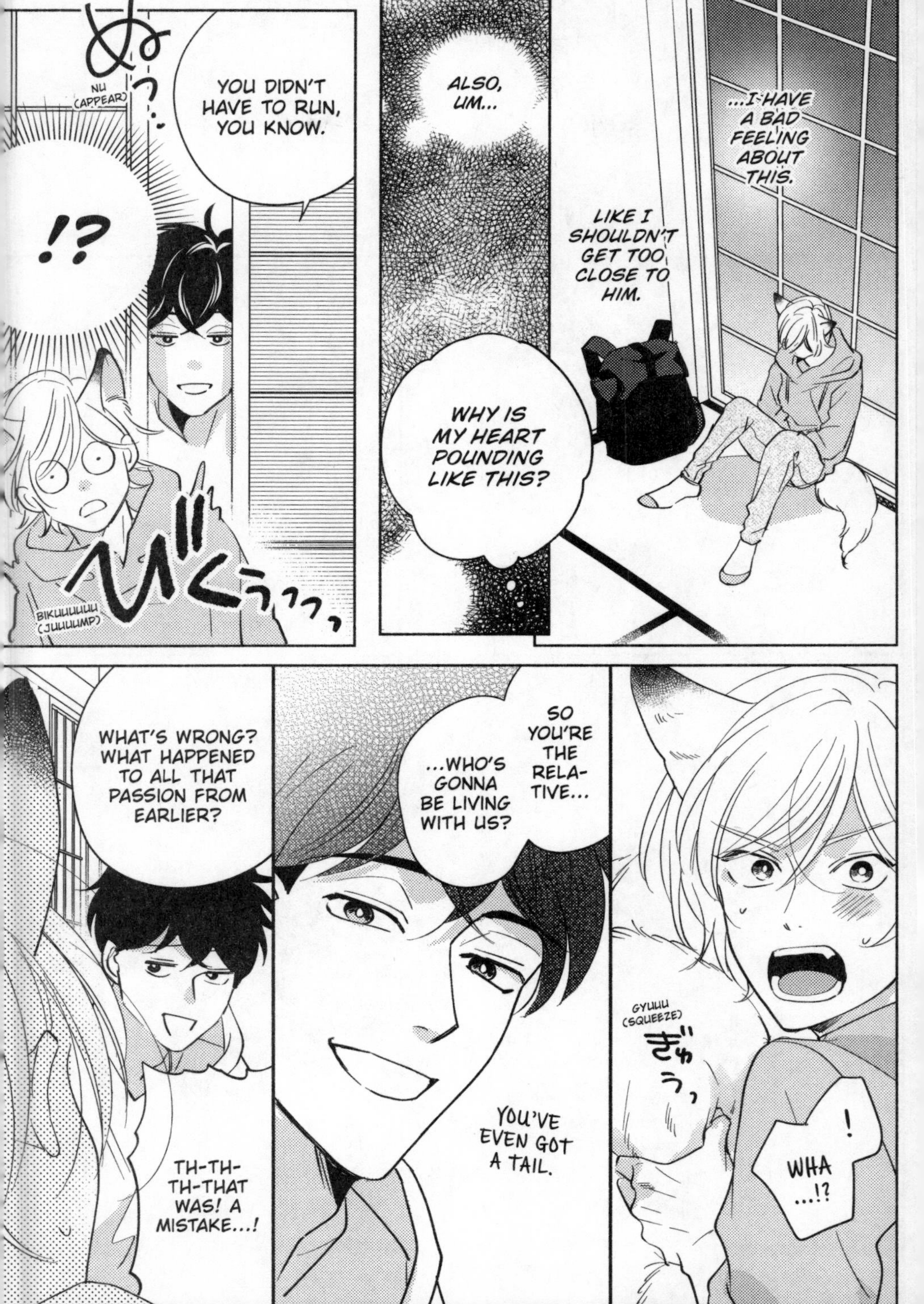
...I HAVE A BAD FEELING ABOUT THIS.
LIKE I SHOULDN'T GET TOO CLOSE TO HIM.
ALSO, UM...
WHY IS MY HEART POUNDING LIKE THIS?
ぬっ
NU (APPEAR)
YOU DIDN'T HAVE TO RUN, YOU KNOW.
!?
BIKUUUUUU (JUUUUMP)
GYUUU (SQUEEZE)
ぎゅうっ
!
WHA ...!?
SO YOU'RE THE RELATIVE...
...WHO'S GONNA BE LIVING WITH US?
YOU'VE EVEN GOT A TAIL.
WHAT'S WRONG? WHAT HAPPENED TO ALL THAT PASSION FROM EARLIER?
TH-TH-TH-THAT WAS! A MISTAKE...!

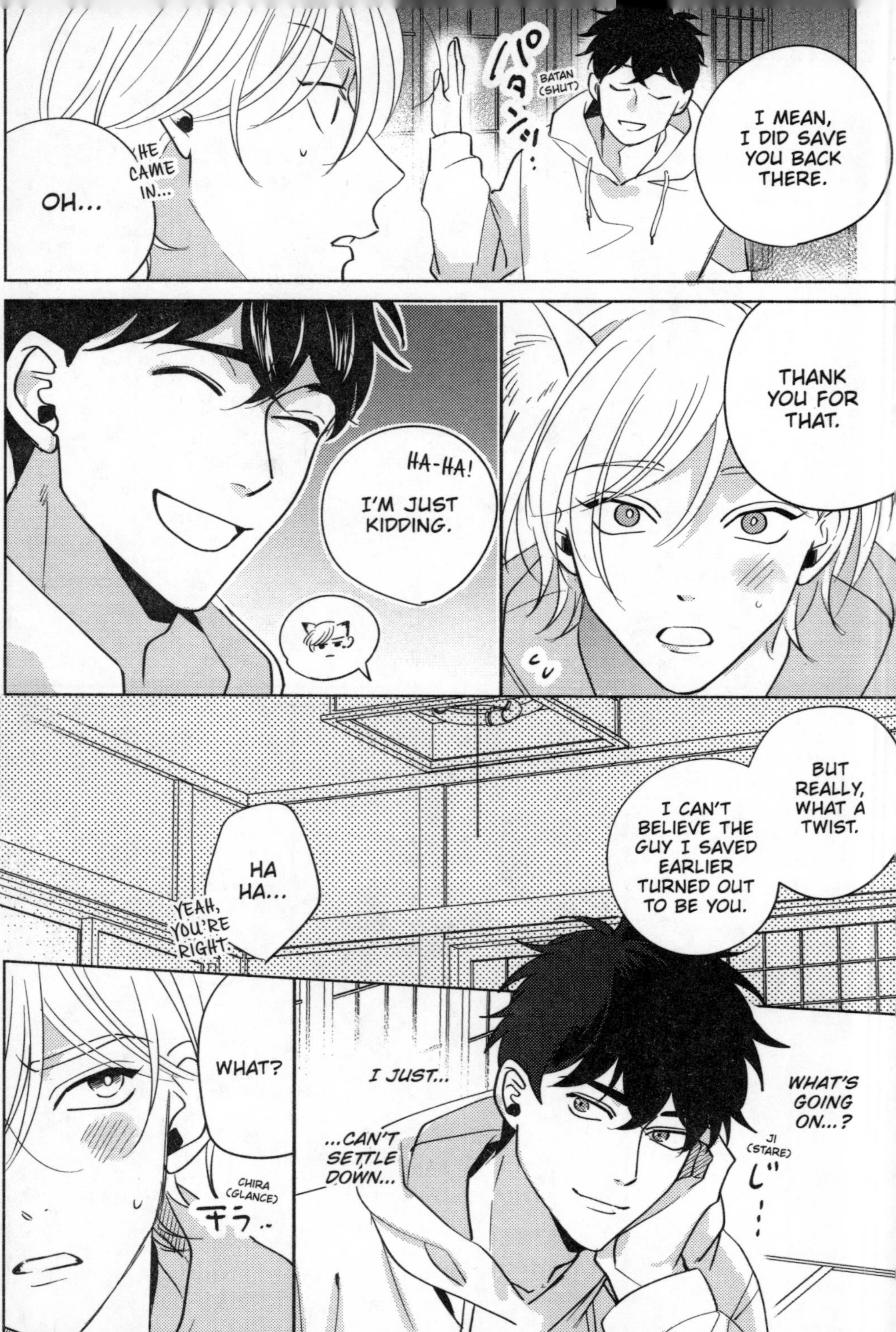
I MEAN, I DID SAVE YOU BACK THERE.
BATAN (SHUT)
HE CAME IN...
OH...
THANK YOU FOR THAT.
HA-HA!
I'M JUST KIDDING.
BUT REALLY, WHAT A TWIST.
I CAN'T BELIEVE THE GUY I SAVED EARLIER TURNED OUT TO BE YOU.
HA HA...
YEAH, YOU'RE RIGHT.
WHAT'S GOING ON...?
JI (STARE)
I JUST...
...CAN'T SETTLE DOWN...
WHAT?
CHIRA (GLANCE)

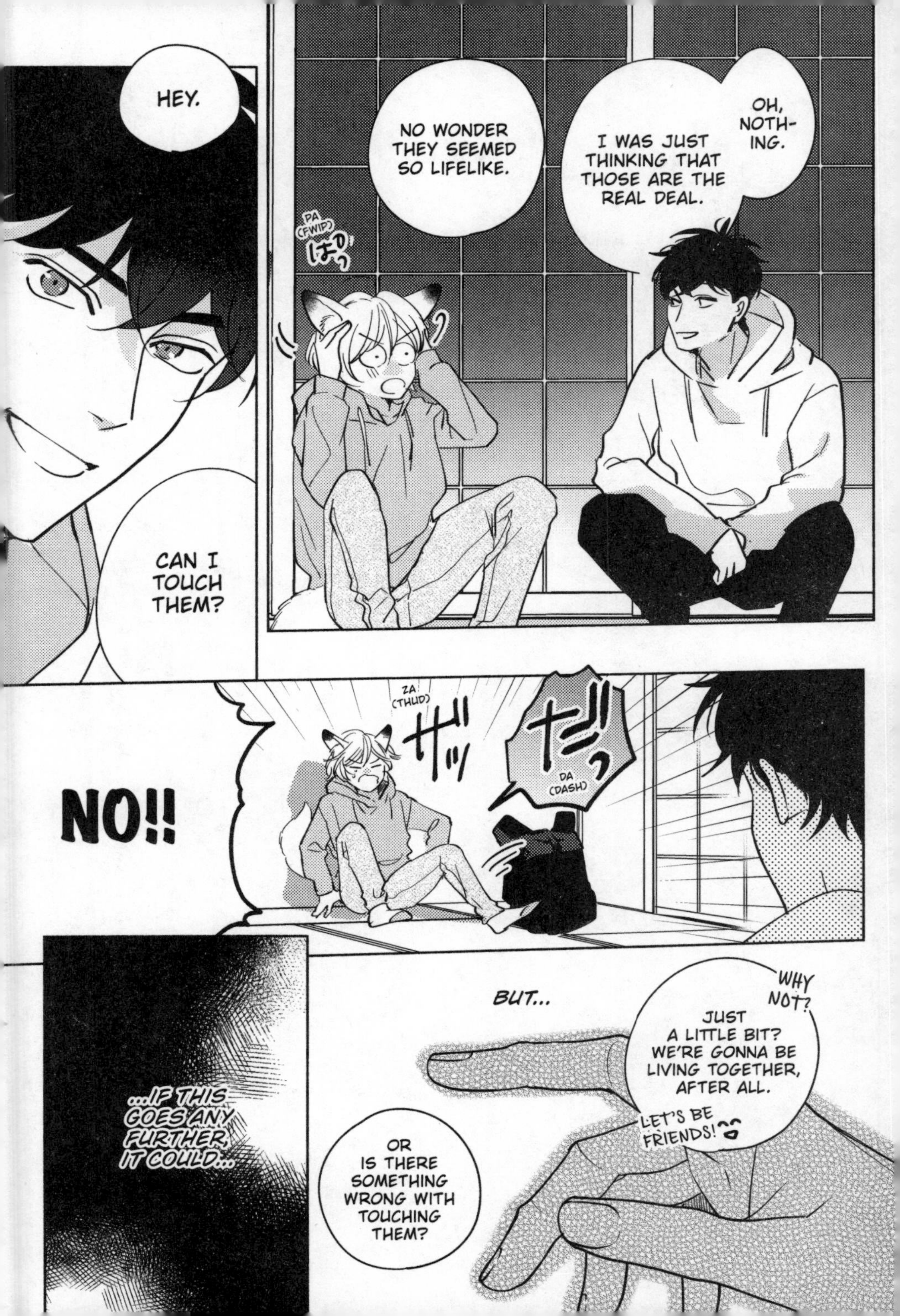
OH, NOTHING.
I WAS JUST THINKING THAT THOSE ARE THE REAL DEAL.
NO WONDER THEY SEEMED SO LIFELIKE.
PA (FWIP)
HEY.
CAN I TOUCH THEM?
DA (DASH)
ZA (THUD)
NO!!
WHY NOT?
JUST A LITTLE BIT? WE'RE GONNA BE LIVING TOGETHER, AFTER ALL.
LET'S BE FRIENDS!
BUT...
OR IS THERE SOMETHING WRONG WITH TOUCHING THEM?
...IF THIS GOES ANY FURTHER, IT COULD...

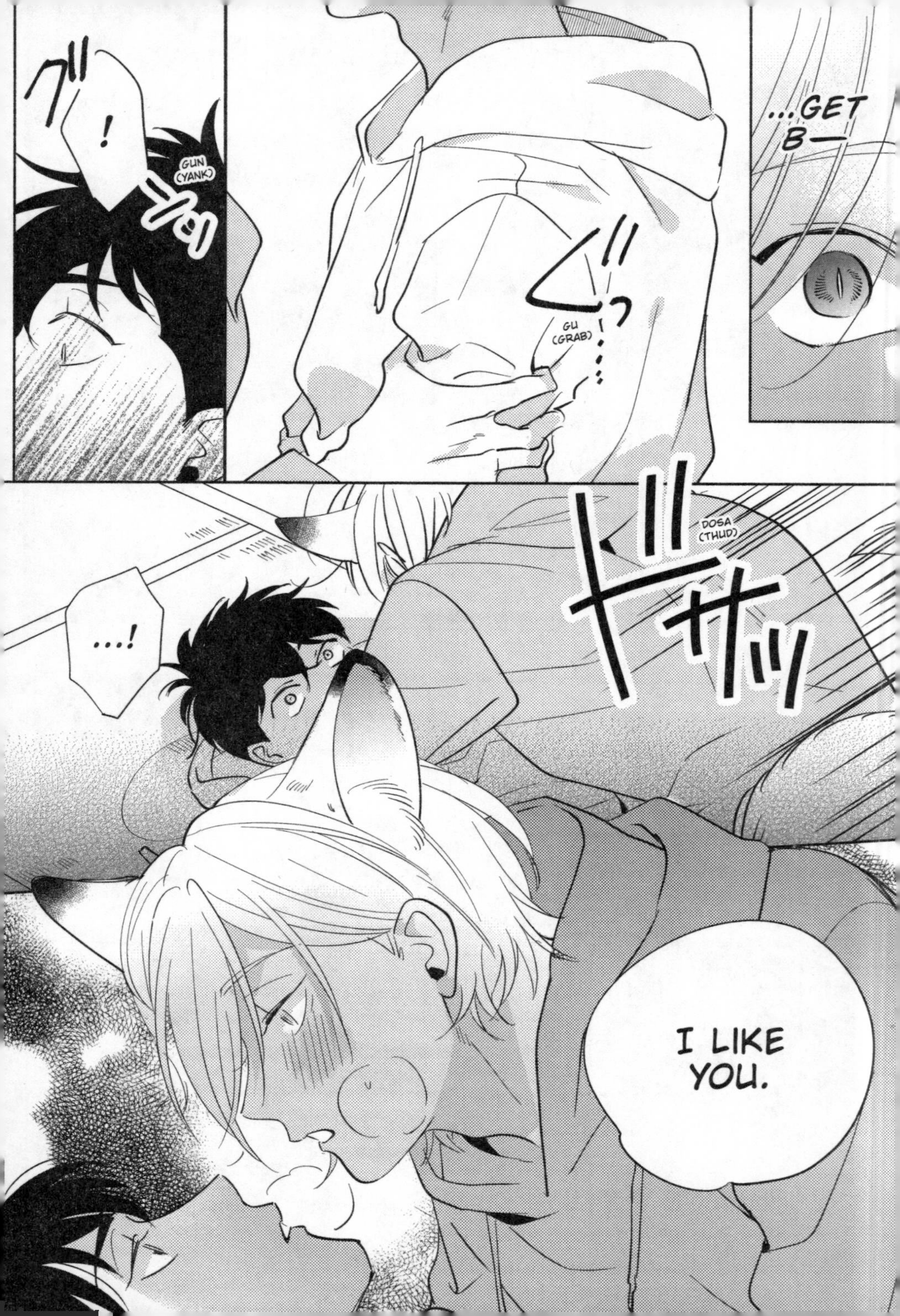
...GET B—
GU (GRAB)
!
GUN (YANK)
DOSA (THUD)
...!
I LIKE YOU.

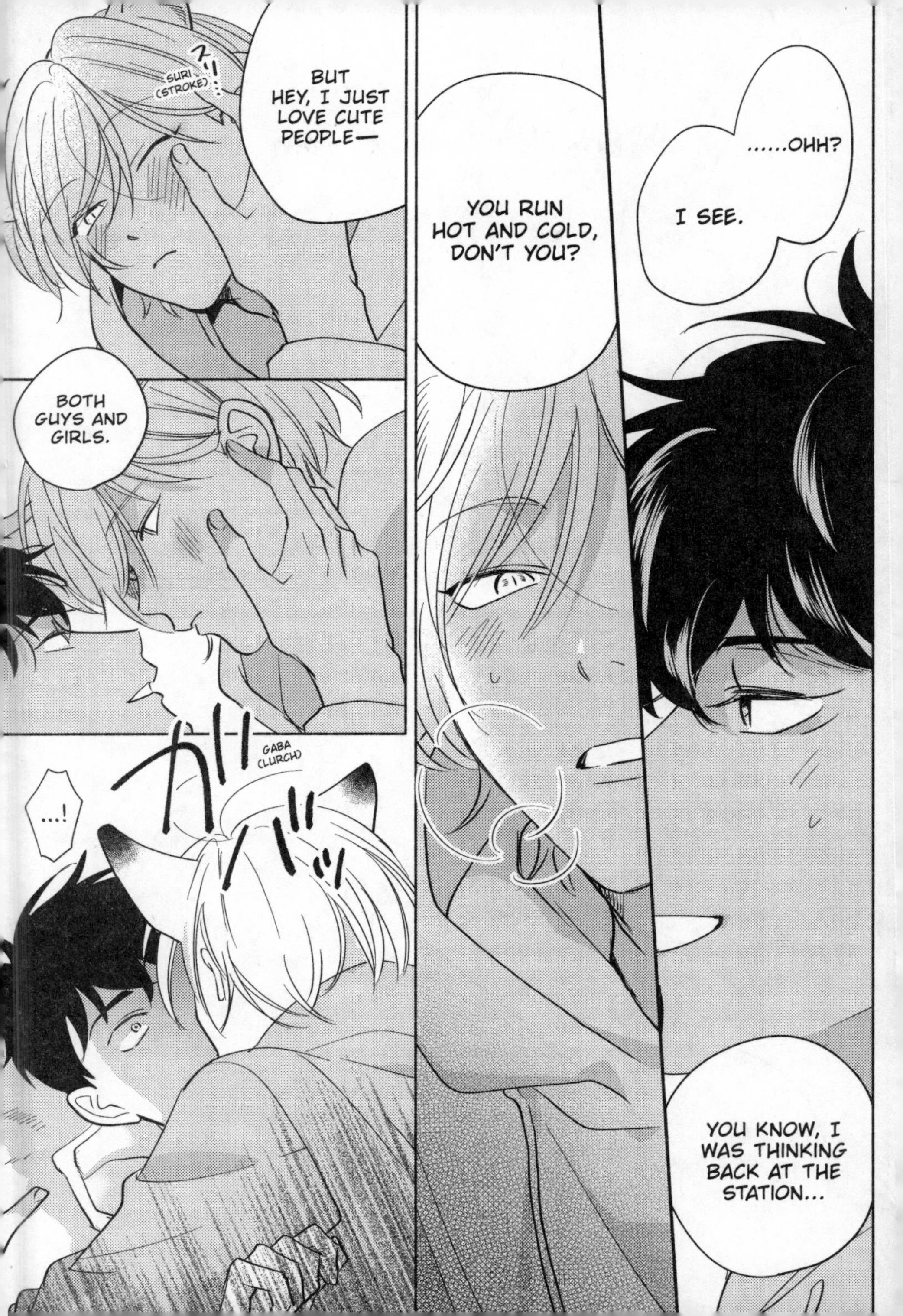
......OHH?
I SEE.
YOU KNOW, I WAS THINKING BACK AT THE STATION...
YOU RUN HOT AND COLD, DON'T YOU?
スリ
SURI (STROKE)
BUT HEY, I JUST LOVE CUTE PEOPLE—
BOTH GUYS AND GIRLS.
ガバッ
GABA (LURCH)
...!

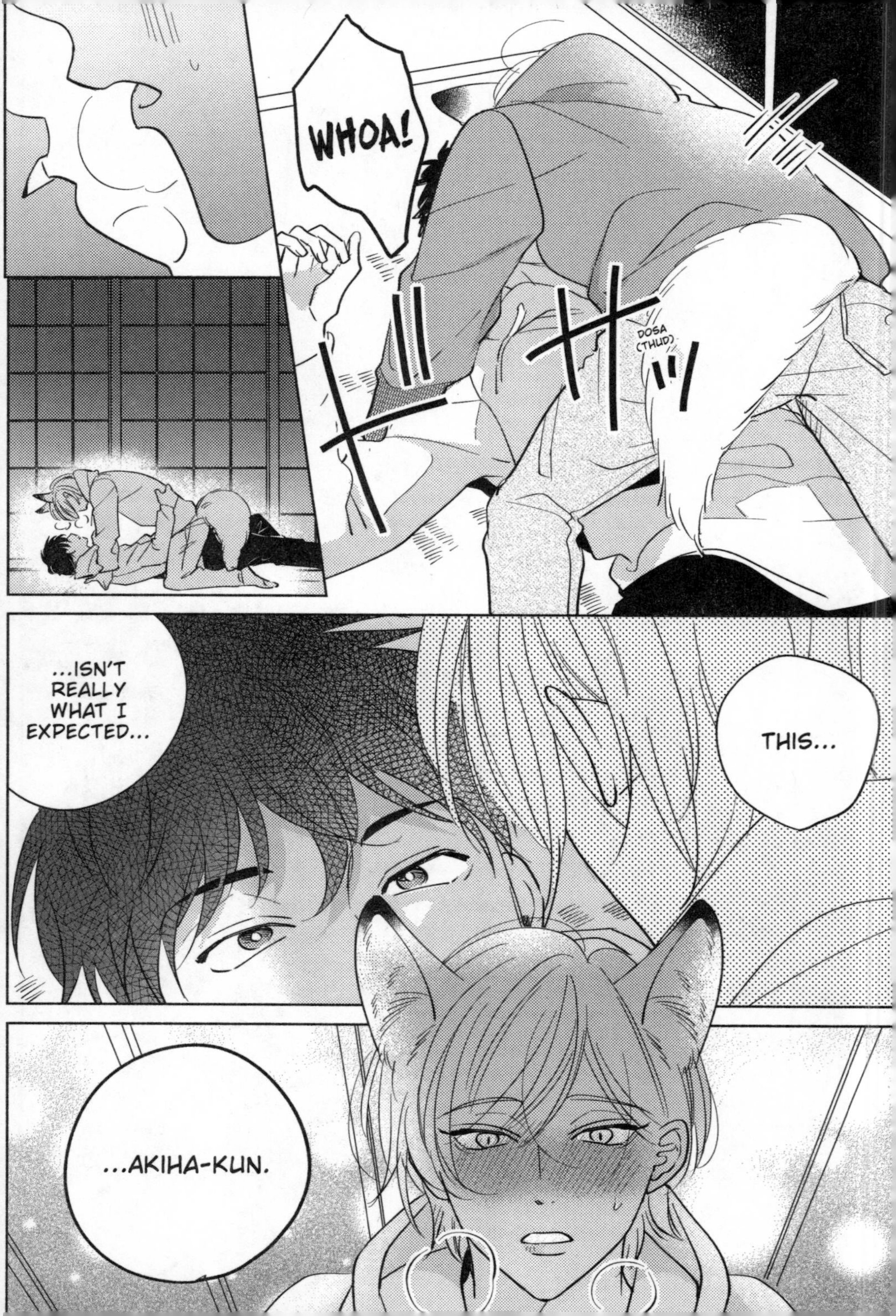
WHOA!
DOSA (THUD)
THIS...
...ISN'T REALLY WHAT I EXPECTED...
...AKIHA-KUN.

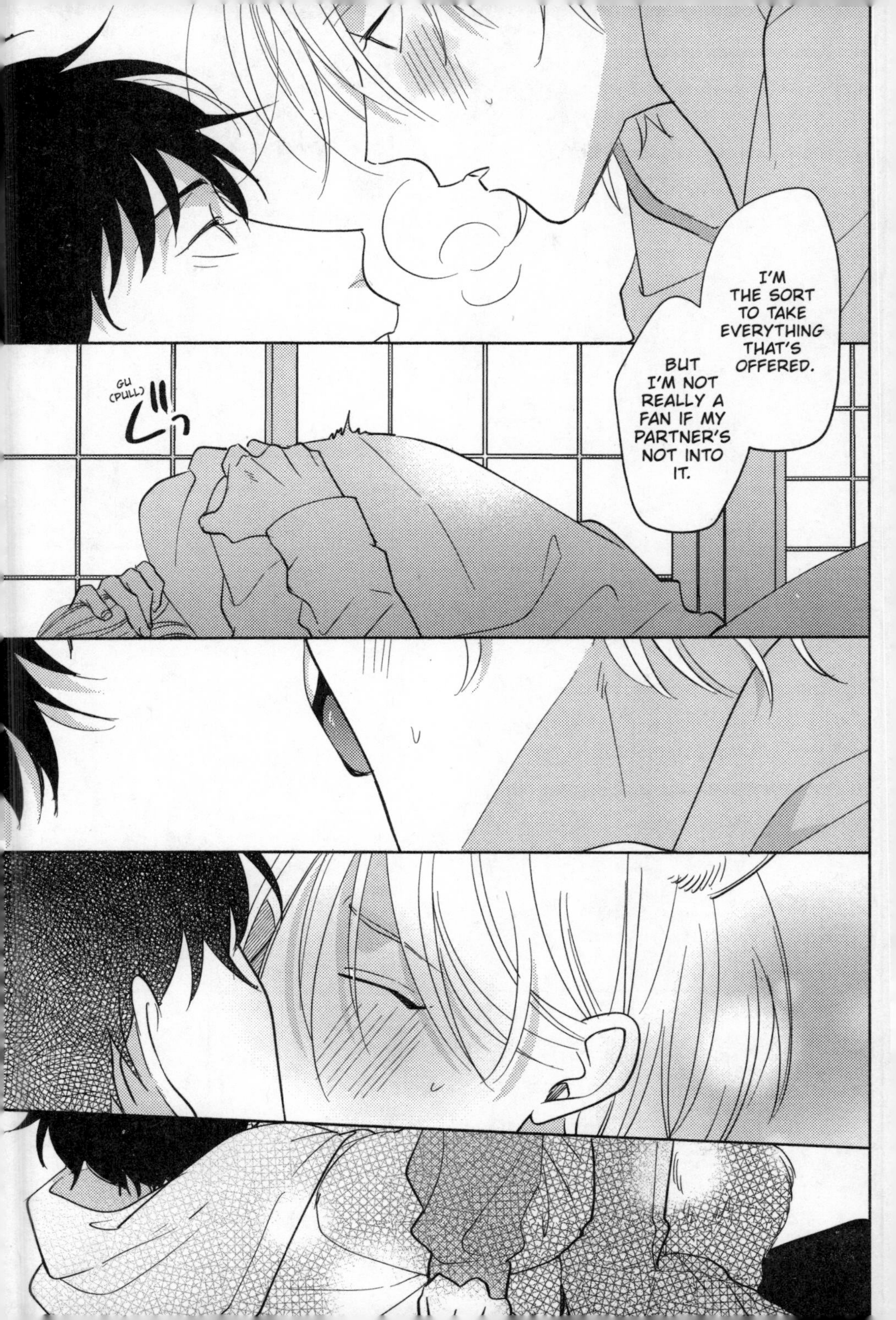
I'M THE SORT TO TAKE EVERYTHING THAT'S OFFERED.
BUT I'M NOT REALLY A FAN IF MY PARTNER'S NOT INTO IT.
GU (PULL)

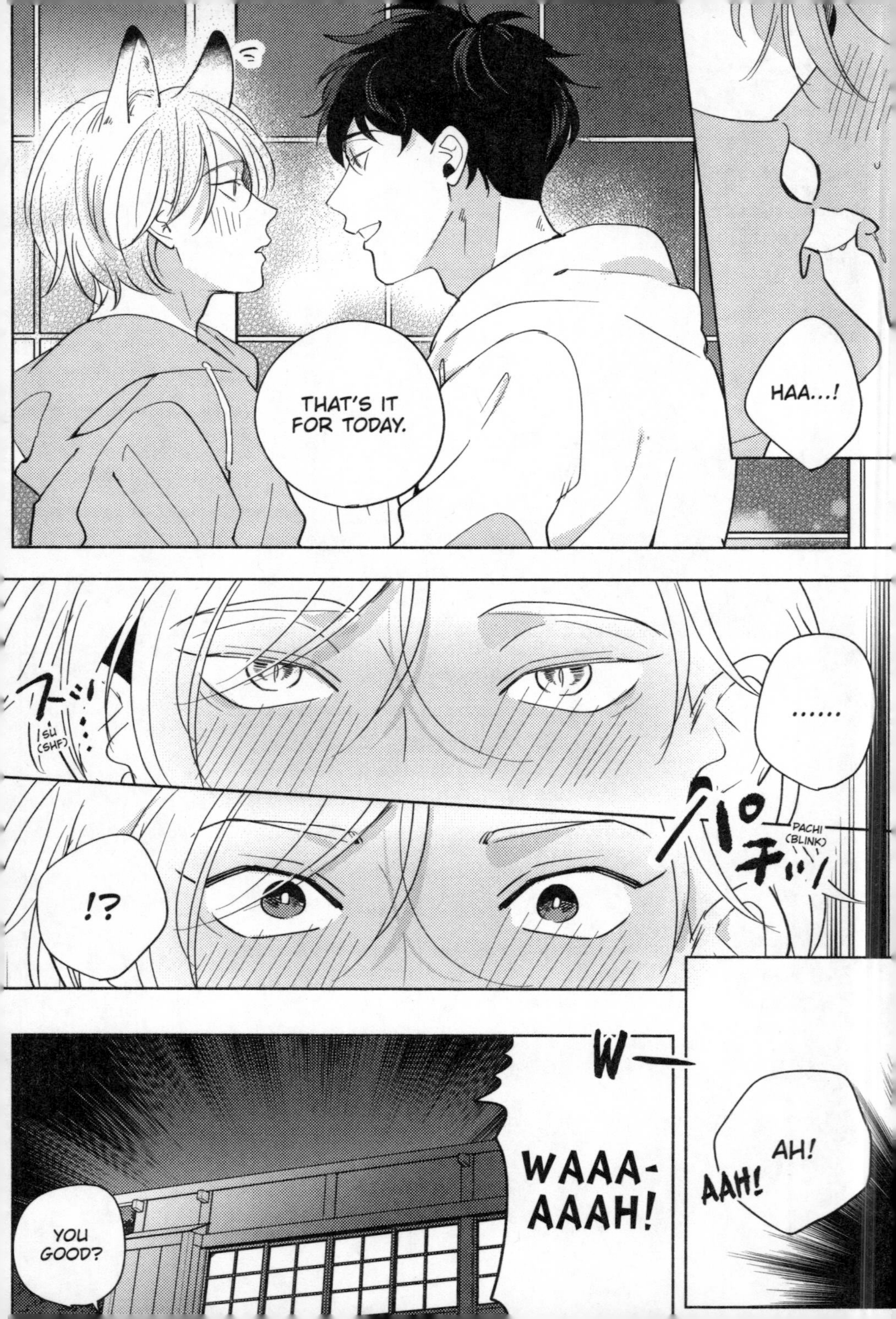
HAA...!
THAT'S IT FOR TODAY.
......
スッ
SU (SHF)
パチッ
PACHI (BLINK)
!?
AH!
AAH!
W—
WAAA-AAAH!
YOU GOOD?

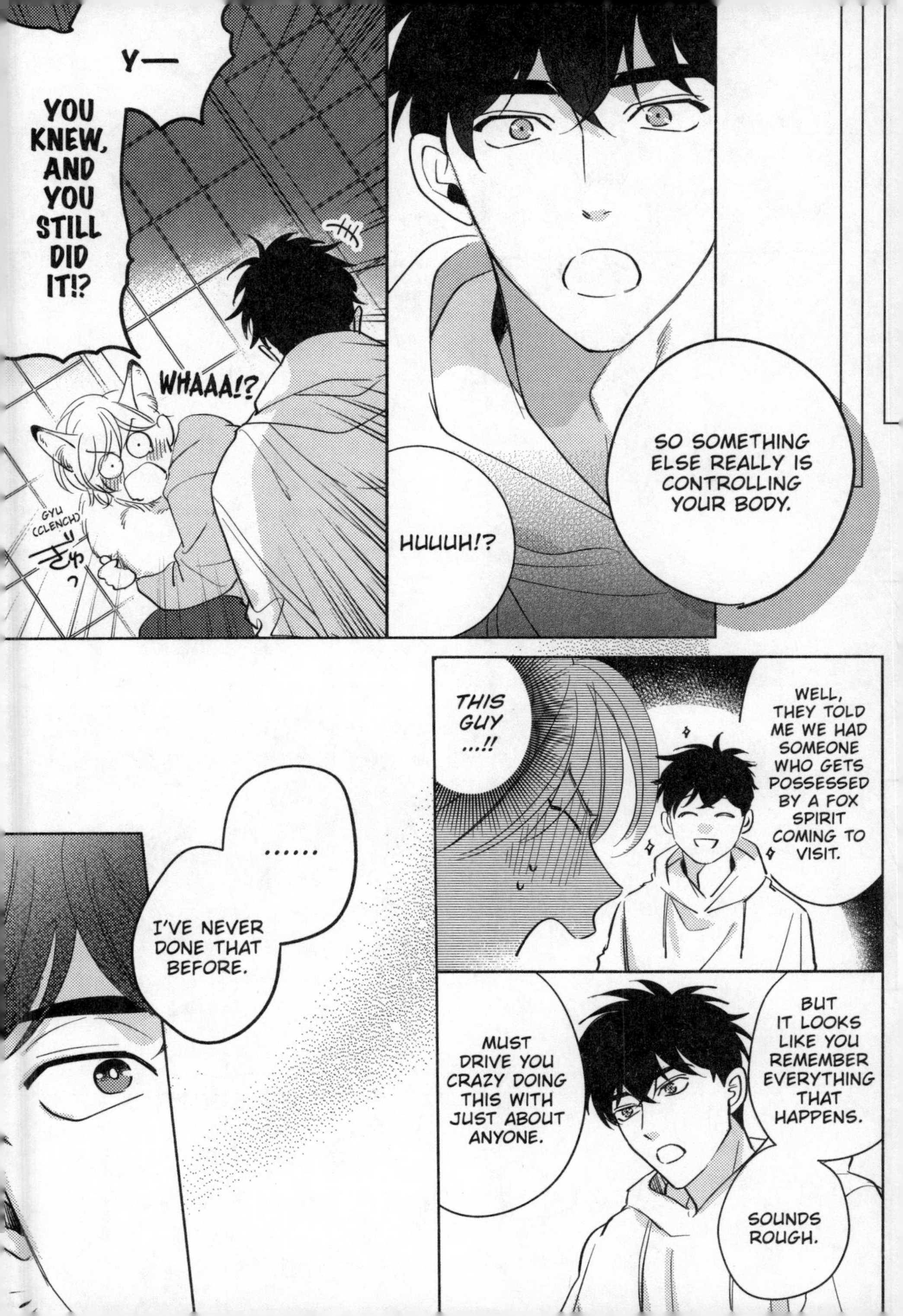
SO SOMETHING ELSE REALLY IS CONTROLLING YOUR BODY.
HUUUH!?
Y—
YOU KNEW, AND YOU STILL DID IT!?
WHAAA!?
GYU (CLENCH)
WELL, THEY TOLD ME WE HAD SOMEONE WHO GETS POSSESSED BY A FOX SPIRIT COMING TO VISIT.
THIS GUY ...!!
BUT IT LOOKS LIKE YOU REMEMBER EVERYTHING THAT HAPPENS.
MUST DRIVE YOU CRAZY DOING THIS WITH JUST ABOUT ANYONE.
SOUNDS ROUGH.
......
I'VE NEVER DONE THAT BEFORE.

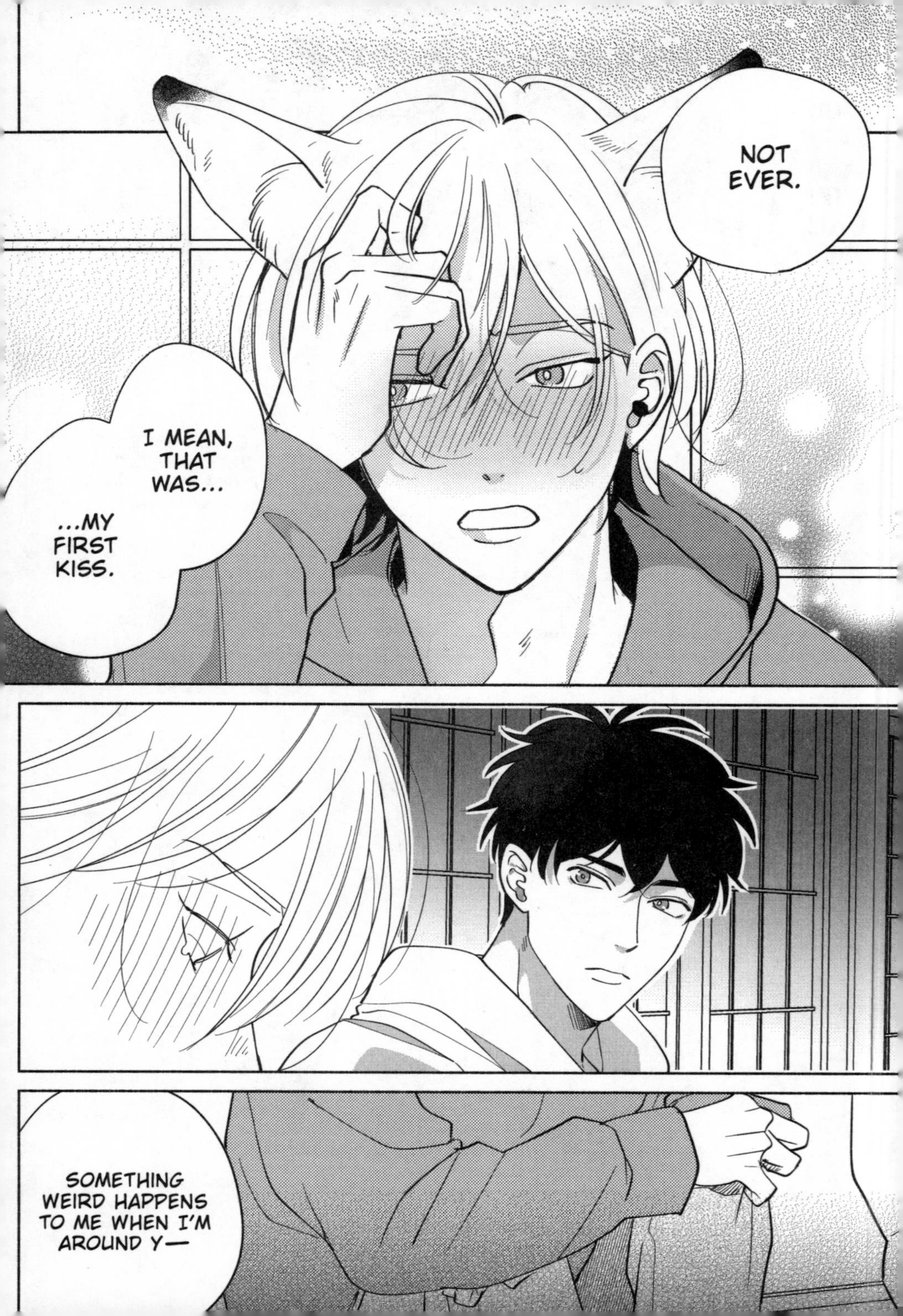
NOT EVER.
I MEAN, THAT WAS...
...MY FIRST KISS.
SOMETHING WEIRD HAPPENS TO ME WHEN I'M AROUND Y—

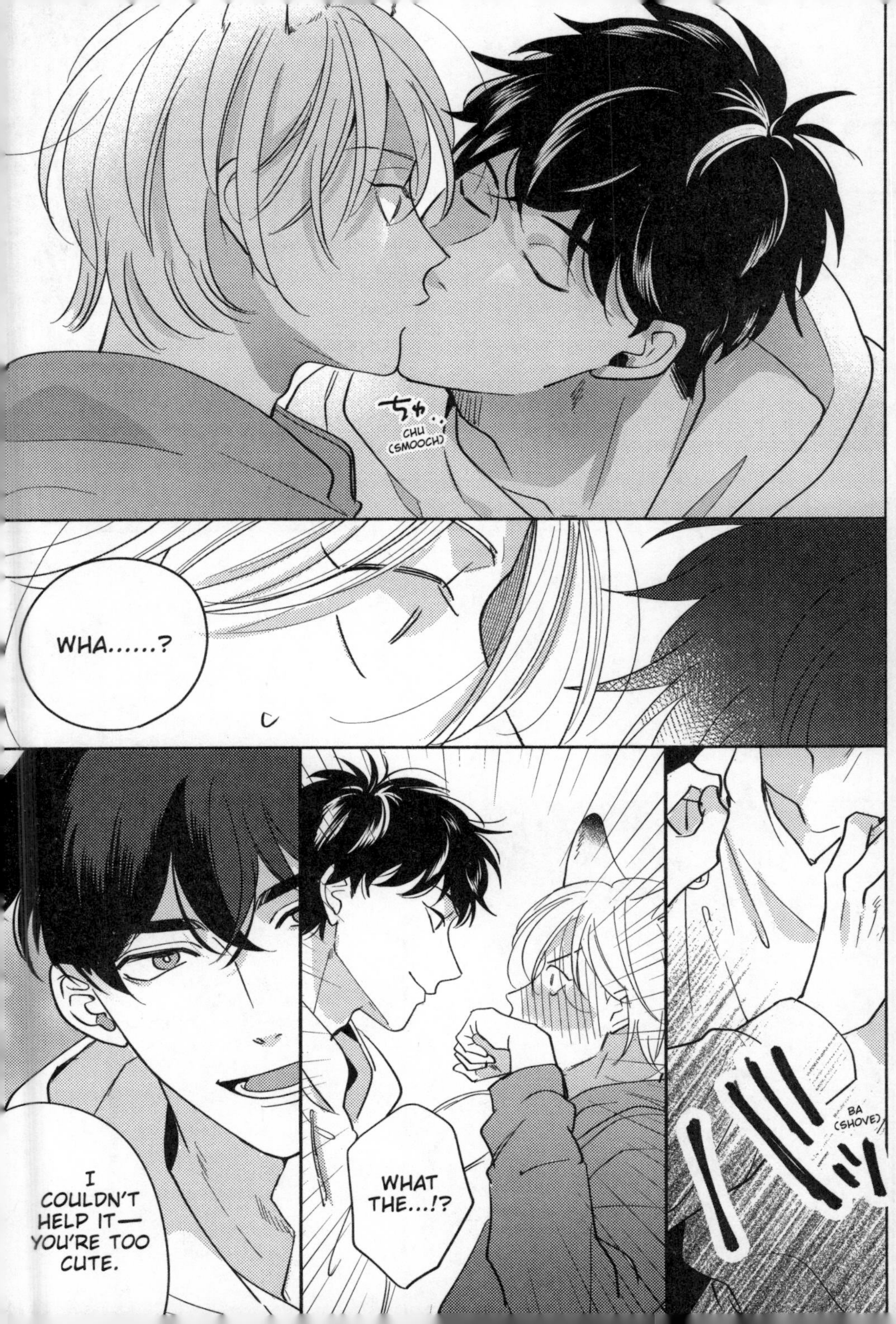
ちゅ…
CHU
(SMOOCH)
WHA......?
バッ
BA
(SHOVE)
WHAT THE...!?
I COULDN'T HELP IT— YOU'RE TOO CUTE.

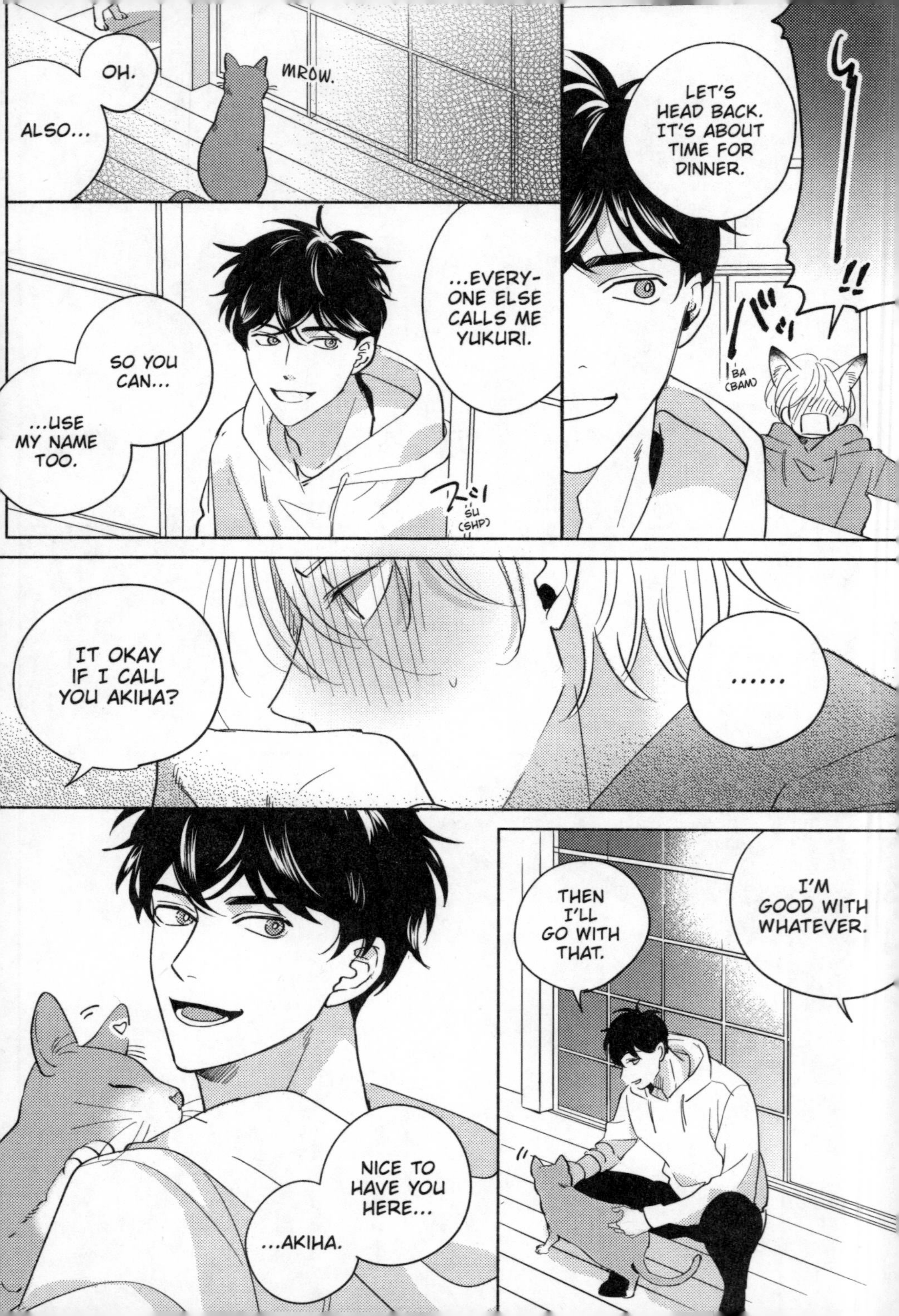
LET'S HEAD BACK. IT'S ABOUT TIME FOR DINNER.
!!
BA (BAM)
OH.
MROW.
ALSO...
...EVERY-ONE ELSE CALLS ME YUKURI.
SO YOU CAN...
...USE MY NAME TOO.
SU (SHP)
IT OKAY IF I CALL YOU AKIHA?
......
I'M GOOD WITH WHATEVER.
THEN I'LL GO WITH THAT.
NICE TO HAVE YOU HERE...
...AKIHA.

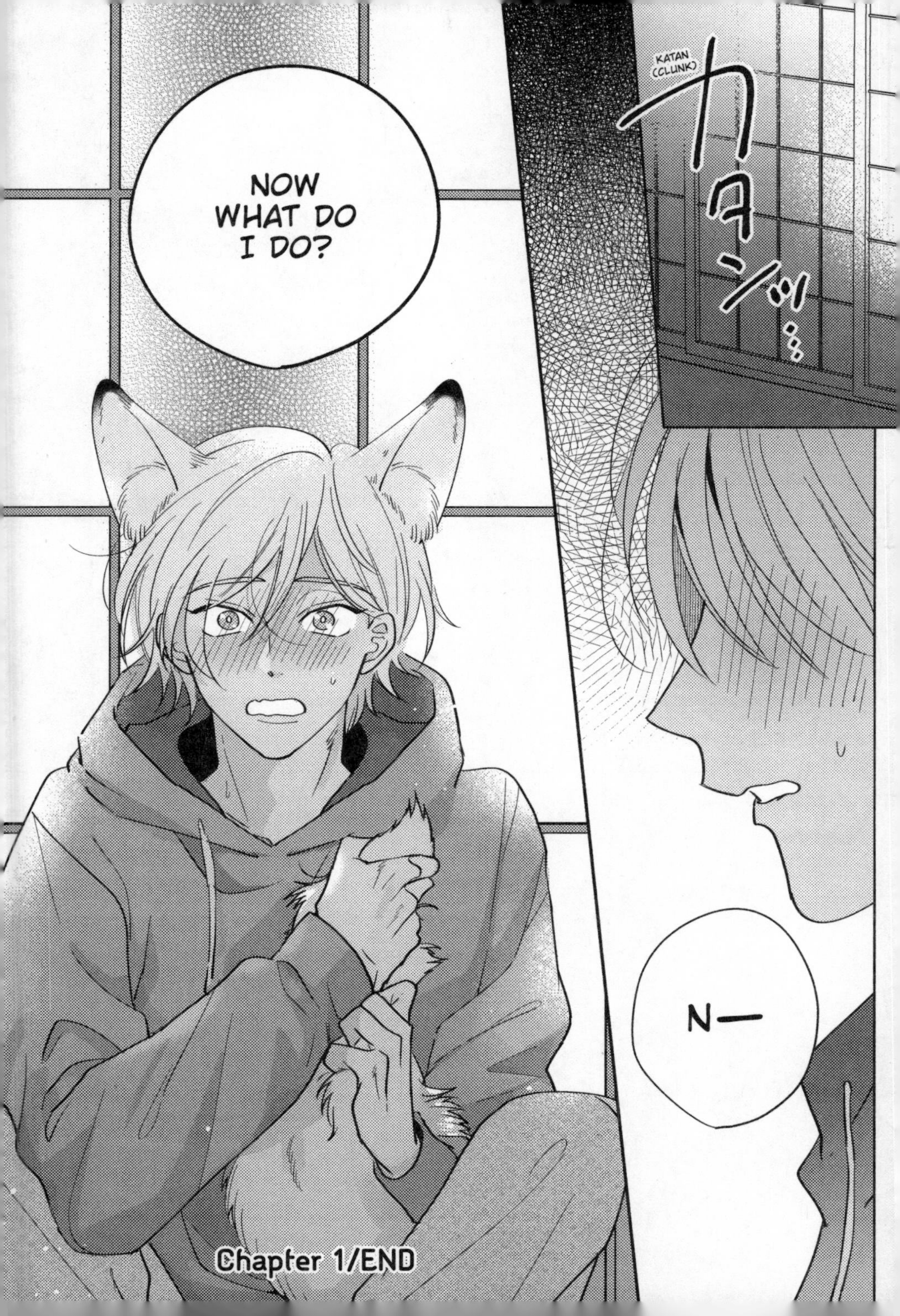
KATAN (CLUNK)
カタンッ…
N—
NOW WHAT DO I DO?
Chapter 1/END

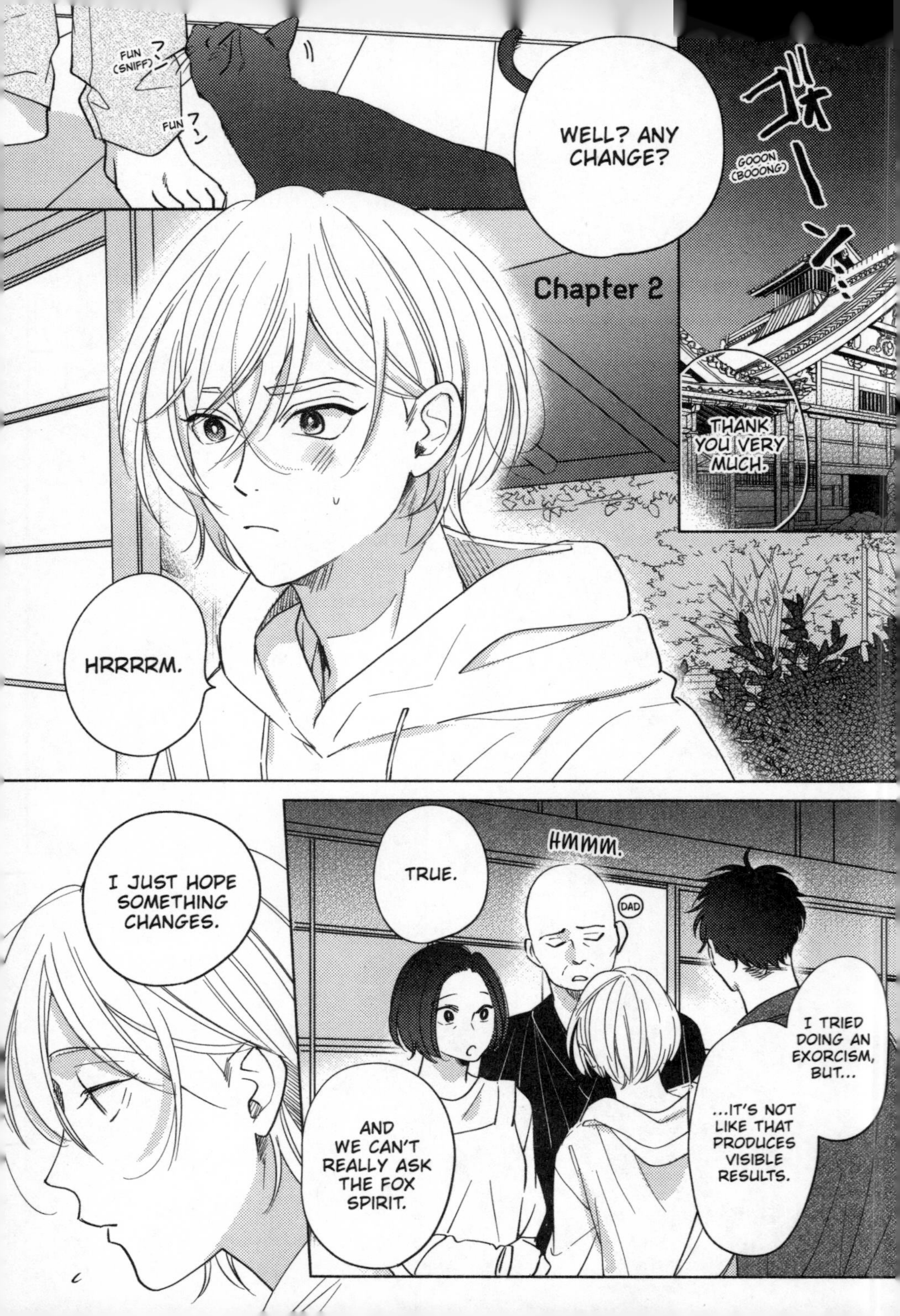
GOOON (BOOONG)
THANK YOU VERY MUCH.
FUN (SNIFF)
FUN
WELL? ANY CHANGE?
Chapter 2
HRRRRM.
HMMM.
TRUE.
DAD
I TRIED DOING AN EXORCISM, BUT...
...IT'S NOT LIKE THAT PRODUCES VISIBLE RESULTS.
AND WE CAN'T REALLY ASK THE FOX SPIRIT.
I JUST HOPE SOMETHING CHANGES.

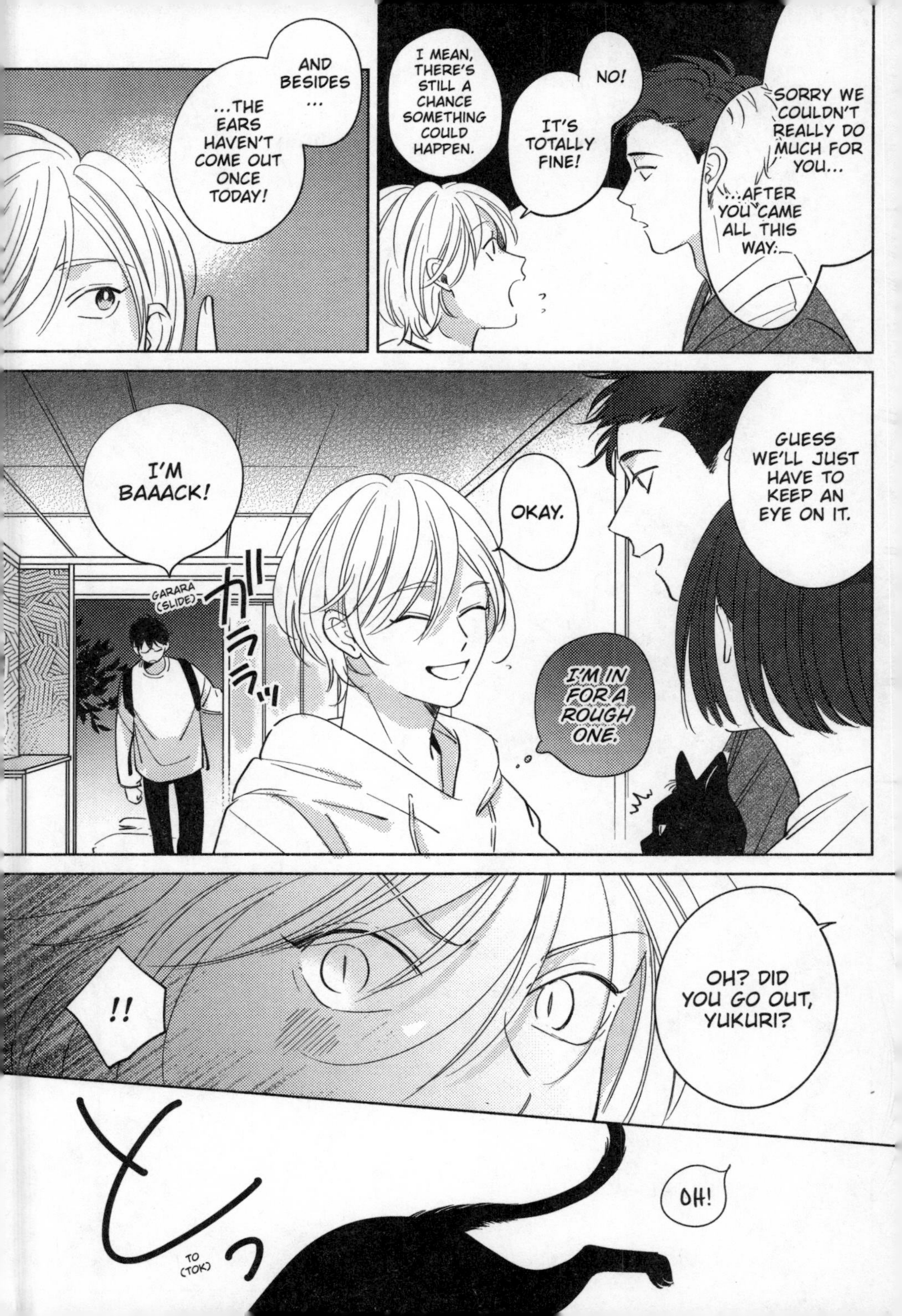
SORRY WE COULDN'T REALLY DO MUCH FOR YOU...
...AFTER YOU CAME ALL THIS WAY.
NO!
IT'S TOTALLY FINE!
I MEAN, THERE'S STILL A CHANCE SOMETHING COULD HAPPEN.
AND BESIDES...
...THE EARS HAVEN'T COME OUT ONCE TODAY!
GUESS WE'LL JUST HAVE TO KEEP AN EYE ON IT.
OKAY.
I'M IN FOR A ROUGH ONE.
I'M BAAACK!
ガラララッ
GARARA (SLIDE)
OH? DID YOU GO OUT, YUKURI?
!!
OH!
とっ
TO (TOK)

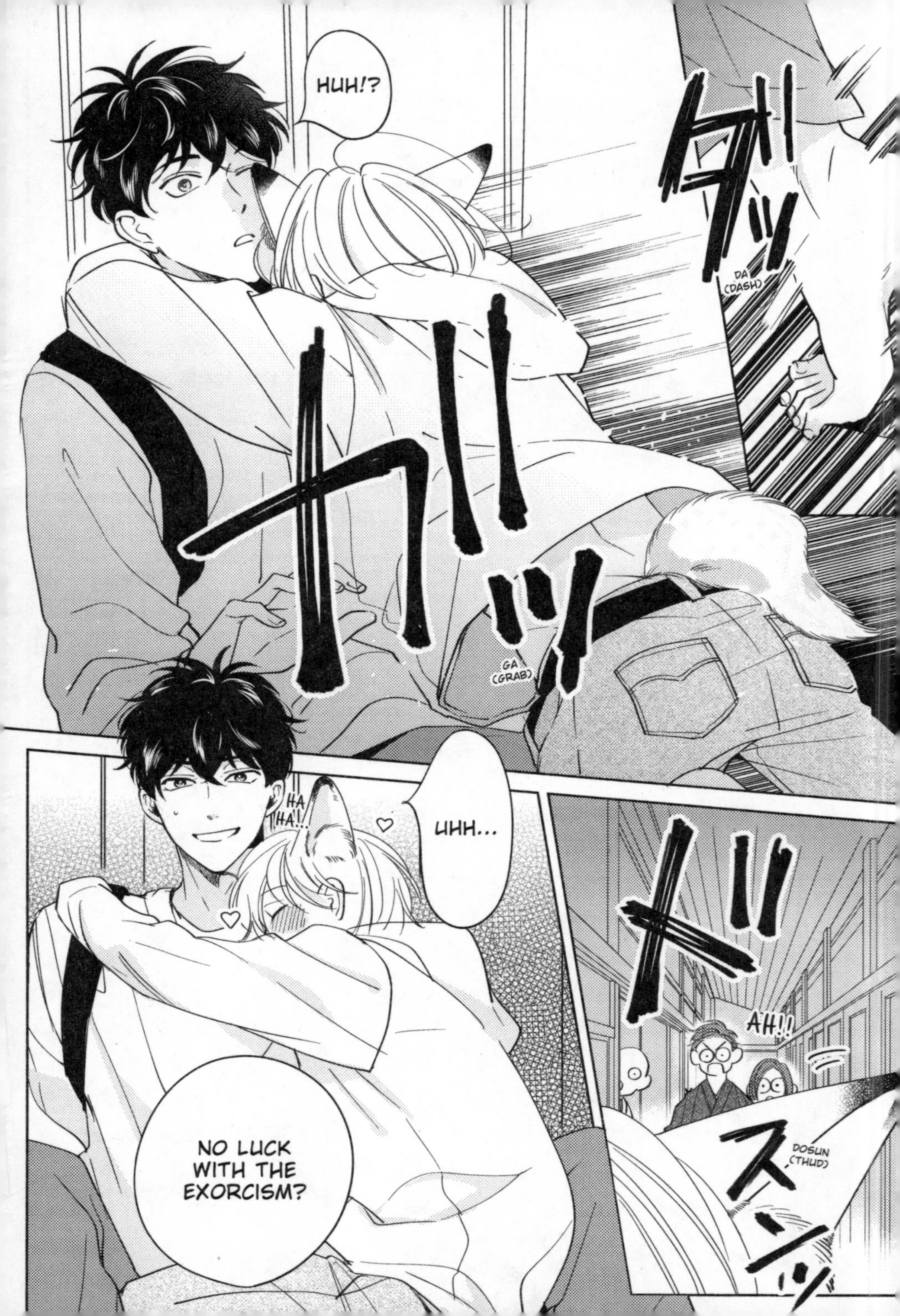
DA
(DASH)
HUH!?
GA
(GRAB)
AH!!
DOSUN
(THUD)
HA
HA!
UHH...
NO LUCK
WITH THE
EXORCISM?

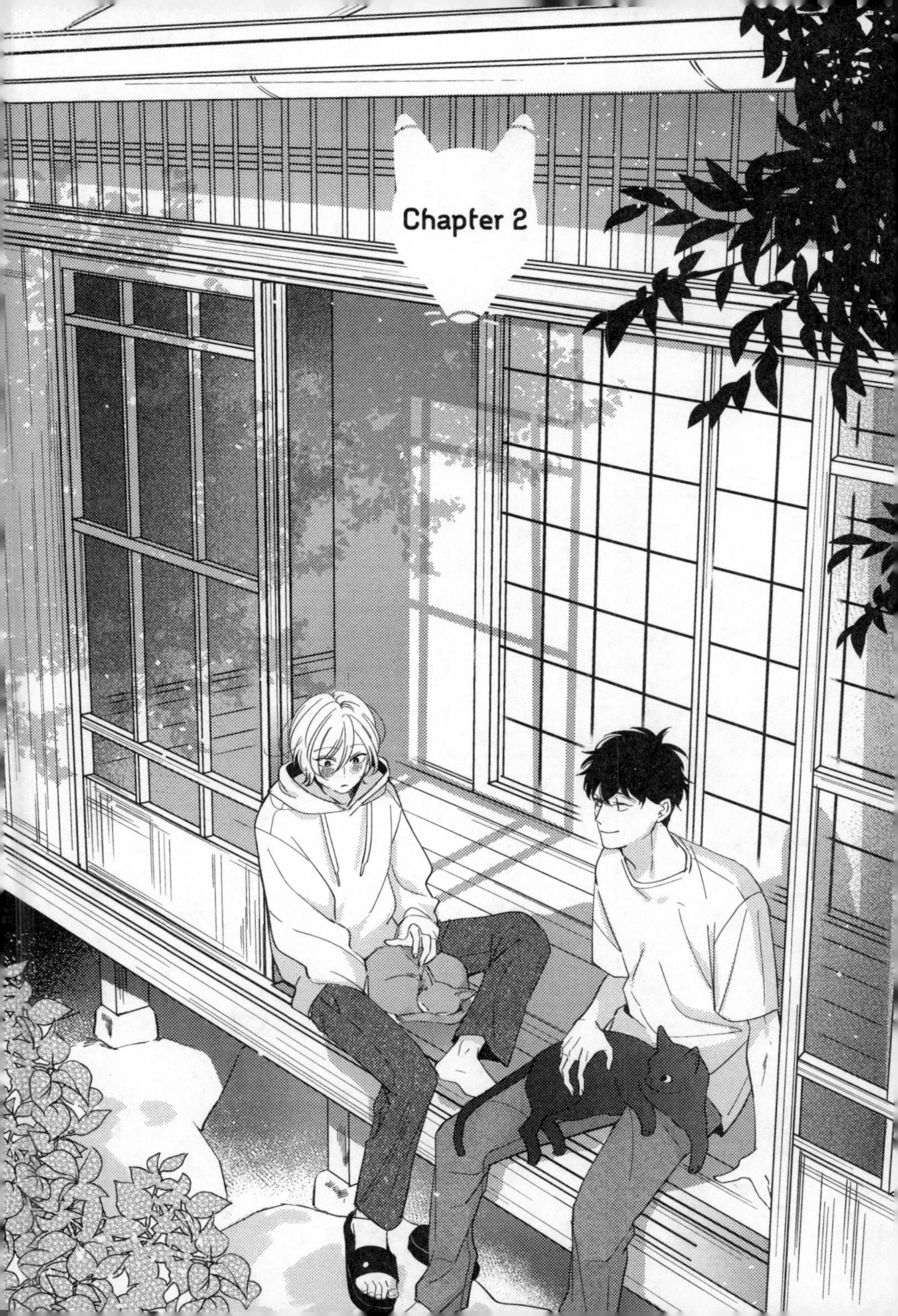
Chapter 2

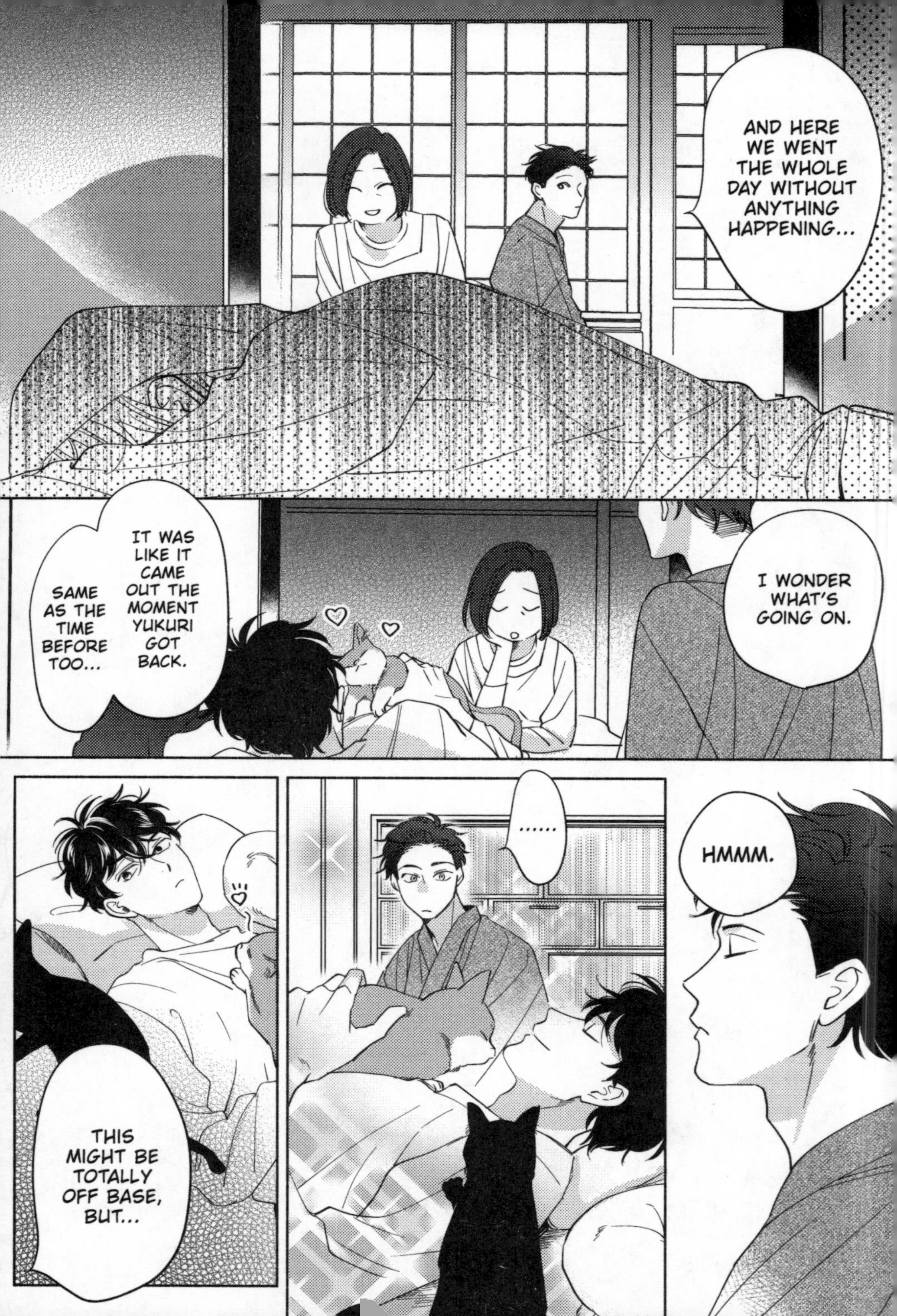
AND HERE WE WENT THE WHOLE DAY WITHOUT ANYTHING HAPPENING...
I WONDER WHAT'S GOING ON.
IT WAS LIKE IT CAME OUT THE MOMENT YUKURI GOT BACK.
SAME AS THE TIME BEFORE TOO...
HMMM.
......
THIS MIGHT BE TOTALLY OFF BASE, BUT...

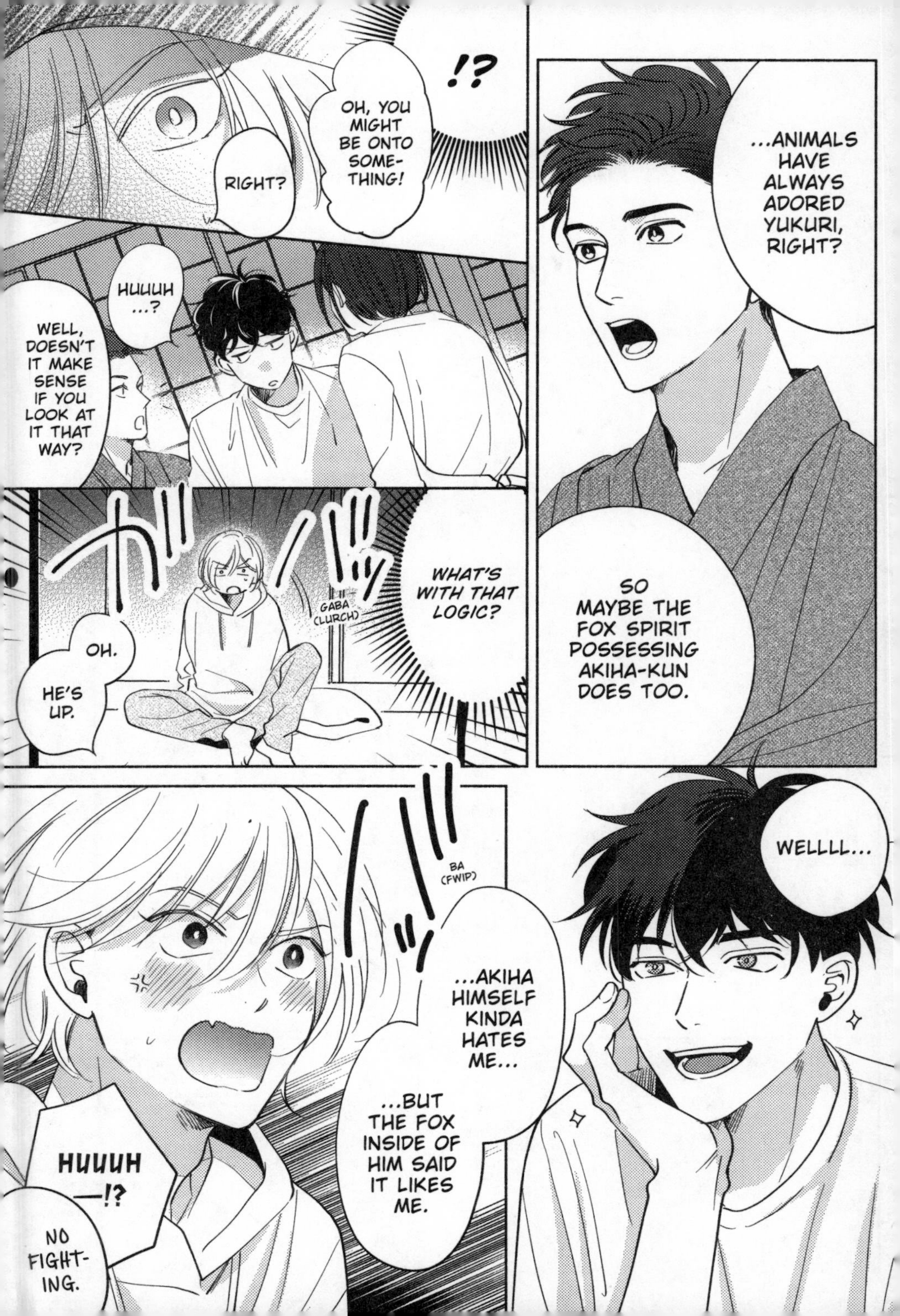
...ANIMALS HAVE ALWAYS ADORED YUKURI, RIGHT?
SO MAYBE THE FOX SPIRIT POSSESSING AKIHA-KUN DOES TOO.
!?
OH, YOU MIGHT BE ONTO SOME-THING!
RIGHT?
HUUUH ...?
WELL, DOESN'T IT MAKE SENSE IF YOU LOOK AT IT THAT WAY?
WHAT'S WITH THAT LOGIC?
GABA (CLURCH)
OH.
HE'S UP.
WELLLL...
...AKIHA HIMSELF KINDA HATES ME...
...BUT THE FOX INSIDE OF HIM SAID IT LIKES ME.
BA (FWIP)
HUUUH —!?
NO FIGHT-ING.

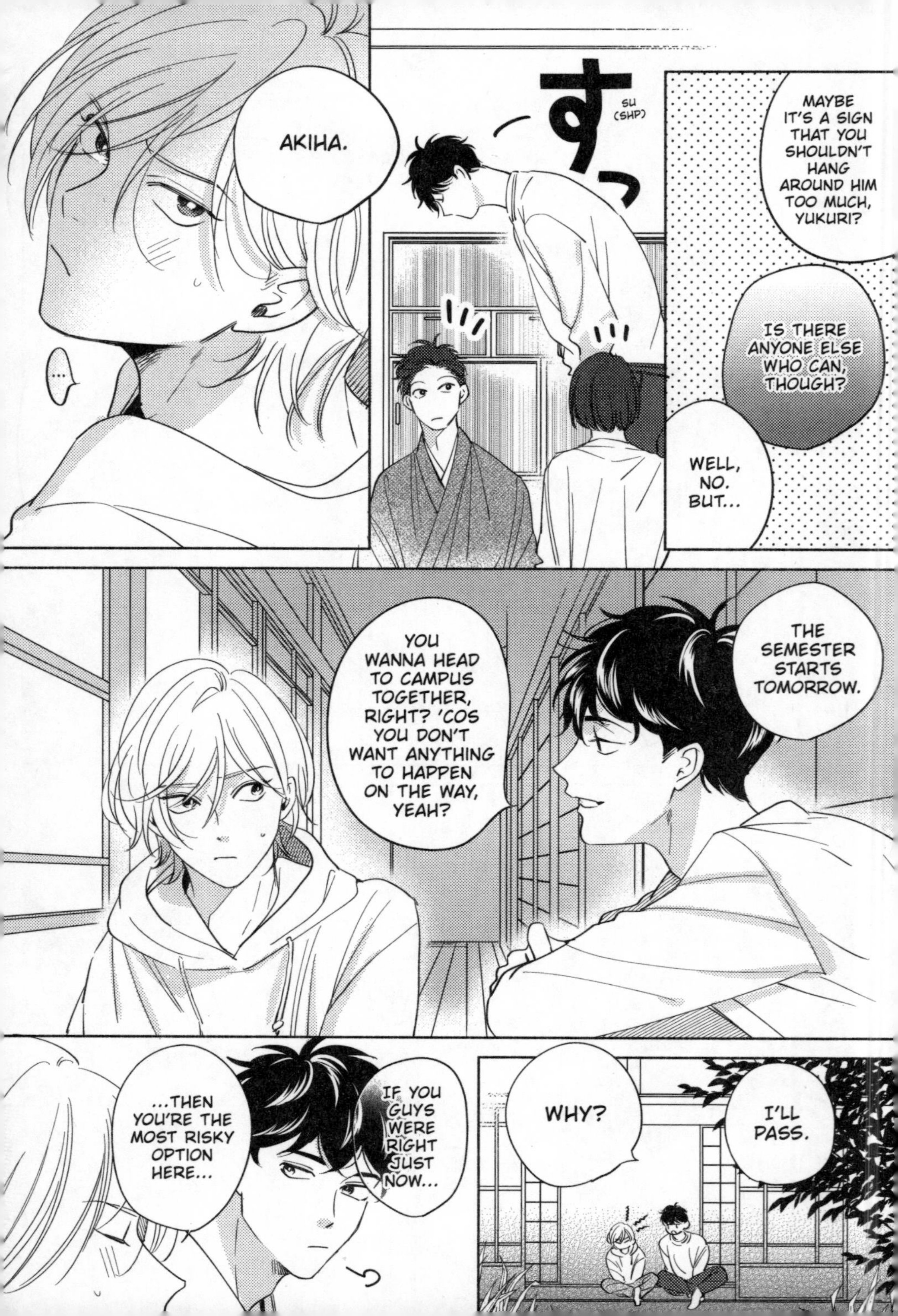
MAYBE IT'S A SIGN THAT YOU SHOULDN'T HANG AROUND HIM TOO MUCH, YUKURI?
IS THERE ANYONE ELSE WHO CAN, THOUGH?
WELL, NO. BUT...
すっ
SU (SHP)
AKIHA.
....
THE SEMESTER STARTS TOMORROW.
YOU WANNA HEAD TO CAMPUS TOGETHER, RIGHT? 'COS YOU DON'T WANT ANYTHING TO HAPPEN ON THE WAY, YEAH?
I'LL PASS.
WHY?
IF YOU GUYS WERE RIGHT JUST NOW...
...THEN YOU'RE THE MOST RISKY OPTION HERE...

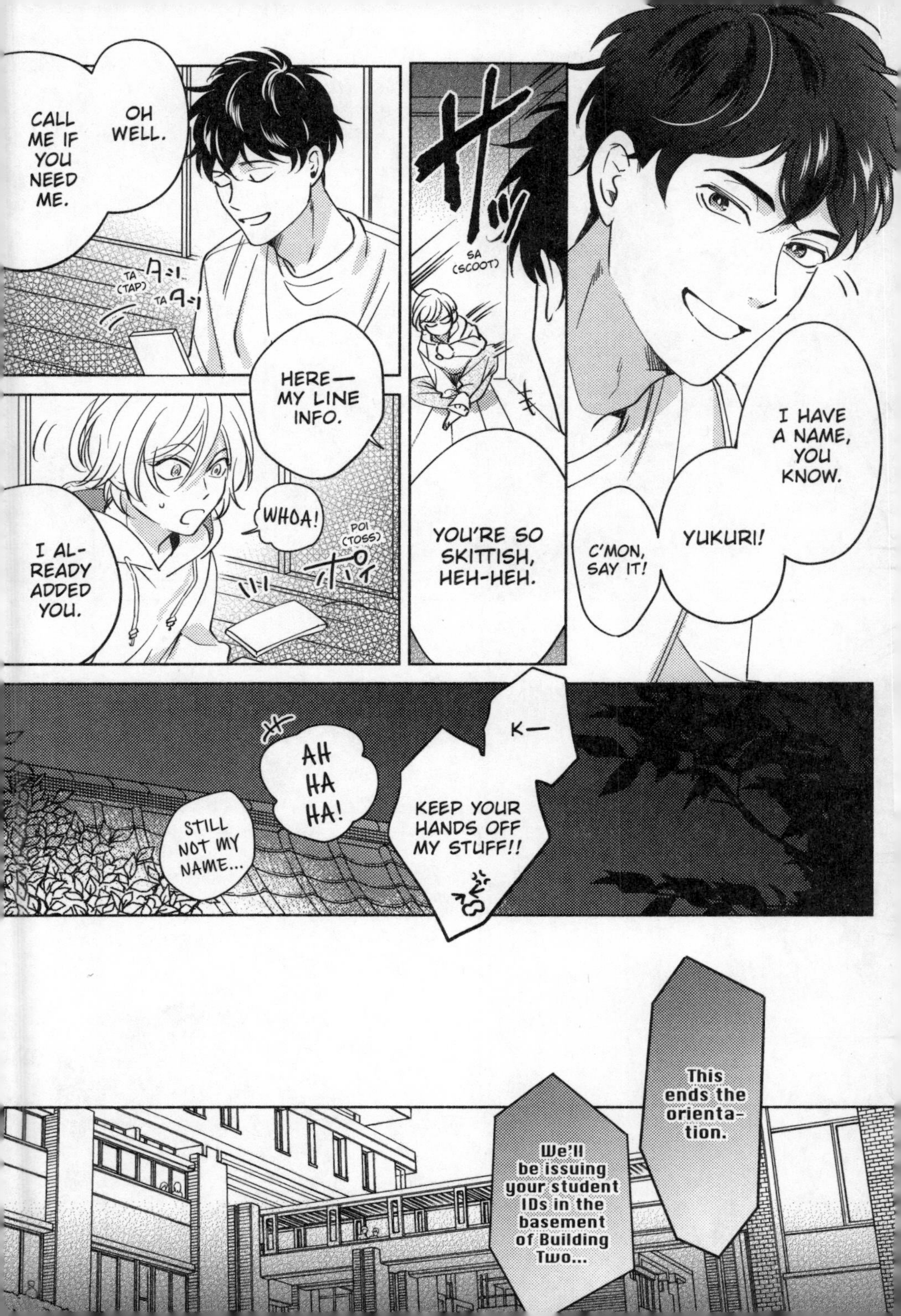
I HAVE A NAME, YOU KNOW.
YUKURI!
C'MON, SAY IT!
SA (SCOOT)
YOU'RE SO SKITTISH, HEH-HEH.
OH WELL.
CALL ME IF YOU NEED ME.
TA (TAP)
TA
HERE— MY LINE INFO.
POI (TOSS)
WHOA!
I AL- READY ADDED YOU.
K—
KEEP YOUR HANDS OFF MY STUFF!!
AH HA HA!
STILL NOT MY NAME...
This ends the orienta- tion.
We'll be issuing your student IDs in the basement of Building Two...

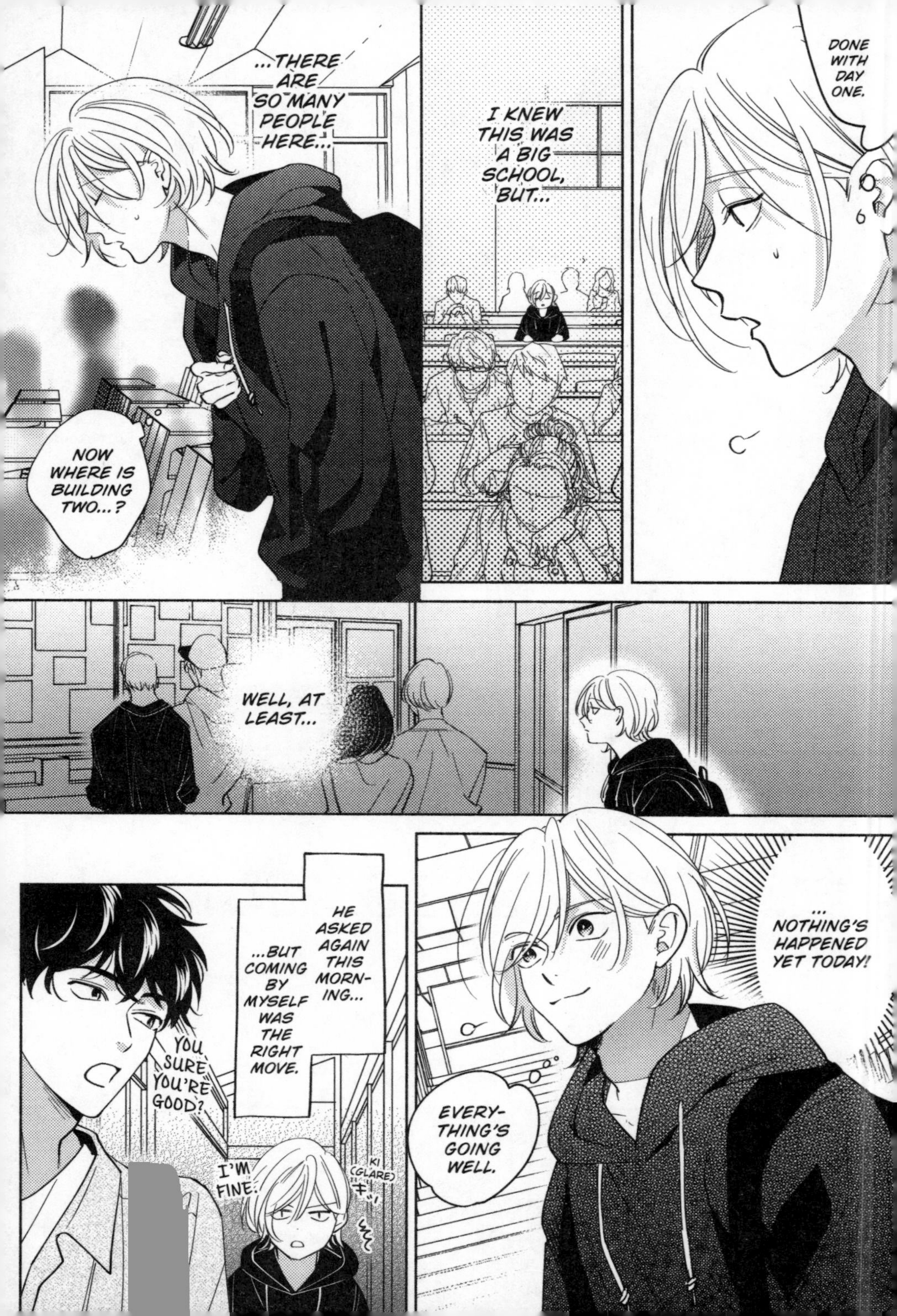
DONE WITH DAY ONE.
I KNEW THIS WAS A BIG SCHOOL, BUT...
...THERE ARE SO MANY PEOPLE HERE...
NOW WHERE IS BUILDING TWO...?
WELL, AT LEAST...
...NOTHING'S HAPPENED YET TODAY!
EVERY-THING'S GOING WELL.
HE ASKED AGAIN THIS MORN-ING...
...BUT COMING BY MYSELF WAS THE RIGHT MOVE.
YOU SURE YOU'RE GOOD?
I'M FINE.
KI (GLARE)

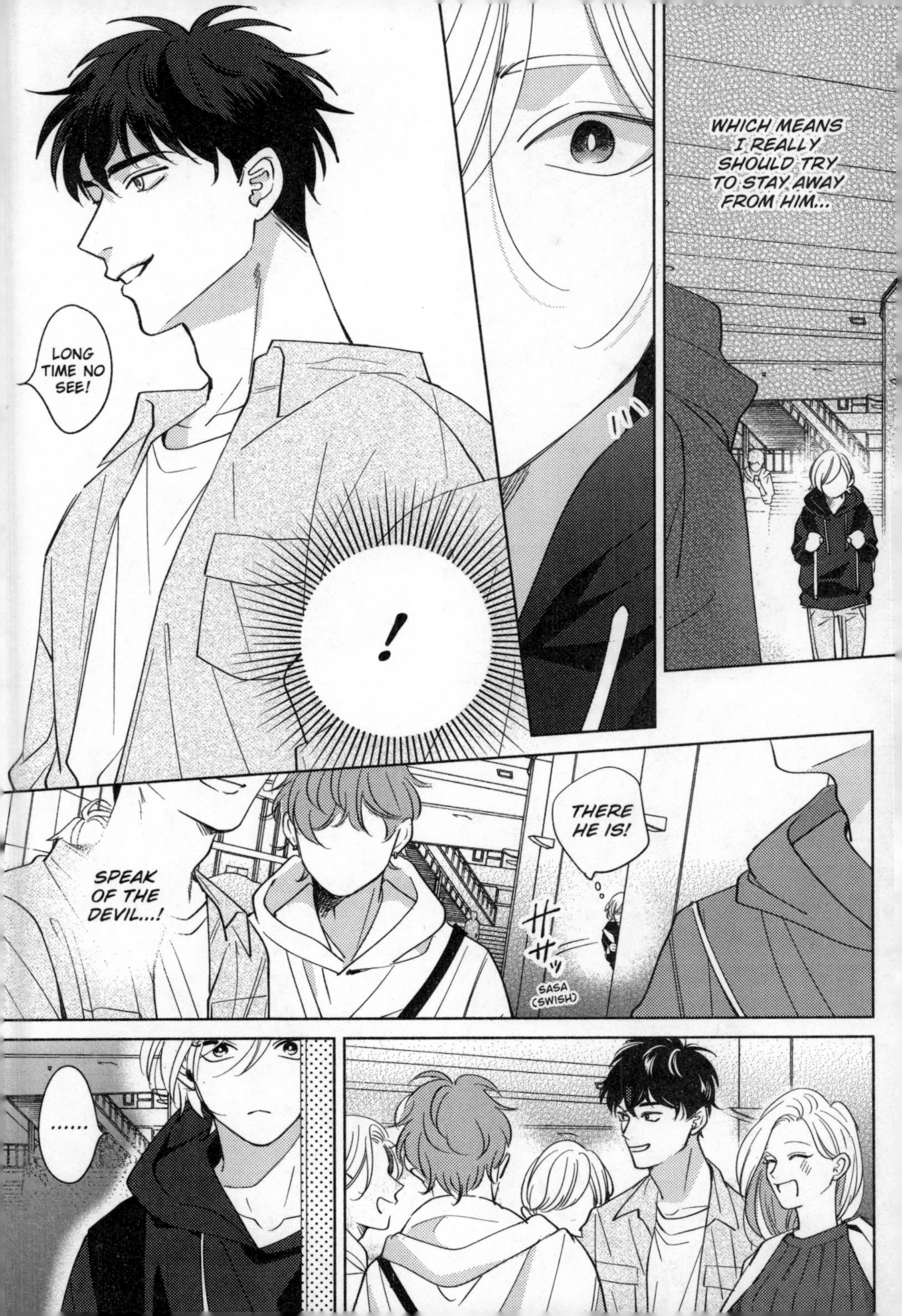

WHICH MEANS I REALLY SHOULD TRY TO STAY AWAY FROM HIM...
LONG TIME NO SEE!
!
THERE HE IS!
ササッ
SASA (SWISH)
SPEAK OF THE DEVIL...!
......

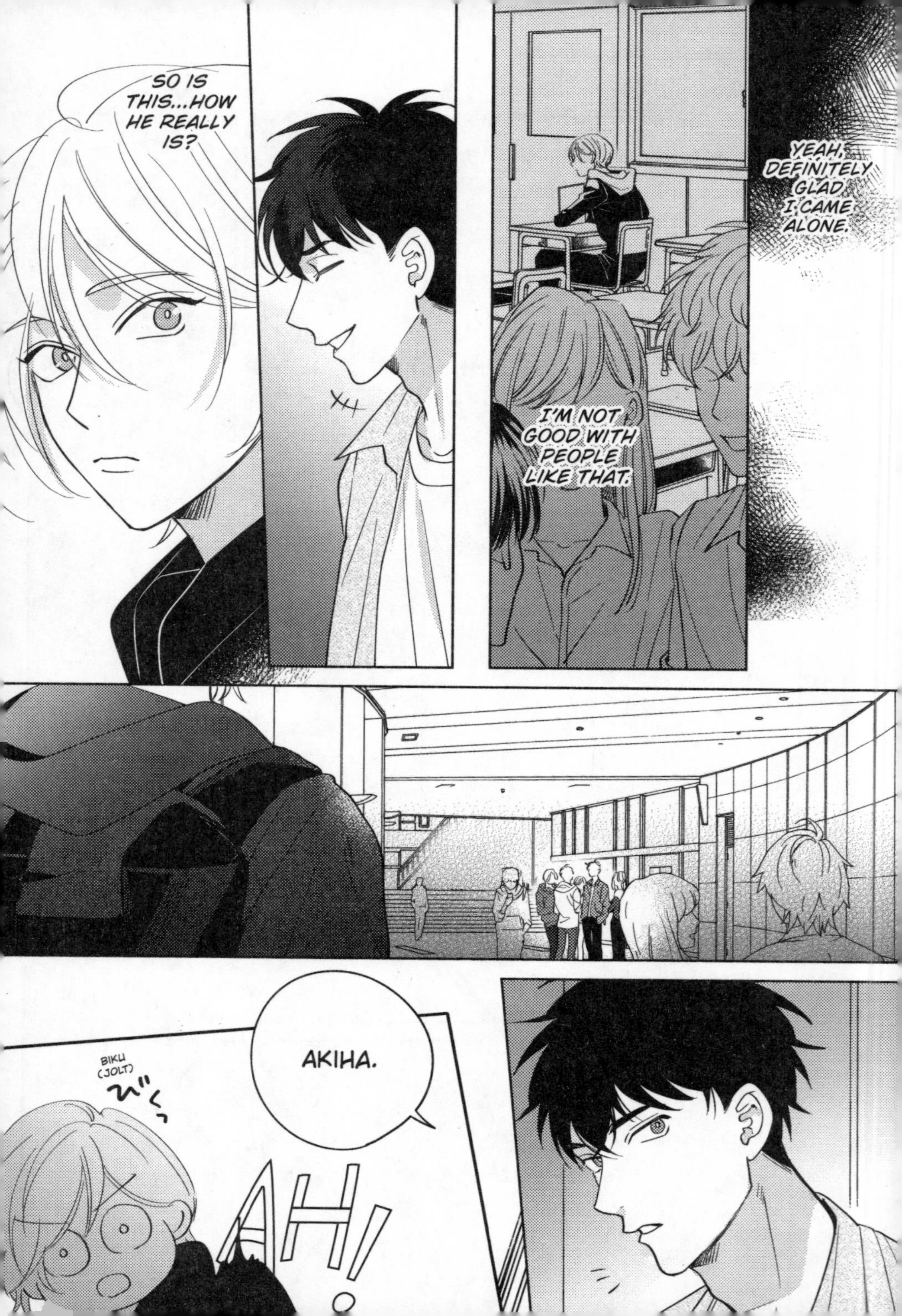
YEAH, DEFINITELY GLAD I CAME ALONE.
I'M NOT GOOD WITH PEOPLE LIKE THAT.
SO IS THIS...HOW HE REALLY IS?
AKIHA.
BIKU (JOLT)
びくっ
AH!

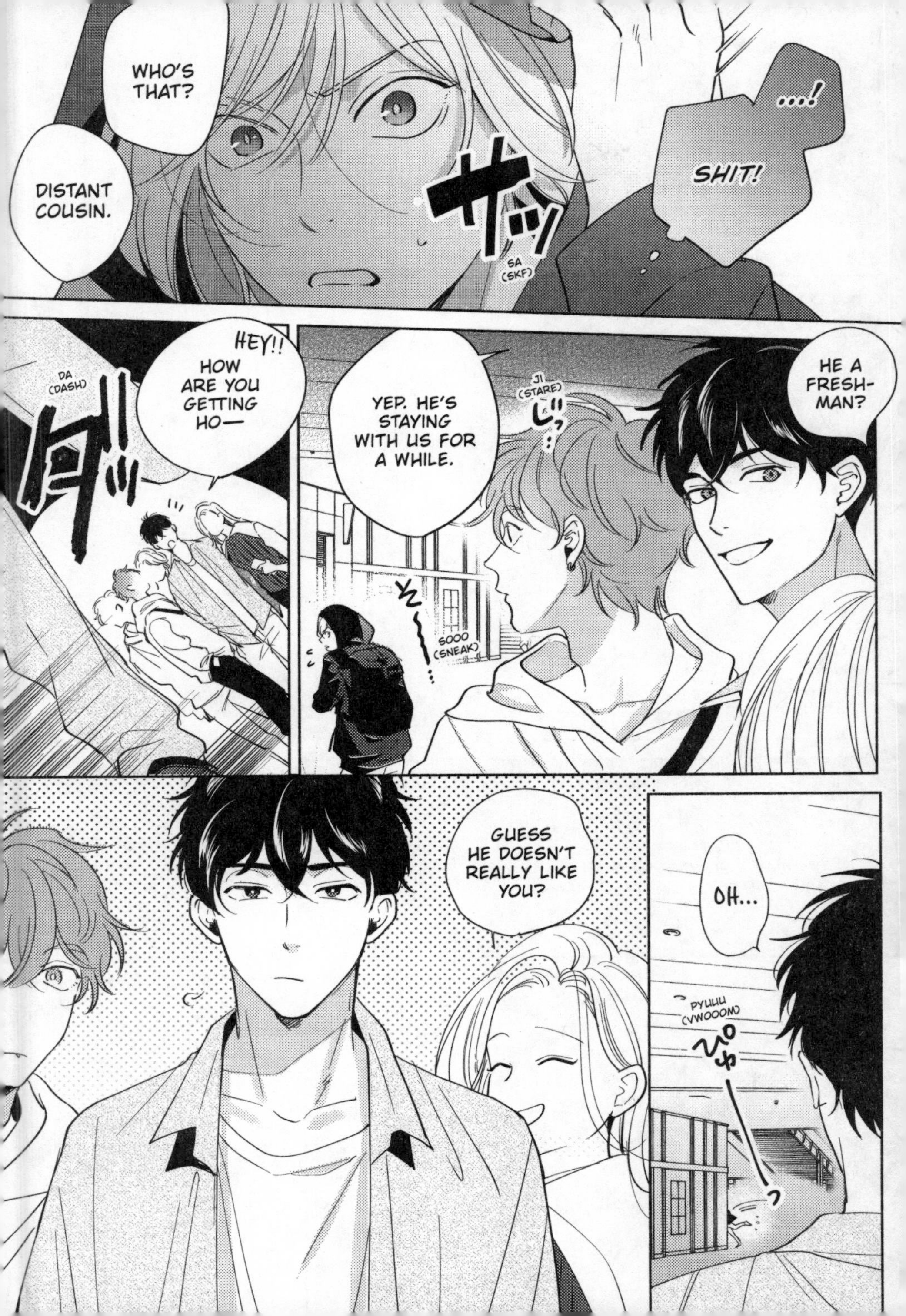
...!
SHIT!
WHO'S THAT?
SA (SKF)
DISTANT COUSIN.
HE A FRESHMAN?
JI (STARE)
YEP. HE'S STAYING WITH US FOR A WHILE.
SOOO (SNEAK)
HEY!! HOW ARE YOU GETTING HO—
DA (DASH)
OH...
PYUUU (VWOOOM)
GUESS HE DOESN'T REALLY LIKE YOU?

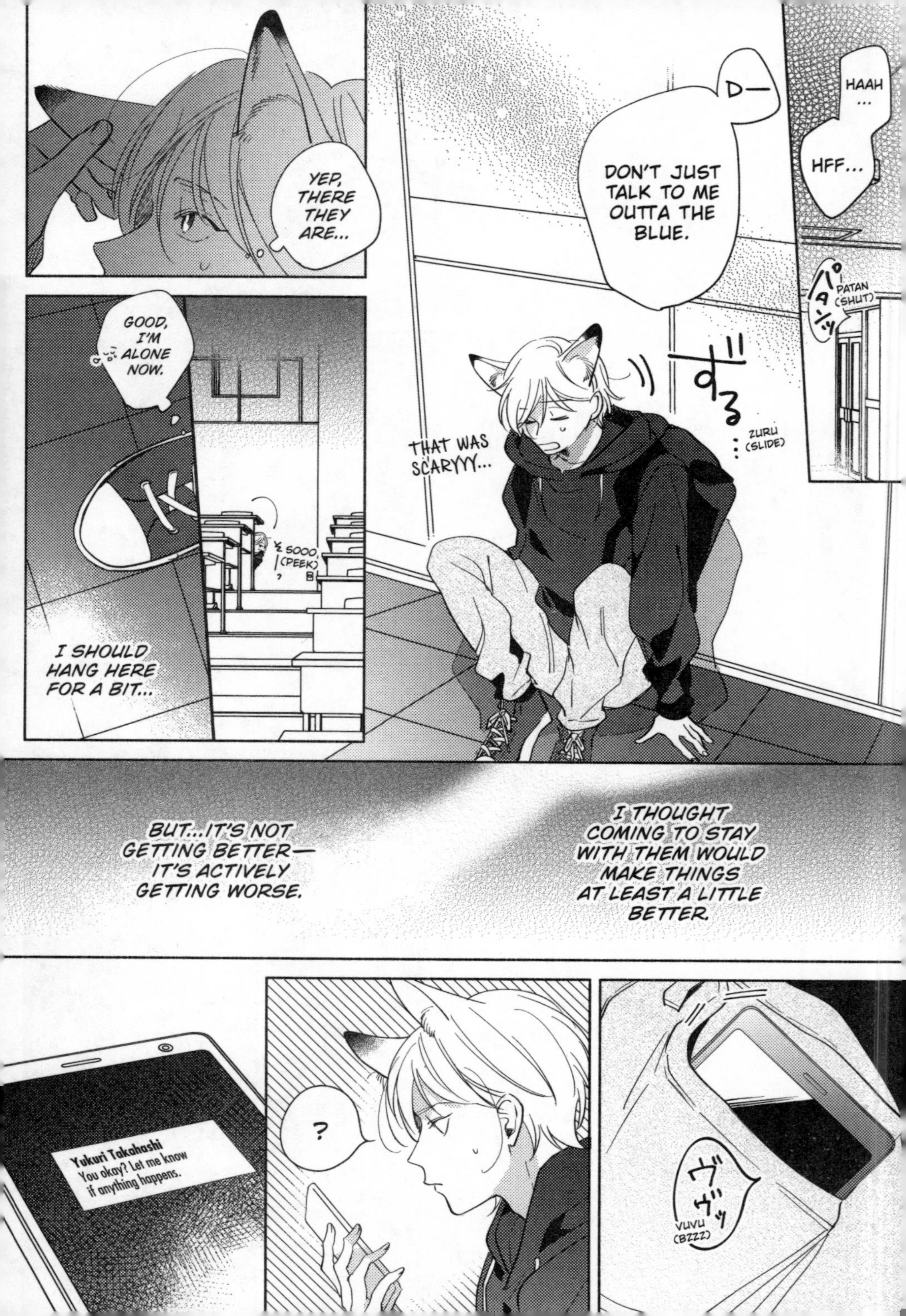
HAAH ...
HFF...
パタン PATAN (SHUT)
D—
DON'T JUST TALK TO ME OUTTA THE BLUE.
ずる ZURU (SLIDE)
THAT WAS SCARYYY...
YEP, THERE THEY ARE...
GOOD, I'M ALONE NOW.
SOOO (PEEK)
I SHOULD HANG HERE FOR A BIT...
I THOUGHT COMING TO STAY WITH THEM WOULD MAKE THINGS AT LEAST A LITTLE BETTER.
BUT...IT'S NOT GETTING BETTER— IT'S ACTIVELY GETTING WORSE.
ヴヴッ VUVU (BZZZ)
?
Yukuri Takahashi
You okay? Let me know if anything happens.

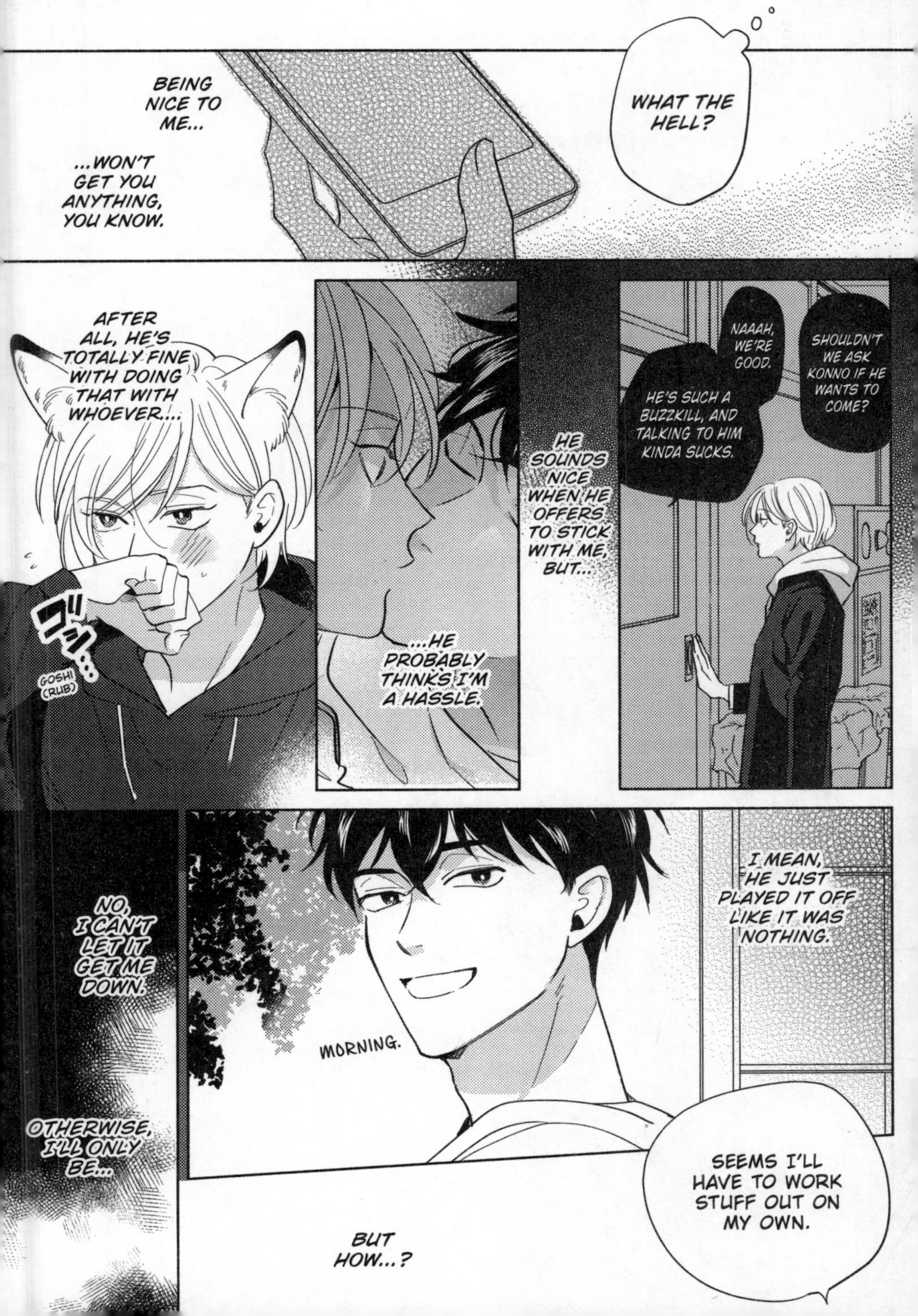
WHAT THE HELL?
BEING NICE TO ME...
...WON'T GET YOU ANYTHING, YOU KNOW.
SHOULDN'T WE ASK KONNO IF HE WANTS TO COME?
NAAAH, WE'RE GOOD.
HE'S SUCH A BUZZKILL, AND TALKING TO HIM KINDA SUCKS.
HE SOUNDS NICE WHEN HE OFFERS TO STICK WITH ME, BUT...
...HE PROBABLY THINKS I'M A HASSLE.
AFTER ALL, HE'S TOTALLY FINE WITH DOING THAT WITH WHOEVER...
ゴシ...
GOSHI (RUB)
I MEAN, HE JUST PLAYED IT OFF LIKE IT WAS NOTHING.
MORNING.
SEEMS I'LL HAVE TO WORK STUFF OUT ON MY OWN.
NO, I CAN'T LET IT GET ME DOWN.
OTHERWISE, I'LL ONLY BE...
BUT HOW...?

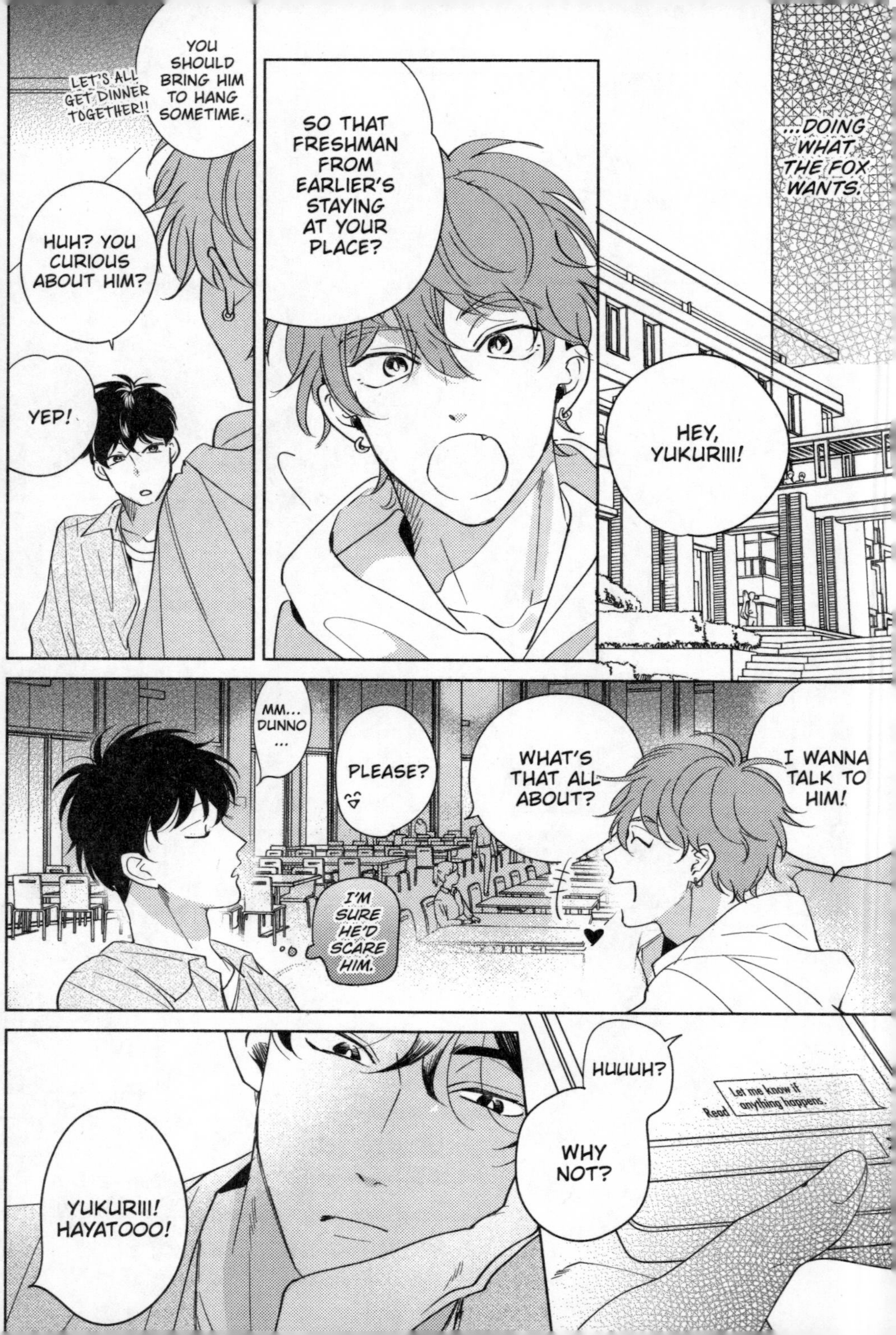
...DOING WHAT THE FOX WANTS.
HEY, YUKURIII!
SO THAT FRESHMAN FROM EARLIER'S STAYING AT YOUR PLACE?
YOU SHOULD BRING HIM TO HANG SOMETIME.
LET'S ALL GET DINNER TOGETHER!!
HUH? YOU CURIOUS ABOUT HIM?
YEP!
I WANNA TALK TO HIM!
WHAT'S THAT ALL ABOUT?
PLEASE?
MM... DUNNO...
I'M SURE HE'D SCARE HIM.
HUUUH?
WHY NOT?
Read
Let me know if anything happens.
YUKURIII! HAYATOOO!

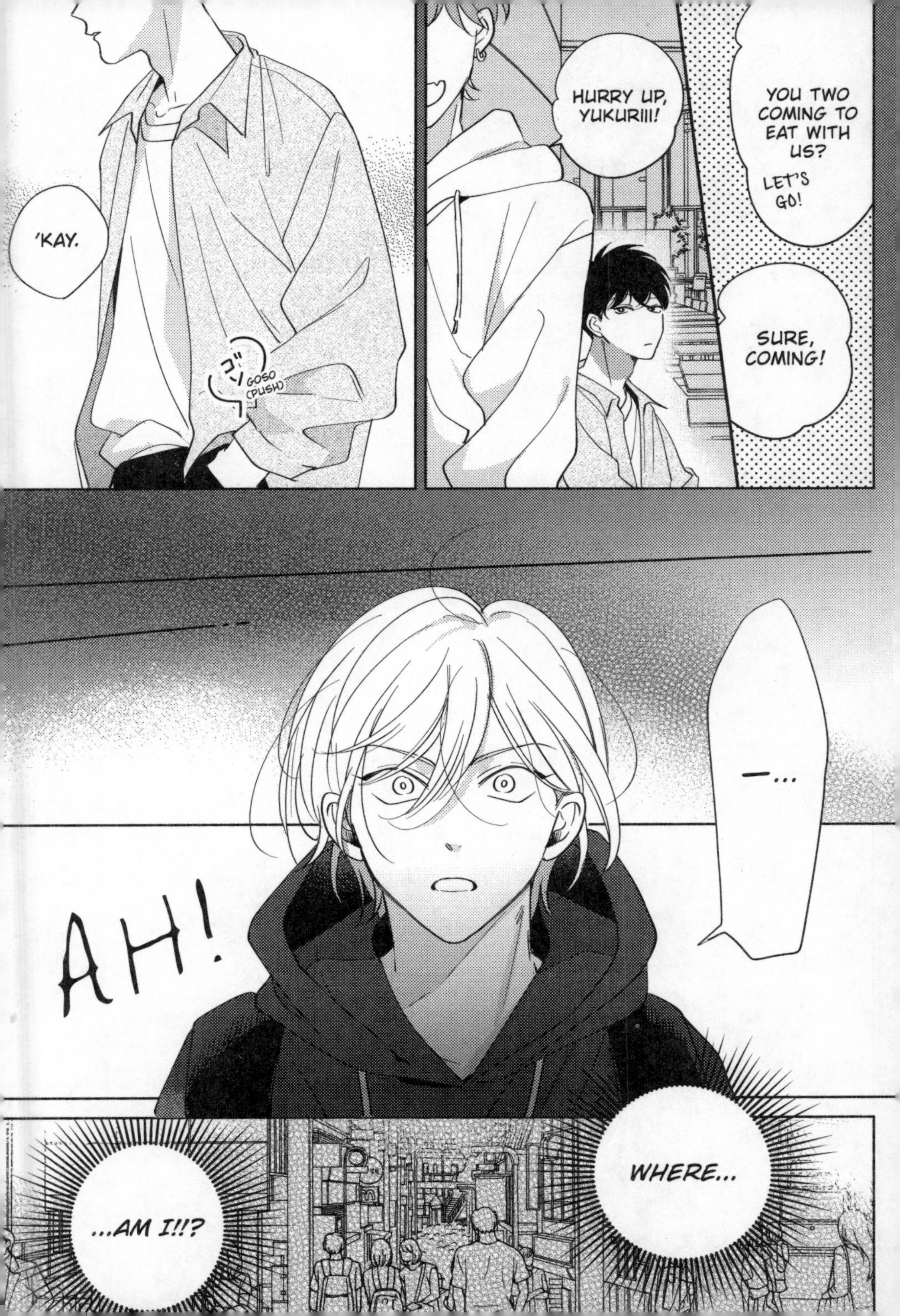
YOU TWO COMING TO EAT WITH US?
LET'S GO!
HURRY UP, YUKURIIII!
SURE, COMING!
'KAY.
GOSO (PUSH)
—...
AH!
WHERE...
...AM I!!?

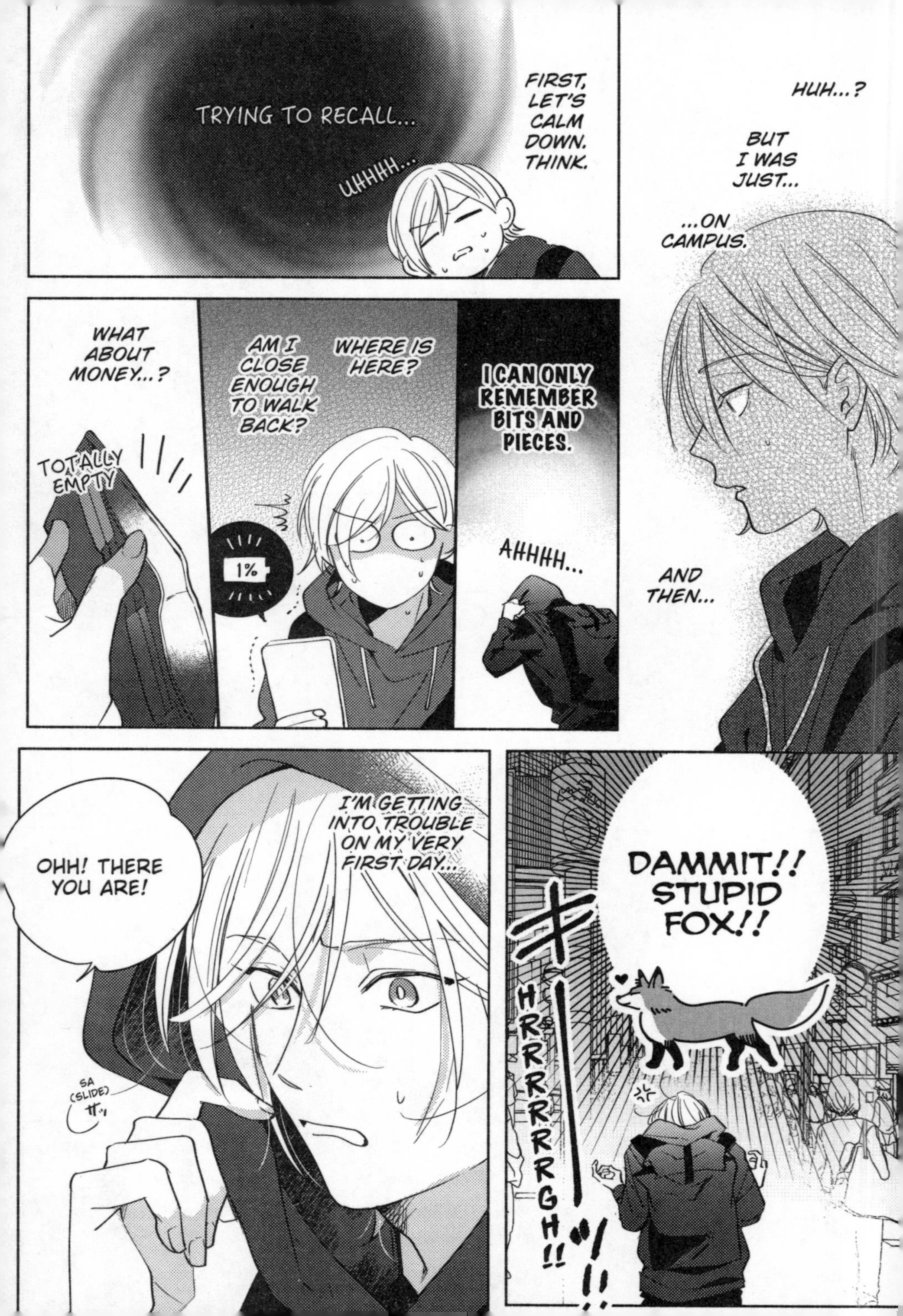
HUH...?
BUT I WAS JUST...
...ON CAMPUS.
AND THEN...
FIRST, LET'S CALM DOWN. THINK.
TRYING TO RECALL...
UHHHH...
I CAN ONLY REMEMBER BITS AND PIECES.
AHHHH...
WHERE IS HERE?
AM I CLOSE ENOUGH TO WALK BACK?
1%
WHAT ABOUT MONEY...?
TOTALLY EMPTY
DAMMIT!! STUPID FOX!!
HRRRRRRRGH!!
I'M GETTING INTO TROUBLE ON MY VERY FIRST DAY...
OHH! THERE YOU ARE!
SA (SLIDE)

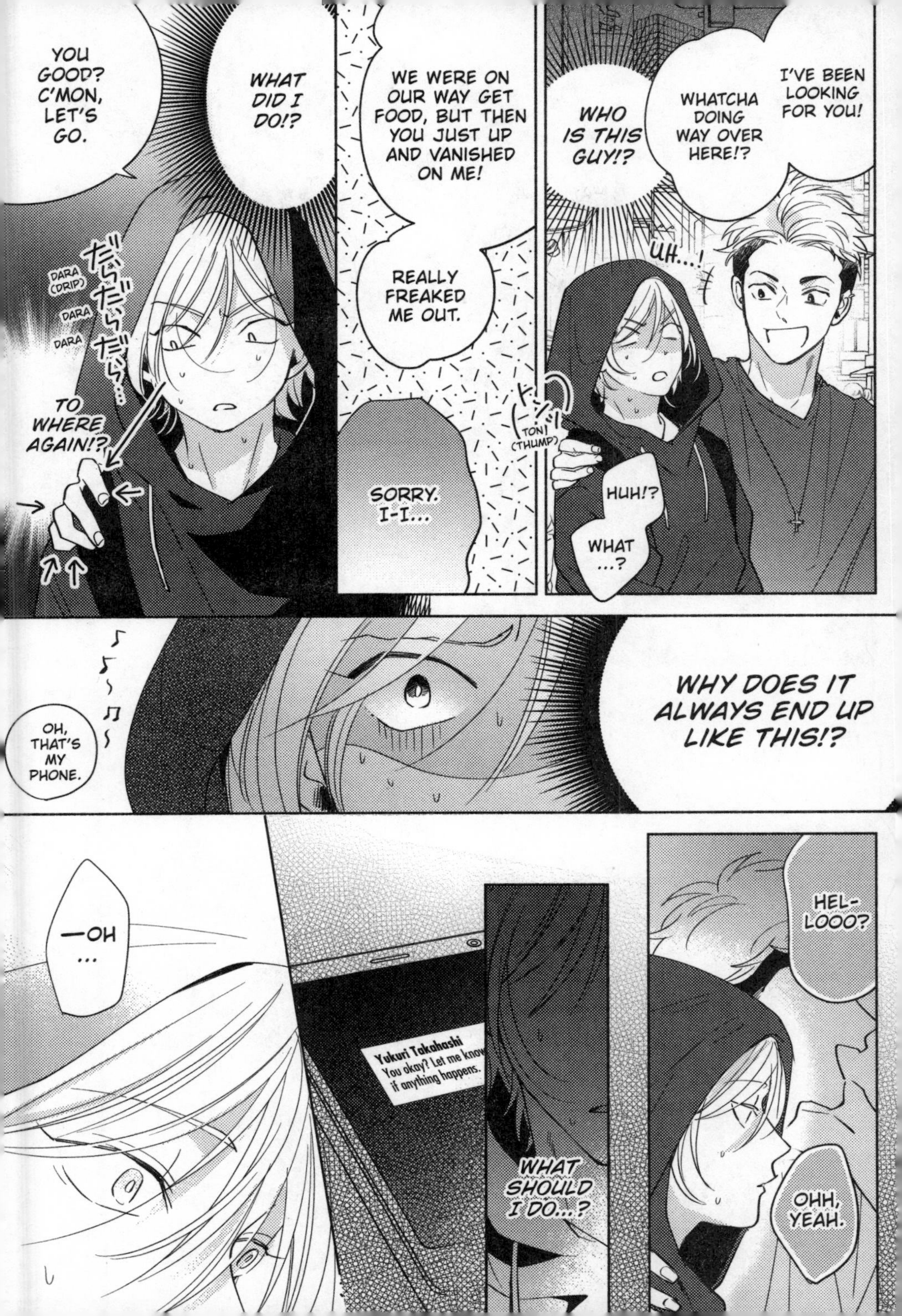
I'VE BEEN LOOKING FOR YOU!
WHATCHA DOING WAY OVER HERE!?
WHO IS THIS GUY!?
UH...!
ドン
TON (THUMP)
HUH!?
WHAT ...?
WE WERE ON OUR WAY GET FOOD, BUT THEN YOU JUST UP AND VANISHED ON ME!
REALLY FREAKED ME OUT.
SORRY. I-I...
WHAT DID I DO!?
YOU GOOD? C'MON, LET'S GO.
だらだらだら…
DARA (DRIP) DARA DARA
TO WHERE AGAIN!?
WHY DOES IT ALWAYS END UP LIKE THIS!?
OH, THAT'S MY PHONE.
HEL-LOOO?
OHH, YEAH.
Yukuri Takahashi
You okay? Let me know if anything happens.
WHAT SHOULD I DO...?
—OH ...

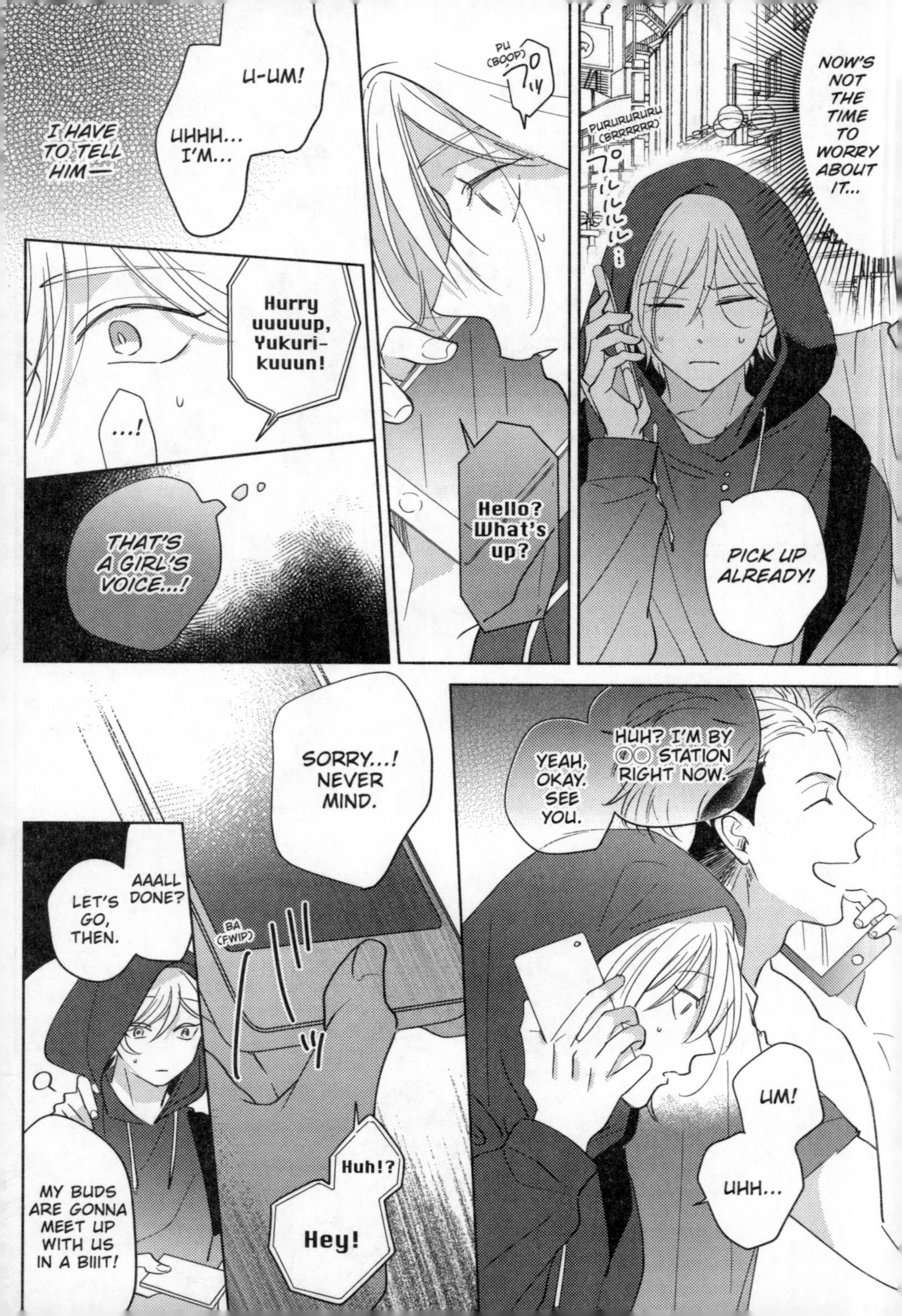
NOW'S NOT THE TIME TO WORRY ABOUT IT...
PURURURURU (BRRRRRR)
PICK UP ALREADY!
PU (BOOP)
Hello? What's up?
U-UM!
UHHH... I'M...
I HAVE TO TELL HIM—
Hurry uuuuup, Yukuri-kuuun!
...!
THAT'S A GIRL'S VOICE...!
HUH? I'M BY ◎◎ STATION RIGHT NOW.
YEAH, OKAY. SEE YOU.
UM!
UHH...
SORRY...! NEVER MIND.
BA (FWIP)
Huh!?
Hey!
AAALL DONE?
LET'S GO, THEN.
MY BUDS ARE GONNA MEET UP WITH US IN A BIIIT!

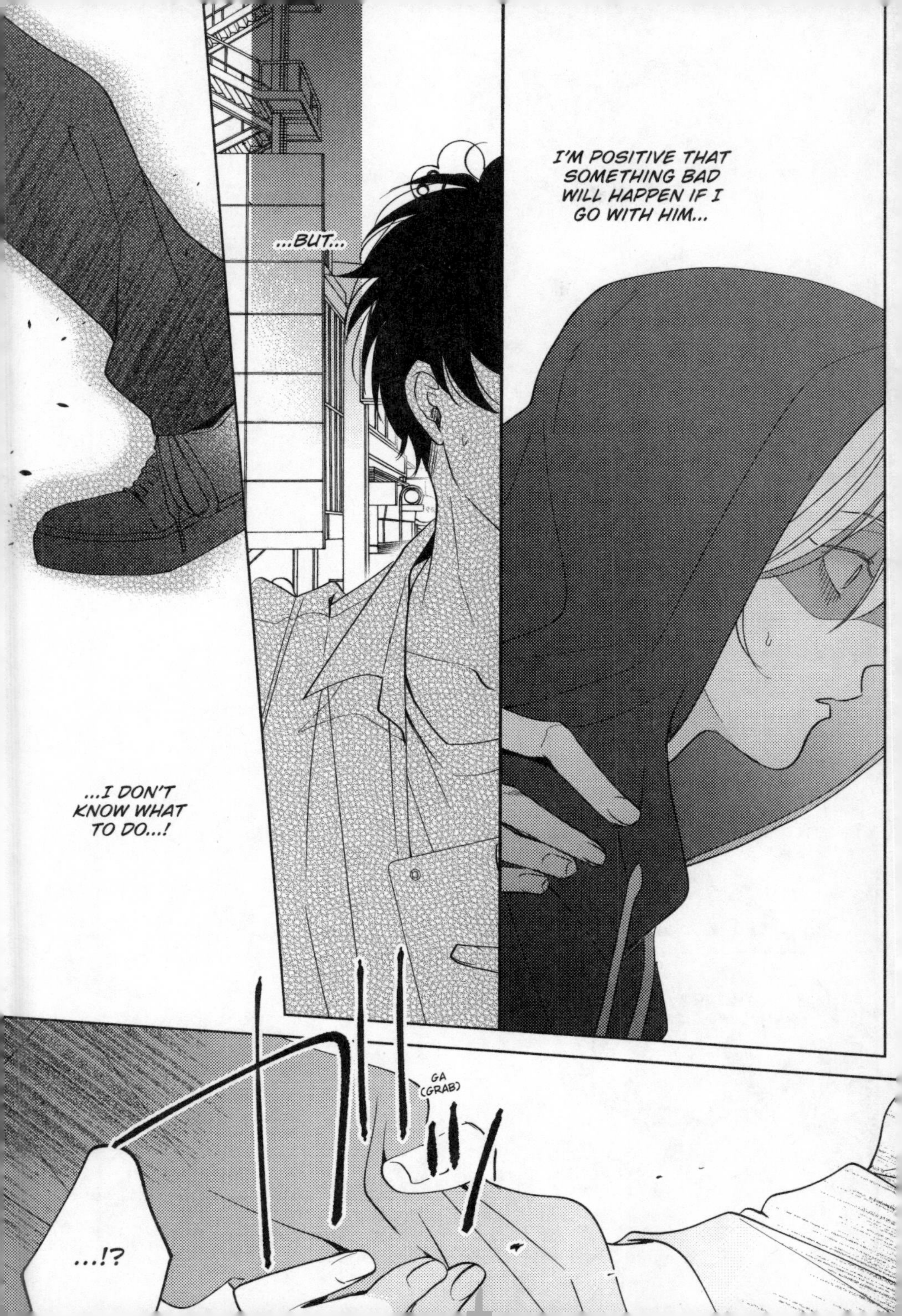
I'M POSITIVE THAT SOMETHING BAD WILL HAPPEN IF I GO WITH HIM...
...BUT...
...I DON'T KNOW WHAT TO DO...!
GA (GRAB)
...!?

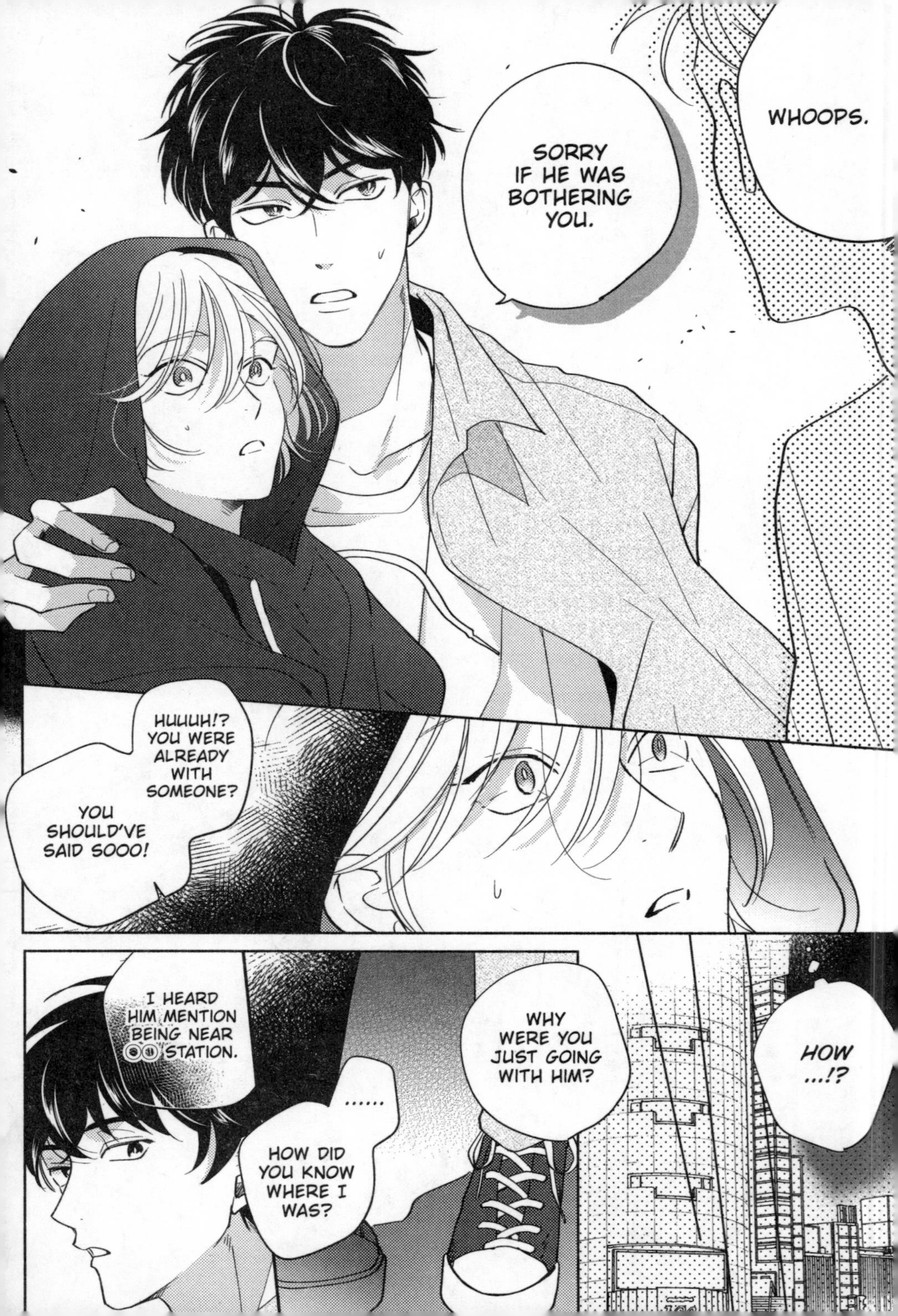
WHOOPS.
SORRY IF HE WAS BOTHERING YOU.
HUUUH!? YOU WERE ALREADY WITH SOMEONE? YOU SHOULD'VE SAID SOOO!
HOW ...!?
WHY WERE YOU JUST GOING WITH HIM?
......
HOW DID YOU KNOW WHERE I WAS?
I HEARD HIM MENTION BEING NEAR ◎◎ STATION.

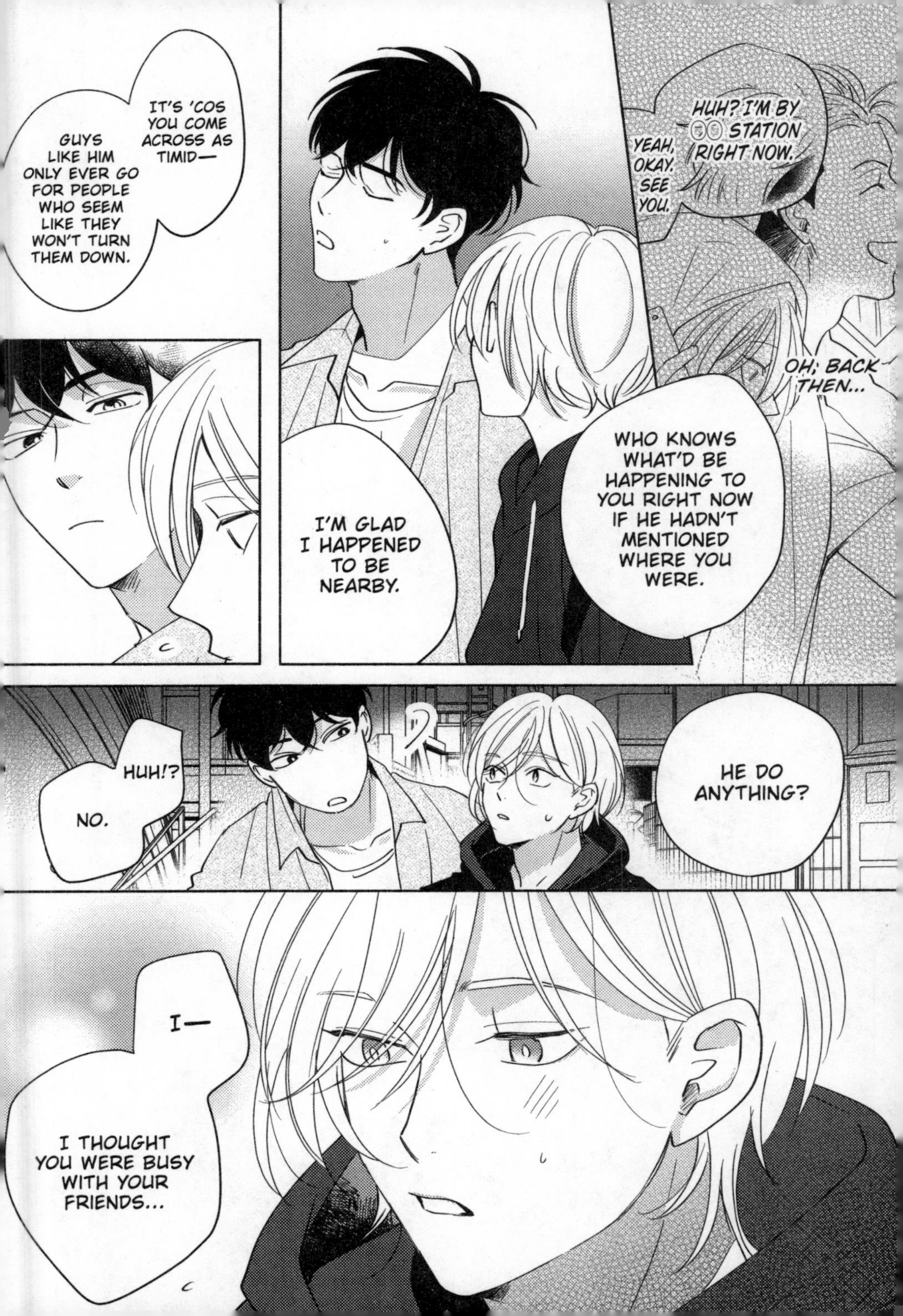
HUH? I'M BY ○○ STATION RIGHT NOW.
YEAH, OKAY. SEE YOU.
OH; BACK THEN...
WHO KNOWS WHAT'D BE HAPPENING TO YOU RIGHT NOW IF HE HADN'T MENTIONED WHERE YOU WERE.
I'M GLAD I HAPPENED TO BE NEARBY.
IT'S 'COS YOU COME ACROSS AS TIMID—
GUYS LIKE HIM ONLY EVER GO FOR PEOPLE WHO SEEM LIKE THEY WON'T TURN THEM DOWN.
HE DO ANYTHING?
HUH!?
NO.
I—
I THOUGHT YOU WERE BUSY WITH YOUR FRIENDS...

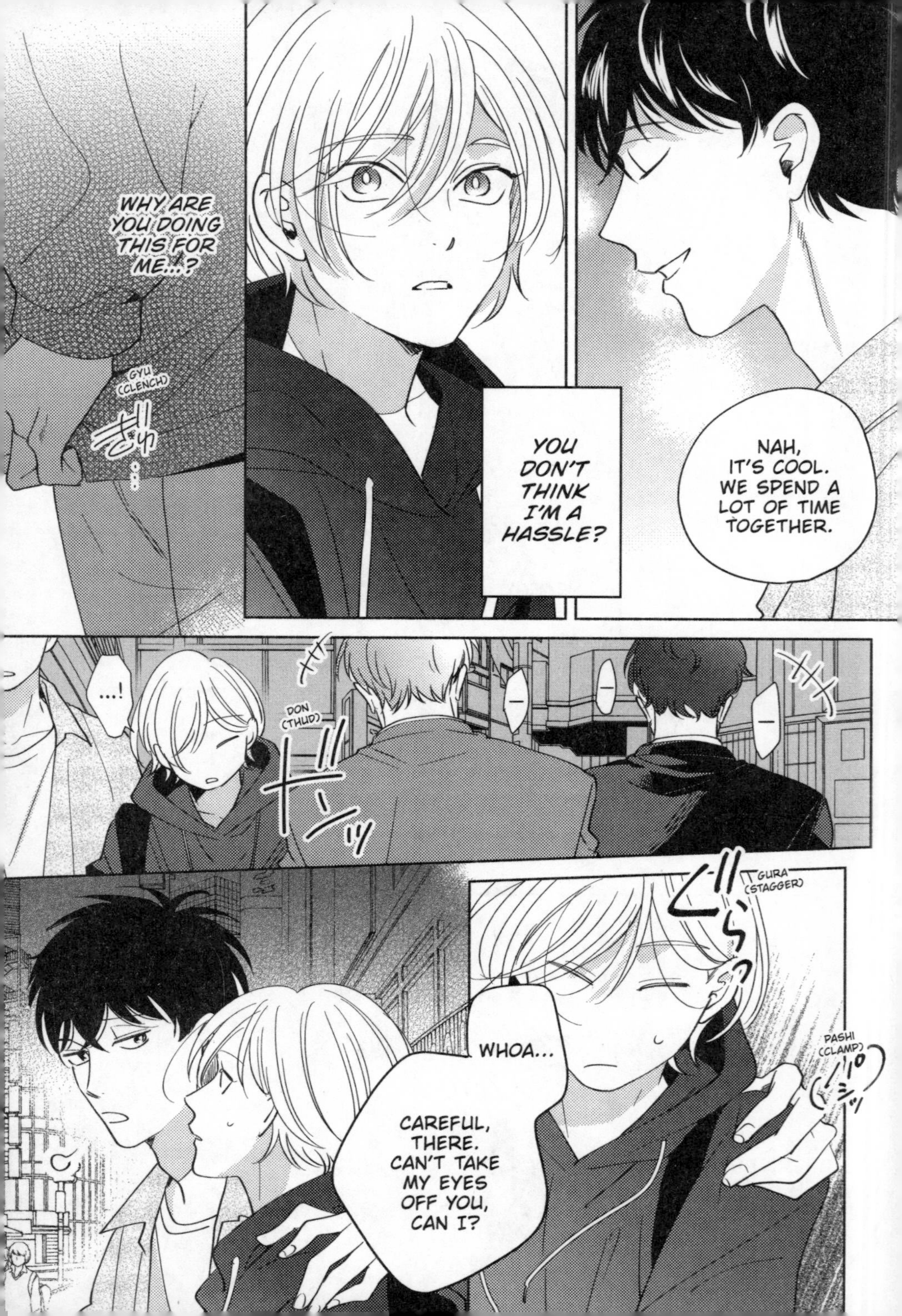
NAH, IT'S COOL. WE SPEND A LOT OF TIME TOGETHER.
YOU DON'T THINK I'M A HASSLE?
WHY ARE YOU DOING THIS FOR ME...?
GYU (CLENCH)
—
—
—
DON (THUD)
...!
GURA (STAGGER)
PASHI (CLAMP)
WHOA...
CAREFUL, THERE. CAN'T TAKE MY EYES OFF YOU, CAN I?

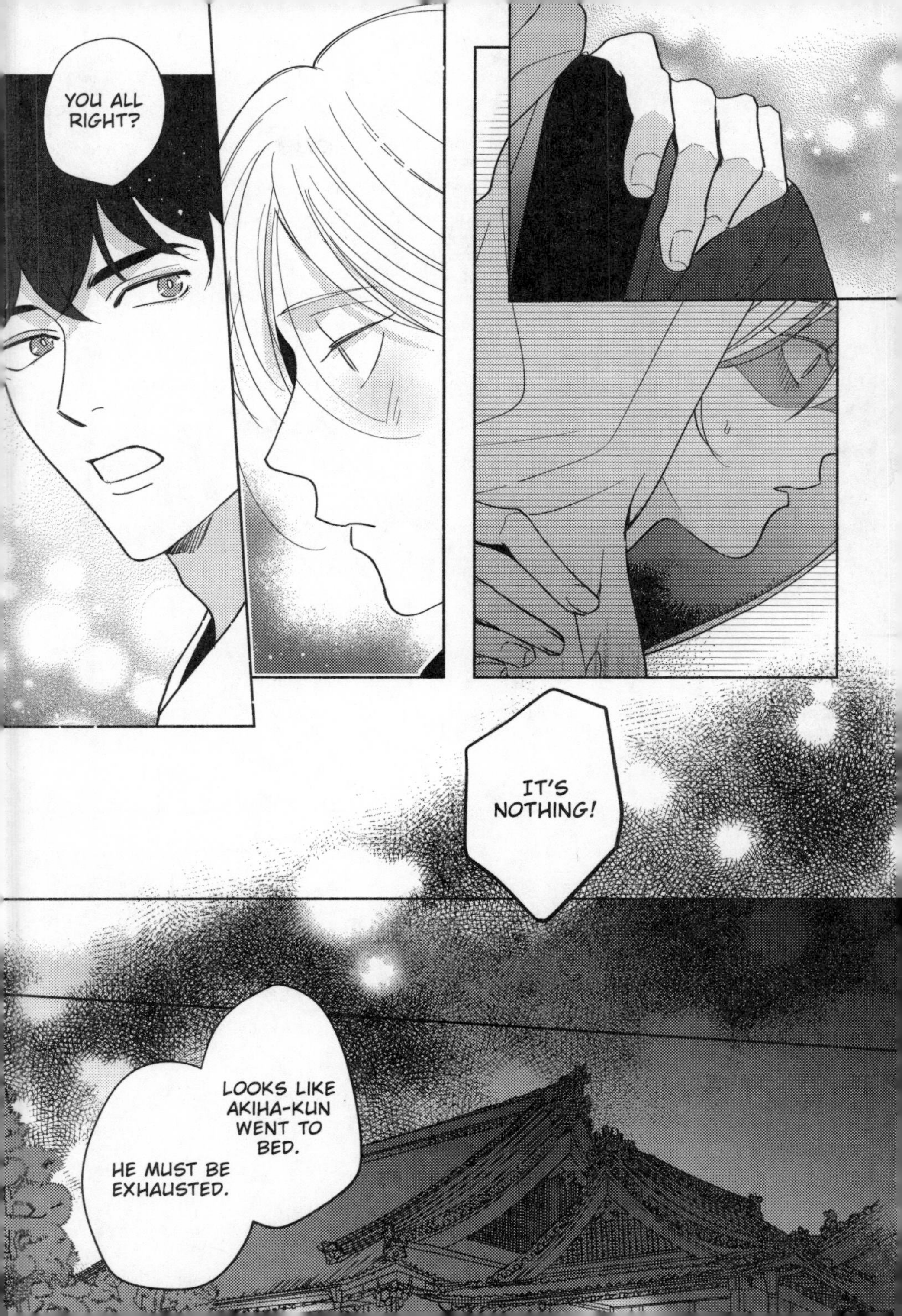
YOU ALL RIGHT?
IT'S NOTHING!
LOOKS LIKE AKIHA-KUN WENT TO BED.
HE MUST BE EXHAUSTED.

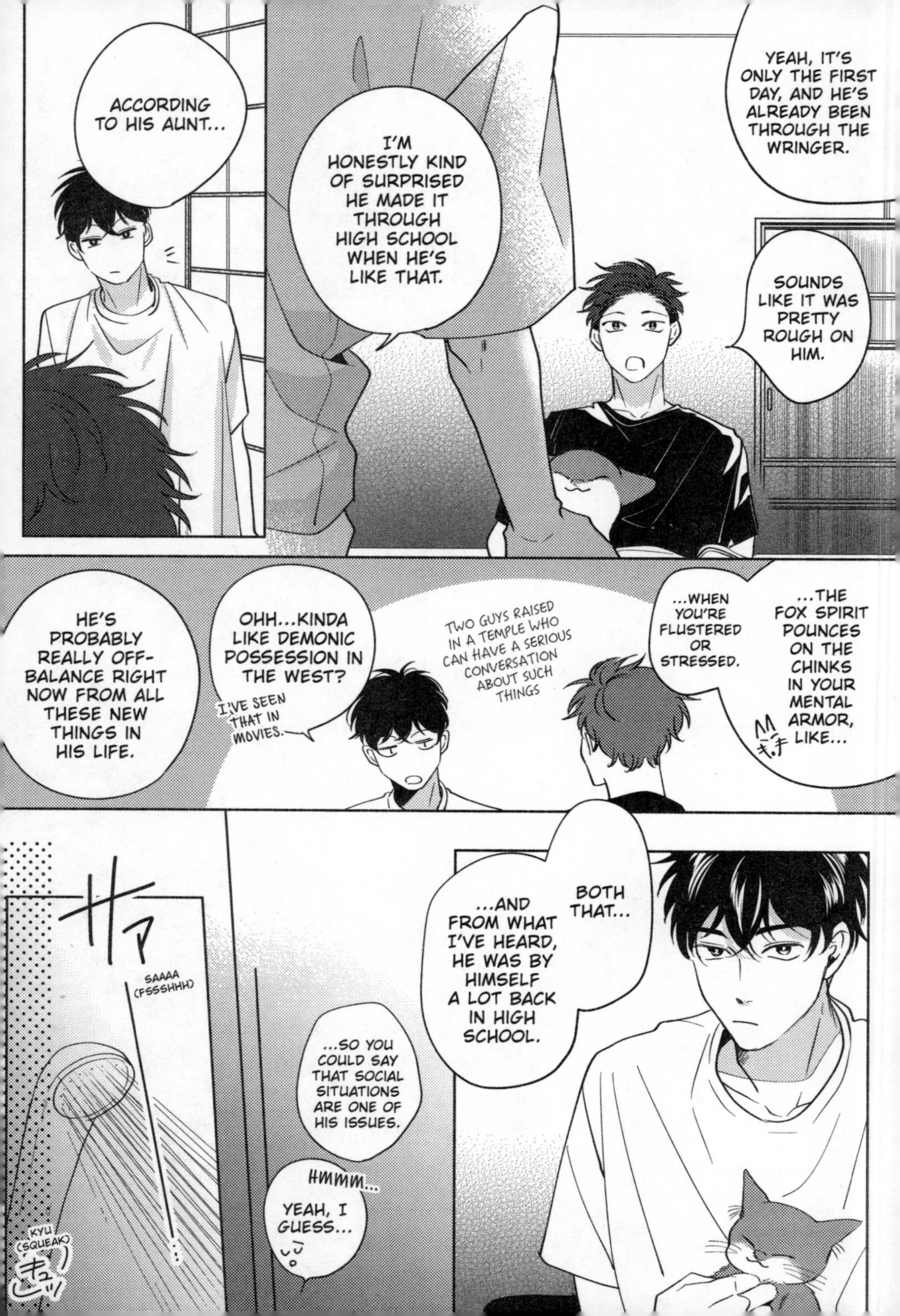
YEAH, IT'S ONLY THE FIRST DAY, AND HE'S ALREADY BEEN THROUGH THE WRINGER.
SOUNDS LIKE IT WAS PRETTY ROUGH ON HIM.
I'M HONESTLY KIND OF SURPRISED HE MADE IT THROUGH HIGH SCHOOL WHEN HE'S LIKE THAT.
ACCORDING TO HIS AUNT...
...THE FOX SPIRIT POUNCES ON THE CHINKS IN YOUR MENTAL ARMOR, LIKE...
...WHEN YOU'RE FLUSTERED OR STRESSED.
TWO GUYS RAISED IN A TEMPLE WHO CAN HAVE A SERIOUS CONVERSATION ABOUT SUCH THINGS
OHH...KINDA LIKE DEMONIC POSSESSION IN THE WEST?
I'VE SEEN THAT IN MOVIES.
HE'S PROBABLY REALLY OFF-BALANCE RIGHT NOW FROM ALL THESE NEW THINGS IN HIS LIFE.
BOTH THAT...
...AND FROM WHAT I'VE HEARD, HE WAS BY HIMSELF A LOT BACK IN HIGH SCHOOL.
...SO YOU COULD SAY THAT SOCIAL SITUATIONS ARE ONE OF HIS ISSUES.
HMMM...
YEAH, I GUESS...
SAAAA (FSSSHHH)
KYU (SQUEAK)

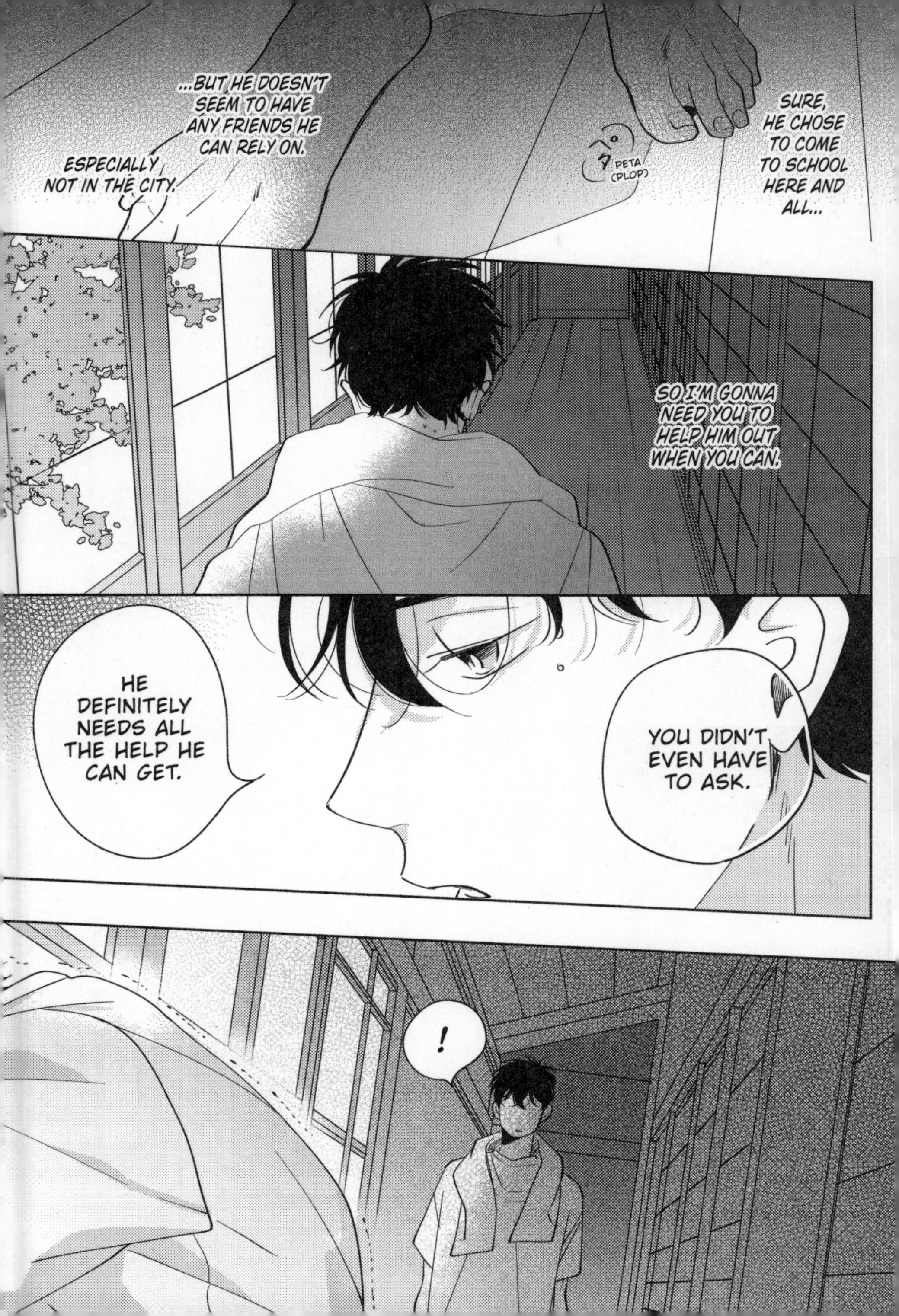
SURE, HE CHOSE TO COME TO SCHOOL HERE AND ALL...
PETA (PLOP)
...BUT HE DOESN'T SEEM TO HAVE ANY FRIENDS HE CAN RELY ON.
ESPECIALLY NOT IN THE CITY.
SO I'M GONNA NEED YOU TO HELP HIM OUT WHEN YOU CAN.
YOU DIDN'T EVEN HAVE TO ASK.
HE DEFINITELY NEEDS ALL THE HELP HE CAN GET.
!

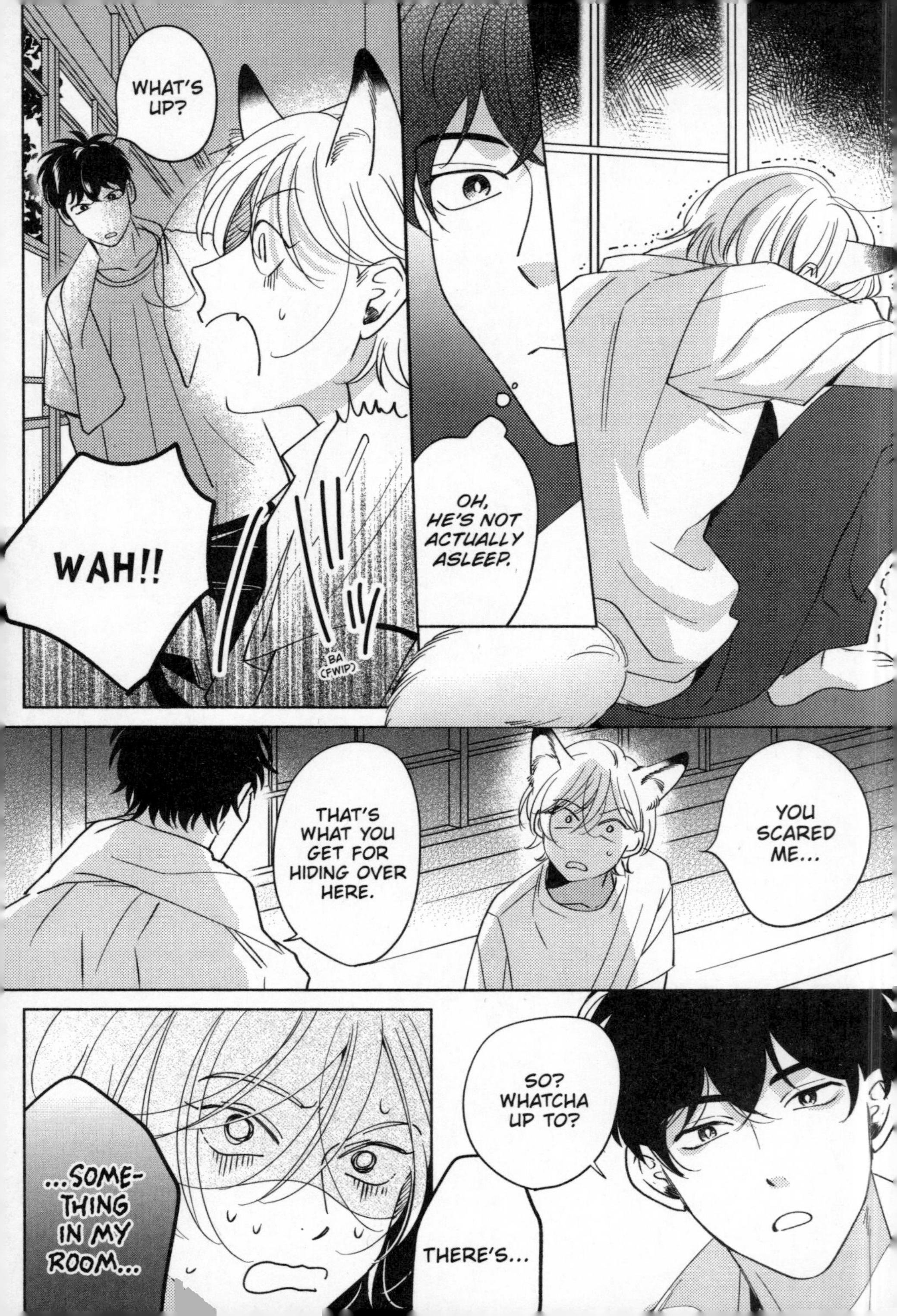
OH, HE'S NOT ACTUALLY ASLEEP.
WHAT'S UP?
WAH!!
BA (FWIP)
YOU SCARED ME...
THAT'S WHAT YOU GET FOR HIDING OVER HERE.
SO? WHATCHA UP TO?
THERE'S...
...SOME-THING IN MY ROOM...

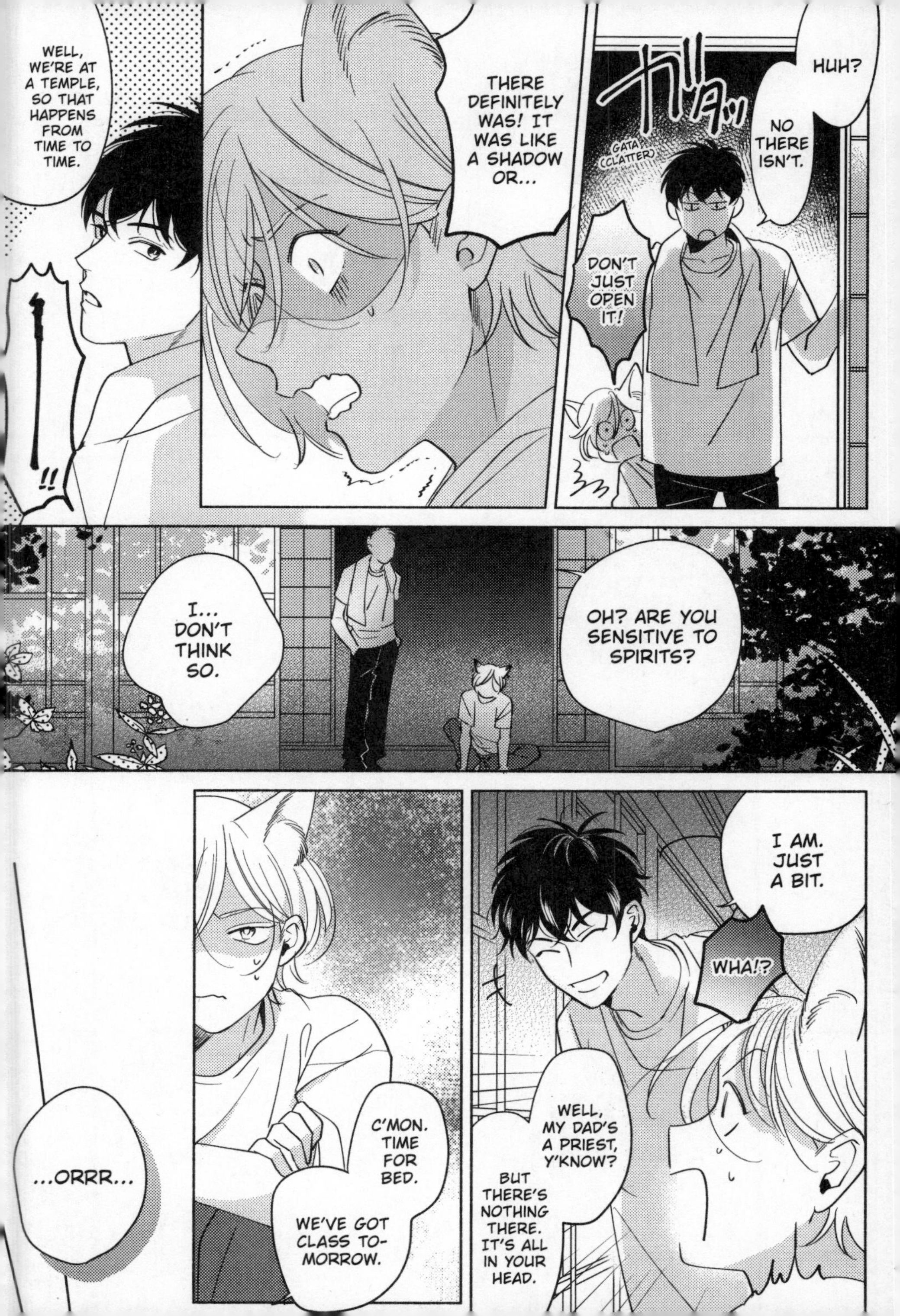
HUH?
NO THERE ISN'T.
GATA (CLATTER)
DON'T JUST OPEN IT!
THERE DEFINITELY WAS! IT WAS LIKE A SHADOW OR...
WELL, WE'RE AT A TEMPLE, SO THAT HAPPENS FROM TIME TO TIME.
!!
OH? ARE YOU SENSITIVE TO SPIRITS?
I... DON'T THINK SO.
I AM. JUST A BIT.
WHA!?
WELL, MY DAD'S A PRIEST, Y'KNOW?
BUT THERE'S NOTHING THERE. IT'S ALL IN YOUR HEAD.
C'MON. TIME FOR BED.
WE'VE GOT CLASS TO-MORROW.
...ORRR...

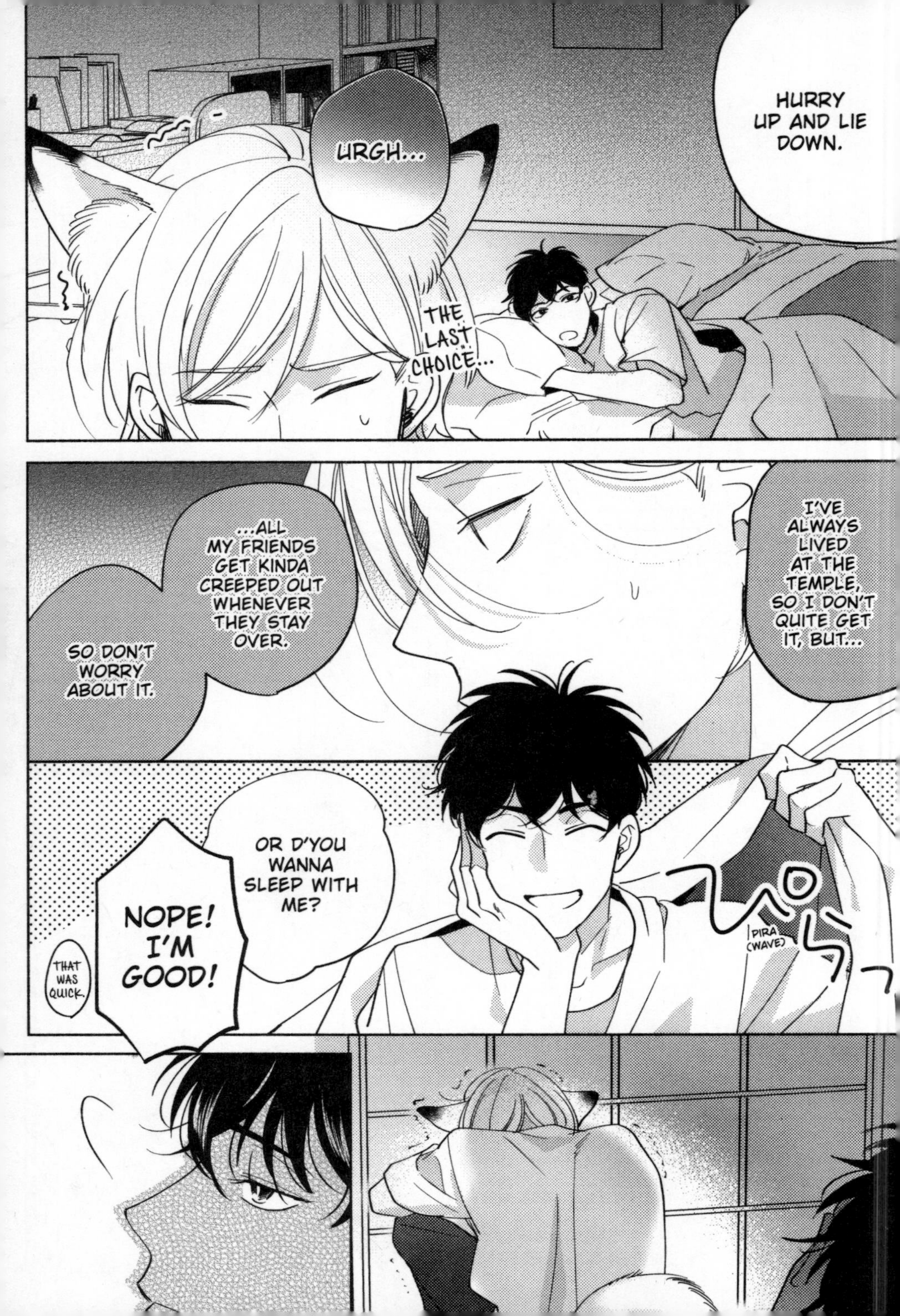
HURRY UP AND LIE DOWN.
URGH...
THE LAST CHOICE...
I'VE ALWAYS LIVED AT THE TEMPLE, SO I DON'T QUITE GET IT, BUT...
...ALL MY FRIENDS GET KINDA CREEPED OUT WHENEVER THEY STAY OVER.
SO DON'T WORRY ABOUT IT.
PIRA (WAVE)
OR D'YOU WANNA SLEEP WITH ME?
NOPE! I'M GOOD!
THAT WAS QUICK.

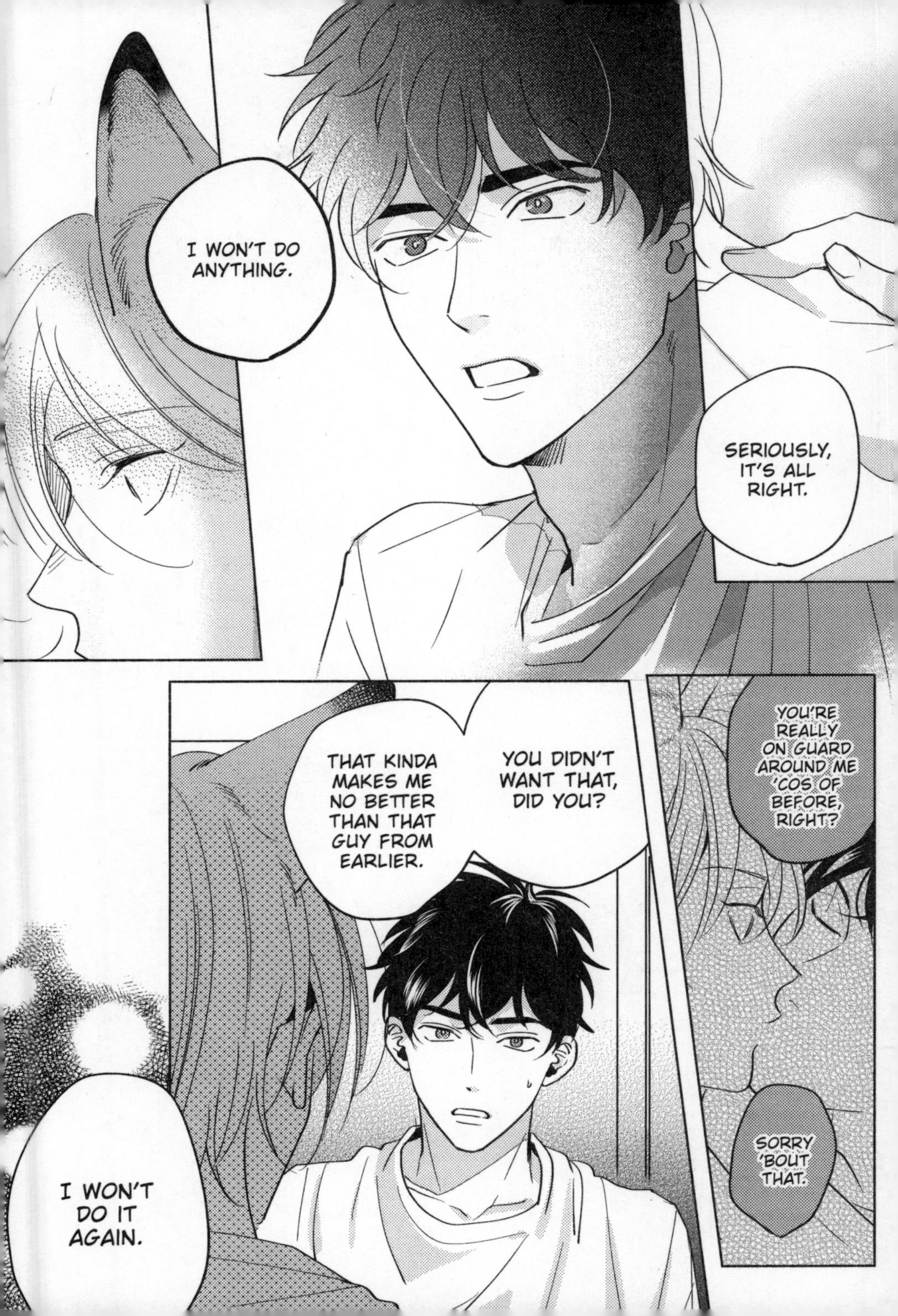
I WON'T DO ANYTHING.
SERIOUSLY, IT'S ALL RIGHT.
YOU'RE REALLY ON GUARD AROUND ME 'COS OF BEFORE, RIGHT?
SORRY 'BOUT THAT.
YOU DIDN'T WANT THAT, DID YOU?
THAT KINDA MAKES ME NO BETTER THAN THAT GUY FROM EARLIER.
I WON'T DO IT AGAIN.

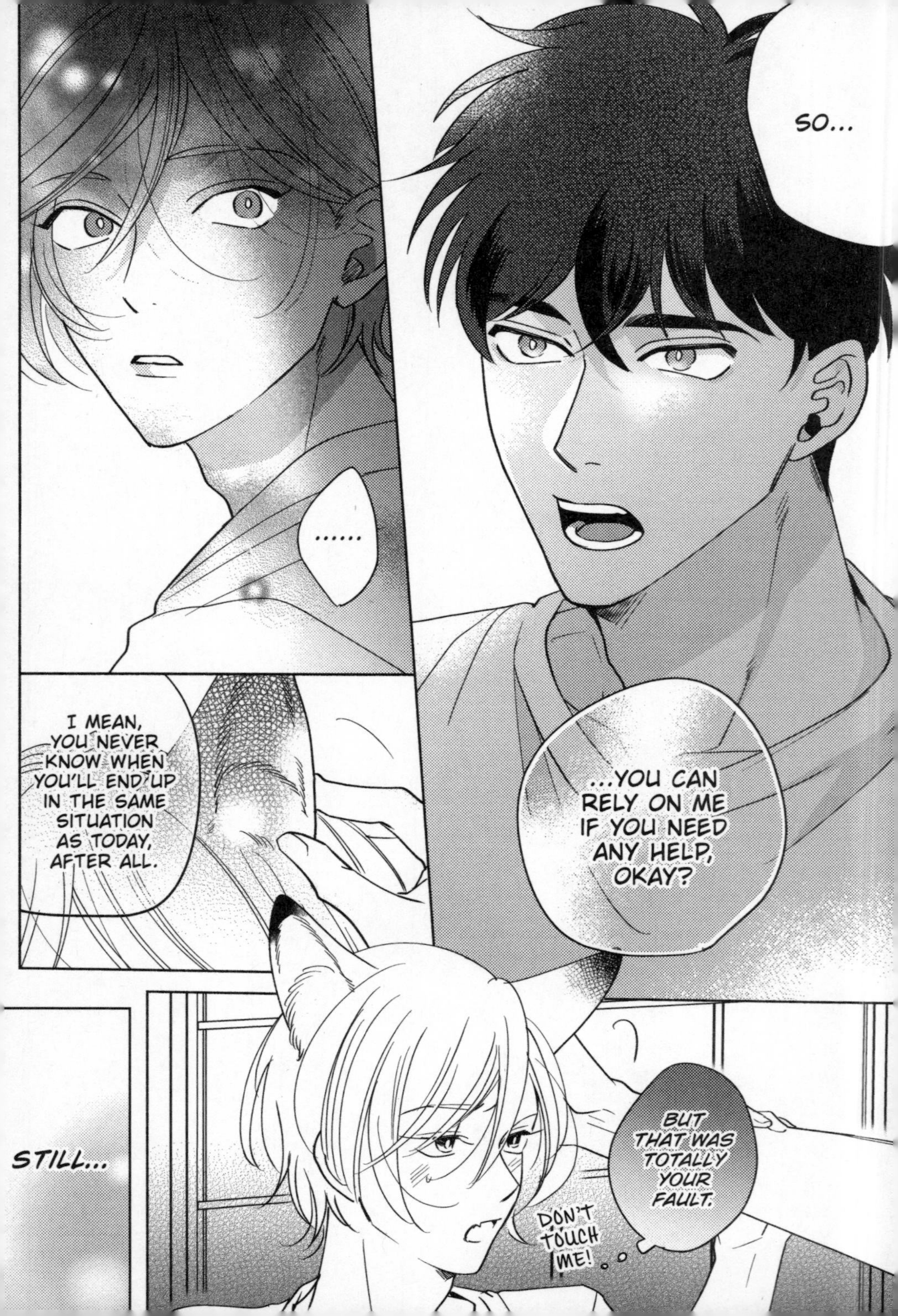
SO...
...YOU CAN RELY ON ME IF YOU NEED ANY HELP, OKAY?
......
I MEAN, YOU NEVER KNOW WHEN YOU'LL END UP IN THE SAME SITUATION AS TODAY, AFTER ALL.
BUT THAT WAS TOTALLY YOUR FAULT.
DON'T TOUCH ME!
STILL...

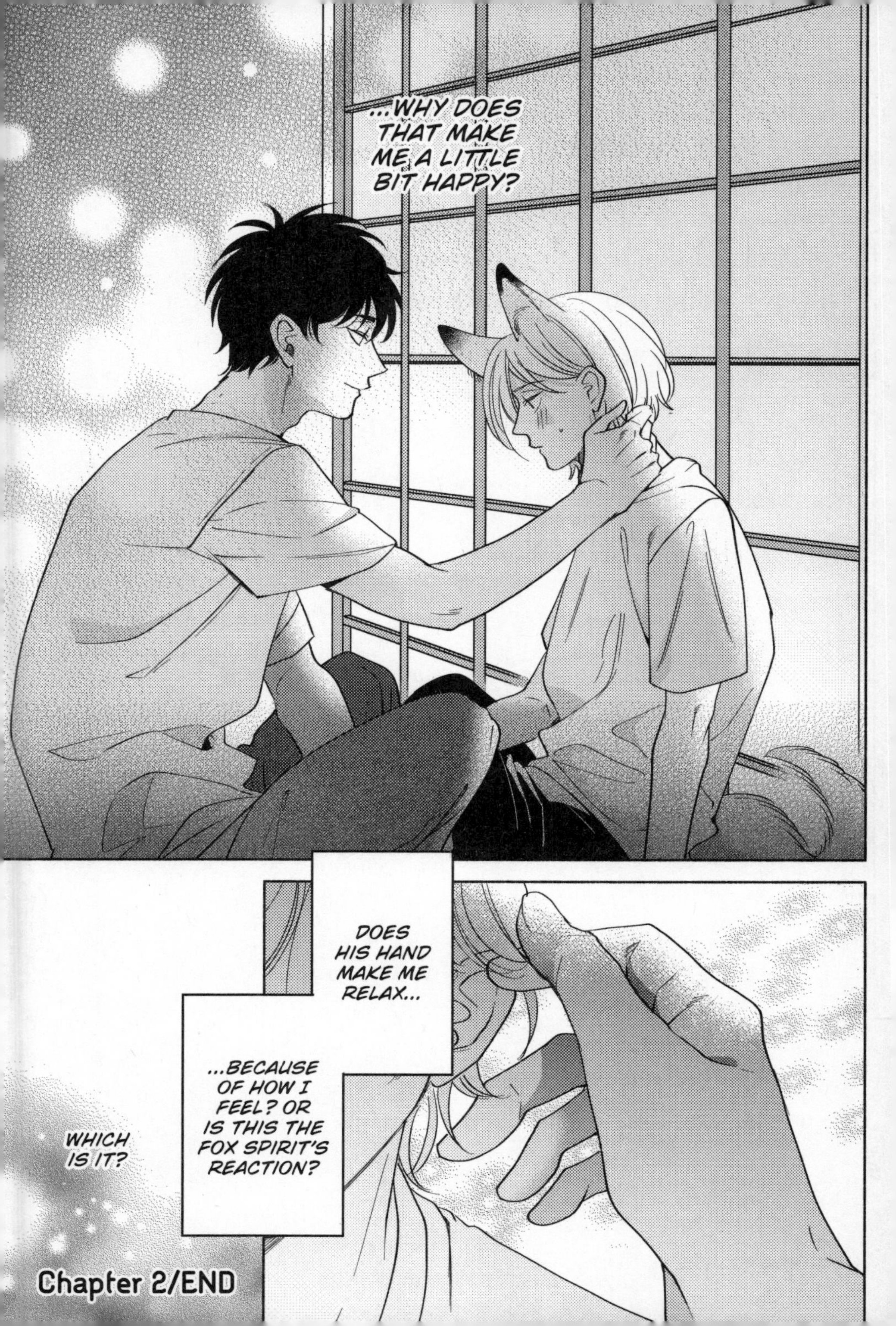
...WHY DOES THAT MAKE ME A LITTLE BIT HAPPY?
DOES HIS HAND MAKE ME RELAX...
...BECAUSE OF HOW I FEEL? OR IS THIS THE FOX SPIRIT'S REACTION?
WHICH IS IT?
Chapter 2/END

Fox-Colored Jealousy

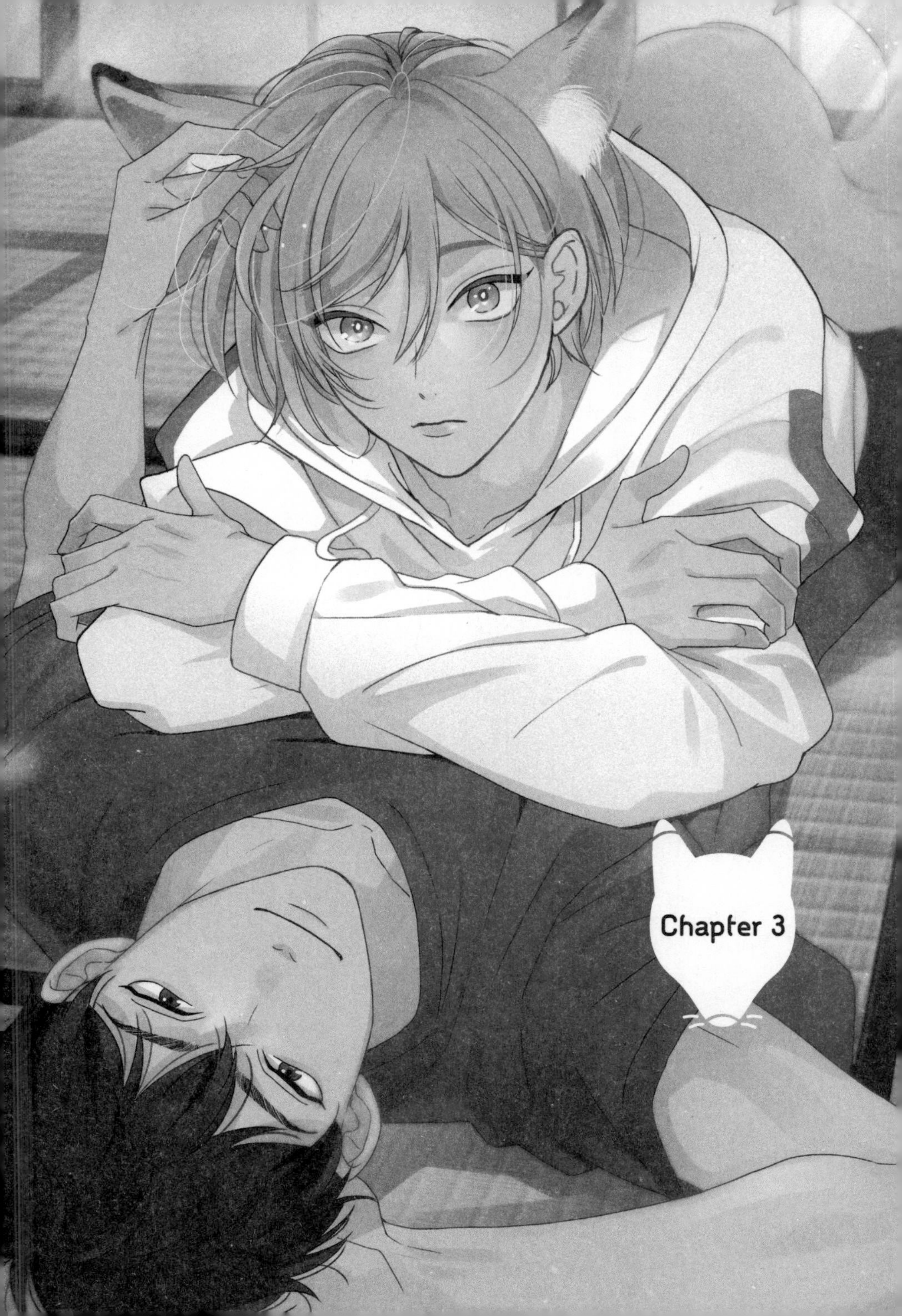
Chapter 3

Fox-
Colored
Jealousy

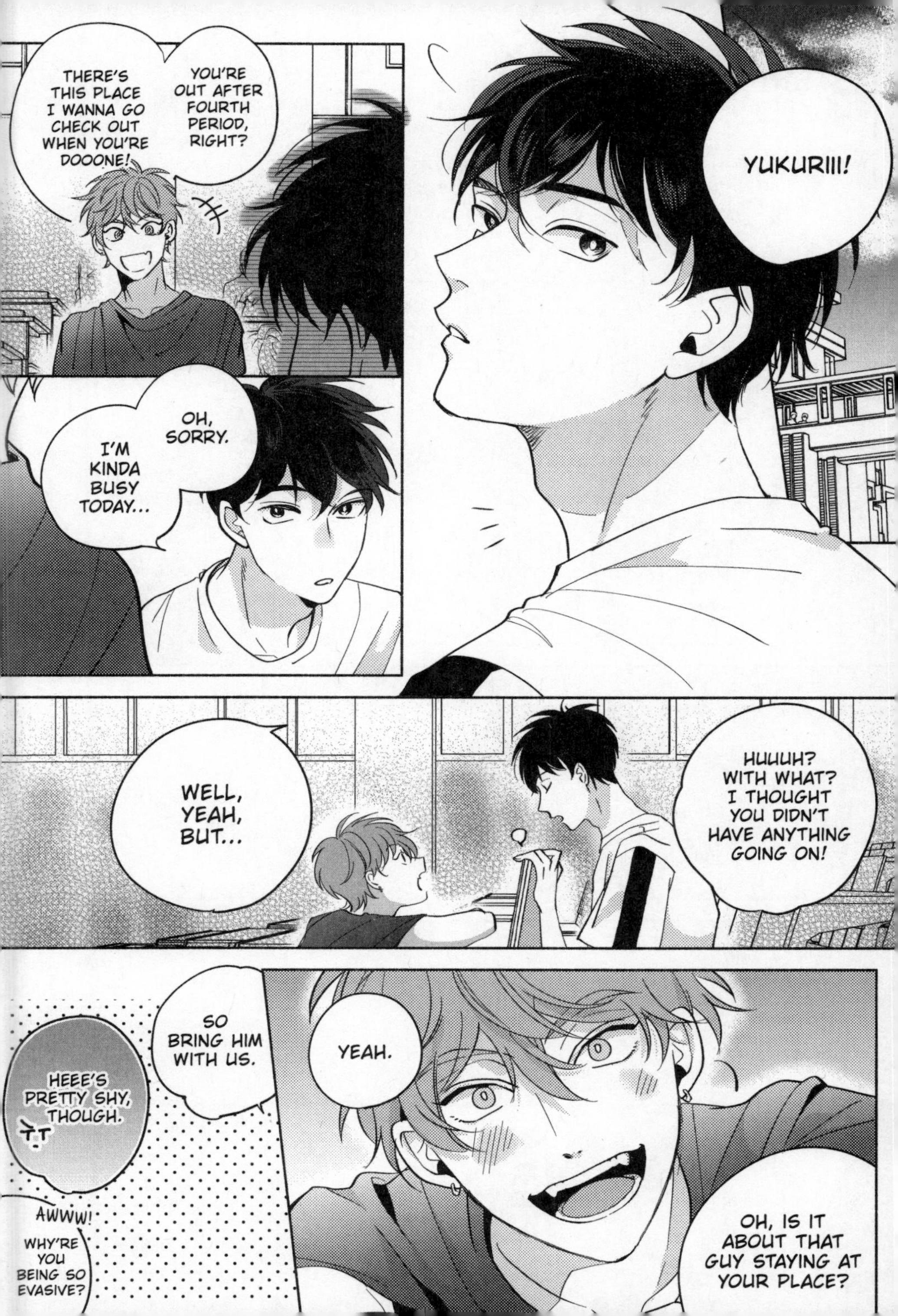
YUKURIII!
YOU'RE OUT AFTER FOURTH PERIOD, RIGHT?
THERE'S THIS PLACE I WANNA GO CHECK OUT WHEN YOU'RE DOOONE!
OH, SORRY.
I'M KINDA BUSY TODAY...
HUUUH? WITH WHAT? I THOUGHT YOU DIDN'T HAVE ANYTHING GOING ON!
WELL, YEAH, BUT...
OH, IS IT ABOUT THAT GUY STAYING AT YOUR PLACE?
YEAH.
SO BRING HIM WITH US.
HEEE'S PRETTY SHY, THOUGH.
AWWW!
WHY'RE YOU BEING SO EVASIVE?

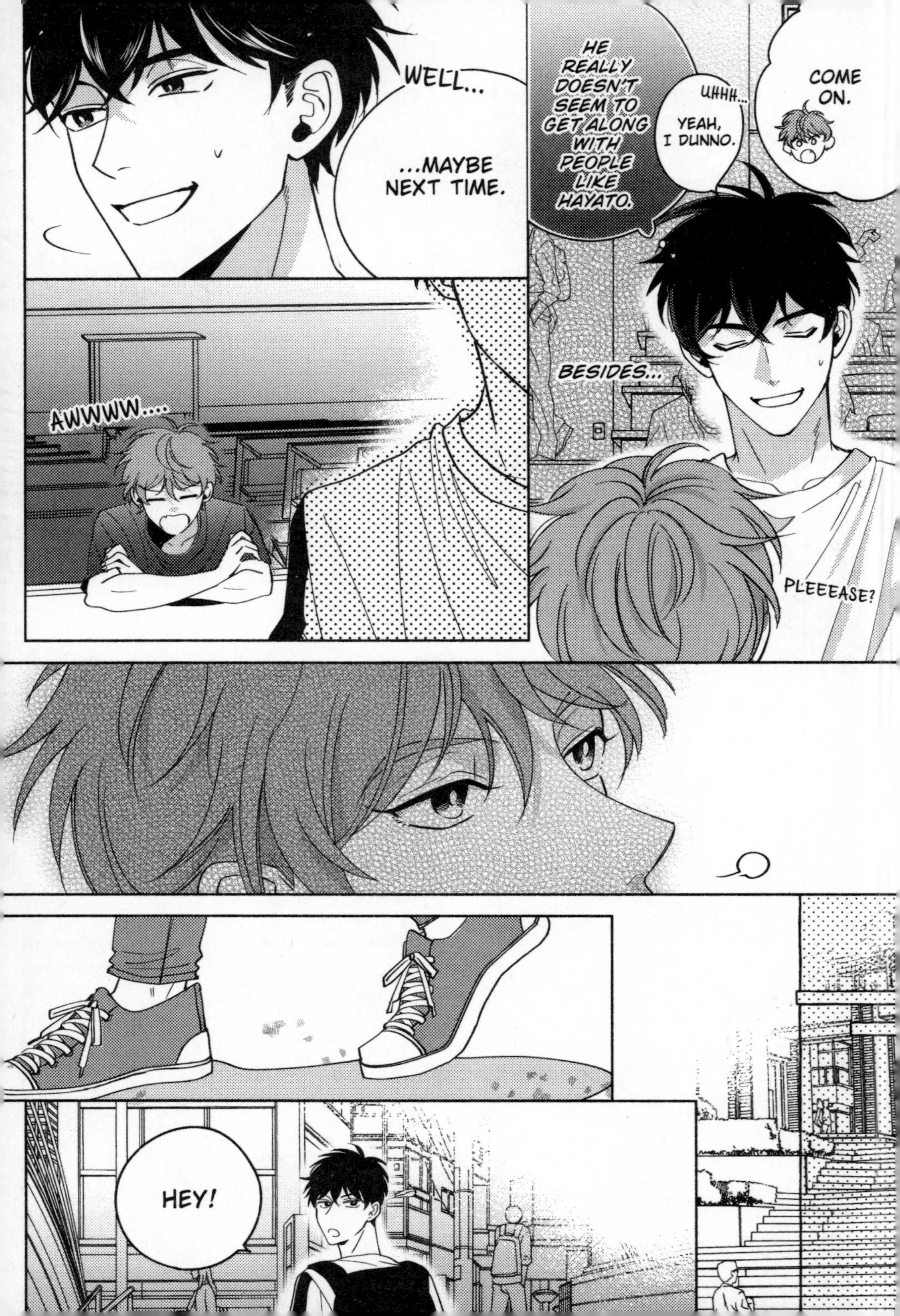
COME ON.
UHHH... YEAH, I DUNNO.
HE REALLY DOESN'T SEEM TO GET ALONG WITH PEOPLE LIKE HAYATO.
BESIDES...
PLEEEASE?
WELL...
...MAYBE NEXT TIME.
AWWWW....
HEY!

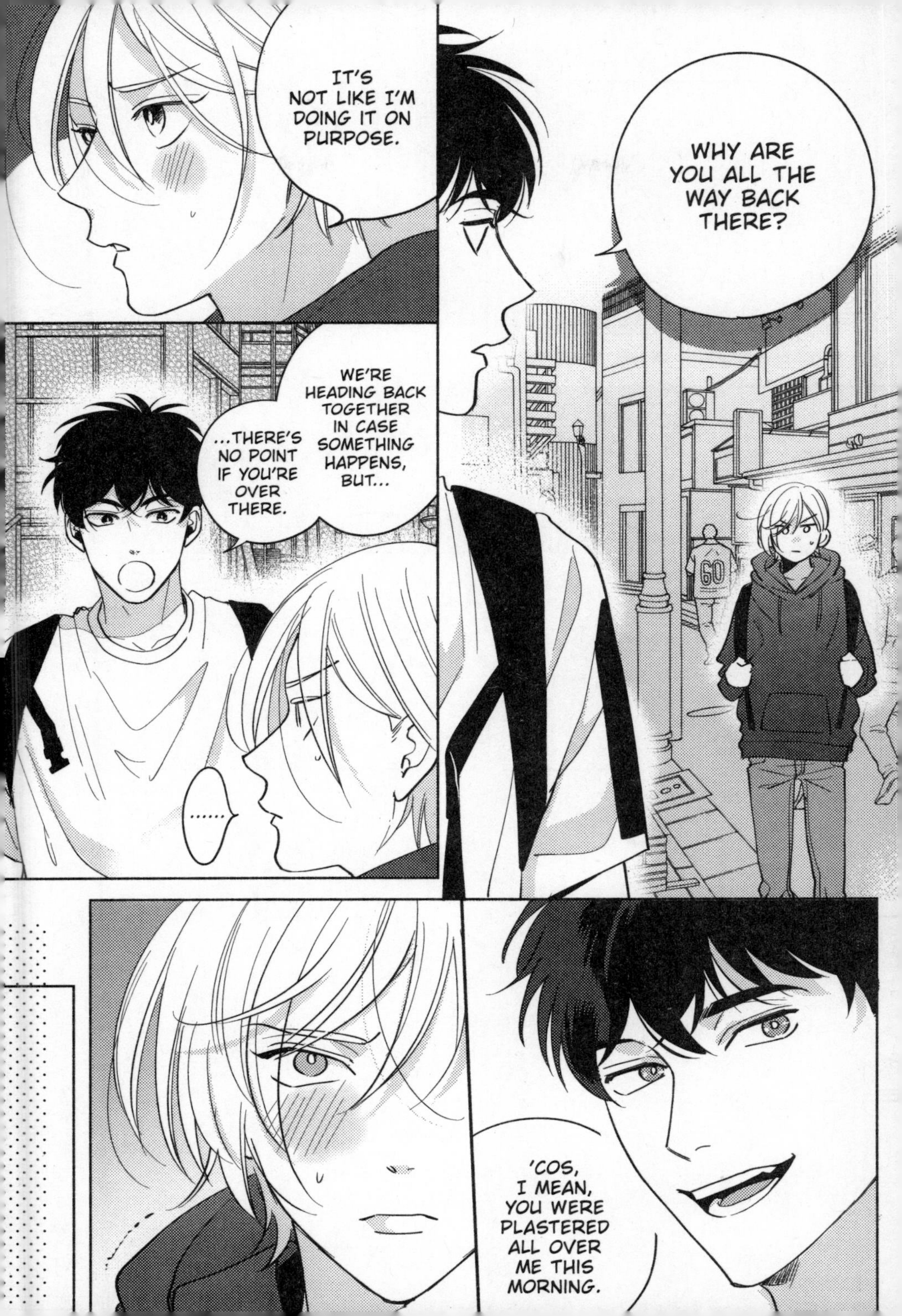
WHY ARE YOU ALL THE WAY BACK THERE?
IT'S NOT LIKE I'M DOING IT ON PURPOSE.
WE'RE HEADING BACK TOGETHER IN CASE SOMETHING HAPPENS, BUT...
...THERE'S NO POINT IF YOU'RE OVER THERE.
......
'COS, I MEAN, YOU WERE PLASTERED ALL OVER ME THIS MORNING.

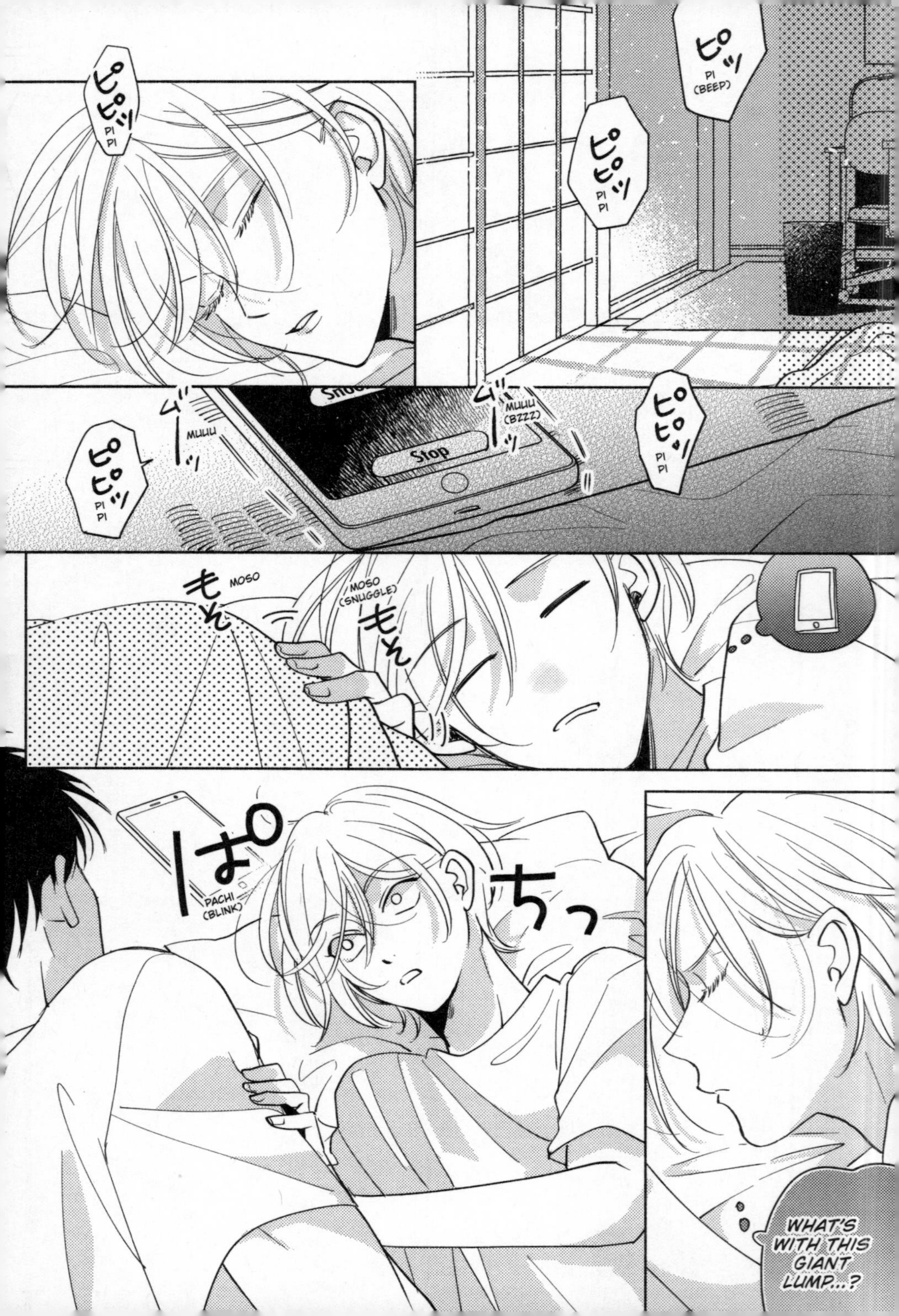
ピッ
PI (BEEP)
ピピッ
PI PI
ピピッ
PI PI
ピピッ
PI PI
ムーッ
MUUU (BZZZ)
Stop
ムーッ
MUUU
ピピッ
PI PI
もそ
MOSO (SNUGGLE)
もそ
MOSO
WHAT'S WITH THIS GIANT LUMP...?
ぱ
ちっ
PACHI (BLINK)

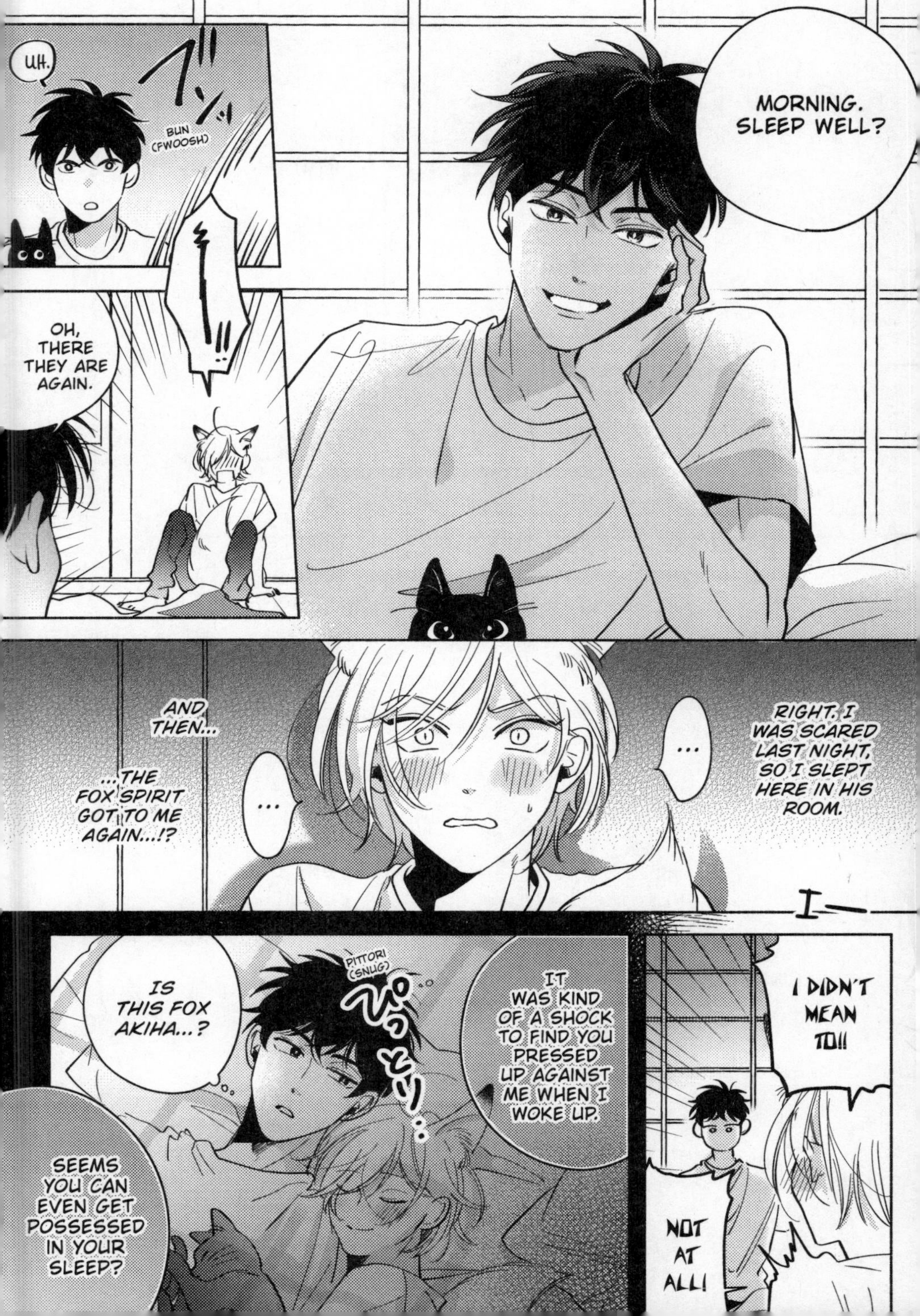
MORNING. SLEEP WELL?
UH.
BUN (FWOOSH)
OH, THERE THEY ARE AGAIN.
RIGHT. I WAS SCARED LAST NIGHT, SO I SLEPT HERE IN HIS ROOM.
...
AND THEN...
...THE FOX SPIRIT GOT TO ME AGAIN...!?
...
I—
I DIDN'T MEAN TO!!
NOT AT ALL!
IT WAS KIND OF A SHOCK TO FIND YOU PRESSED UP AGAINST ME WHEN I WOKE UP.
PITTORI (SNUG)
IS THIS FOX AKIHA...?
SEEMS YOU CAN EVEN GET POSSESSED IN YOUR SLEEP?

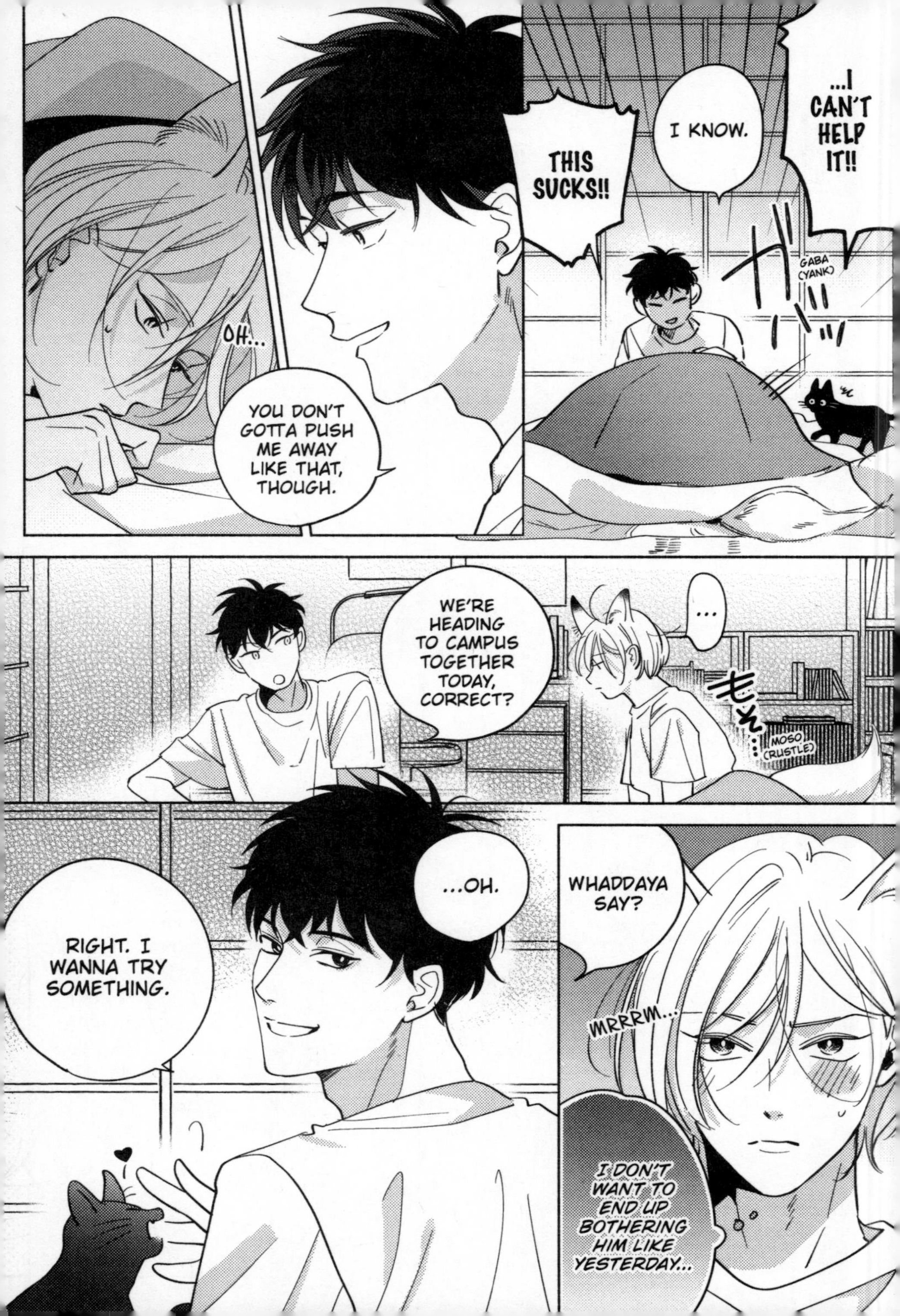
...I CAN'T HELP IT!!
I KNOW.
THIS SUCKS!!
GABA (YANK)
OH...
YOU DON'T GOTTA PUSH ME AWAY LIKE THAT, THOUGH.
...
MOSO (RUSTLE)
WE'RE HEADING TO CAMPUS TOGETHER TODAY, CORRECT?
WHADDAYA SAY?
MRRRM...
I DON'T WANT TO END UP BOTHERING HIM LIKE YESTERDAY...
...OH.
RIGHT. I WANNA TRY SOMETHING.

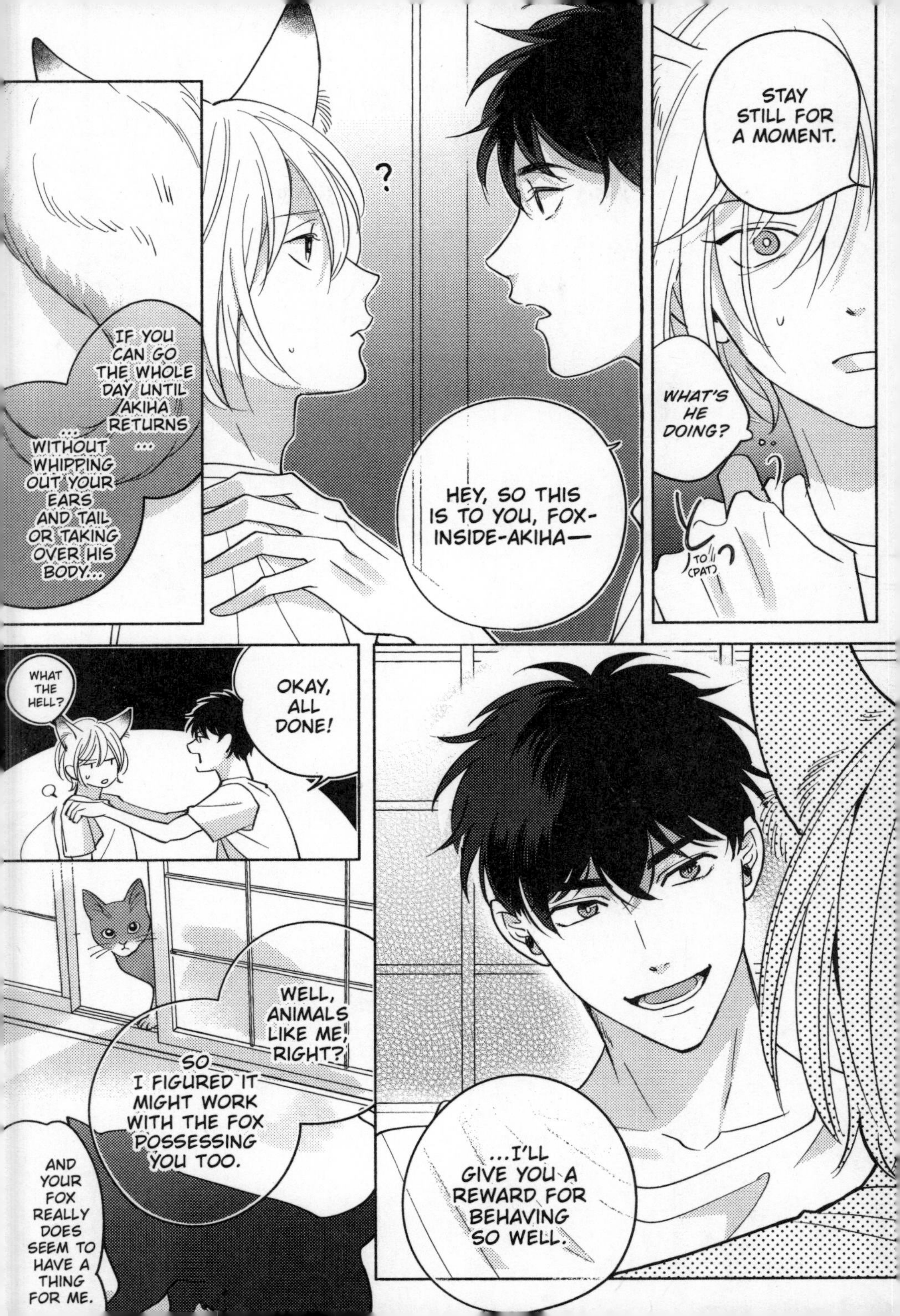

STAY STILL FOR A MOMENT.
WHAT'S HE DOING?
TO (PAT)
?
HEY, SO THIS IS TO YOU, FOX-INSIDE-AKIHA—
IF YOU CAN GO THE WHOLE DAY UNTIL AKIHA RETURNS ...
... WITHOUT WHIPPING OUT YOUR EARS AND TAIL OR TAKING OVER HIS BODY...
...I'LL GIVE YOU A REWARD FOR BEHAVING SO WELL.
OKAY, ALL DONE!
WHAT THE HELL?
WELL, ANIMALS LIKE ME, RIGHT?
SO I FIGURED IT MIGHT WORK WITH THE FOX POSSESSING YOU TOO.
AND YOUR FOX REALLY DOES SEEM TO HAVE A THING FOR ME.

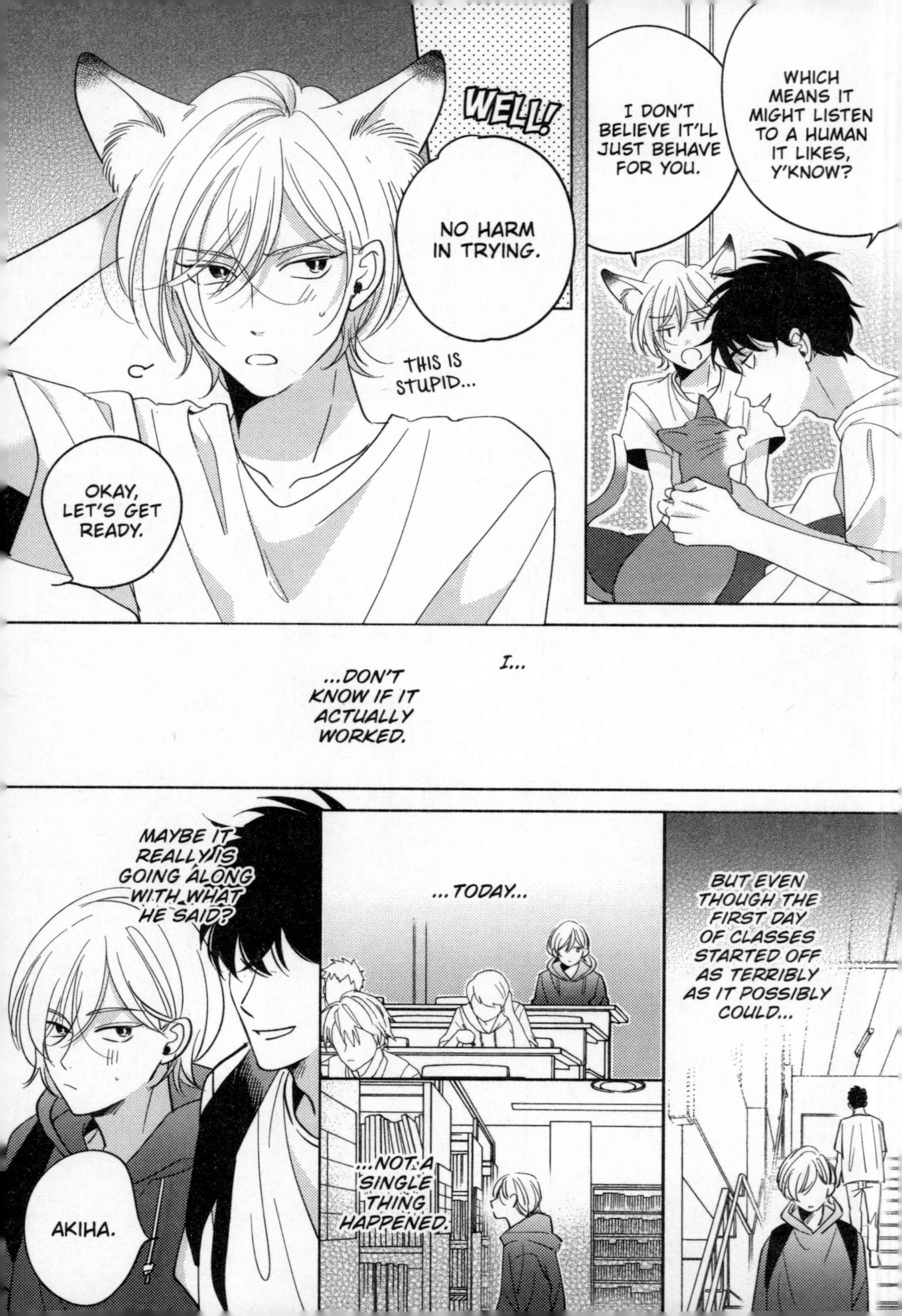
WHICH MEANS IT MIGHT LISTEN TO A HUMAN IT LIKES, Y'KNOW?
I DON'T BELIEVE IT'LL JUST BEHAVE FOR YOU.
WELL!
NO HARM IN TRYING.
THIS IS STUPID...
OKAY, LET'S GET READY.
I...
...DON'T KNOW IF IT ACTUALLY WORKED.
BUT EVEN THOUGH THE FIRST DAY OF CLASSES STARTED OFF AS TERRIBLY AS IT POSSIBLY COULD...
...TODAY...
...NOT A SINGLE THING HAPPENED.
MAYBE IT REALLY IS GOING ALONG WITH WHAT HE SAID?
AKIHA.

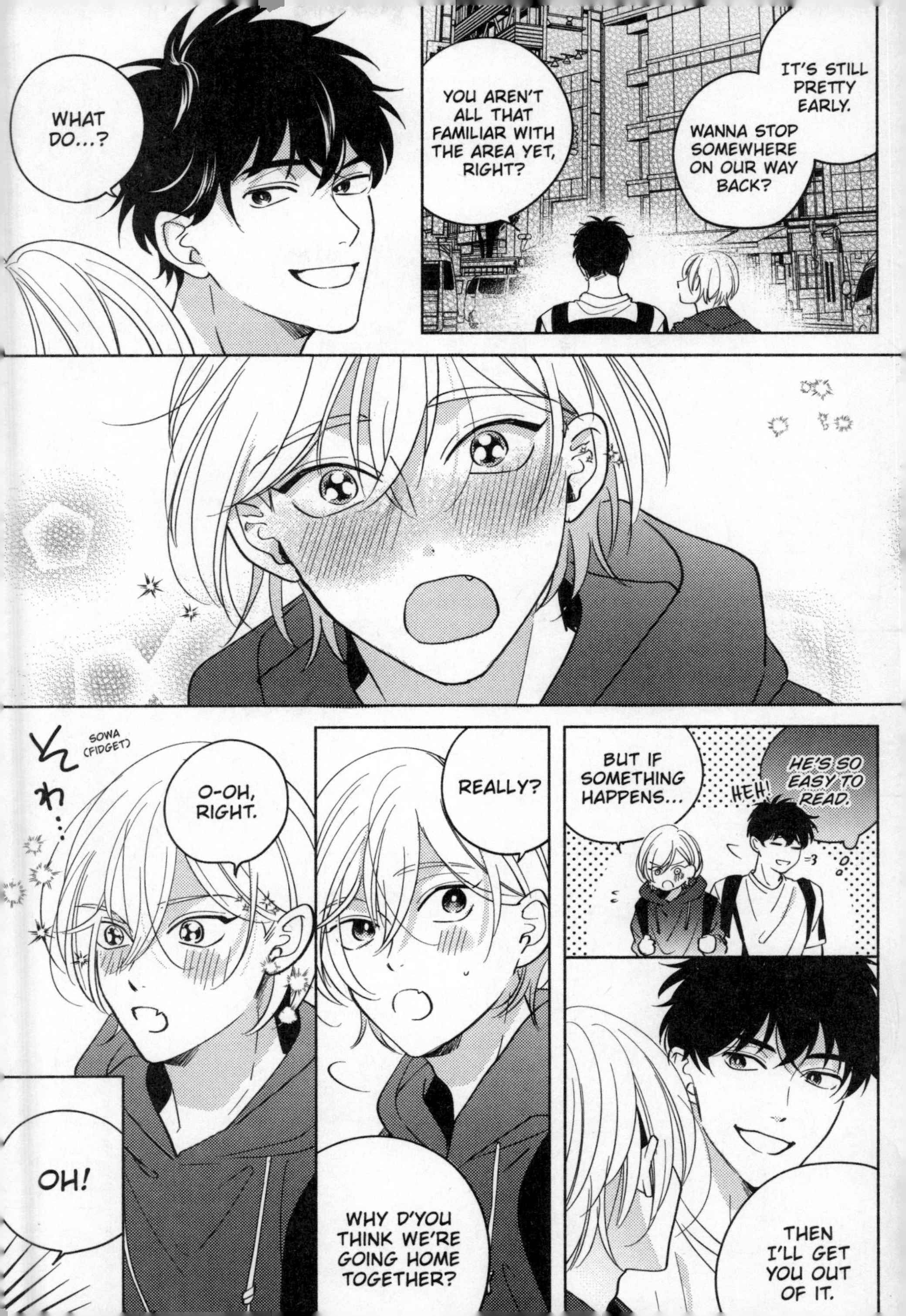
IT'S STILL PRETTY EARLY.
WANNA STOP SOMEWHERE ON OUR WAY BACK?
YOU AREN'T ALL THAT FAMILIAR WITH THE AREA YET, RIGHT?
WHAT DO...?
HE'S SO EASY TO READ.
HEH!
BUT IF SOMETHING HAPPENS...
THEN I'LL GET YOU OUT OF IT.
REALLY?
WHY D'YOU THINK WE'RE GOING HOME TOGETHER?
そわ…
SOWA (FIDGET)
O-OH, RIGHT.
OH!

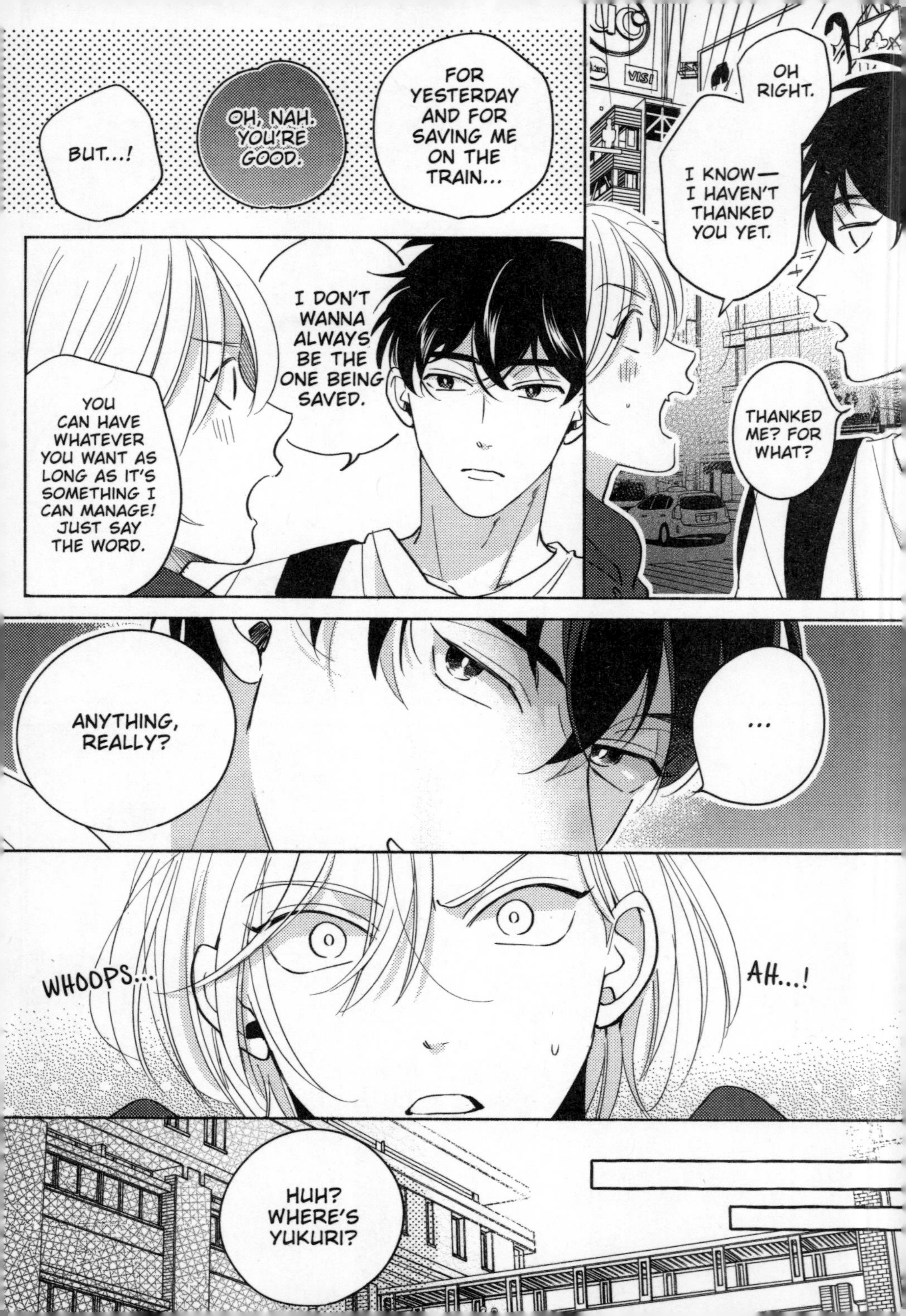
OH RIGHT.
I KNOW— I HAVEN'T THANKED YOU YET.
THANKED ME? FOR WHAT?
FOR YESTERDAY AND FOR SAVING ME ON THE TRAIN...
OH, NAH. YOU'RE GOOD.
BUT...!
I DON'T WANNA ALWAYS BE THE ONE BEING SAVED.
YOU CAN HAVE WHATEVER YOU WANT AS LONG AS IT'S SOMETHING I CAN MANAGE! JUST SAY THE WORD.
...
ANYTHING, REALLY?
AH...!
WHOOPS...
HUH? WHERE'S YUKURI?

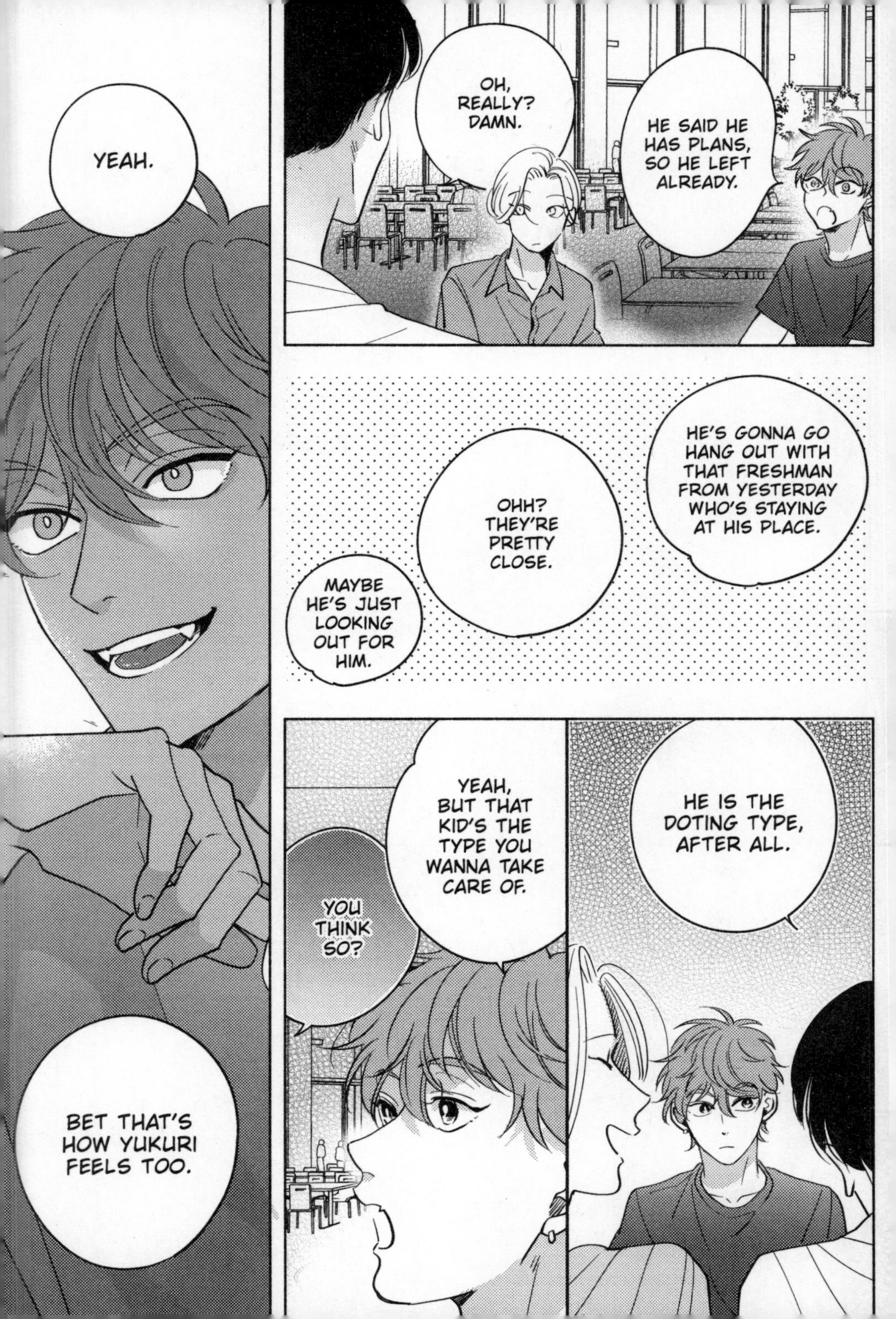
HE SAID HE HAS PLANS, SO HE LEFT ALREADY.
OH, REALLY? DAMN.
HE'S GONNA GO HANG OUT WITH THAT FRESHMAN FROM YESTERDAY WHO'S STAYING AT HIS PLACE.
OHH? THEY'RE PRETTY CLOSE.
MAYBE HE'S JUST LOOKING OUT FOR HIM.
HE IS THE DOTING TYPE, AFTER ALL.
YEAH, BUT THAT KID'S THE TYPE YOU WANNA TAKE CARE OF.
YOU THINK SO?
YEAH.
BET THAT'S HOW YUKURI FEELS TOO.

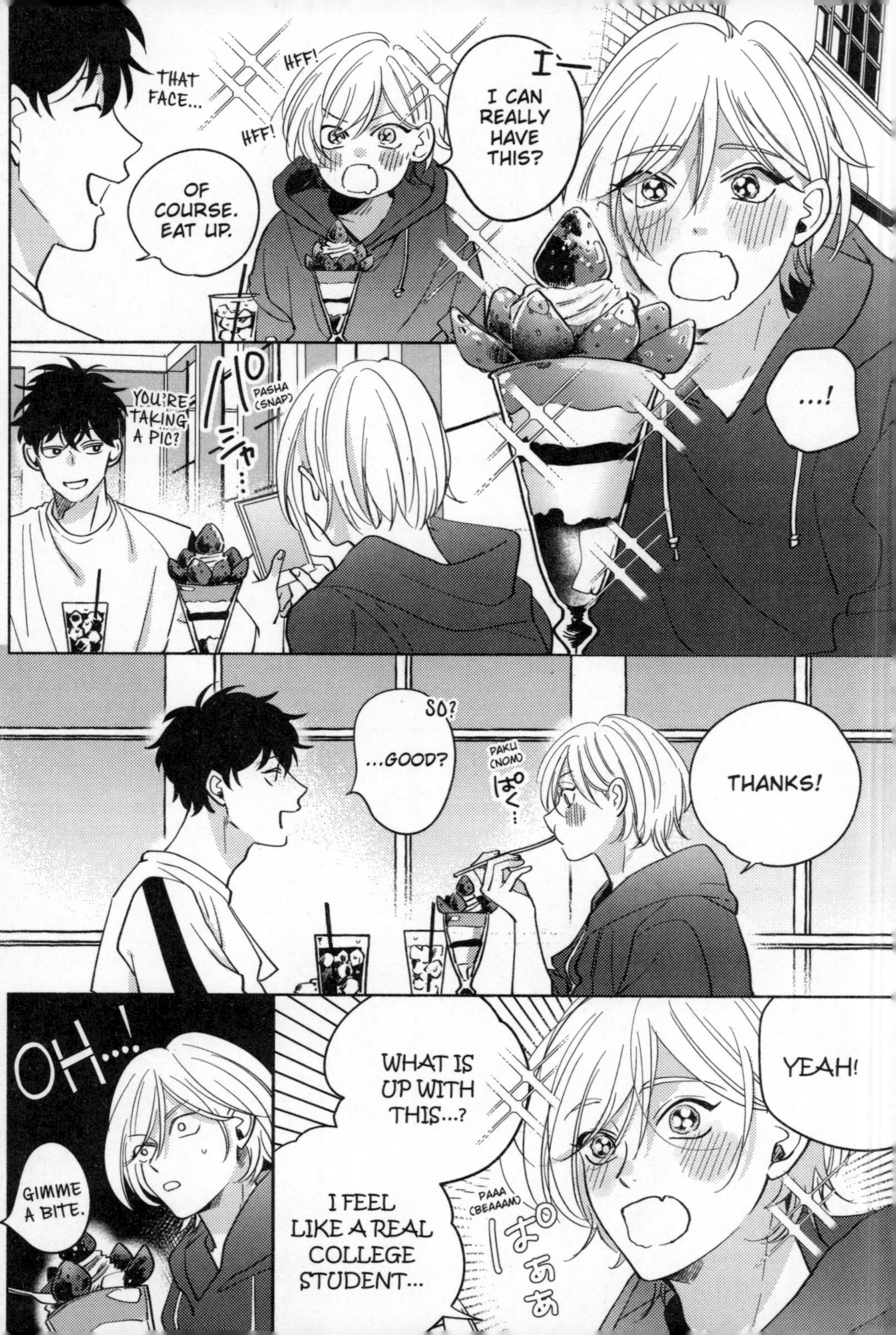
エー
I CAN REALLY HAVE THIS?
...!
HFF!
THAT FACE...
HFF!
OF COURSE. EAT UP.
パシャ
PASHA (SNAP)
YOU'RE TAKING A PIC?
THANKS!
ぱく…
PAKU (NOM)
SO?
...GOOD?
YEAH!
WHAT IS UP WITH THIS...?
ぱぁぁ
PAAA (BEAAAM)
I FEEL LIKE A REAL COLLEGE STUDENT...
OH...!
GIMME A BITE.

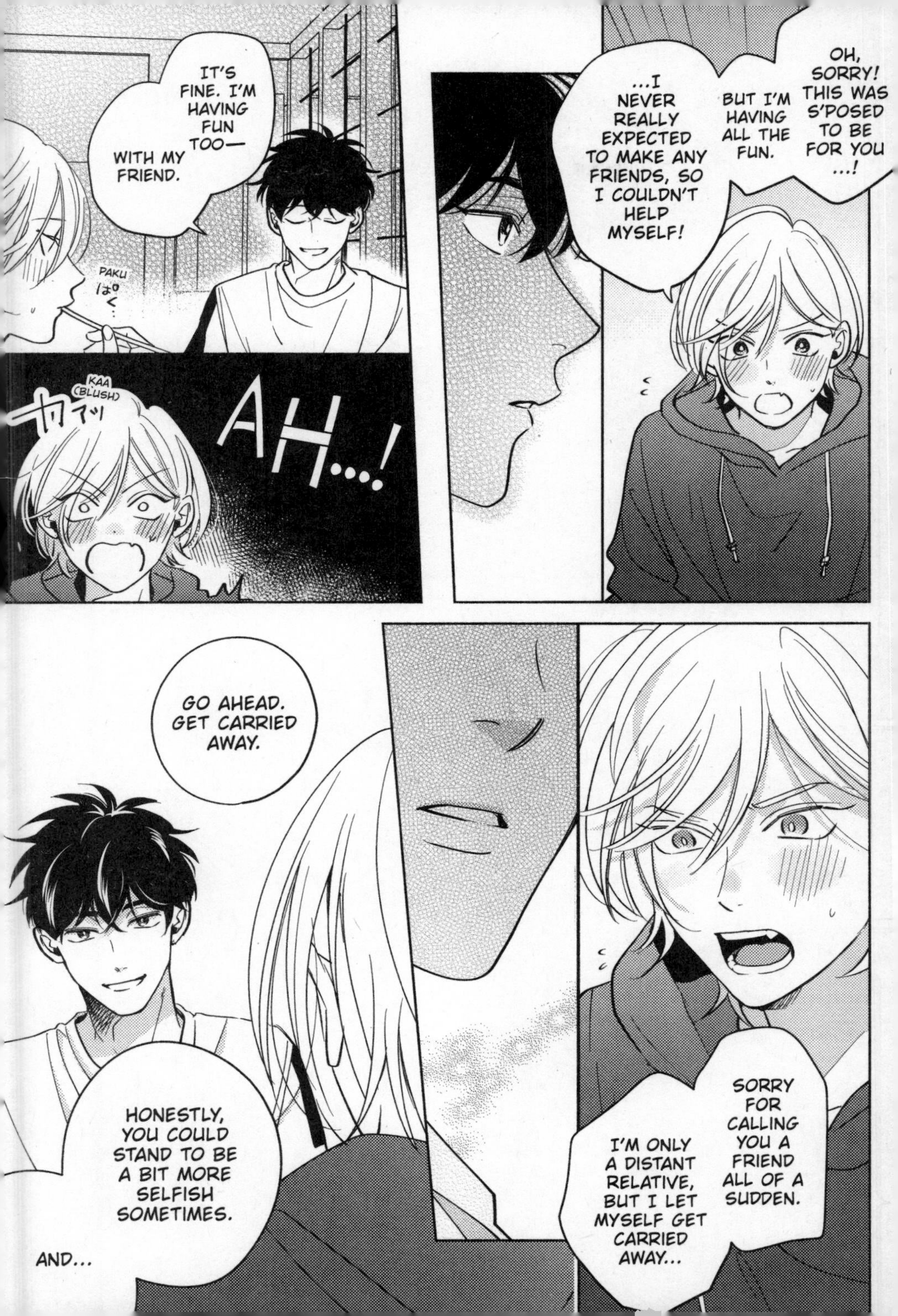

OH, SORRY! THIS WAS S'POSED TO BE FOR YOU ...!
BUT I'M HAVING ALL THE FUN.
...I NEVER REALLY EXPECTED TO MAKE ANY FRIENDS, SO I COULDN'T HELP MYSELF!
IT'S FINE. I'M HAVING FUN TOO— WITH MY FRIEND.
PAKU
ぱく…
KAA (BLUSH)
カァッ
AH...!
SORRY FOR CALLING YOU A FRIEND ALL OF A SUDDEN.
I'M ONLY A DISTANT RELATIVE, BUT I LET MYSELF GET CARRIED AWAY...
GO AHEAD. GET CARRIED AWAY.
HONESTLY, YOU COULD STAND TO BE A BIT MORE SELFISH SOMETIMES.
AND...

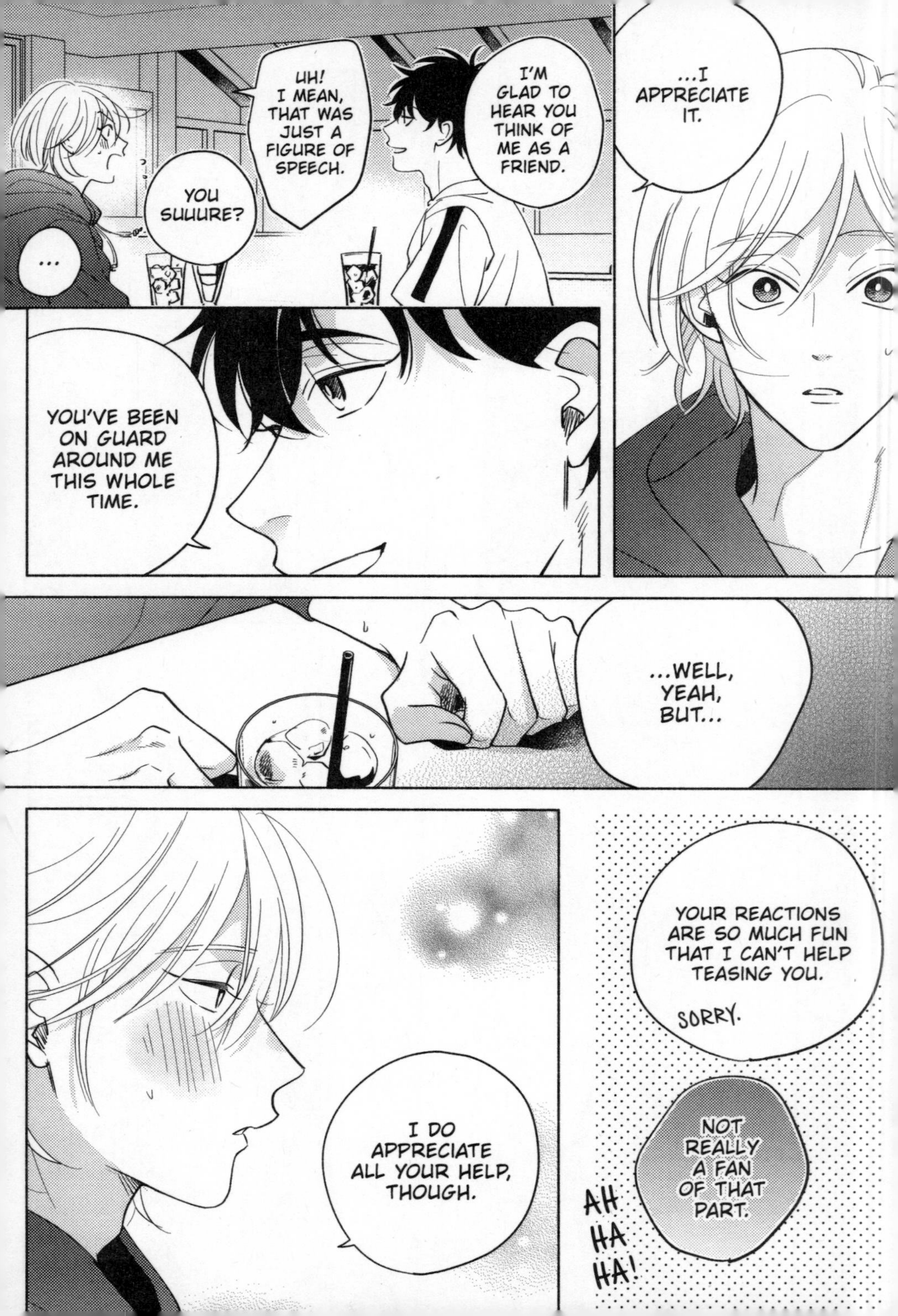
...I APPRECIATE IT.
I'M GLAD TO HEAR YOU THINK OF ME AS A FRIEND.
UH! I MEAN, THAT WAS JUST A FIGURE OF SPEECH.
YOU SUUURE?
...
YOU'VE BEEN ON GUARD AROUND ME THIS WHOLE TIME.
...WELL, YEAH, BUT...
YOUR REACTIONS ARE SO MUCH FUN THAT I CAN'T HELP TEASING YOU.
SORRY.
NOT REALLY A FAN OF THAT PART.
AH HA HA!
I DO APPRECIATE ALL YOUR HELP, THOUGH.

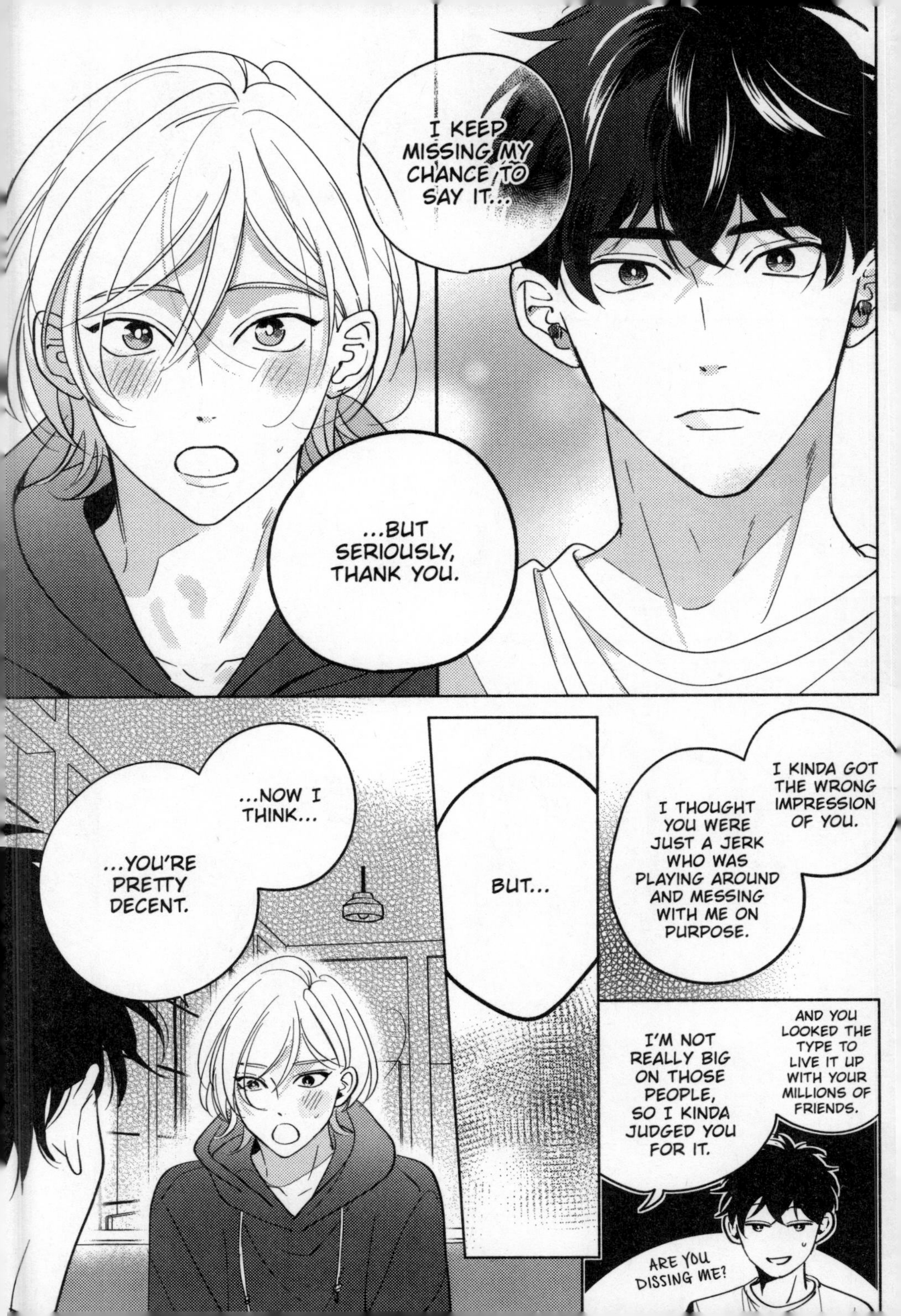
I KEEP MISSING MY CHANCE TO SAY IT...
...BUT SERIOUSLY, THANK YOU.
I KINDA GOT THE WRONG IMPRESSION OF YOU.
I THOUGHT YOU WERE JUST A JERK WHO WAS PLAYING AROUND AND MESSING WITH ME ON PURPOSE.
AND YOU LOOKED THE TYPE TO LIVE IT UP WITH YOUR MILLIONS OF FRIENDS.
I'M NOT REALLY BIG ON THOSE PEOPLE, SO I KINDA JUDGED YOU FOR IT.
ARE YOU DISSING ME?
BUT...
...NOW I THINK...
...YOU'RE PRETTY DECENT.

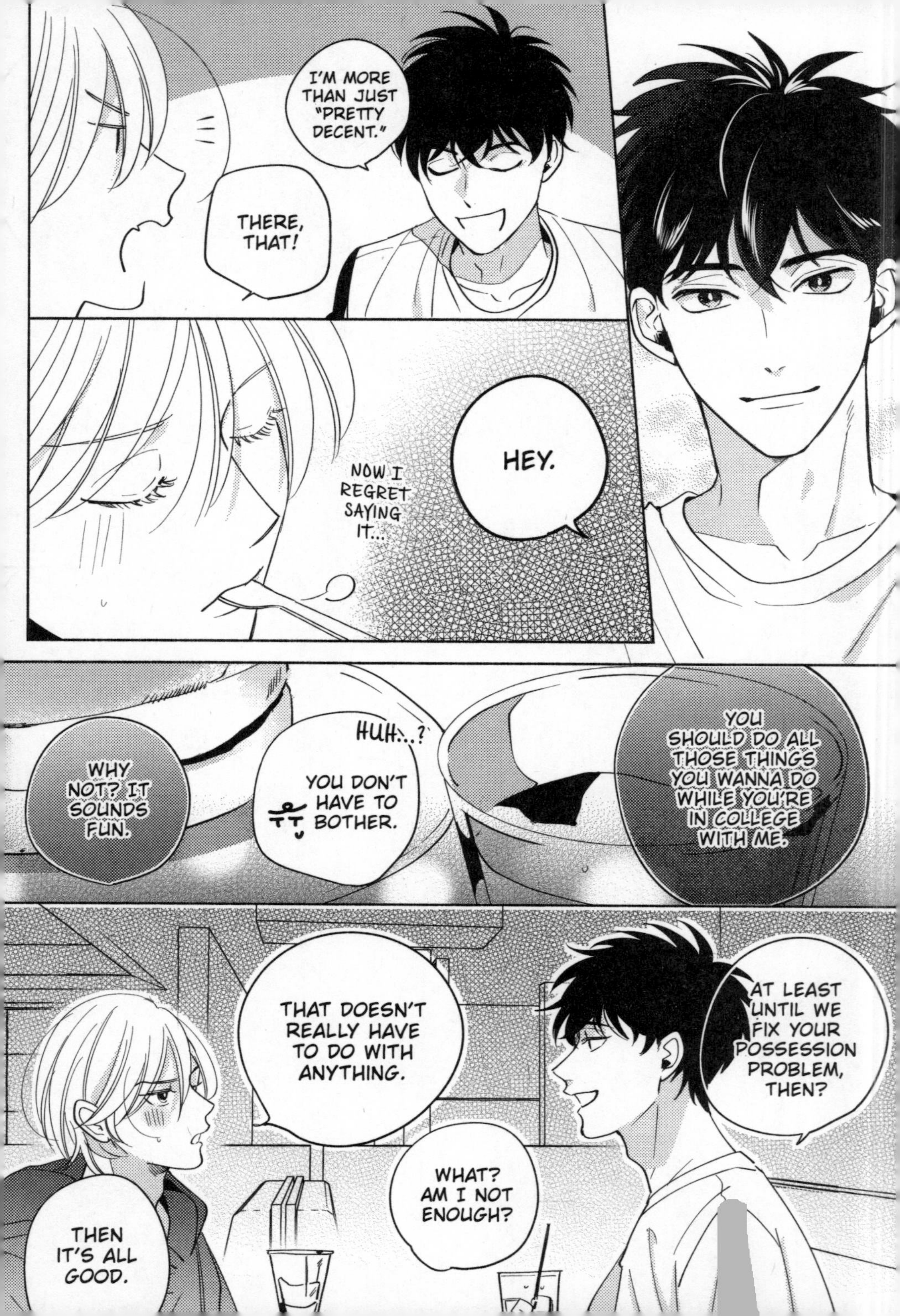
I'M MORE THAN JUST "PRETTY DECENT."
THERE, THAT!
HEY.
NOW I REGRET SAYING IT...
YOU SHOULD DO ALL THOSE THINGS YOU WANNA DO WHILE YOU'RE IN COLLEGE WITH ME.
HUH...?
YOU DON'T HAVE TO BOTHER.
WHY NOT? IT SOUNDS FUN.
AT LEAST UNTIL WE FIX YOUR POSSESSION PROBLEM, THEN?
THAT DOESN'T REALLY HAVE TO DO WITH ANYTHING.
WHAT? AM I NOT ENOUGH?
THEN IT'S ALL GOOD.

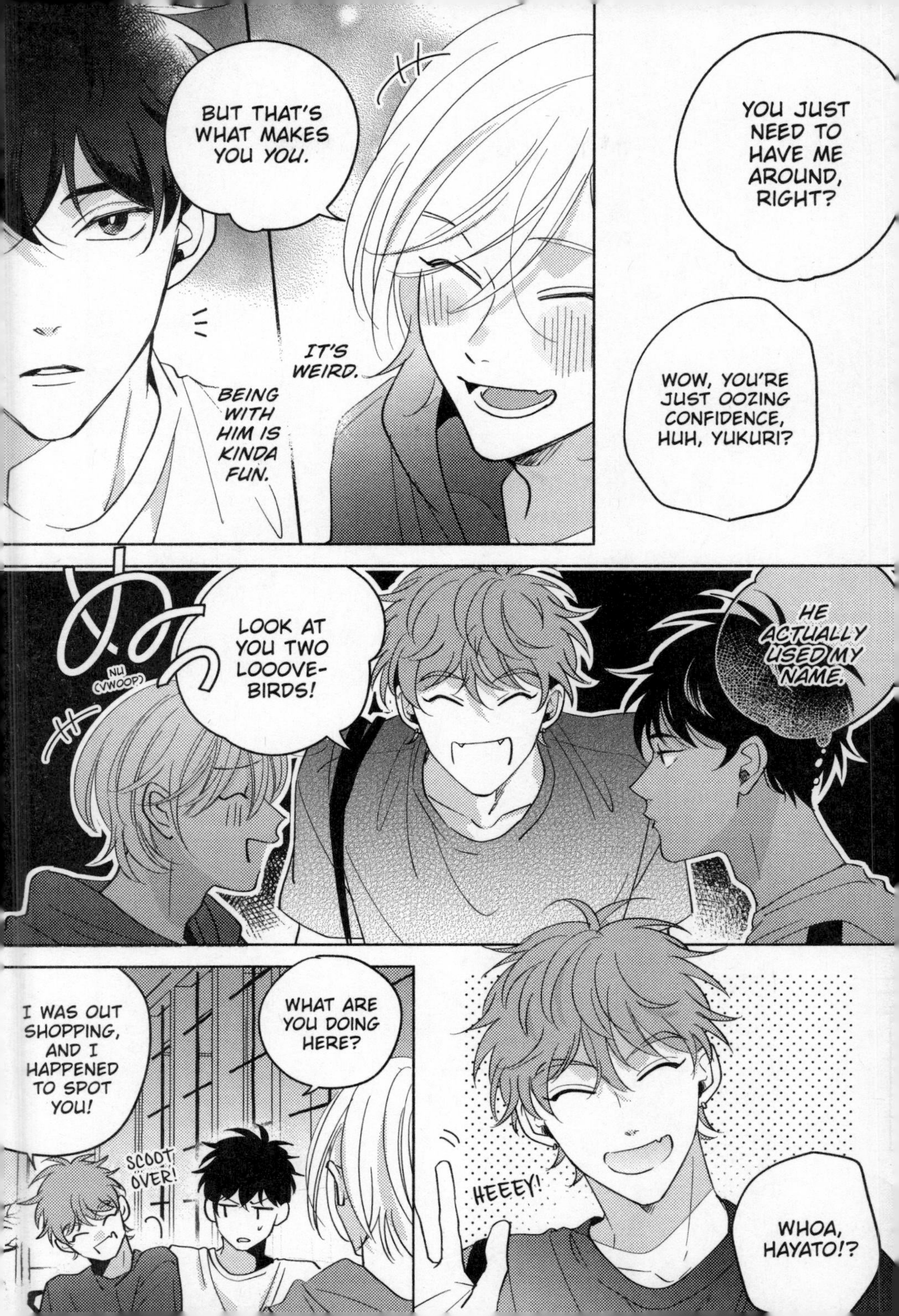
YOU JUST NEED TO HAVE ME AROUND, RIGHT?
WOW, YOU'RE JUST OOZING CONFIDENCE, HUH, YUKURI?
BUT THAT'S WHAT MAKES YOU YOU.
IT'S WEIRD.
BEING WITH HIM IS KINDA FUN.
HE ACTUALLY USED MY NAME.
LOOK AT YOU TWO LOOOVE-BIRDS!
NU (VWOOP)
WHOA, HAYATO!?
HEEEY!
WHAT ARE YOU DOING HERE?
I WAS OUT SHOPPING, AND I HAPPENED TO SPOT YOU!
SCOOT OVER!

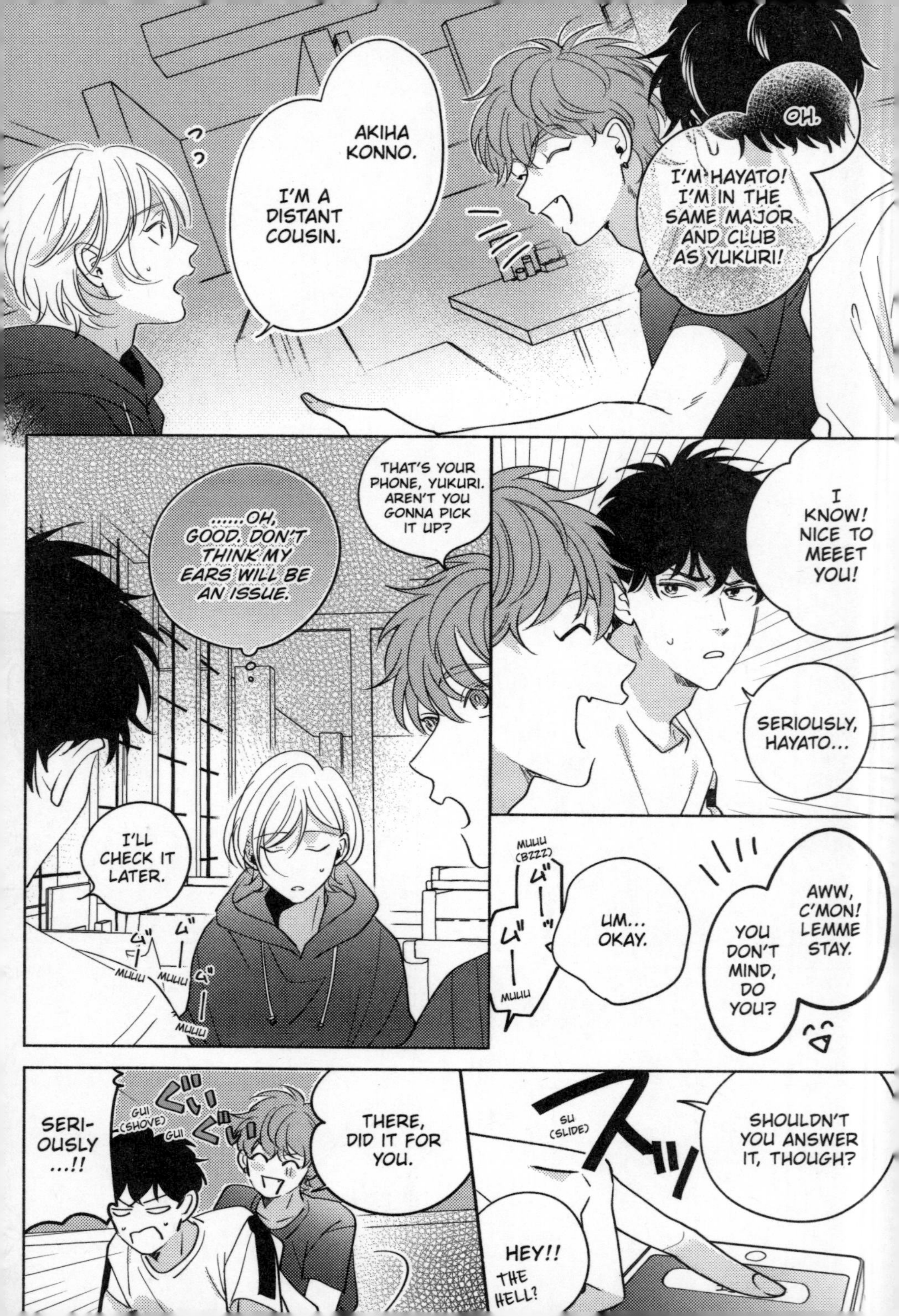
OH.
I'M HAYATO! I'M IN THE SAME MAJOR AND CLUB AS YUKURI!
AKIHA KONNO.
I'M A DISTANT COUSIN.
I KNOW! NICE TO MEEET YOU!
SERIOUSLY, HAYATO...
AWW, C'MON! LEMME STAY.
YOU DON'T MIND, DO YOU?
UM... OKAY.
MUUU (BZZZ)
MUUU
THAT'S YOUR PHONE, YUKURI. AREN'T YOU GONNA PICK IT UP?
......OH, GOOD. DON'T THINK MY EARS WILL BE AN ISSUE.
I'LL CHECK IT LATER.
MUUU MUUU
MUUU
SHOULDN'T YOU ANSWER IT, THOUGH?
SU (SLIDE)
HEY!!
THE HELL?
THERE, DID IT FOR YOU.
GUI (SHOVE) GUI
SERIOUSLY...!!

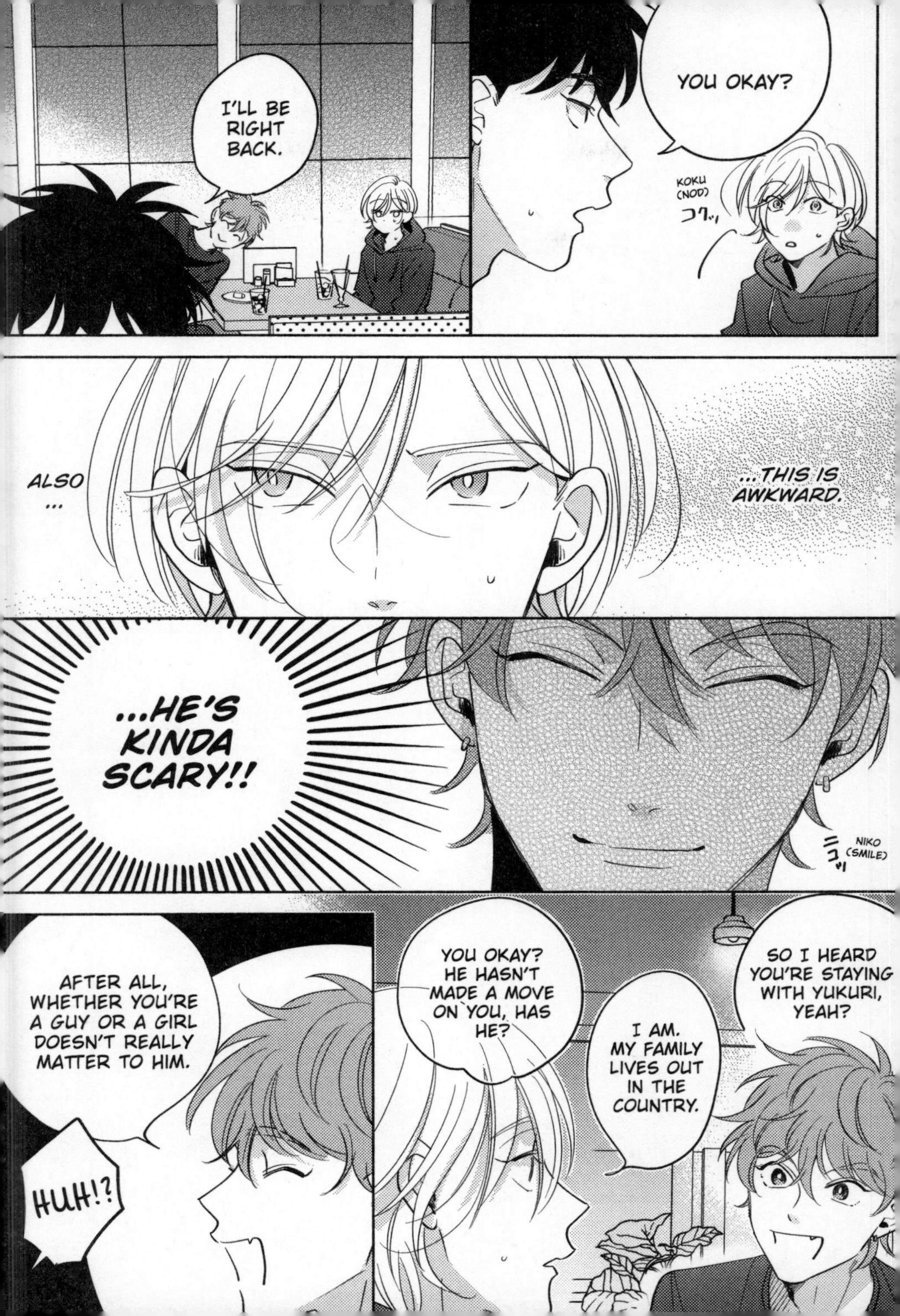
YOU OKAY?
KOKU (NOD)
コクッ
I'LL BE RIGHT BACK.
...THIS IS AWKWARD.
ALSO ...
NIKO (SMILE)
ニコッ
...HE'S KINDA SCARY!!
SO I HEARD YOU'RE STAYING WITH YUKURI, YEAH?
I AM. MY FAMILY LIVES OUT IN THE COUNTRY.
YOU OKAY? HE HASN'T MADE A MOVE ON YOU, HAS HE?
AFTER ALL, WHETHER YOU'RE A GUY OR A GIRL DOESN'T REALLY MATTER TO HIM.
HUH!?

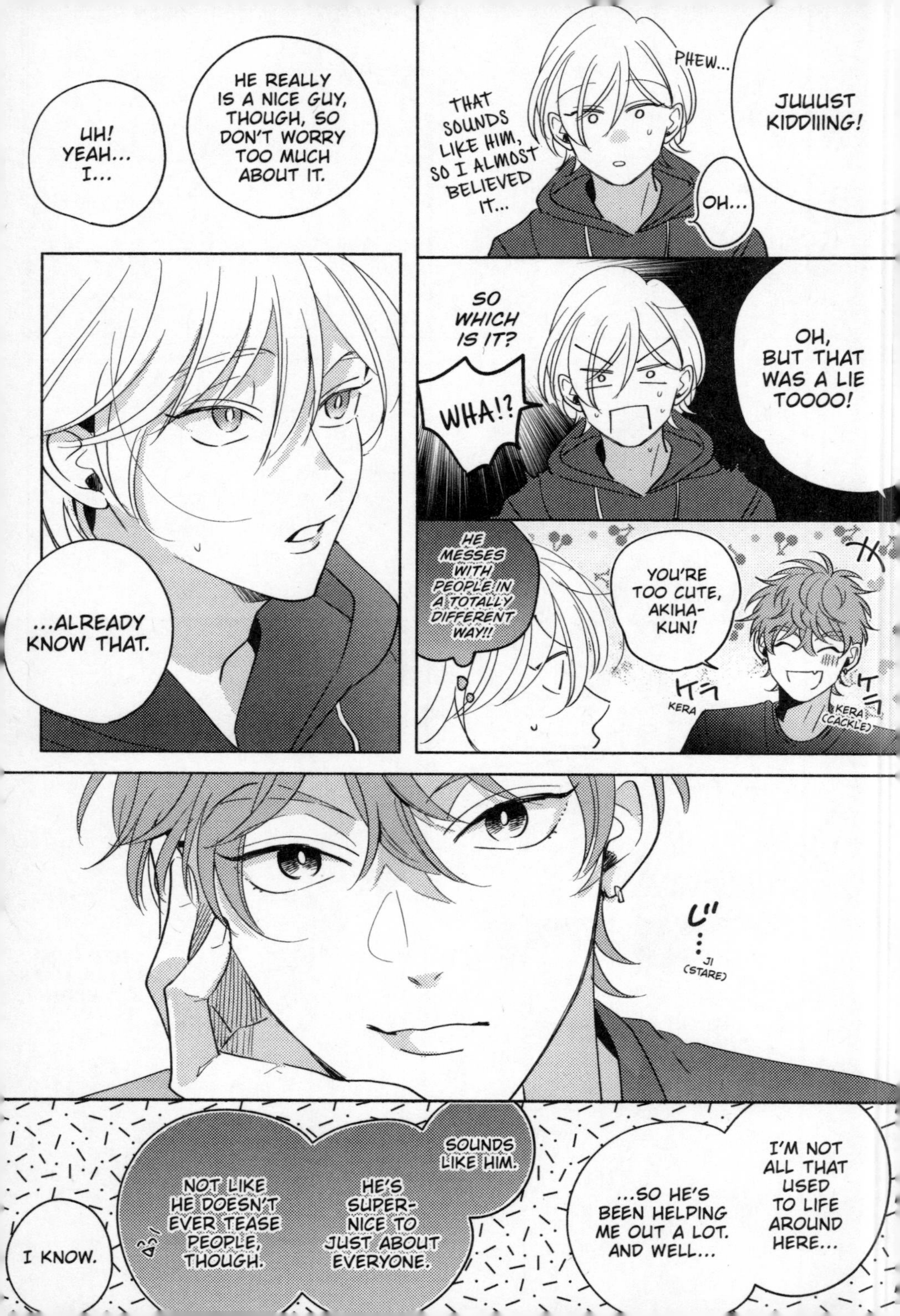
JUUUST KIDDIIING!
OH...
PHEW...
THAT SOUNDS LIKE HIM, SO I ALMOST BELIEVED IT...
HE REALLY IS A NICE GUY, THOUGH, SO DON'T WORRY TOO MUCH ABOUT IT.
UH! YEAH... I...
OH, BUT THAT WAS A LIE TOOOO!
SO WHICH IS IT?
WHA!?
YOU'RE TOO CUTE, AKIHA-KUN!
KERA (CACKLE)
KERA
HE MESSES WITH PEOPLE IN A TOTALLY DIFFERENT WAY!!
...ALREADY KNOW THAT.
ジ…
JI (STARE)
I'M NOT ALL THAT USED TO LIFE AROUND HERE...
...SO HE'S BEEN HELPING ME OUT A LOT. AND WELL...
SOUNDS LIKE HIM.
HE'S SUPER-NICE TO JUST ABOUT EVERYONE.
NOT LIKE HE DOESN'T EVER TEASE PEOPLE, THOUGH.
I KNOW.

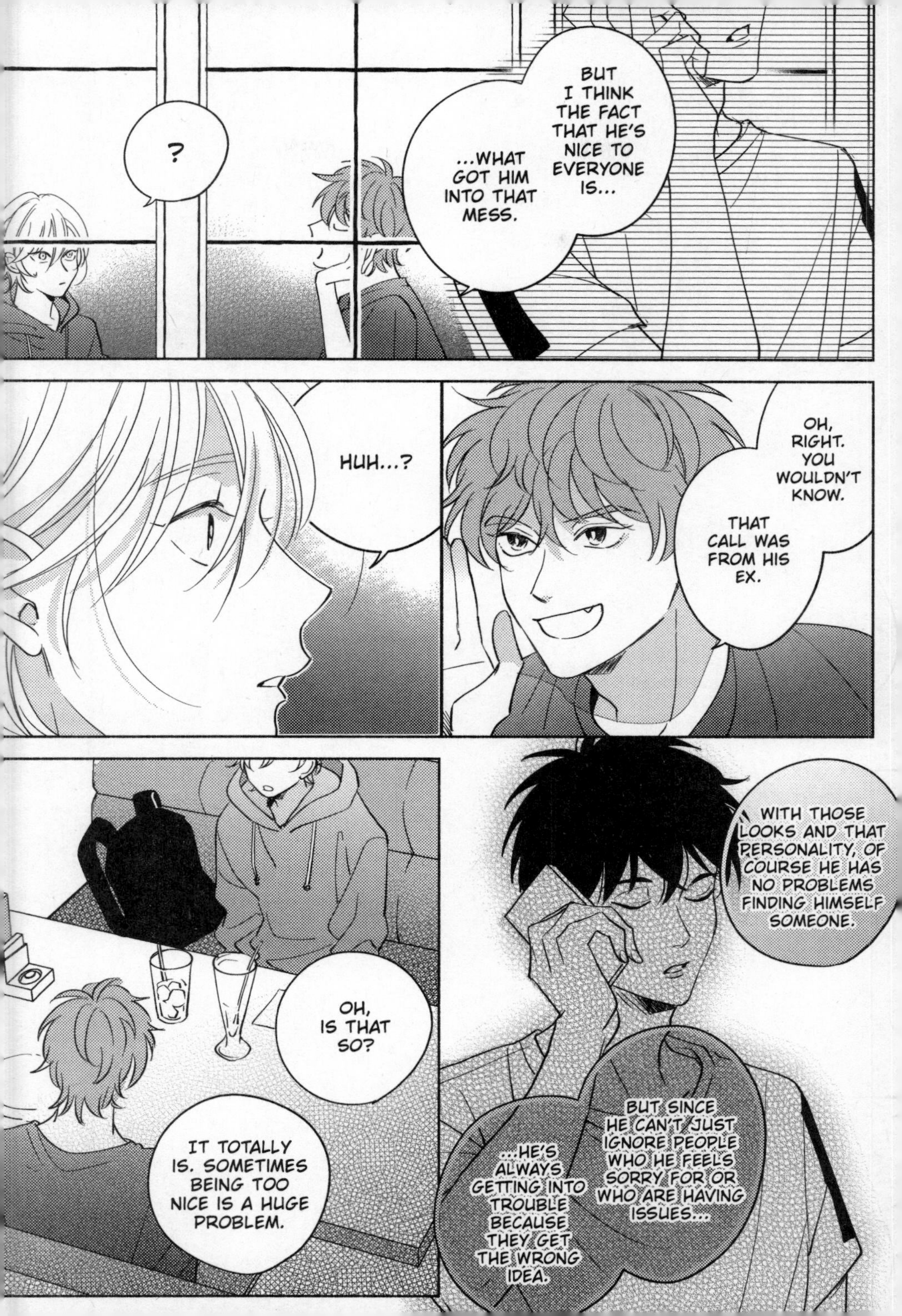
BUT I THINK THE FACT THAT HE'S NICE TO EVERYONE IS...
...WHAT GOT HIM INTO THAT MESS.
?
OH, RIGHT. YOU WOULDN'T KNOW.
THAT CALL WAS FROM HIS EX.
HUH...?
WITH THOSE LOOKS AND THAT PERSONALITY, OF COURSE HE HAS NO PROBLEMS FINDING HIMSELF SOMEONE.
BUT SINCE HE CAN'T JUST IGNORE PEOPLE WHO HE FEELS SORRY FOR OR WHO ARE HAVING ISSUES...
...HE'S ALWAYS GETTING INTO TROUBLE BECAUSE THEY GET THE WRONG IDEA.
OH, IS THAT SO?
IT TOTALLY IS. SOMETIMES BEING TOO NICE IS A HUGE PROBLEM.

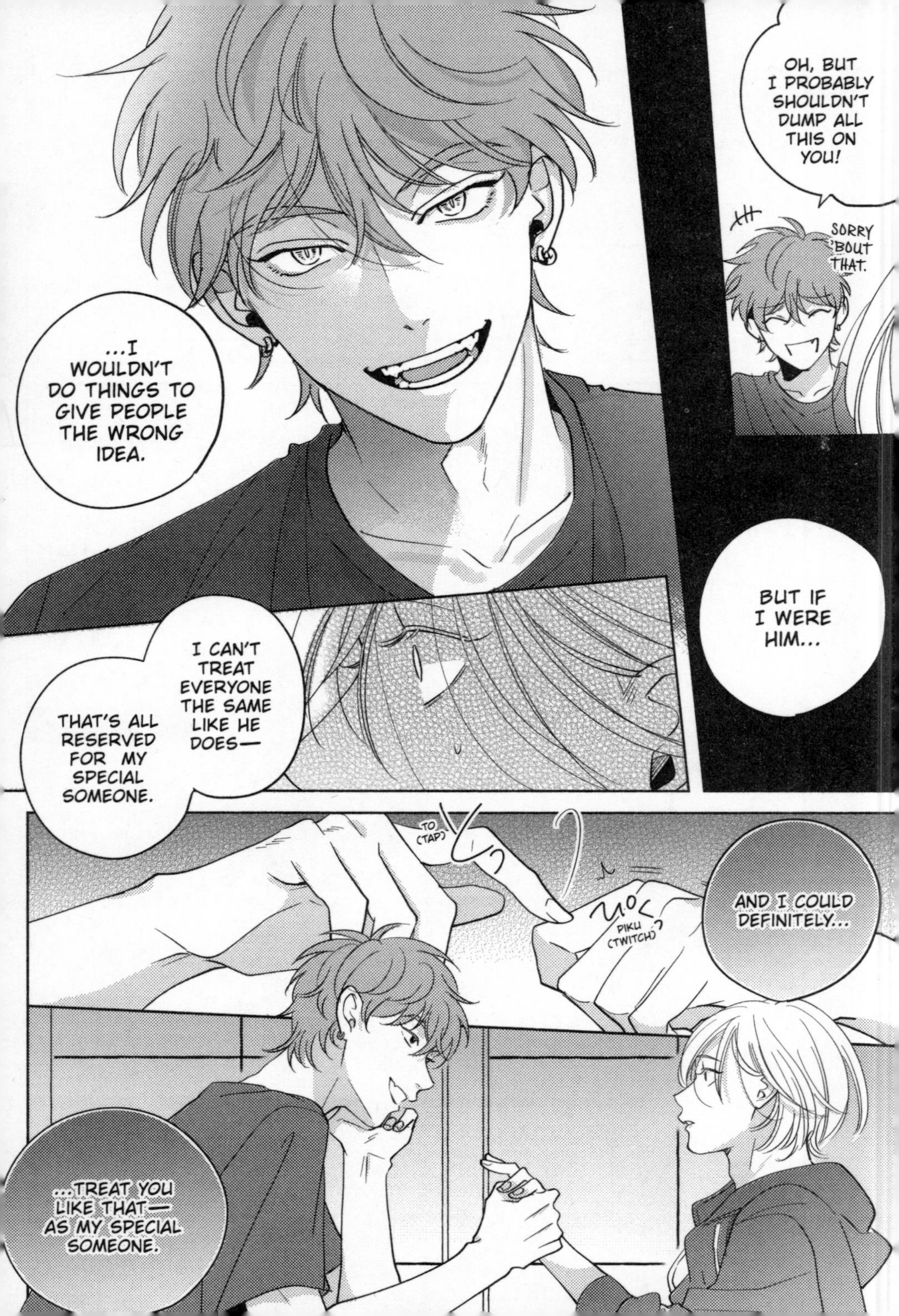
OH, BUT I PROBABLY SHOULDN'T DUMP ALL THIS ON YOU!
SORRY 'BOUT THAT.
BUT IF I WERE HIM...
...I WOULDN'T DO THINGS TO GIVE PEOPLE THE WRONG IDEA.
I CAN'T TREAT EVERYONE THE SAME LIKE HE DOES—
THAT'S ALL RESERVED FOR MY SPECIAL SOMEONE.
TO (TAP)
PIKU (TWITCH)
AND I COULD DEFINITELY...
...TREAT YOU LIKE THAT— AS MY SPECIAL SOMEONE.

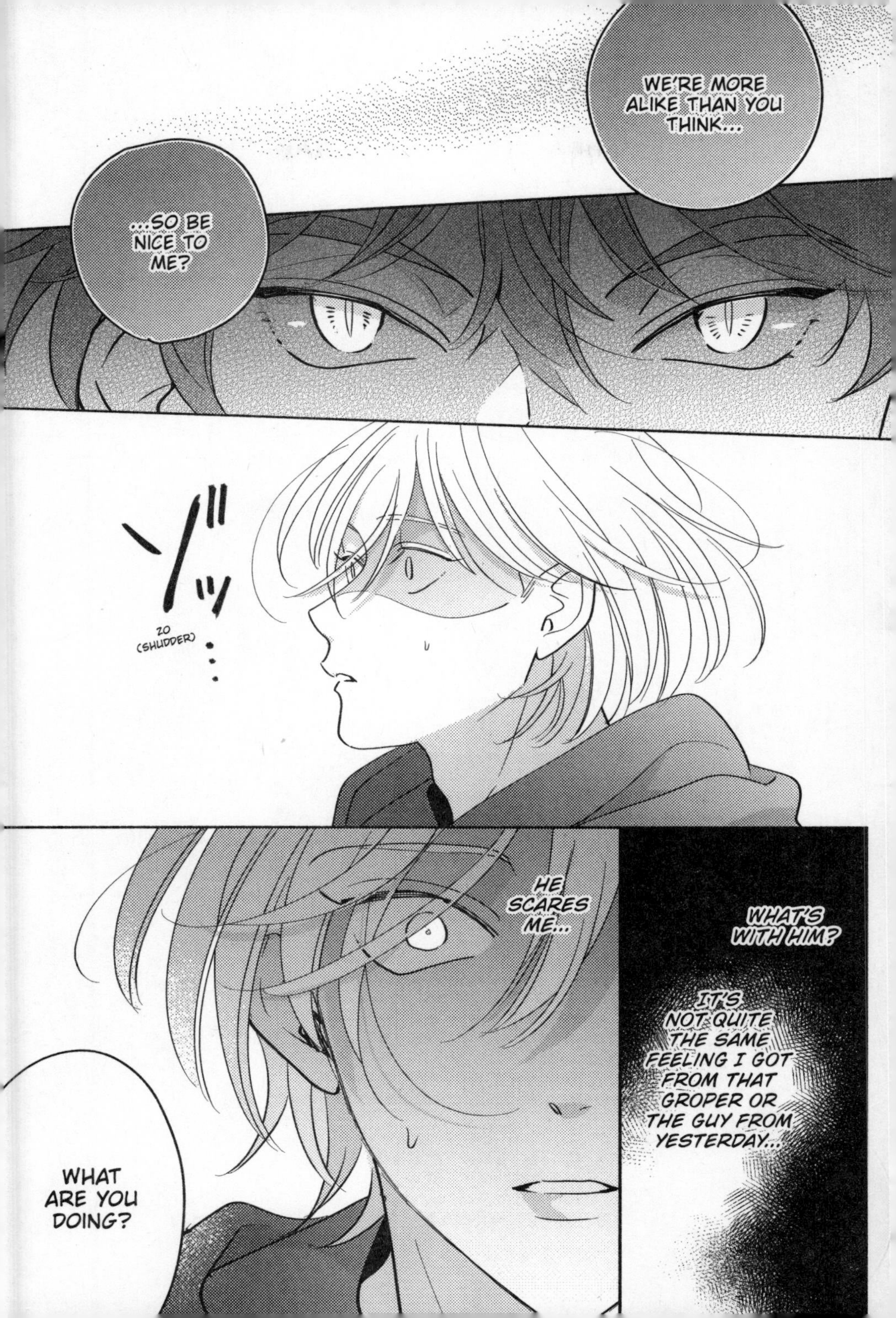
WE'RE MORE ALIKE THAN YOU THINK...
...SO BE NICE TO ME?
ゾッ
ZO (SHUDDER)
WHAT'S WITH HIM?
IT'S NOT QUITE THE SAME FEELING I GOT FROM THAT GROPER OR THE GUY FROM YESTERDAY...
HE SCARES ME...
WHAT ARE YOU DOING?

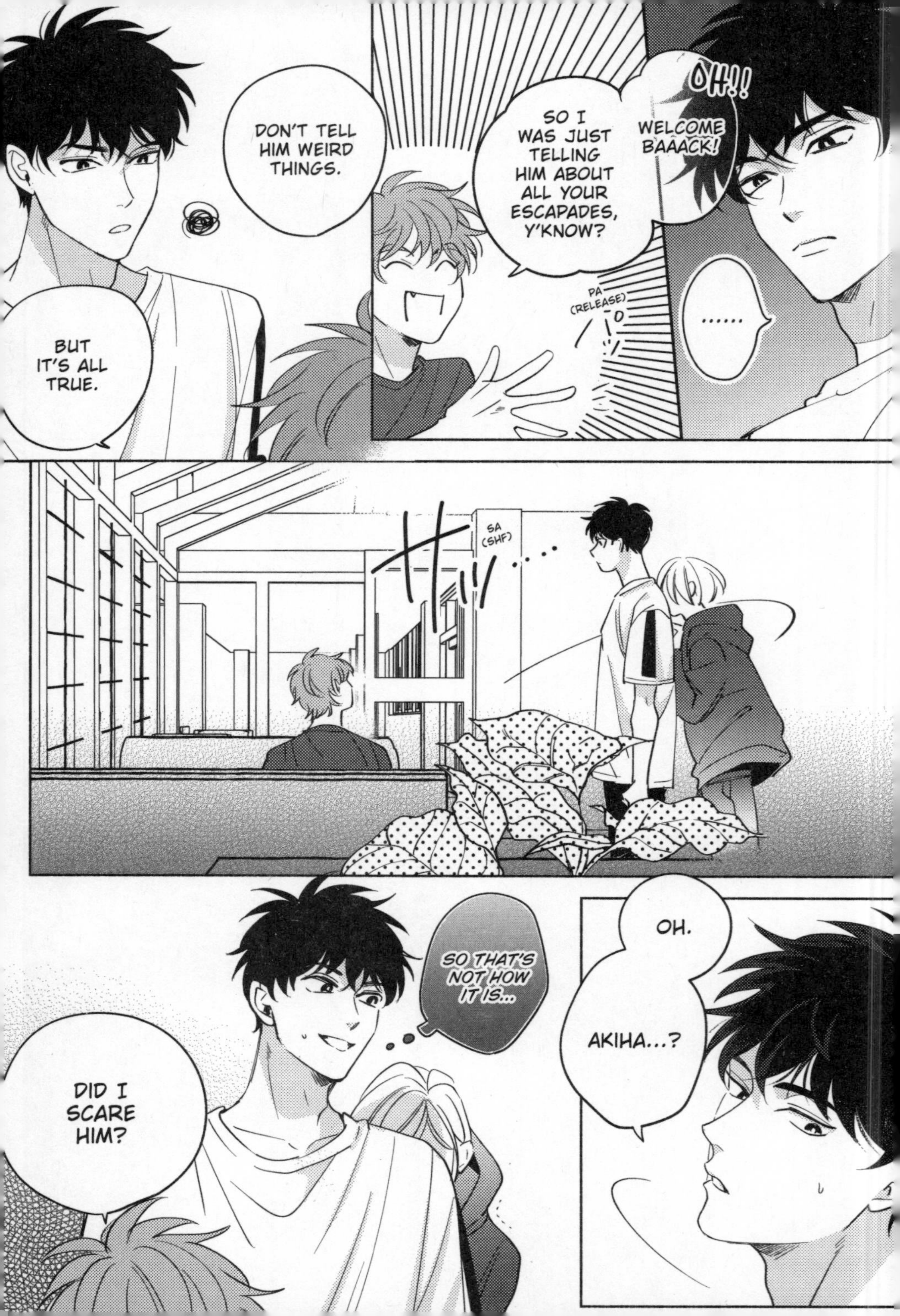
OH!!
WELCOME BAAACK!
SO I WAS JUST TELLING HIM ABOUT ALL YOUR ESCAPADES, Y'KNOW?
PA (RELEASE)
......
DON'T TELL HIM WEIRD THINGS.
BUT IT'S ALL TRUE.
SA (SHF)
...
OH.
AKIHA...?
SO THAT'S NOT HOW IT IS...
DID I SCARE HIM?

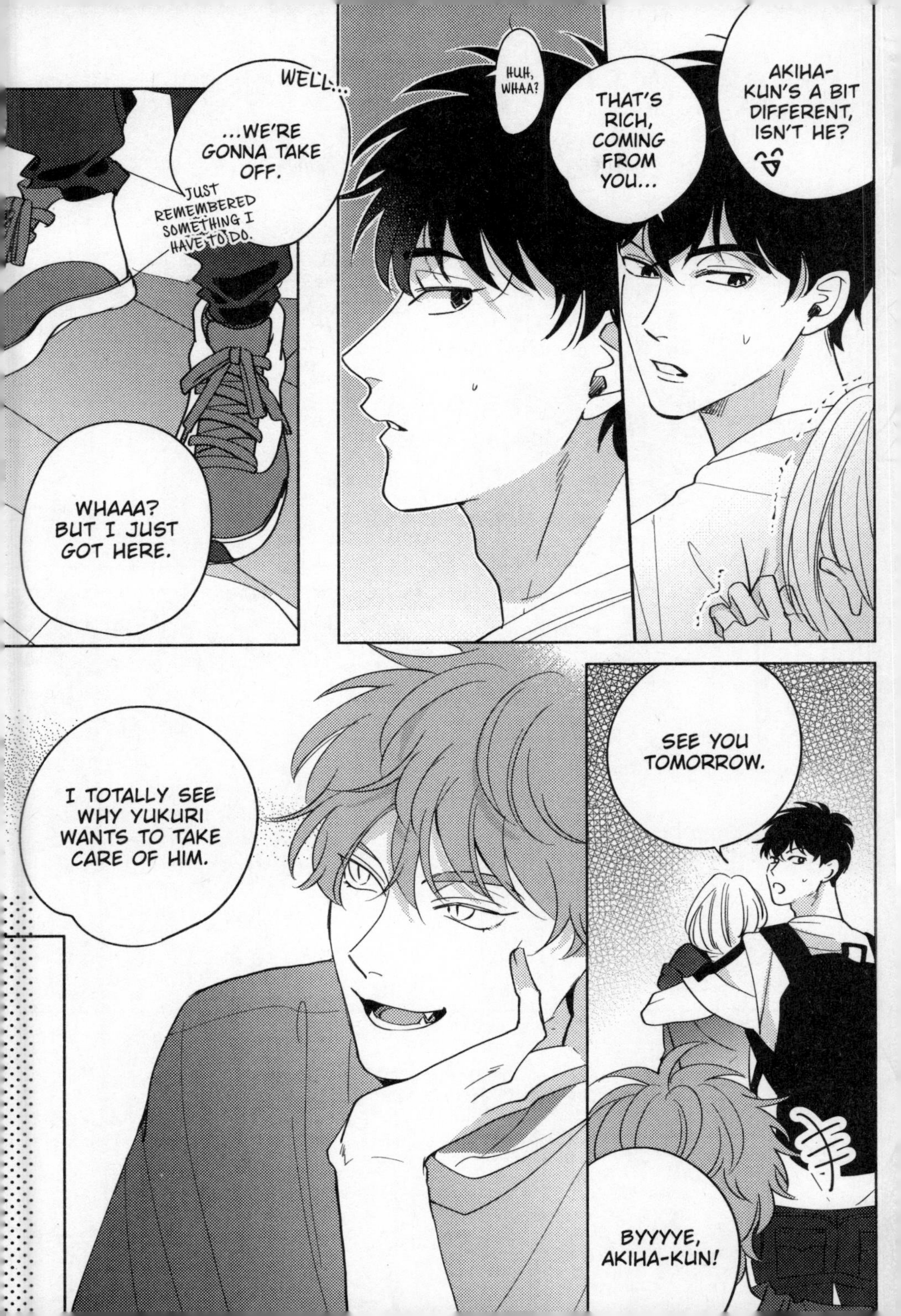
AKIHA-KUN'S A BIT DIFFERENT, ISN'T HE?
THAT'S RICH, COMING FROM YOU...
HUH, WHAA?
WELL...
...WE'RE GONNA TAKE OFF.
JUST REMEMBERED SOMETHING I HAVE TO DO.
WHAAA? BUT I JUST GOT HERE.
SEE YOU TOMORROW.
BYYYYE, AKIHA-KUN!
I TOTALLY SEE WHY YUKURI WANTS TO TAKE CARE OF HIM.

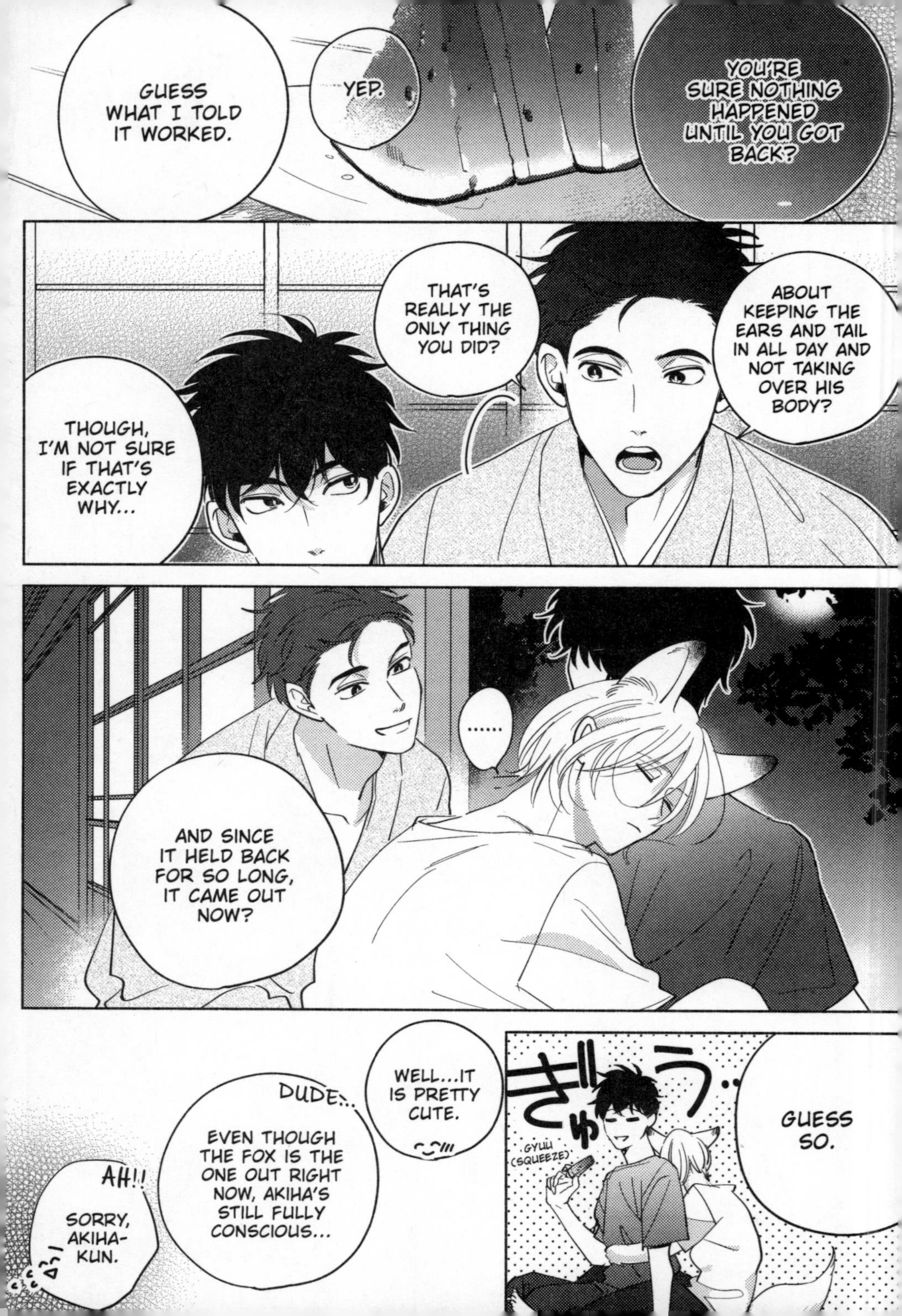
YOU'RE SURE NOTHING HAPPENED UNTIL YOU GOT BACK?
YEP.
GUESS WHAT I TOLD IT WORKED.
ABOUT KEEPING THE EARS AND TAIL IN ALL DAY AND NOT TAKING OVER HIS BODY?
THAT'S REALLY THE ONLY THING YOU DID?
THOUGH, I'M NOT SURE IF THAT'S EXACTLY WHY...
......
AND SINCE IT HELD BACK FOR SO LONG, IT CAME OUT NOW?
GUESS SO.
ぎゅう
GYUU (SQUEEZE)
WELL...IT IS PRETTY CUTE.
DUDE...
EVEN THOUGH THE FOX IS THE ONE OUT RIGHT NOW, AKIHA'S STILL FULLY CONSCIOUS...
AH!!
SORRY, AKIHA-KUN.

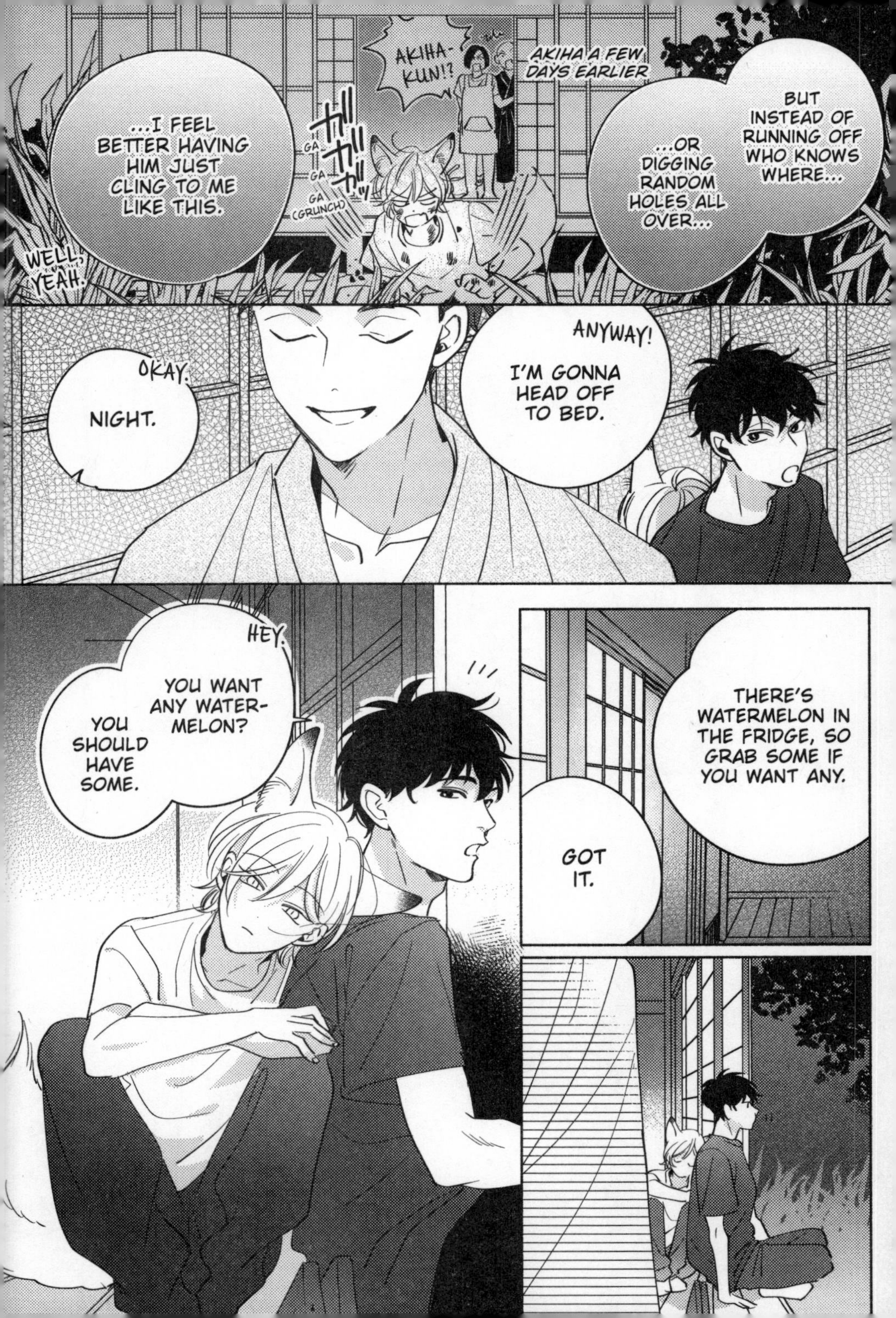
BUT INSTEAD OF RUNNING OFF WHO KNOWS WHERE...
...OR DIGGING RANDOM HOLES ALL OVER...
AKIHA A FEW DAYS EARLIER
AKIHA-KUN!?
GA GA GA (GRUNCH)
...I FEEL BETTER HAVING HIM JUST CLING TO ME LIKE THIS.
WELL, YEAH.
ANYWAY!
I'M GONNA HEAD OFF TO BED.
OKAY.
NIGHT.
THERE'S WATERMELON IN THE FRIDGE, SO GRAB SOME IF YOU WANT ANY.
GOT IT.
HEY.
YOU WANT ANY WATER-MELON?
YOU SHOULD HAVE SOME.

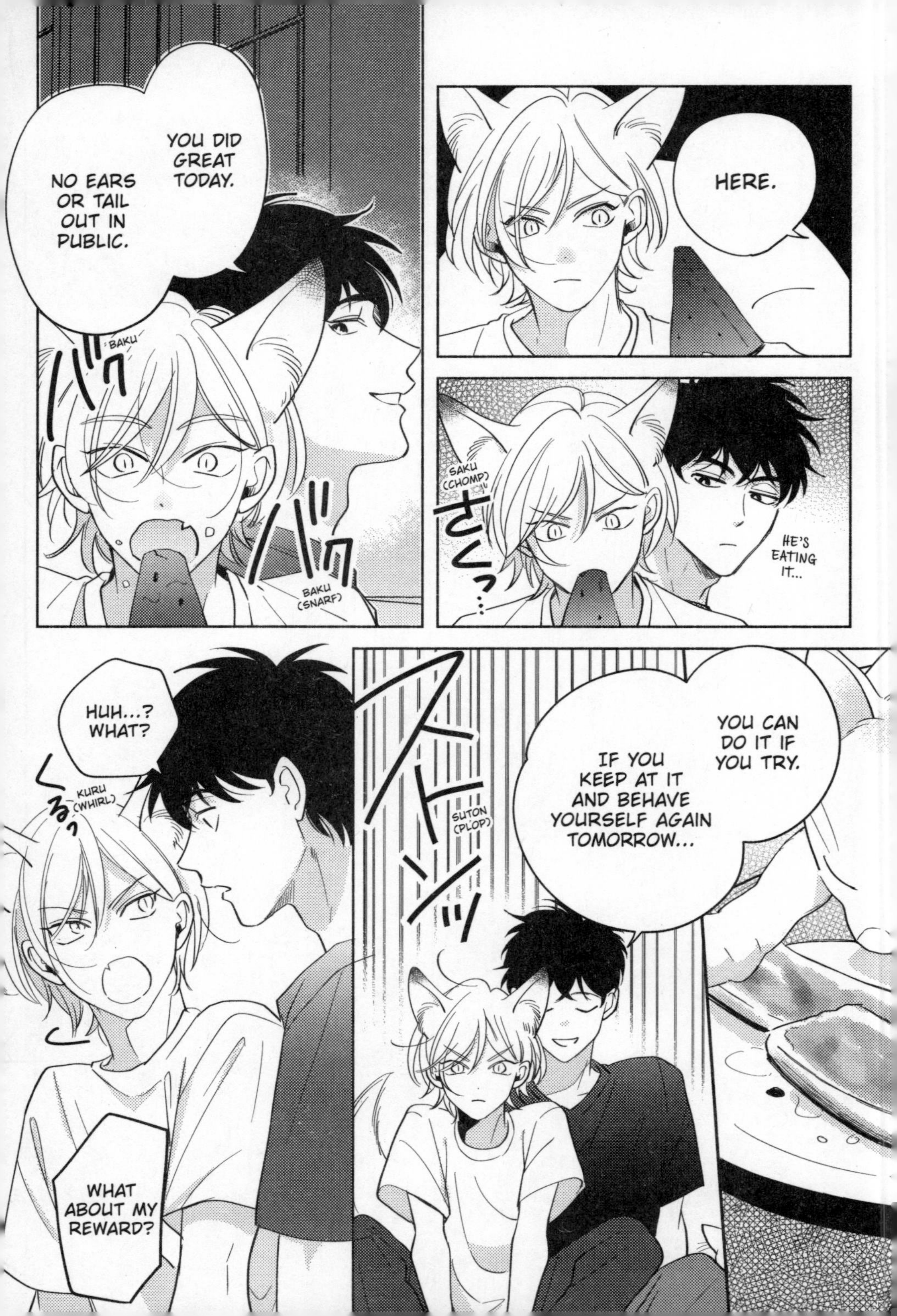
HERE.
SAKU (CHOMP)
HE'S EATING IT...
YOU DID GREAT TODAY.
NO EARS OR TAIL OUT IN PUBLIC.
BAKU
BAKU (SNARF)
YOU CAN DO IT IF YOU TRY.
IF YOU KEEP AT IT AND BEHAVE YOURSELF AGAIN TOMORROW...
SUTON (PLOP)
HUH...? WHAT?
KURU (WHIRL)
WHAT ABOUT MY REWARD?

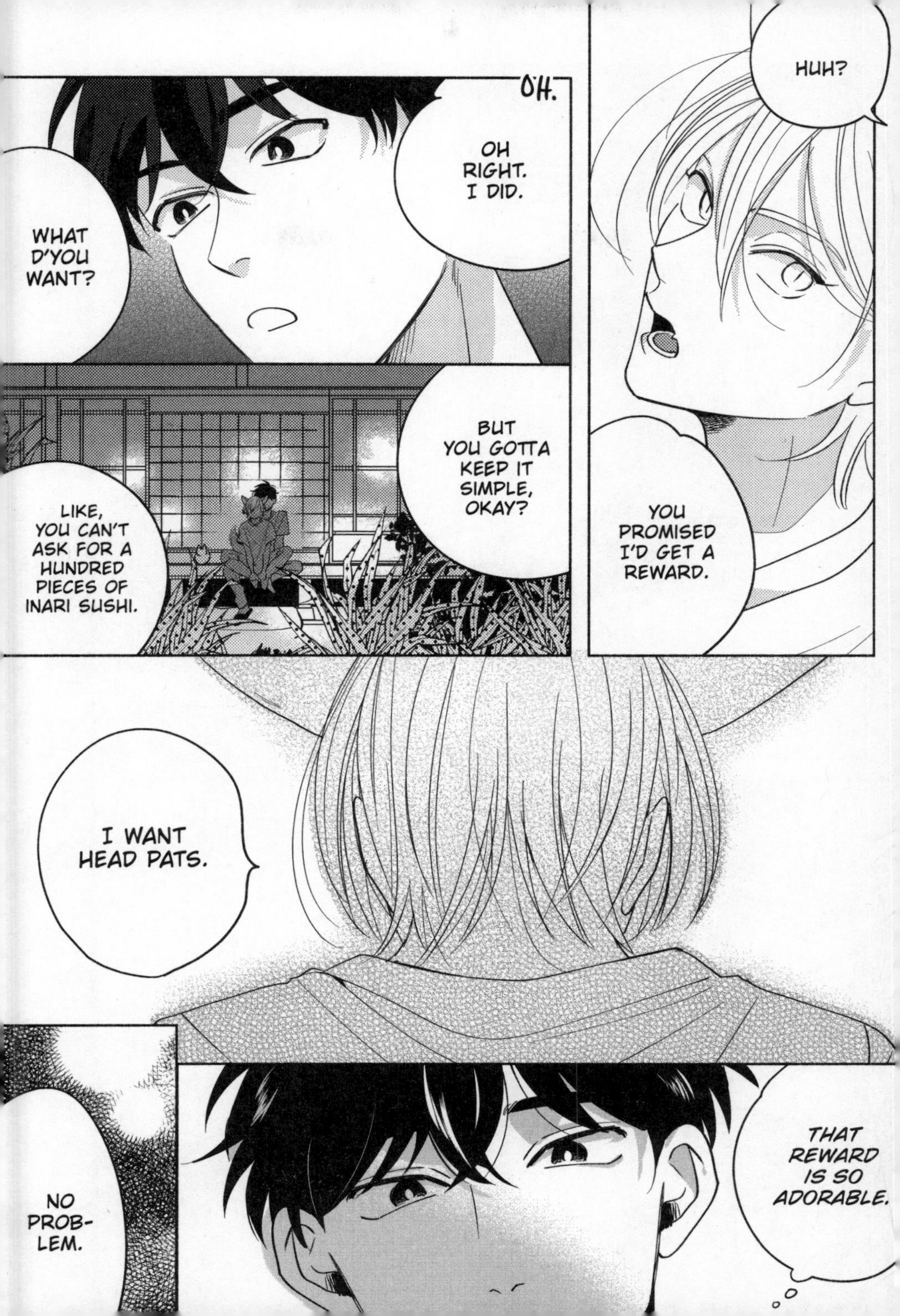
HUH?
YOU PROMISED I'D GET A REWARD.
OH.
OH RIGHT. I DID.
WHAT D'YOU WANT?
BUT YOU GOTTA KEEP IT SIMPLE, OKAY?
LIKE, YOU CAN'T ASK FOR A HUNDRED PIECES OF INARI SUSHI.
I WANT HEAD PATS.
THAT REWARD IS SO ADORABLE.
NO PROB-LEM.

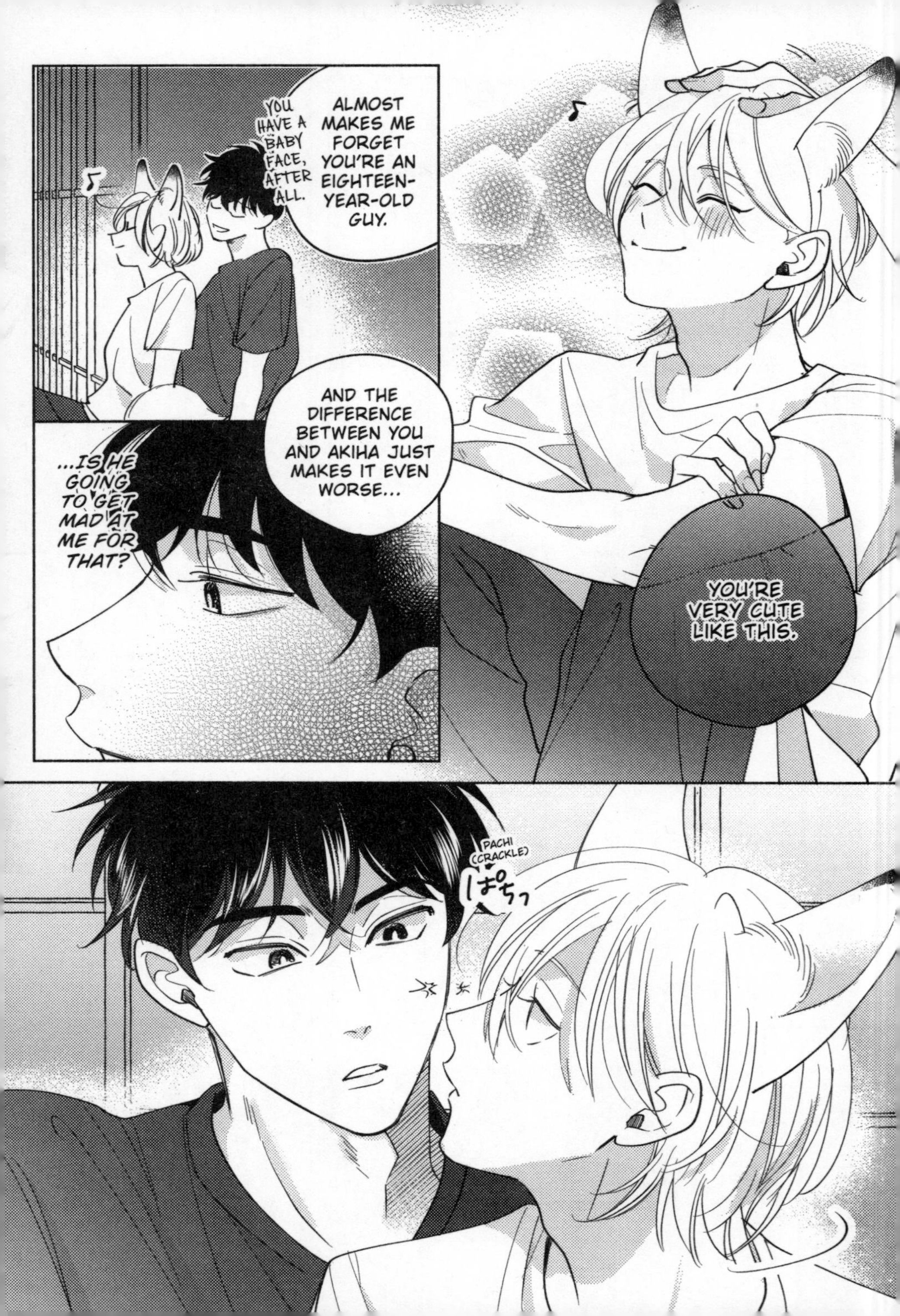
YOU'RE VERY CUTE LIKE THIS.
ALMOST MAKES ME FORGET YOU'RE AN EIGHTEEN-YEAR-OLD GUY.
YOU HAVE A BABY FACE, AFTER ALL.
AND THE DIFFERENCE BETWEEN YOU AND AKIHA JUST MAKES IT EVEN WORSE...
...IS HE GOING TO GET MAD AT ME FOR THAT?
PACHI (CRACKLE)
ぱちっ

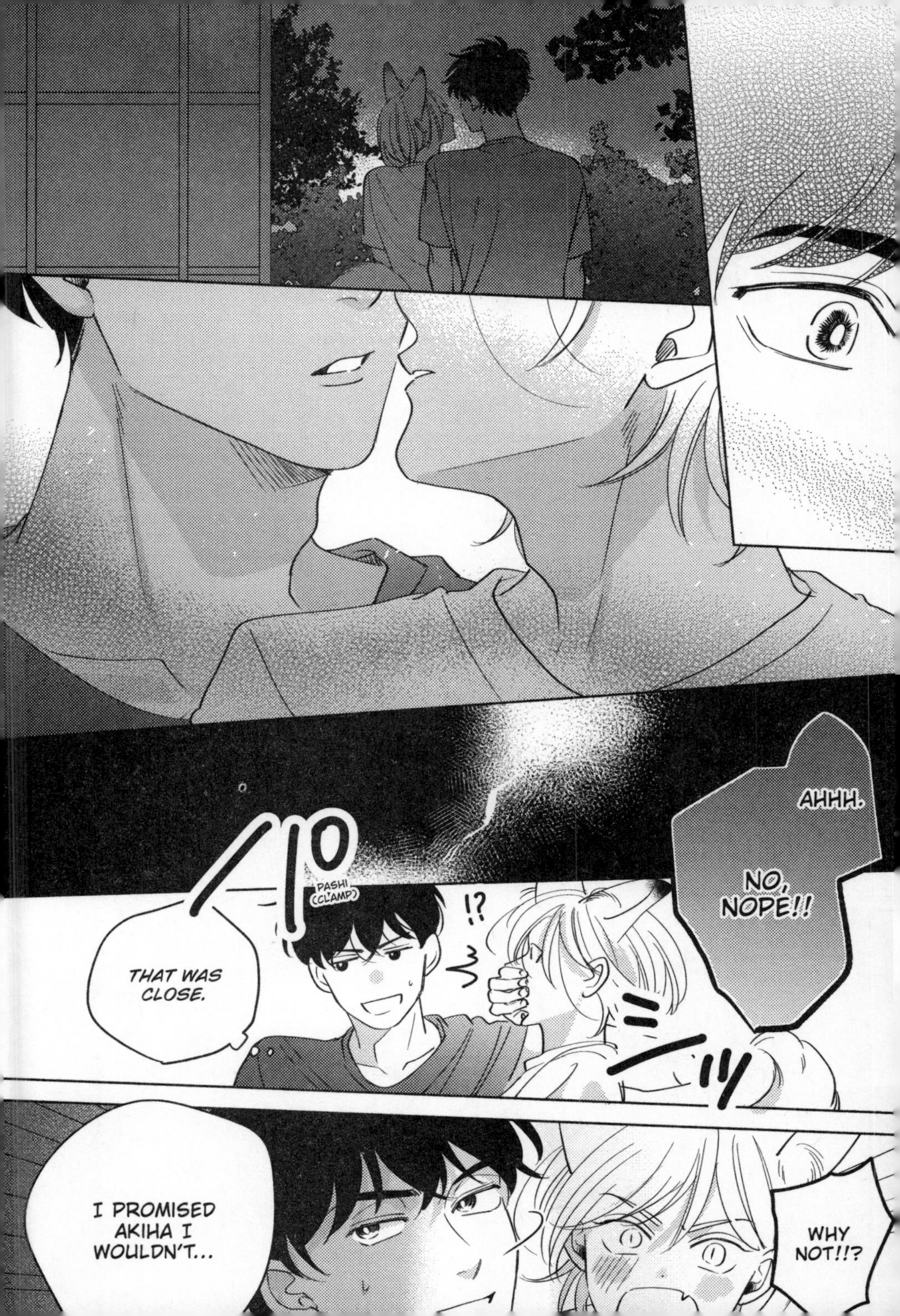
AHHH.
NO, NOPE!!
!?
PASHI (CLAMP)
THAT WAS CLOSE.
WHY NOT!!?
I PROMISED AKIHA I WOULDN'T...

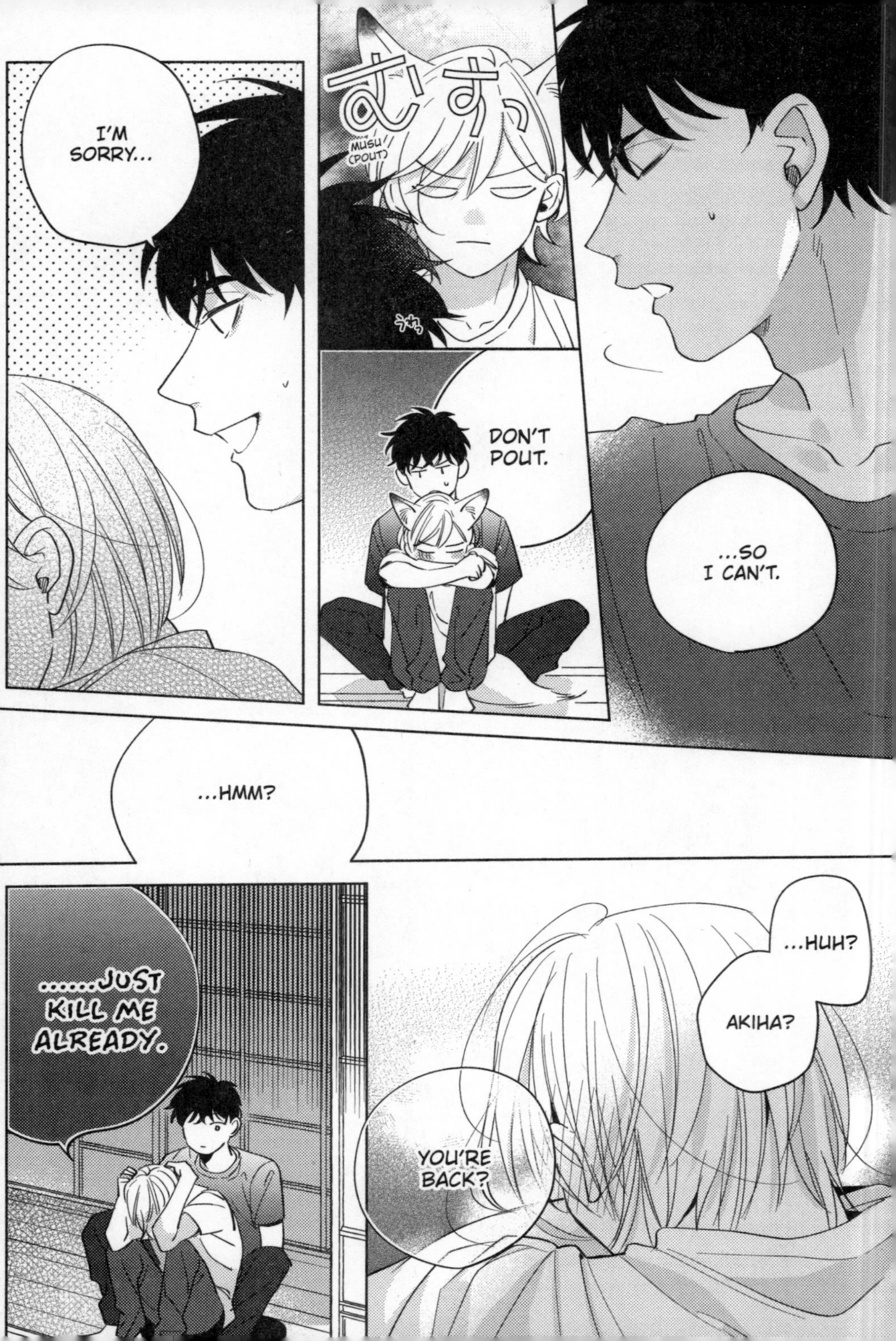
...SO
I CAN'T.
むすっ
MUSU
(POUT)
DON'T
POUT.
I'M
SORRY...
...HMM?
...HUH?
AKIHA?
YOU'RE
BACK?
......JUST
KILL ME
ALREADY.

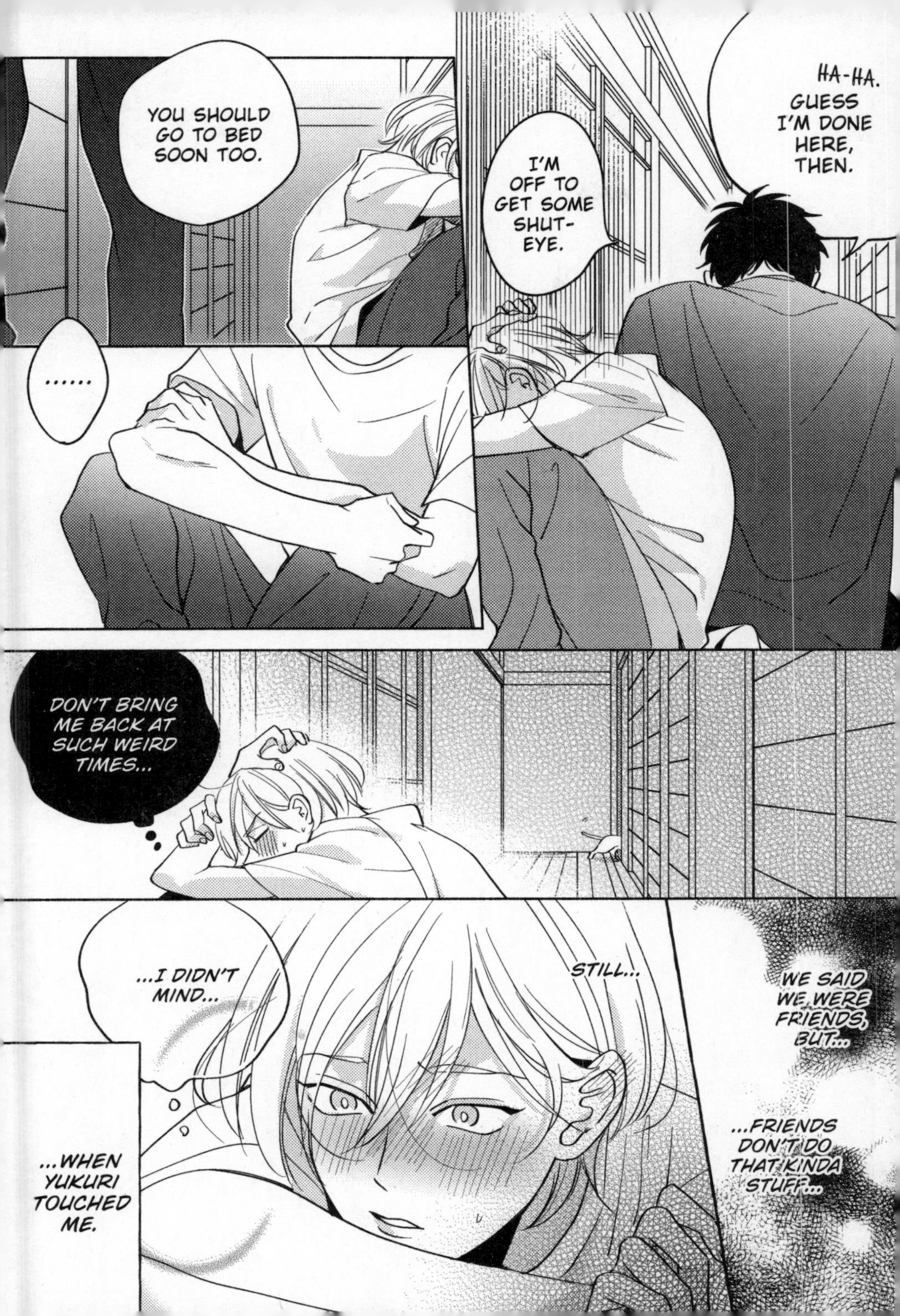
HA-HA. GUESS I'M DONE HERE, THEN.
I'M OFF TO GET SOME SHUT-EYE.
YOU SHOULD GO TO BED SOON TOO.
......
DON'T BRING ME BACK AT SUCH WEIRD TIMES...
WE SAID WE WERE FRIENDS, BUT...
...FRIENDS DON'T DO THAT KINDA STUFF...
STILL...
...I DIDN'T MIND...
...WHEN YUKURI TOUCHED ME.

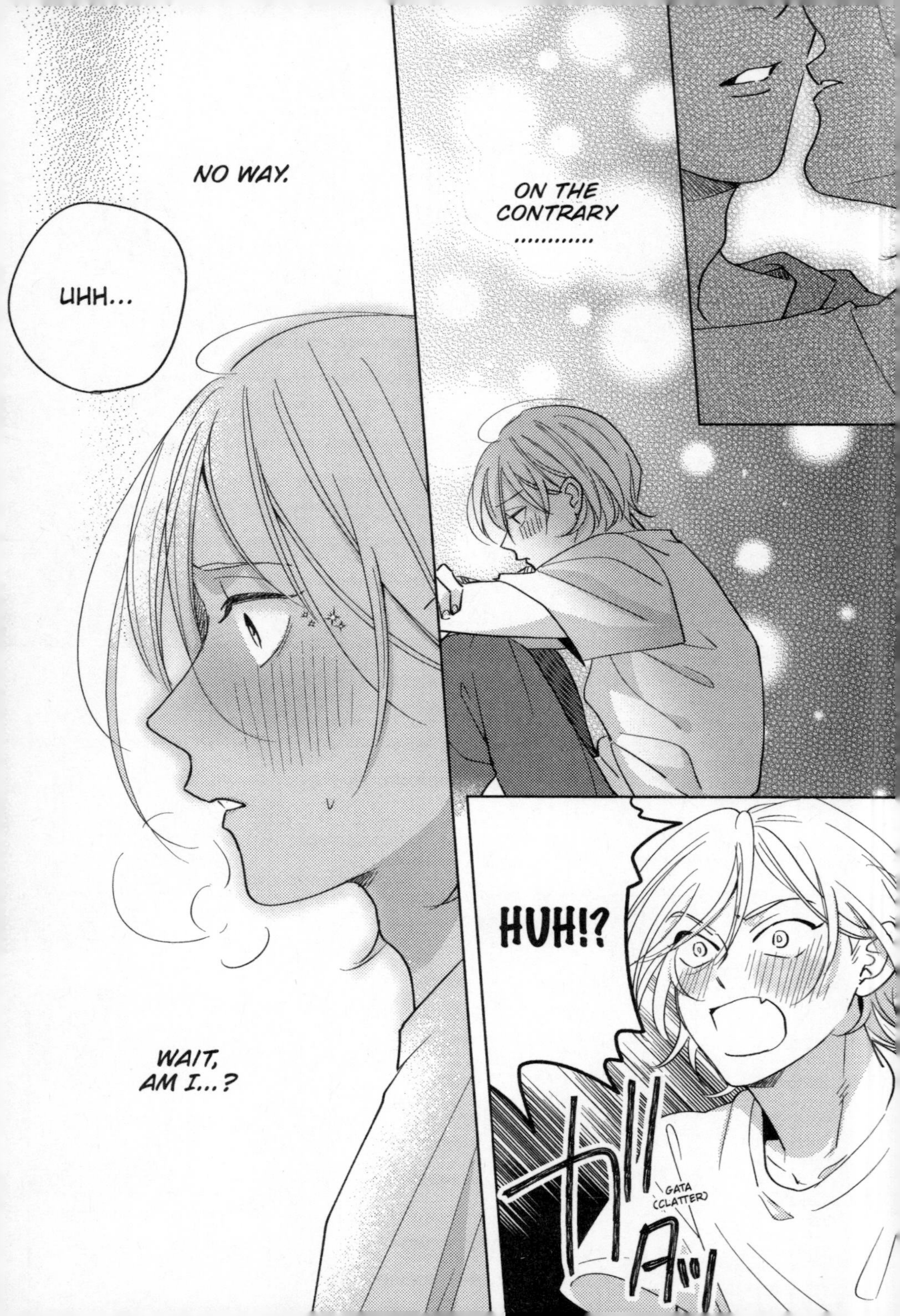
ON THE CONTRARY ....
HUH!?
GATA (CLATTER)
NO WAY.
UHH...
WAIT, AM I...?

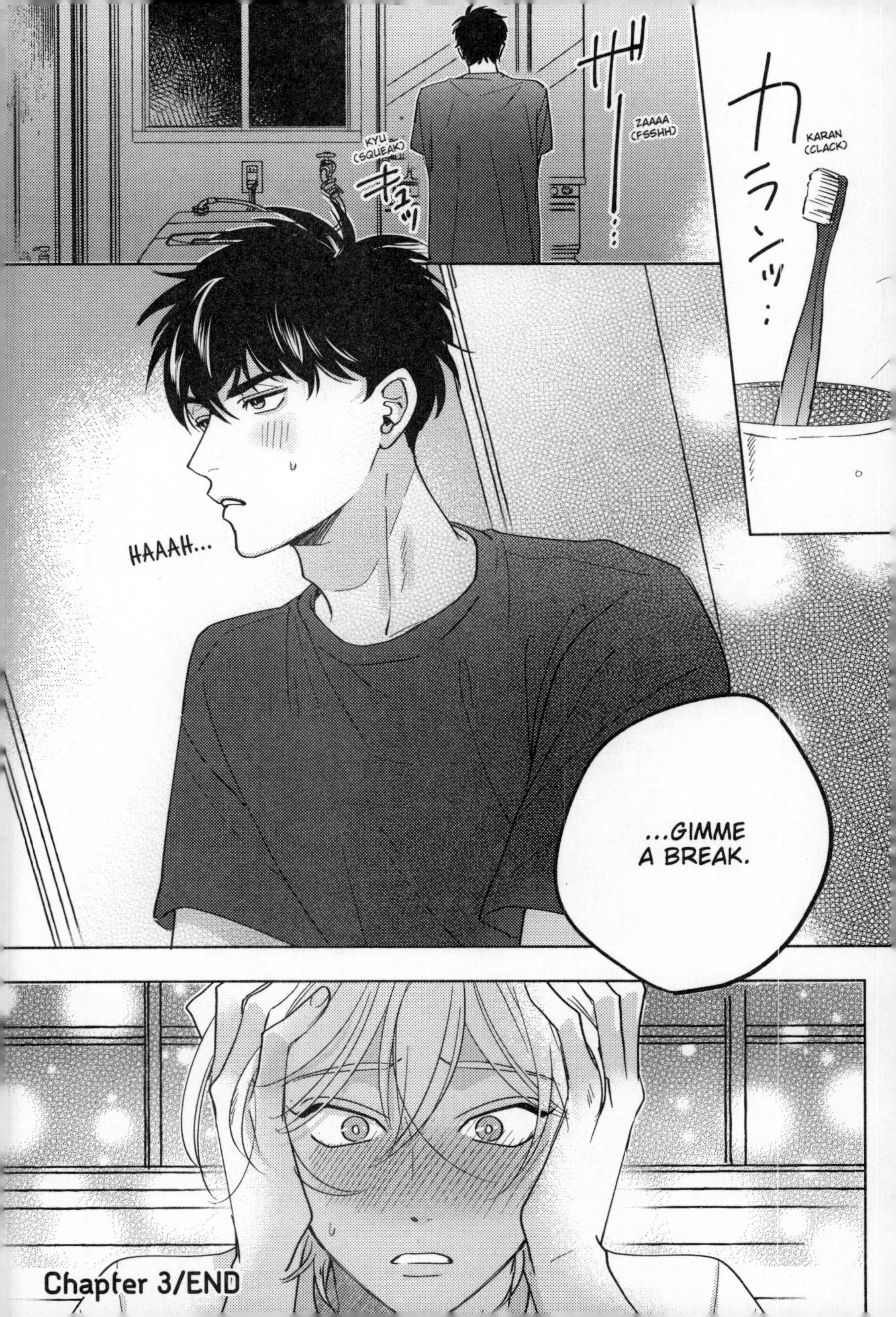
カランッ…
KARAN (CLACK)
ザー……
ZAAAA (FSSHH)
キュッ
KYU (SQUEAK)
HAAAH...
...GIMME A BREAK.
Chapter 3/END

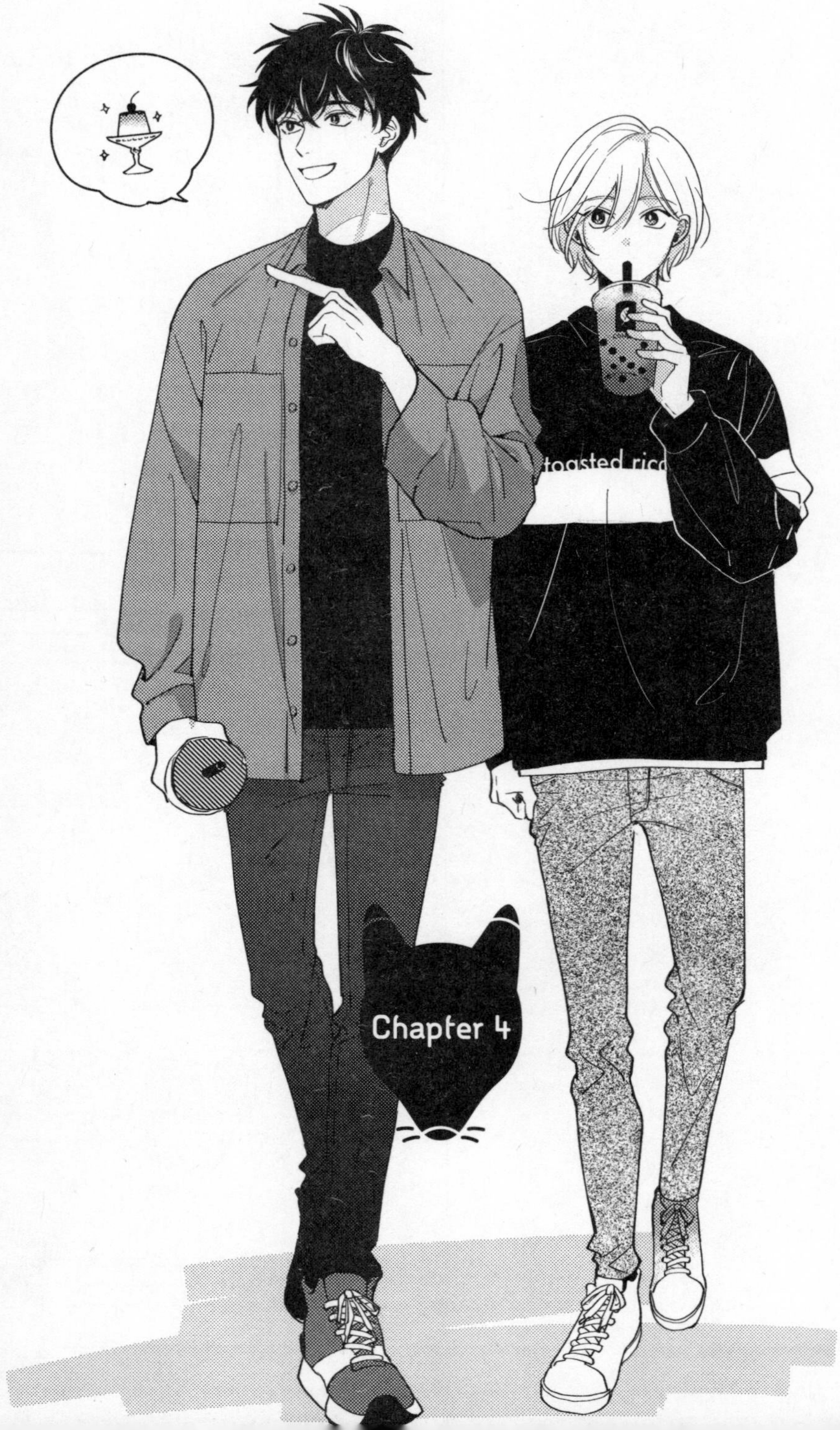
toasted rice
Chapter 4

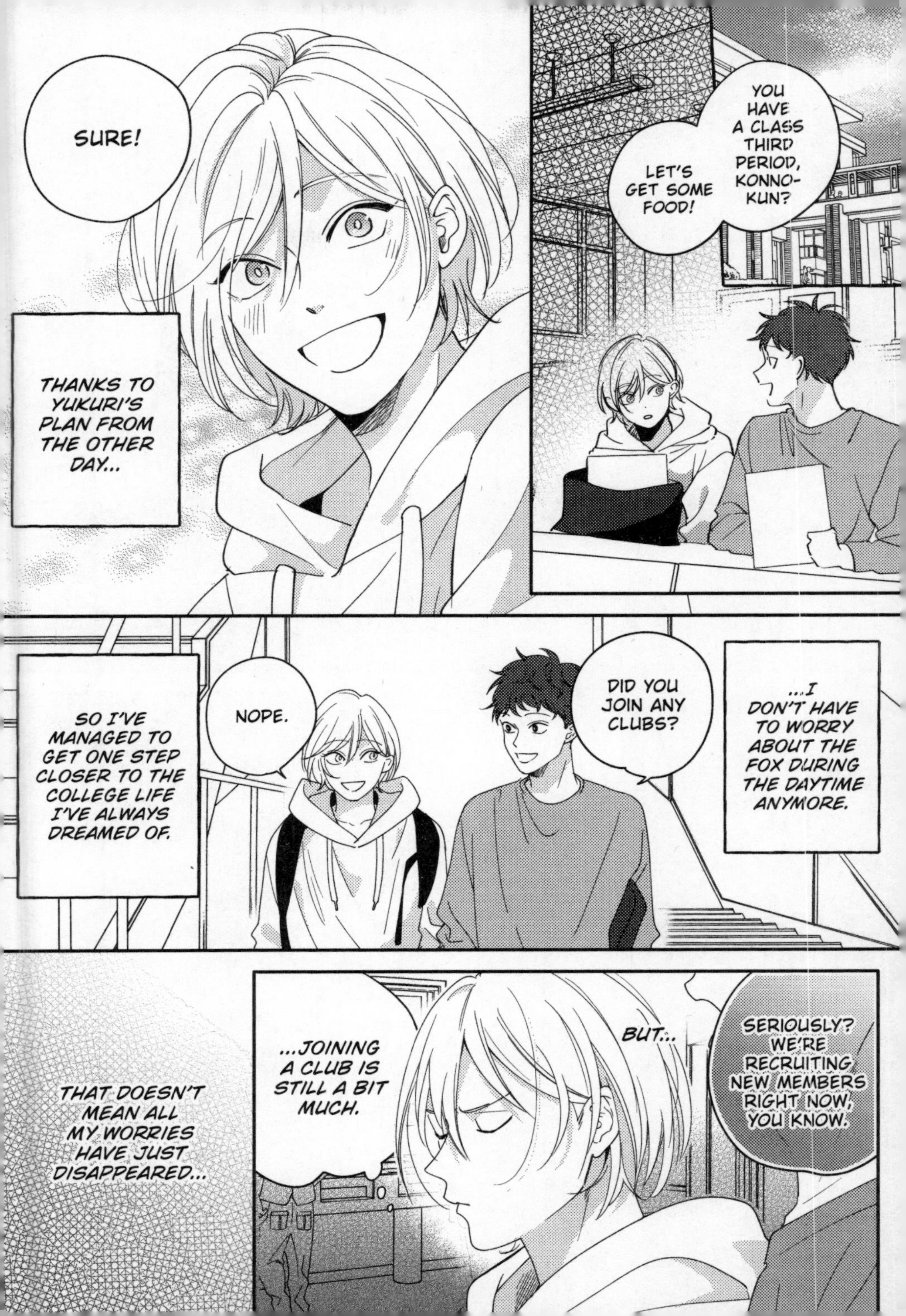
YOU HAVE A CLASS THIRD PERIOD, KONNO-KUN?
LET'S GET SOME FOOD!
SURE!
THANKS TO YUKURI'S PLAN FROM THE OTHER DAY...
...I DON'T HAVE TO WORRY ABOUT THE FOX DURING THE DAYTIME ANYMORE.
DID YOU JOIN ANY CLUBS?
NOPE.
SO I'VE MANAGED TO GET ONE STEP CLOSER TO THE COLLEGE LIFE I'VE ALWAYS DREAMED OF.
SERIOUSLY? WE'RE RECRUITING NEW MEMBERS RIGHT NOW, YOU KNOW.
BUT...
...JOINING A CLUB IS STILL A BIT MUCH.
THAT DOESN'T MEAN ALL MY WORRIES HAVE JUST DISAPPEARED...

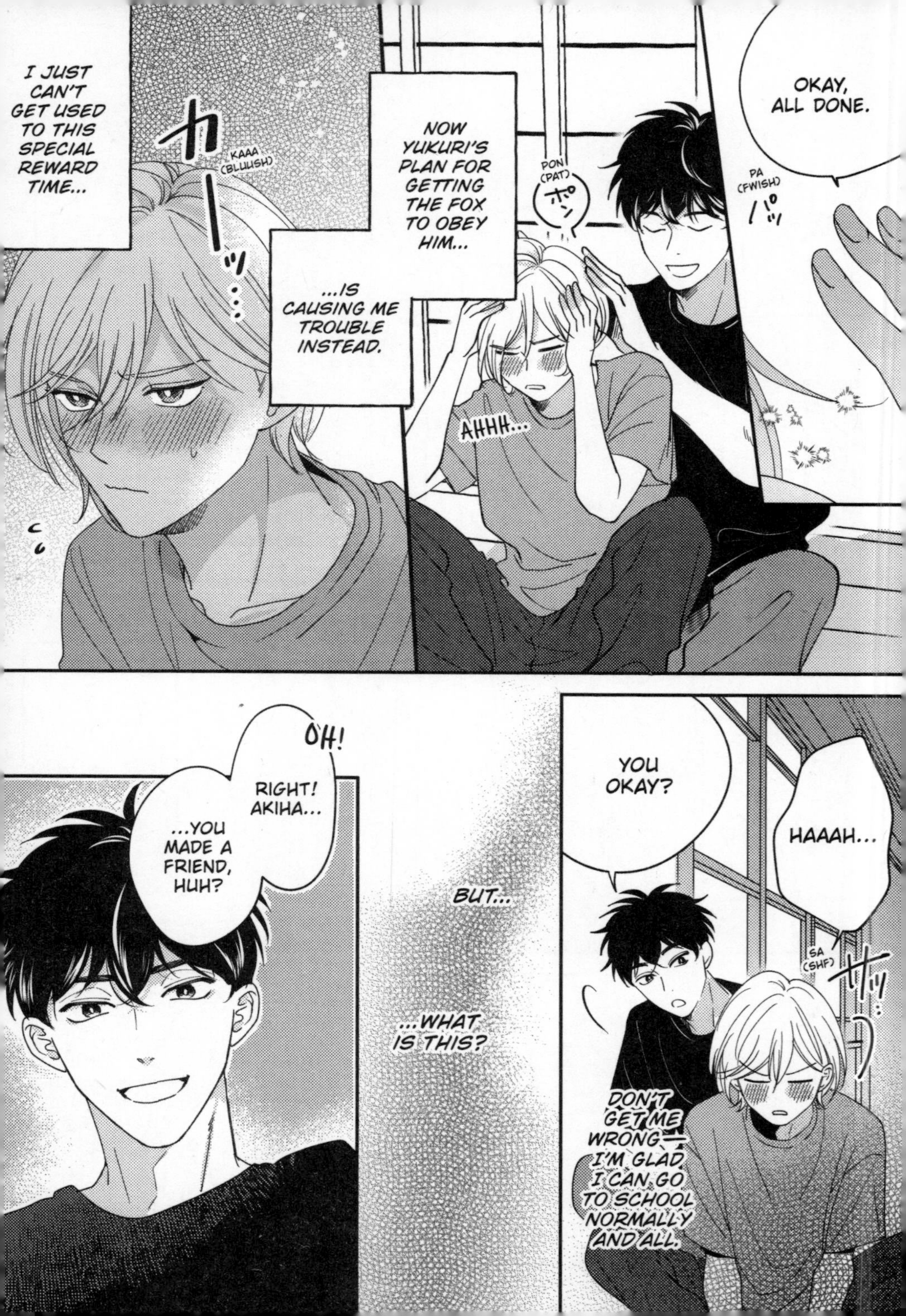
OKAY, ALL DONE.
PA (FWISH)
パッ
NOW YUKURI'S PLAN FOR GETTING THE FOX TO OBEY HIM...
PON (PAT)
ポン
...IS CAUSING ME TROUBLE INSTEAD.
AHHH...
I JUST CAN'T GET USED TO THIS SPECIAL REWARD TIME...
KAAA (BLUUSH)
カーッ...
HAAAH...
YOU OKAY?
SA (SHF)
サッ
DON'T GET ME WRONG— I'M GLAD I CAN GO TO SCHOOL NORMALLY AND ALL.
BUT...
...WHAT IS THIS?
OH!
RIGHT! AKIHA...
...YOU MADE A FRIEND, HUH?

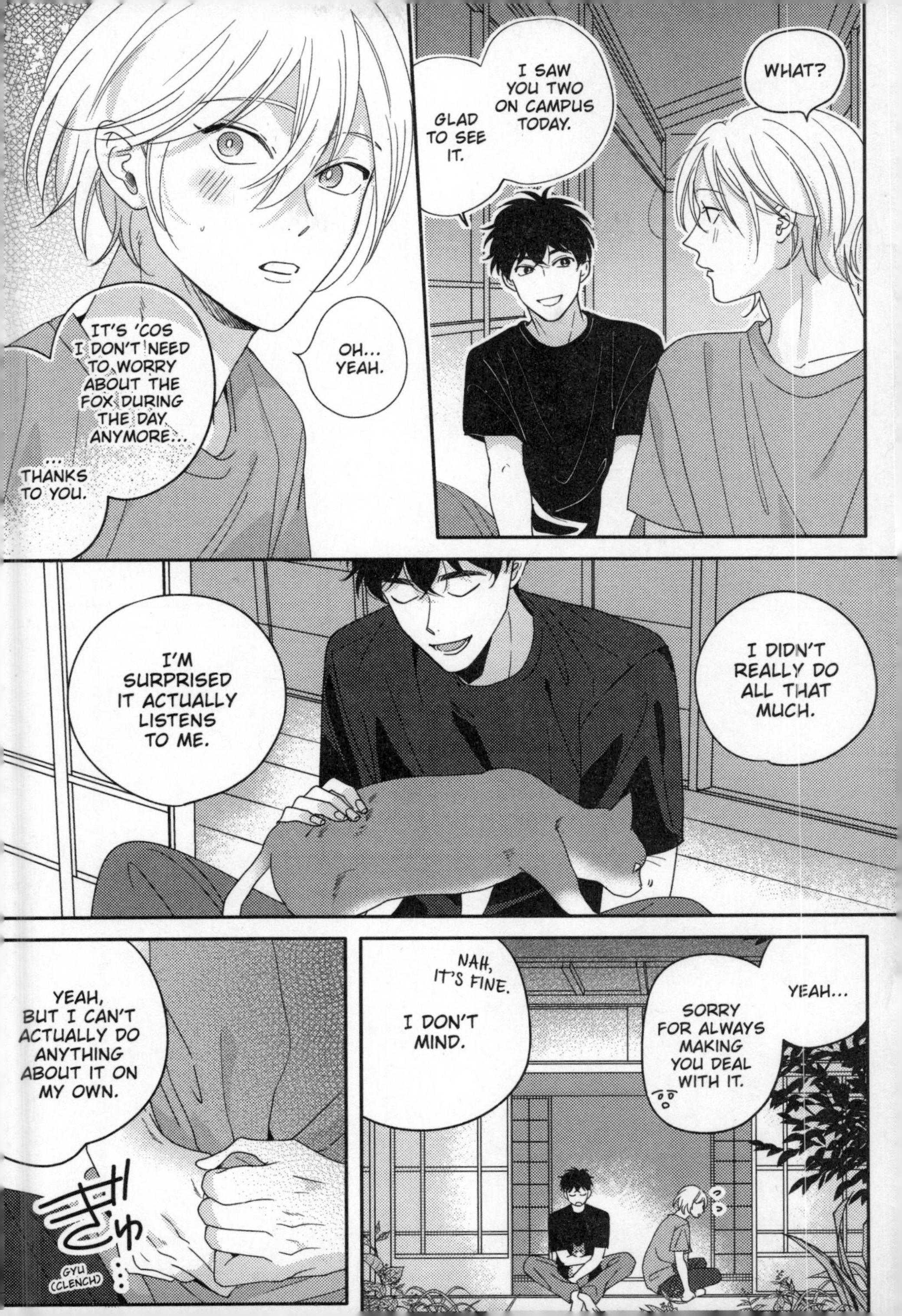
I SAW YOU TWO ON CAMPUS TODAY.
GLAD TO SEE IT.
WHAT?
OH... YEAH.
IT'S 'COS I DON'T NEED TO WORRY ABOUT THE FOX DURING THE DAY ANYMORE...
...THANKS TO YOU.
I DIDN'T REALLY DO ALL THAT MUCH.
I'M SURPRISED IT ACTUALLY LISTENS TO ME.
YEAH...
SORRY FOR ALWAYS MAKING YOU DEAL WITH IT.
NAH, IT'S FINE.
I DON'T MIND.
YEAH, BUT I CAN'T ACTUALLY DO ANYTHING ABOUT IT ON MY OWN.
ぎゅ…
GYU (CLENCH)

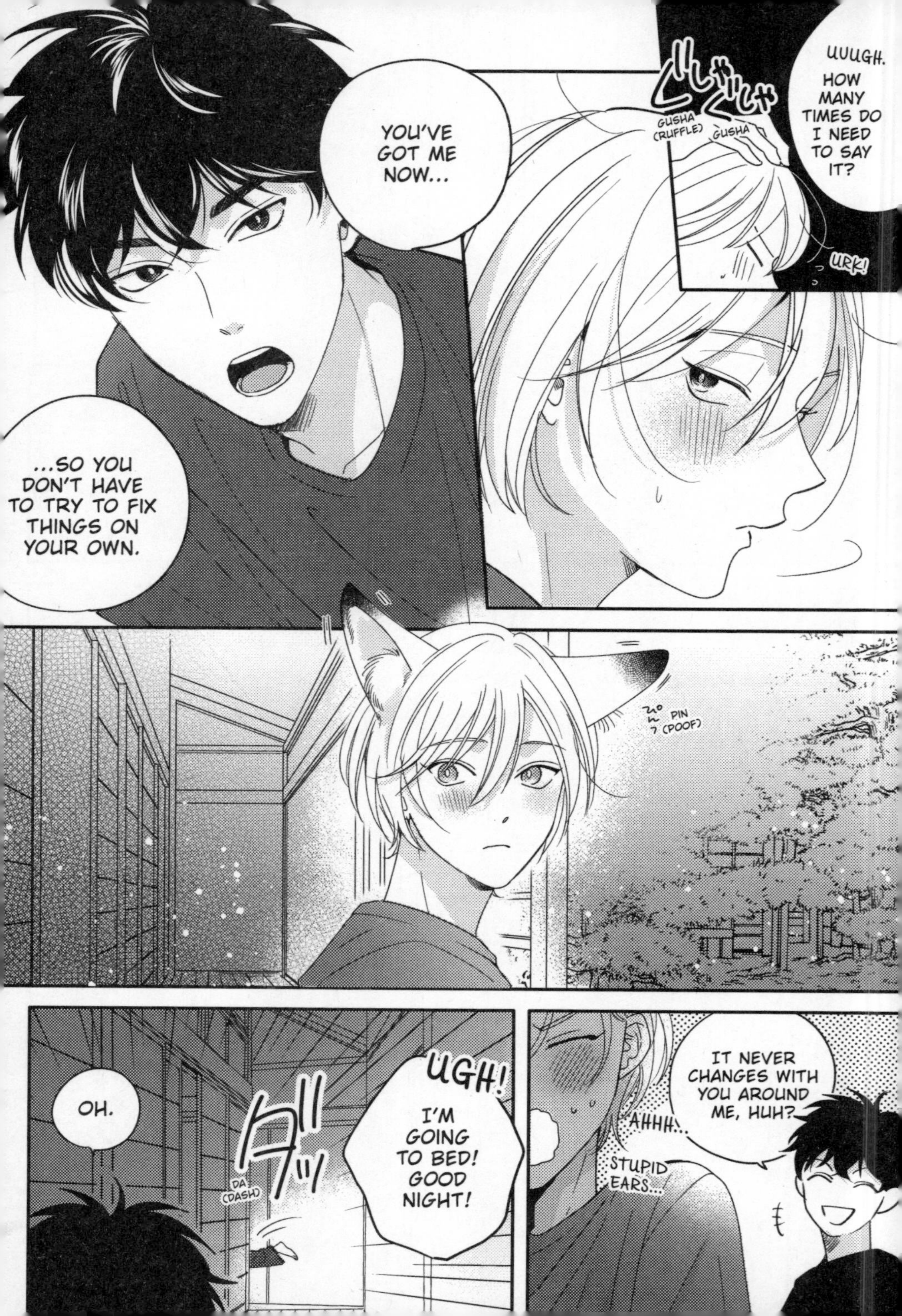
GUSHA (RUFFLE) GUSHA
UUUGH. HOW MANY TIMES DO I NEED TO SAY IT?
URK!
YOU'VE GOT ME NOW...
...SO YOU DON'T HAVE TO TRY TO FIX THINGS ON YOUR OWN.
PIN (POOF)
IT NEVER CHANGES WITH YOU AROUND ME, HUH?
AHHH...
STUPID EARS...
UGH!
I'M GOING TO BED! GOOD NIGHT!
DA (DASH)
OH.

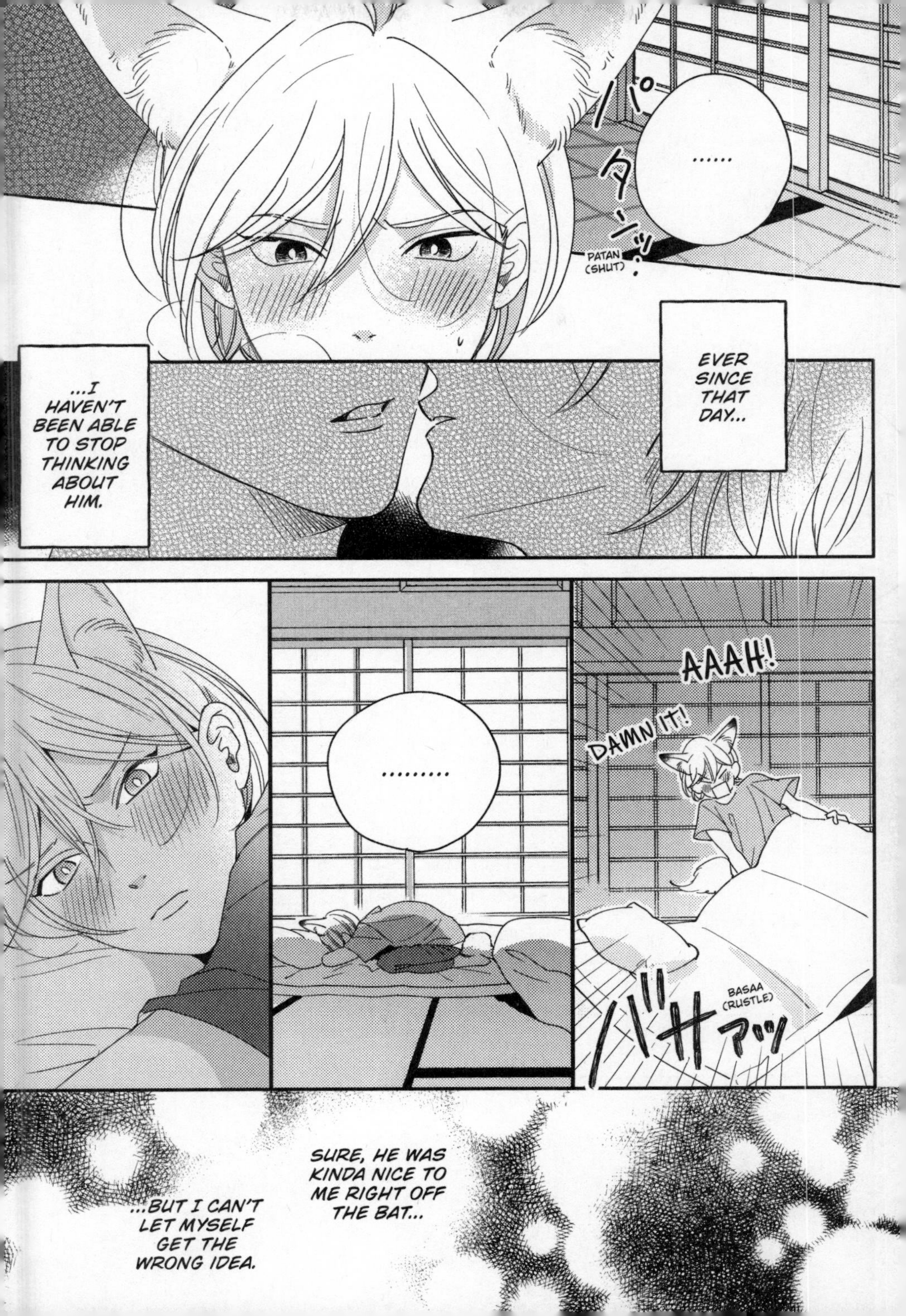
......
PATAN (SHUT)
EVER SINCE THAT DAY...
...I HAVEN'T BEEN ABLE TO STOP THINKING ABOUT HIM.
AAAH!
DAMN IT!
BASAA (RUSTLE)
....
SURE, HE WAS KINDA NICE TO ME RIGHT OFF THE BAT...
...BUT I CAN'T LET MYSELF GET THE WRONG IDEA.

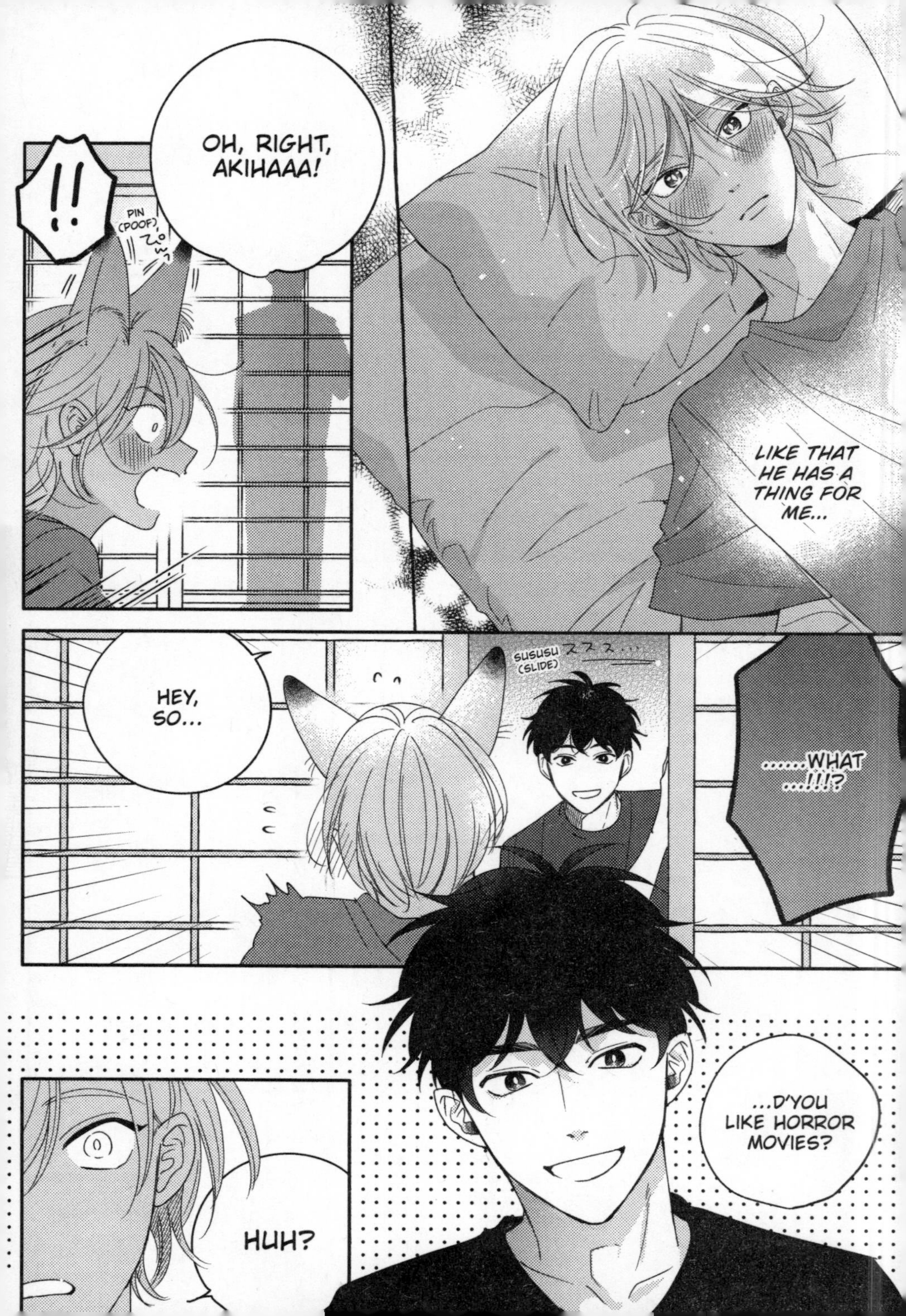
LIKE THAT HE HAS A THING FOR ME...
OH, RIGHT, AKIHAAA!
PIN (POOF)
!!
......WHAT ...!!!?
SUSUSU (SLIDE) ススス…
HEY, SO...
...D'YOU LIKE HORROR MOVIES?
HUH?

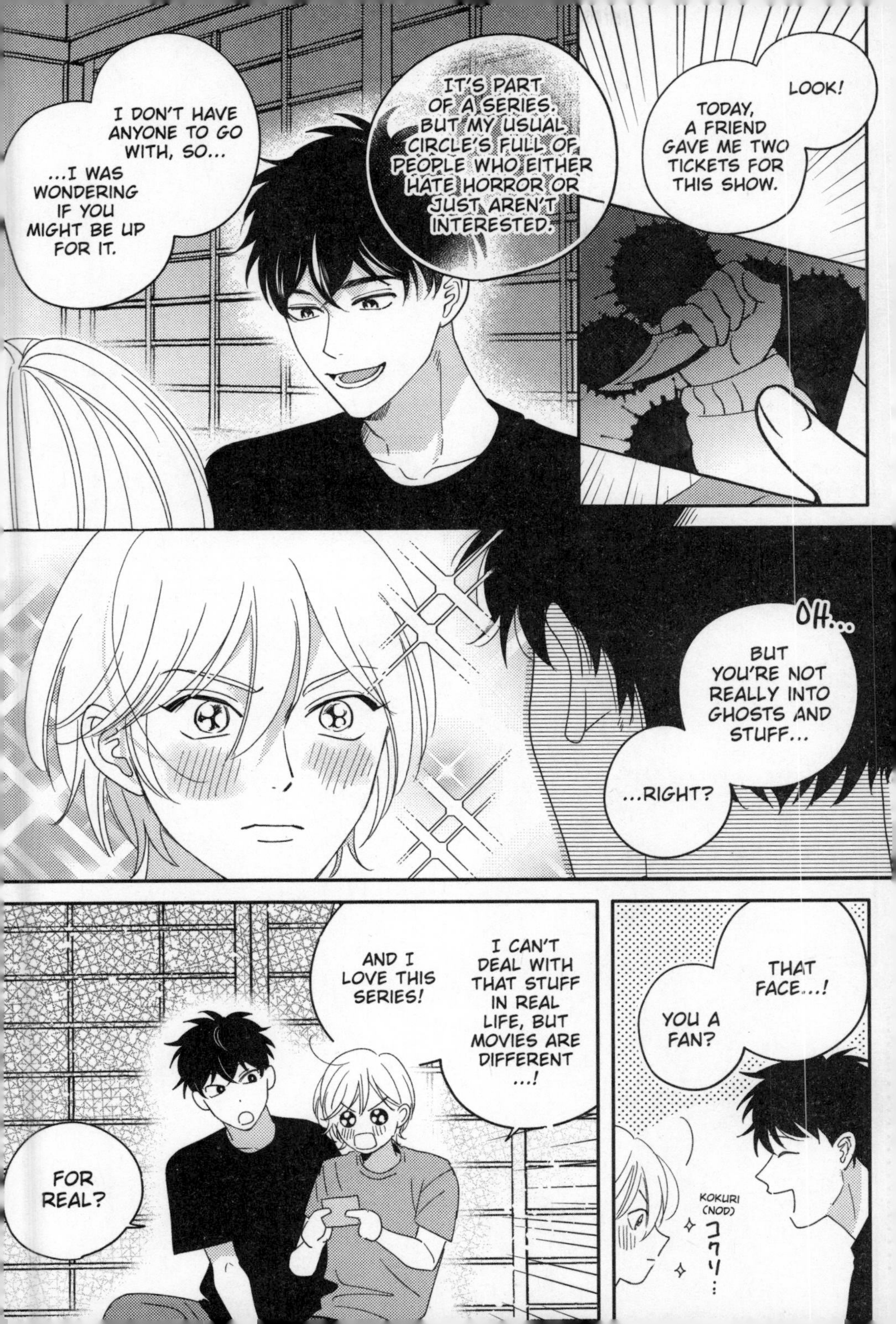
LOOK!
TODAY, A FRIEND GAVE ME TWO TICKETS FOR THIS SHOW.
IT'S PART OF A SERIES. BUT MY USUAL CIRCLE'S FULL OF PEOPLE WHO EITHER HATE HORROR OR JUST AREN'T INTERESTED.
I DON'T HAVE ANYONE TO GO WITH, SO...
...I WAS WONDERING IF YOU MIGHT BE UP FOR IT.
OH...
BUT YOU'RE NOT REALLY INTO GHOSTS AND STUFF...
...RIGHT?
THAT FACE...!
YOU A FAN?
KOKURI (NOD)
コクリ…
I CAN'T DEAL WITH THAT STUFF IN REAL LIFE, BUT MOVIES ARE DIFFERENT...!
AND I LOVE THIS SERIES!
FOR REAL?

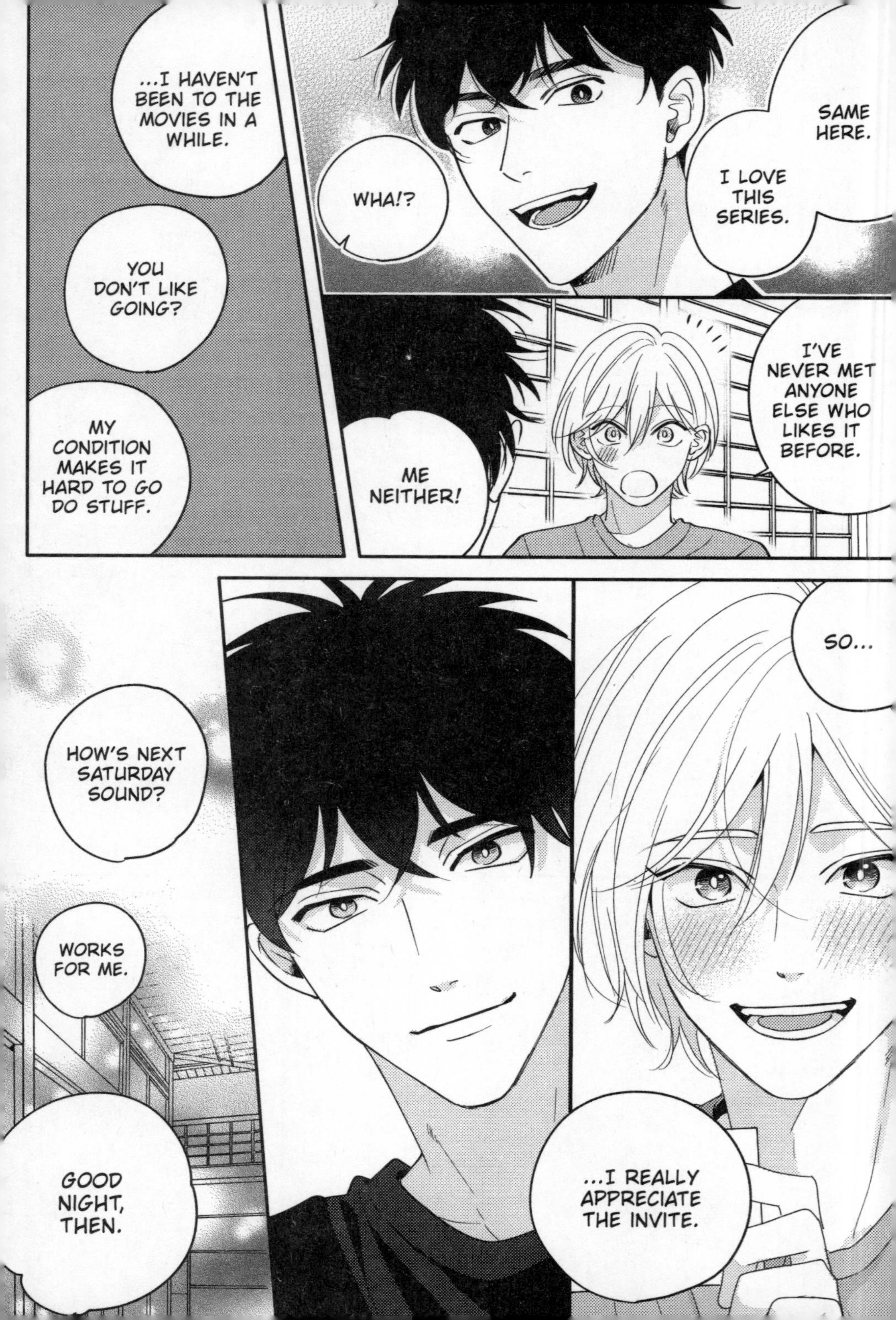
SAME HERE.
I LOVE THIS SERIES.
WHA!?
I'VE NEVER MET ANYONE ELSE WHO LIKES IT BEFORE.
ME NEITHER!
...I HAVEN'T BEEN TO THE MOVIES IN A WHILE.
YOU DON'T LIKE GOING?
MY CONDITION MAKES IT HARD TO GO DO STUFF.
SO...
...I REALLY APPRECIATE THE INVITE.
HOW'S NEXT SATURDAY SOUND?
WORKS FOR ME.
GOOD NIGHT, THEN.

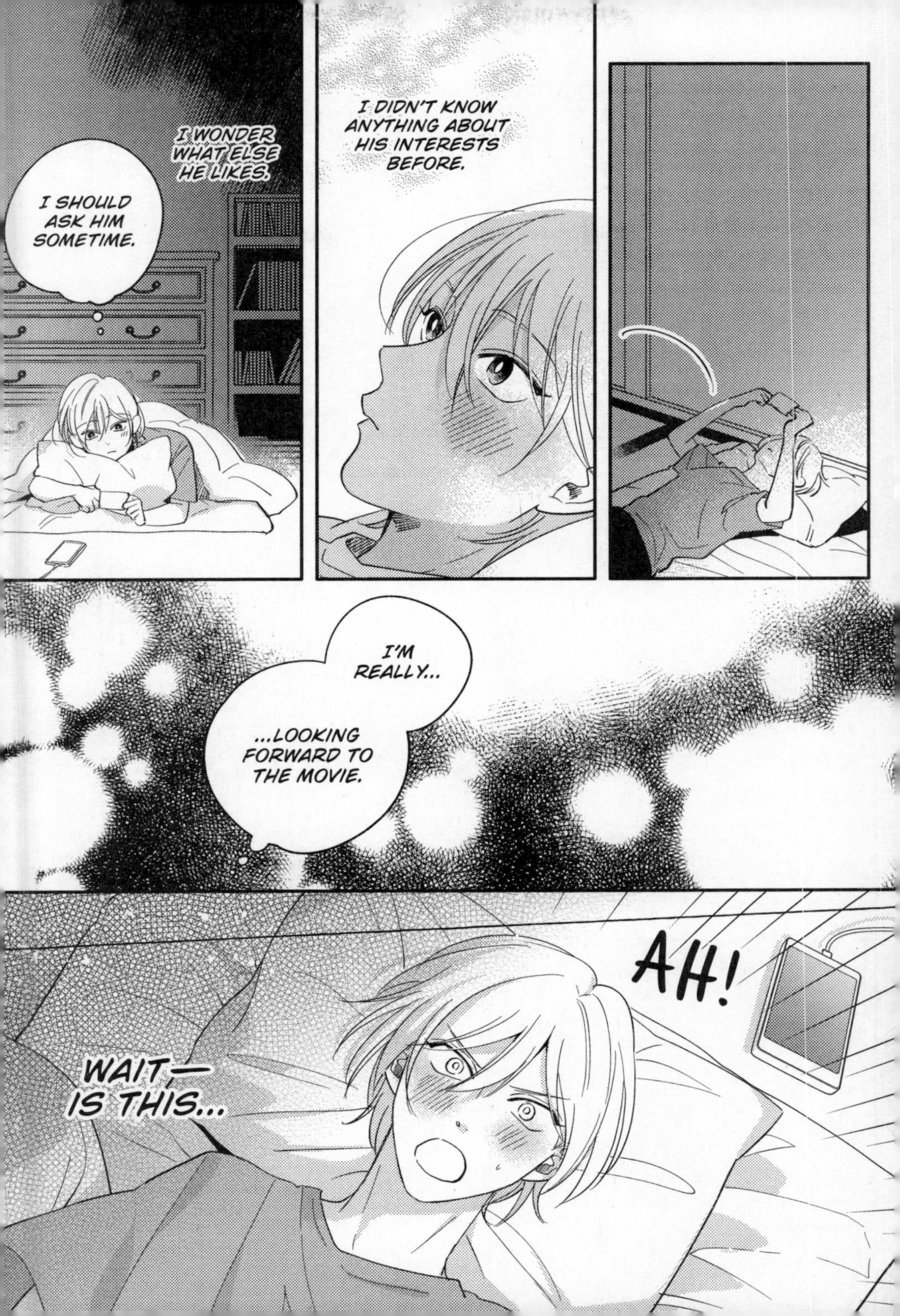
I DIDN'T KNOW ANYTHING ABOUT HIS INTERESTS BEFORE.
I WONDER WHAT ELSE HE LIKES.
I SHOULD ASK HIM SOMETIME.
I'M REALLY...
...LOOKING FORWARD TO THE MOVIE.
AH!
WAIT— IS THIS...

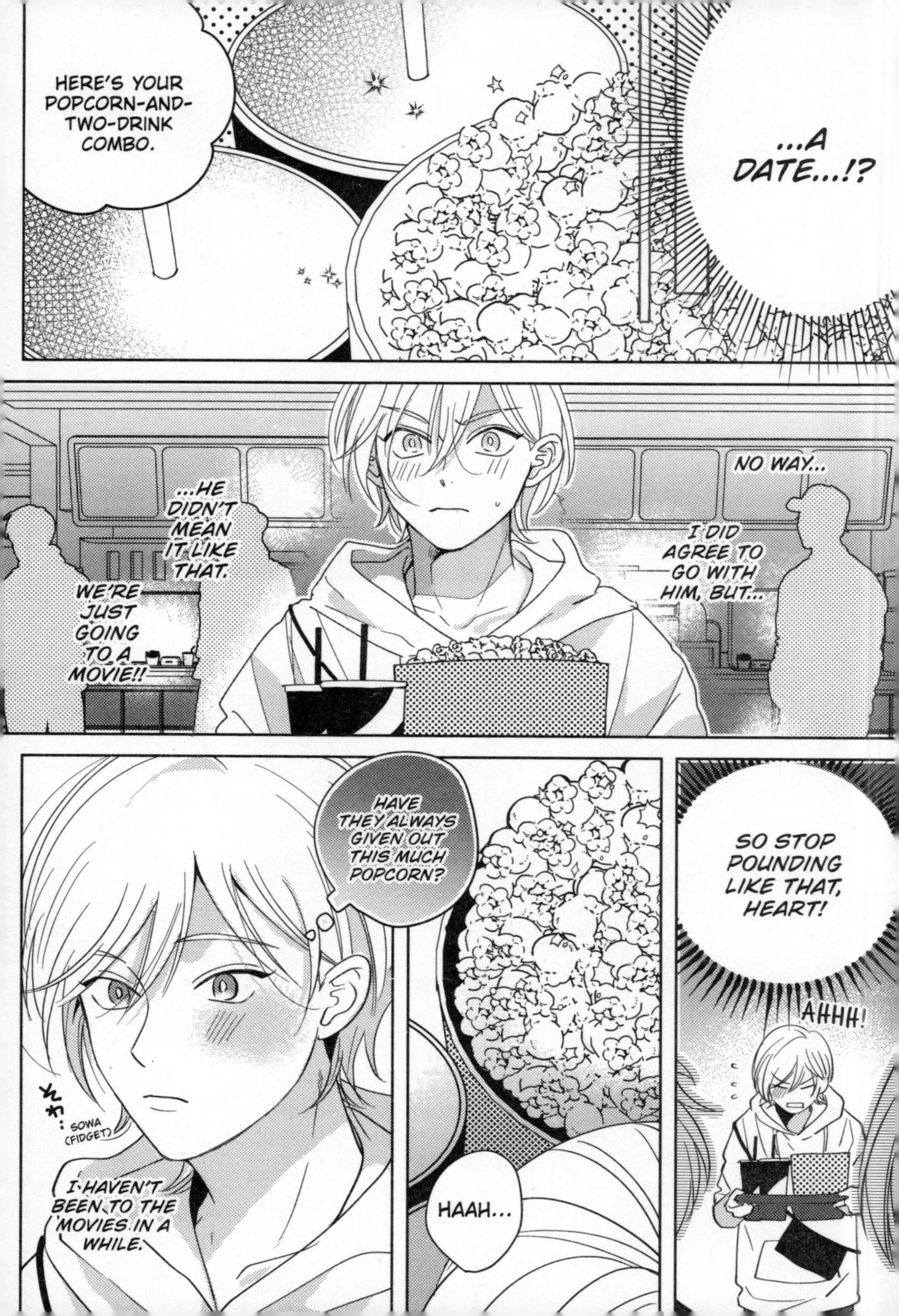
...A DATE...!?
HERE'S YOUR POPCORN-AND-TWO-DRINK COMBO.
NO WAY...
I DID AGREE TO GO WITH HIM, BUT...
...HE DIDN'T MEAN IT LIKE THAT.
WE'RE JUST GOING TO A MOVIE!!
SO STOP POUNDING LIKE THAT, HEART!
AHHH!
HAAH...
HAVE THEY ALWAYS GIVEN OUT THIS MUCH POPCORN?
SOWA (FIDGET)
I HAVEN'T BEEN TO THE MOVIES IN A WHILE.

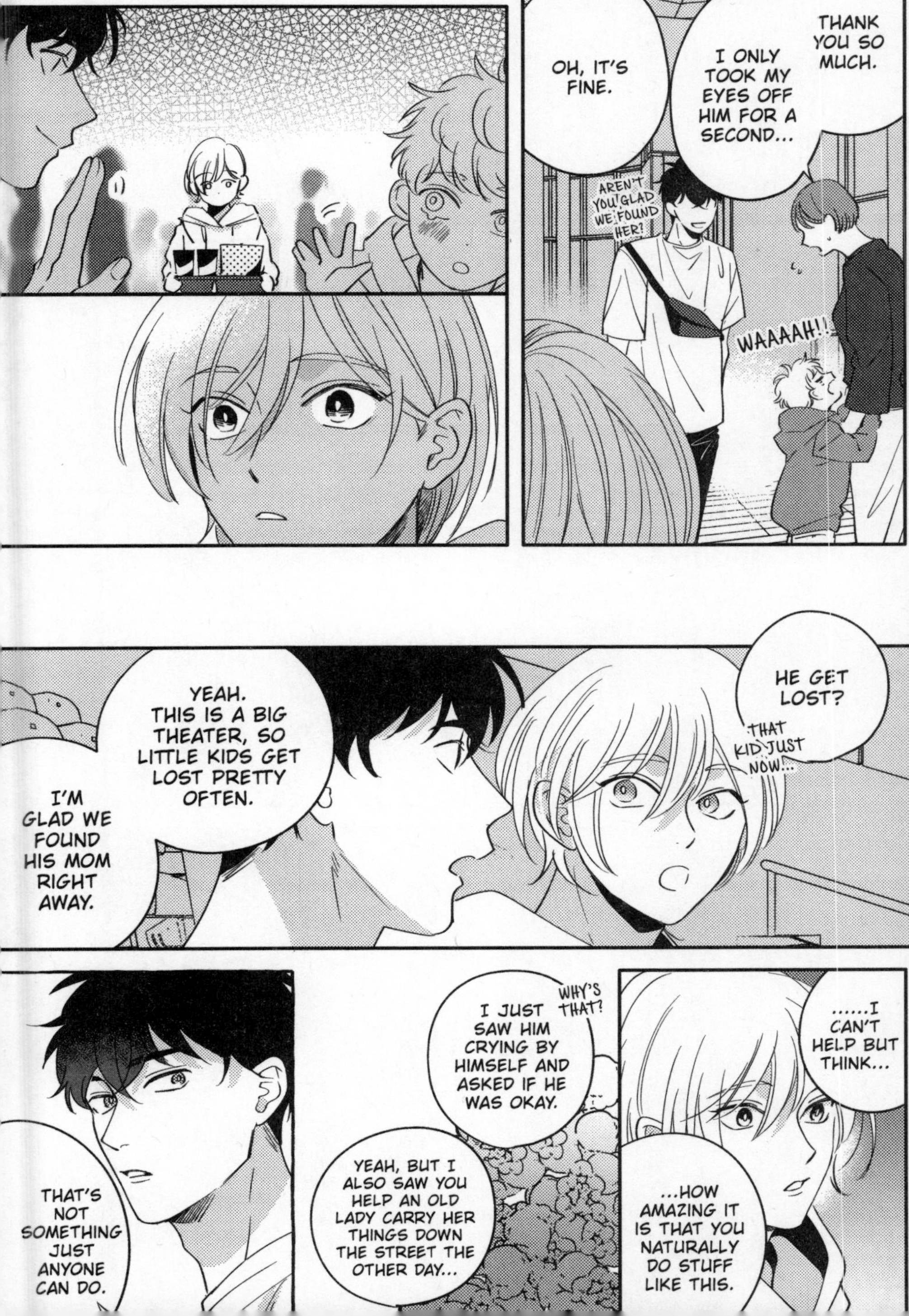
THANK YOU SO MUCH.
I ONLY TOOK MY EYES OFF HIM FOR A SECOND...
OH, IT'S FINE.
AREN'T YOU GLAD WE FOUND HER?
WAAAAH!!
HE GET LOST?
THAT KID JUST NOW...
YEAH. THIS IS A BIG THEATER, SO LITTLE KIDS GET LOST PRETTY OFTEN.
I'M GLAD WE FOUND HIS MOM RIGHT AWAY.
......I CAN'T HELP BUT THINK...
...HOW AMAZING IT IS THAT YOU NATURALLY DO STUFF LIKE THIS.
WHY'S THAT?
I JUST SAW HIM CRYING BY HIMSELF AND ASKED IF HE WAS OKAY.
YEAH, BUT I ALSO SAW YOU HELP AN OLD LADY CARRY HER THINGS DOWN THE STREET THE OTHER DAY...
THAT'S NOT SOMETHING JUST ANYONE CAN DO.

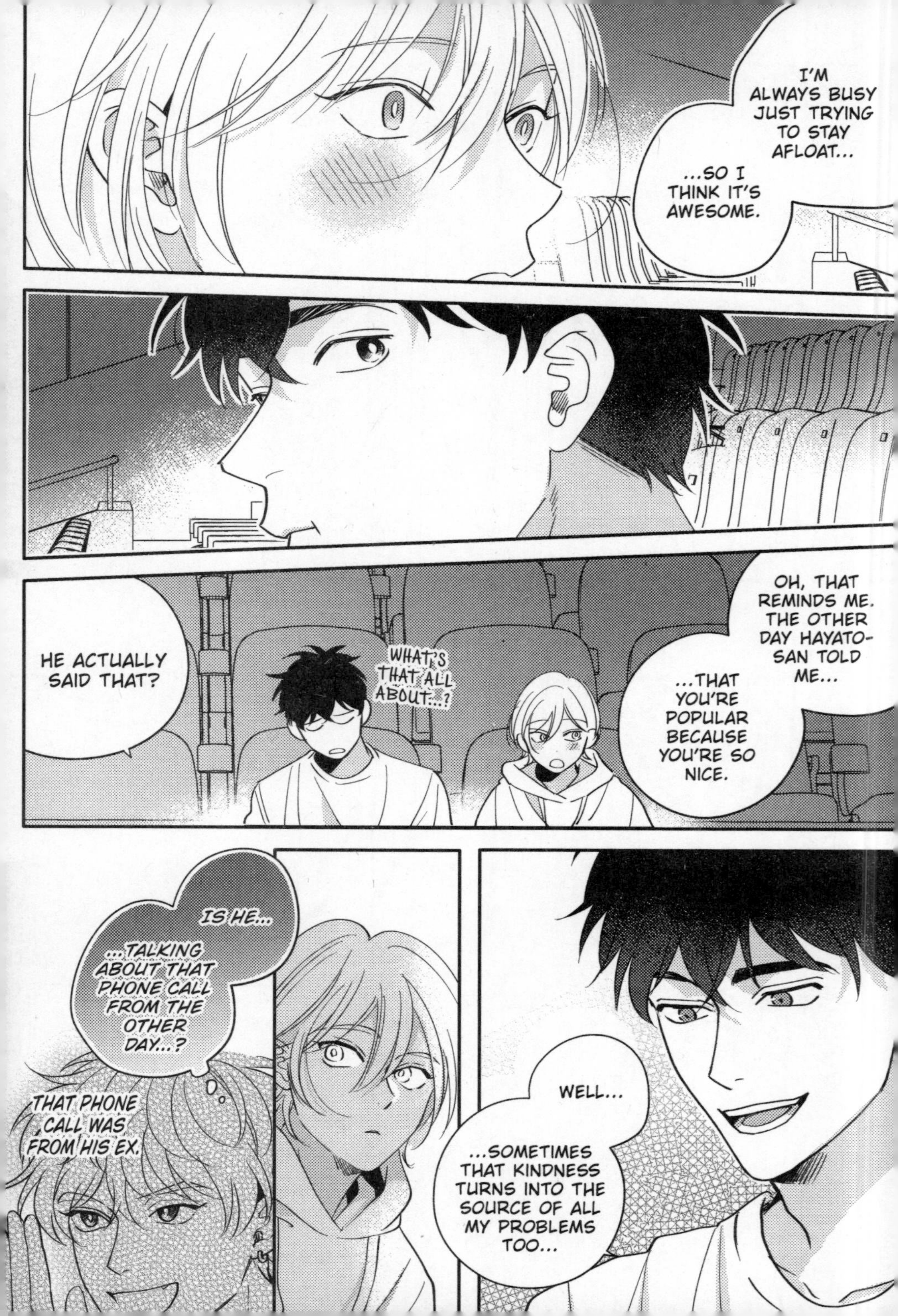
I'M ALWAYS BUSY JUST TRYING TO STAY AFLOAT...
...SO I THINK IT'S AWESOME.
OH, THAT REMINDS ME. THE OTHER DAY HAYATO-SAN TOLD ME...
...THAT YOU'RE POPULAR BECAUSE YOU'RE SO NICE.
WHAT'S THAT ALL ABOUT...?
HE ACTUALLY SAID THAT?
WELL...
...SOMETIMES THAT KINDNESS TURNS INTO THE SOURCE OF ALL MY PROBLEMS TOO...
IS HE...
...TALKING ABOUT THAT PHONE CALL FROM THE OTHER DAY...?
THAT PHONE CALL WAS FROM HIS EX.

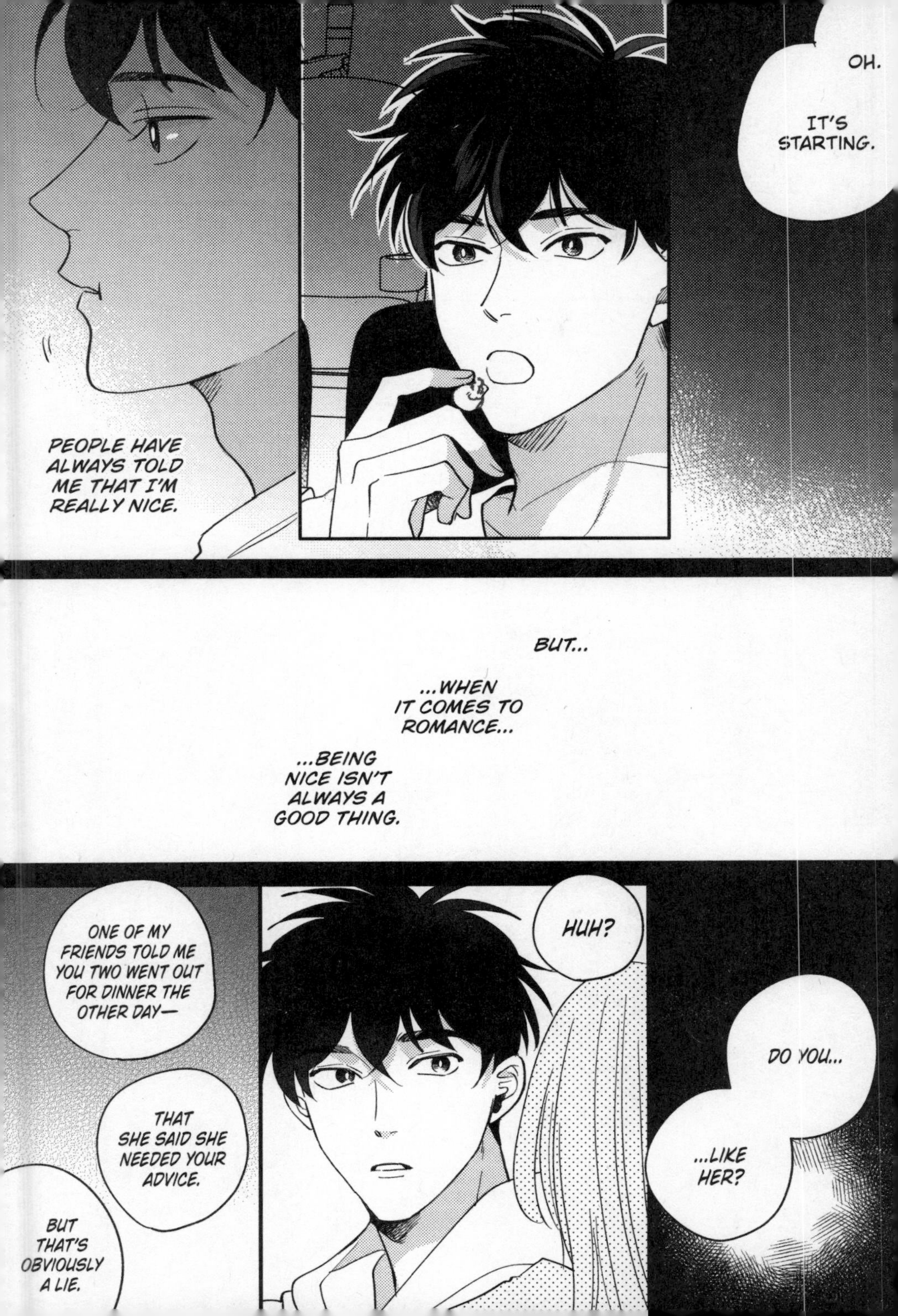
OH.
IT'S STARTING.
PEOPLE HAVE ALWAYS TOLD ME THAT I'M REALLY NICE.
BUT...
...WHEN IT COMES TO ROMANCE...
...BEING NICE ISN'T ALWAYS A GOOD THING.
DO YOU...
...LIKE HER?
HUH?
ONE OF MY FRIENDS TOLD ME YOU TWO WENT OUT FOR DINNER THE OTHER DAY—
THAT SHE SAID SHE NEEDED YOUR ADVICE.
BUT THAT'S OBVIOUSLY A LIE.

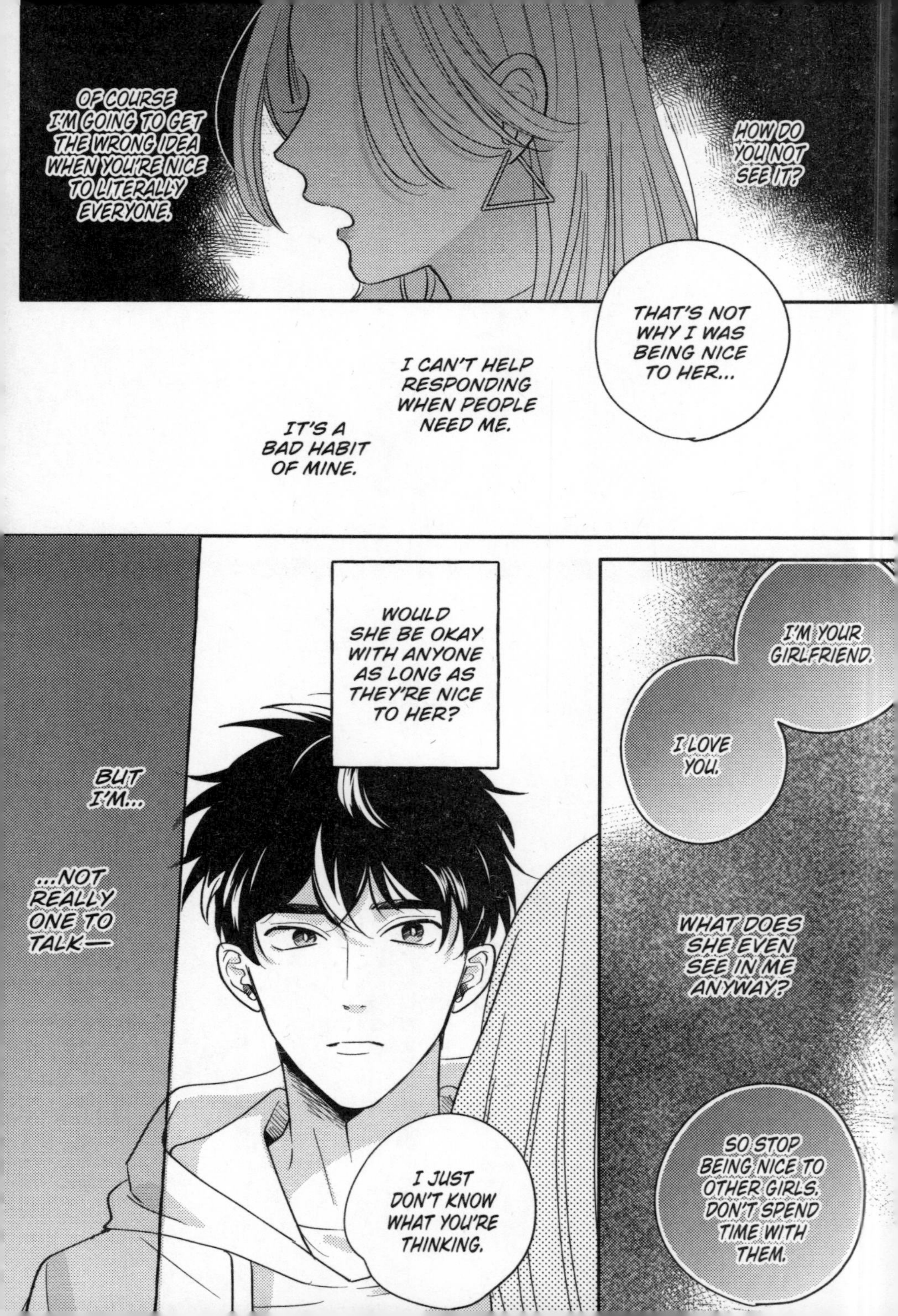
HOW DO YOU NOT SEE IT?
OF COURSE I'M GOING TO GET THE WRONG IDEA WHEN YOU'RE NICE TO LITERALLY EVERYONE.
THAT'S NOT WHY I WAS BEING NICE TO HER...
I CAN'T HELP RESPONDING WHEN PEOPLE NEED ME.
IT'S A BAD HABIT OF MINE.
I'M YOUR GIRLFRIEND.
I LOVE YOU.
WHAT DOES SHE EVEN SEE IN ME ANYWAY?
SO STOP BEING NICE TO OTHER GIRLS. DON'T SPEND TIME WITH THEM.
WOULD SHE BE OKAY WITH ANYONE AS LONG AS THEY'RE NICE TO HER?
BUT I'M...
...NOT REALLY ONE TO TALK—
I JUST DON'T KNOW WHAT YOU'RE THINKING.

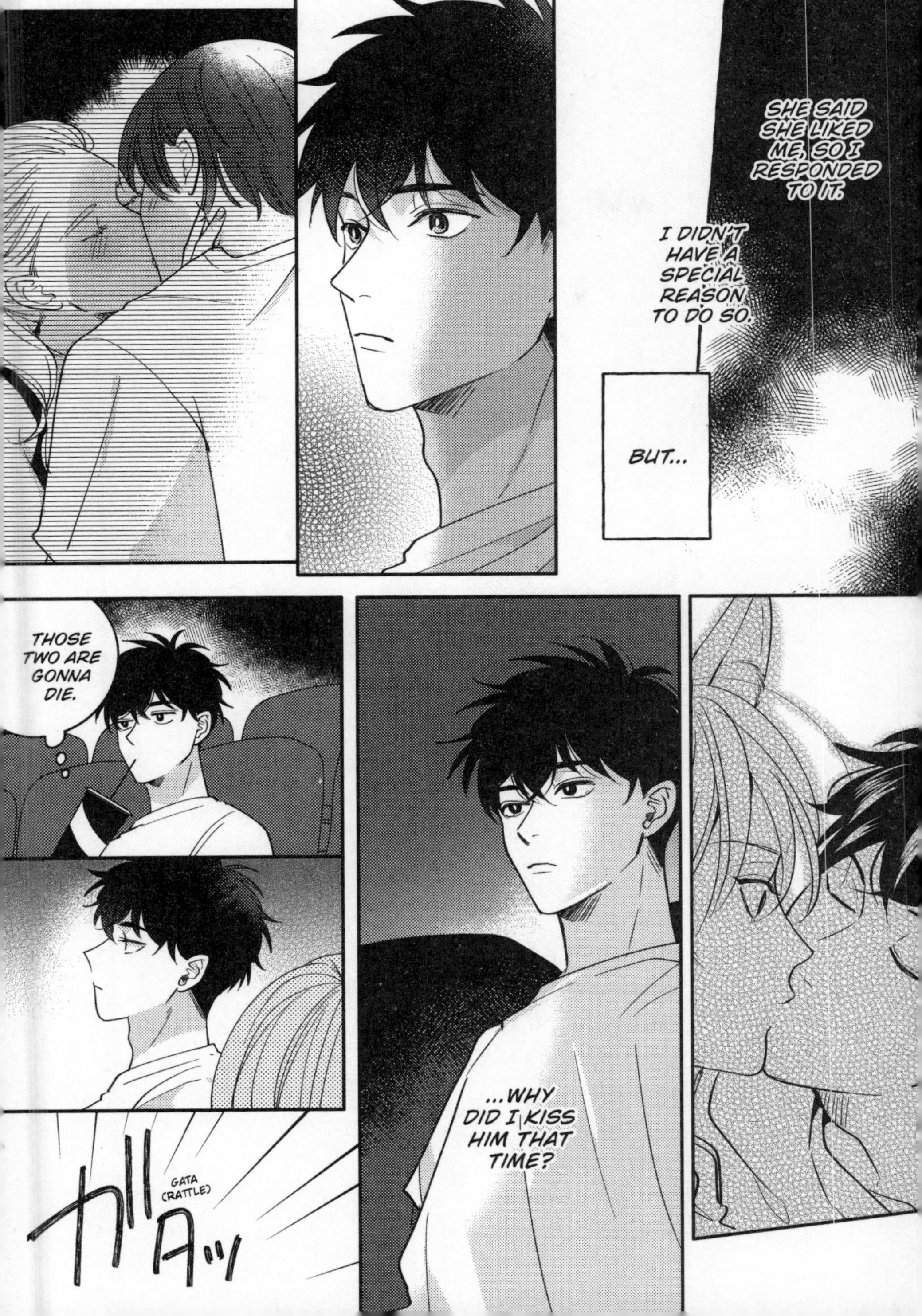
SHE SAID SHE LIKED ME, SO I RESPONDED TO IT.
I DIDN'T HAVE A SPECIAL REASON TO DO SO.
BUT...
...WHY DID I KISS HIM THAT TIME?
THOSE TWO ARE GONNA DIE.
ガタッ
GATA (RATTLE)

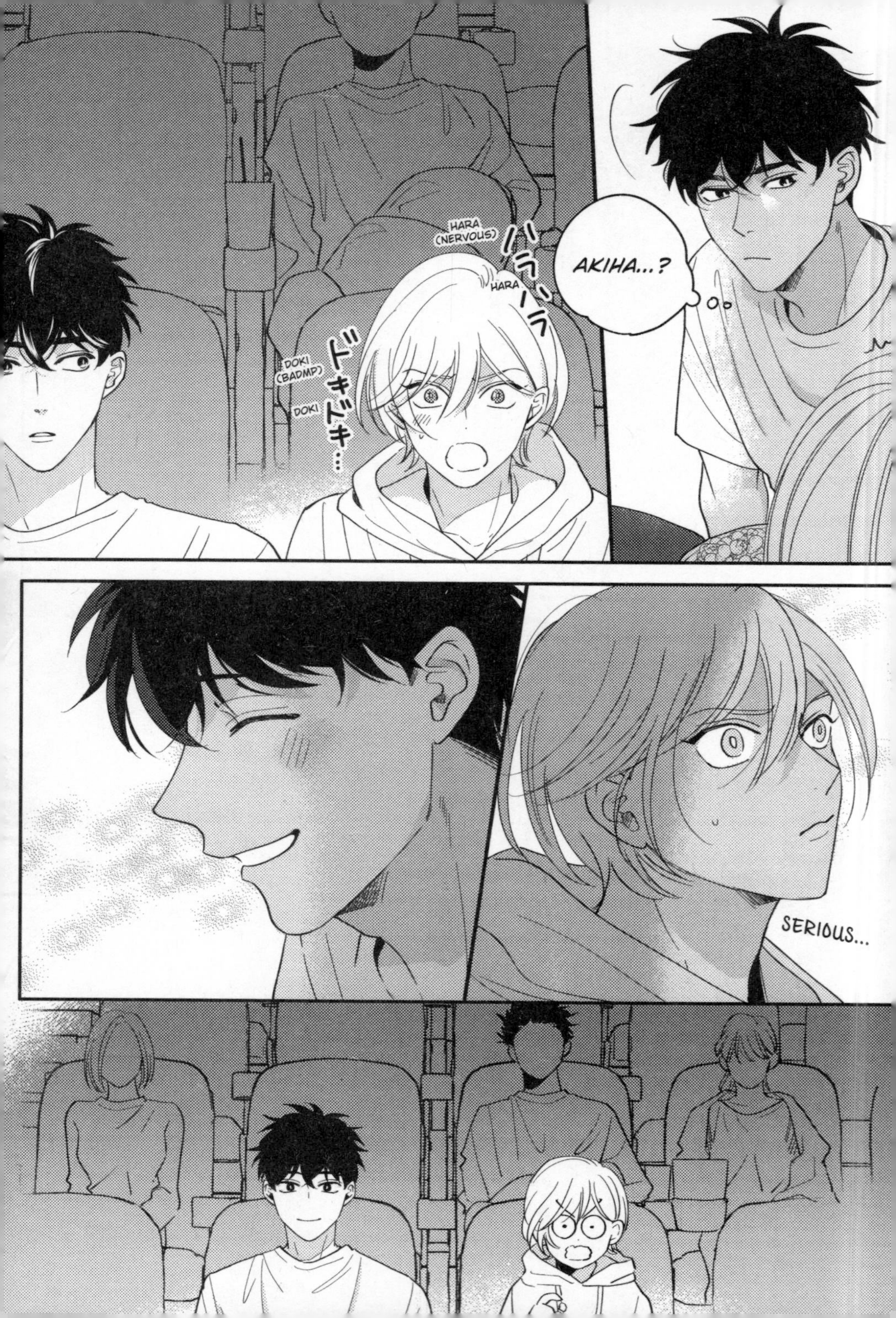
AKIHA...?
HARA (NERVOUS)
ハラ
HARA
ハラ
DOKI (BADMP)
ドキ
DOKI
ドキ…
SERIOUS...

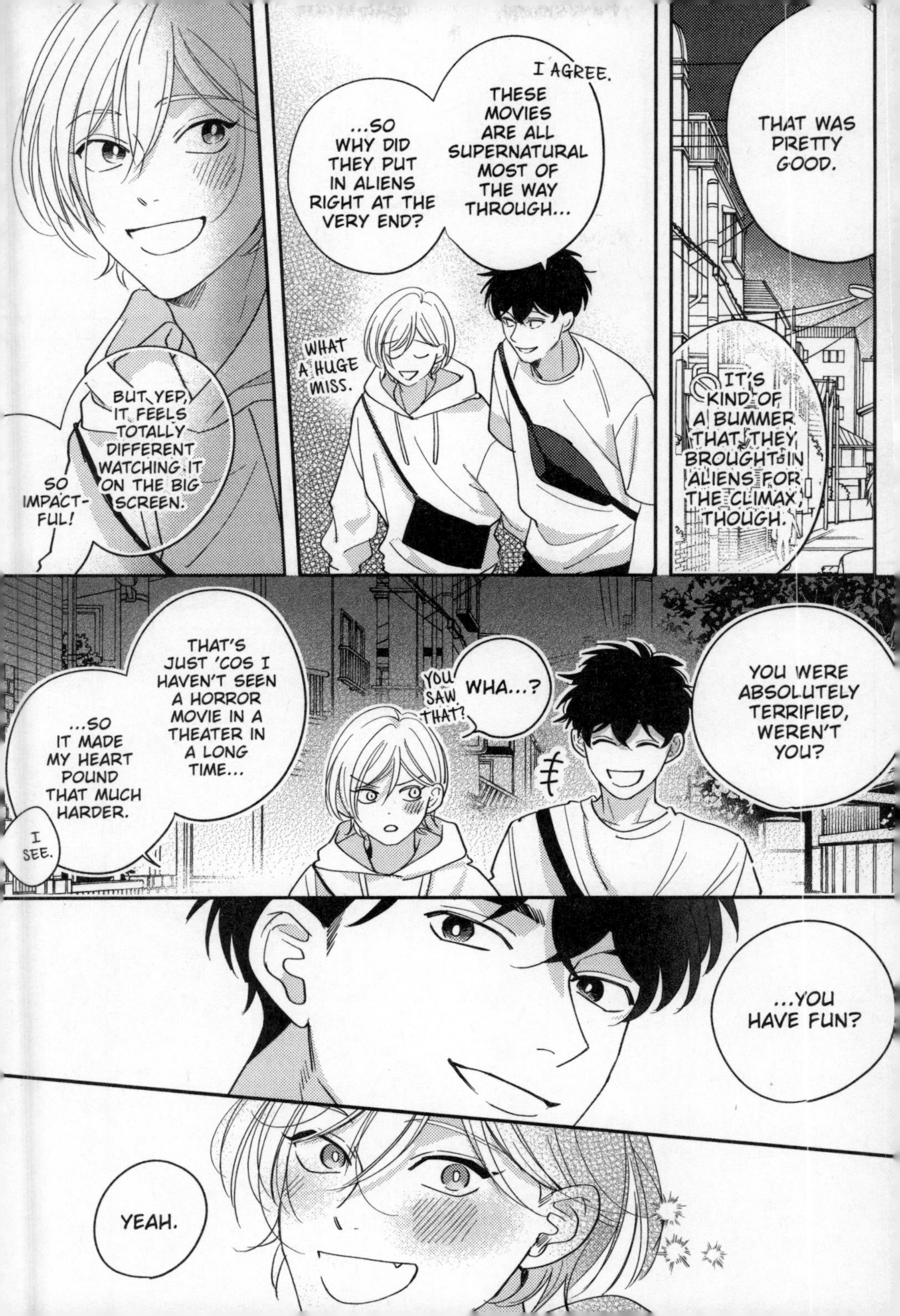
THAT WAS PRETTY GOOD.
IT'S KIND OF A BUMMER THAT THEY BROUGHT IN ALIENS FOR THE CLIMAX, THOUGH.
I AGREE.
THESE MOVIES ARE ALL SUPERNATURAL MOST OF THE WAY THROUGH...
...SO WHY DID THEY PUT IN ALIENS RIGHT AT THE VERY END?
WHAT A HUGE MISS.
BUT YEP, IT FEELS TOTALLY DIFFERENT WATCHING IT ON THE BIG SCREEN.
SO IMPACTFUL!
YOU WERE ABSOLUTELY TERRIFIED, WEREN'T YOU?
WHA...?
YOU SAW THAT?
THAT'S JUST 'COS I HAVEN'T SEEN A HORROR MOVIE IN A THEATER IN A LONG TIME...
...SO IT MADE MY HEART POUND THAT MUCH HARDER.
I SEE.
...YOU HAVE FUN?
YEAH.

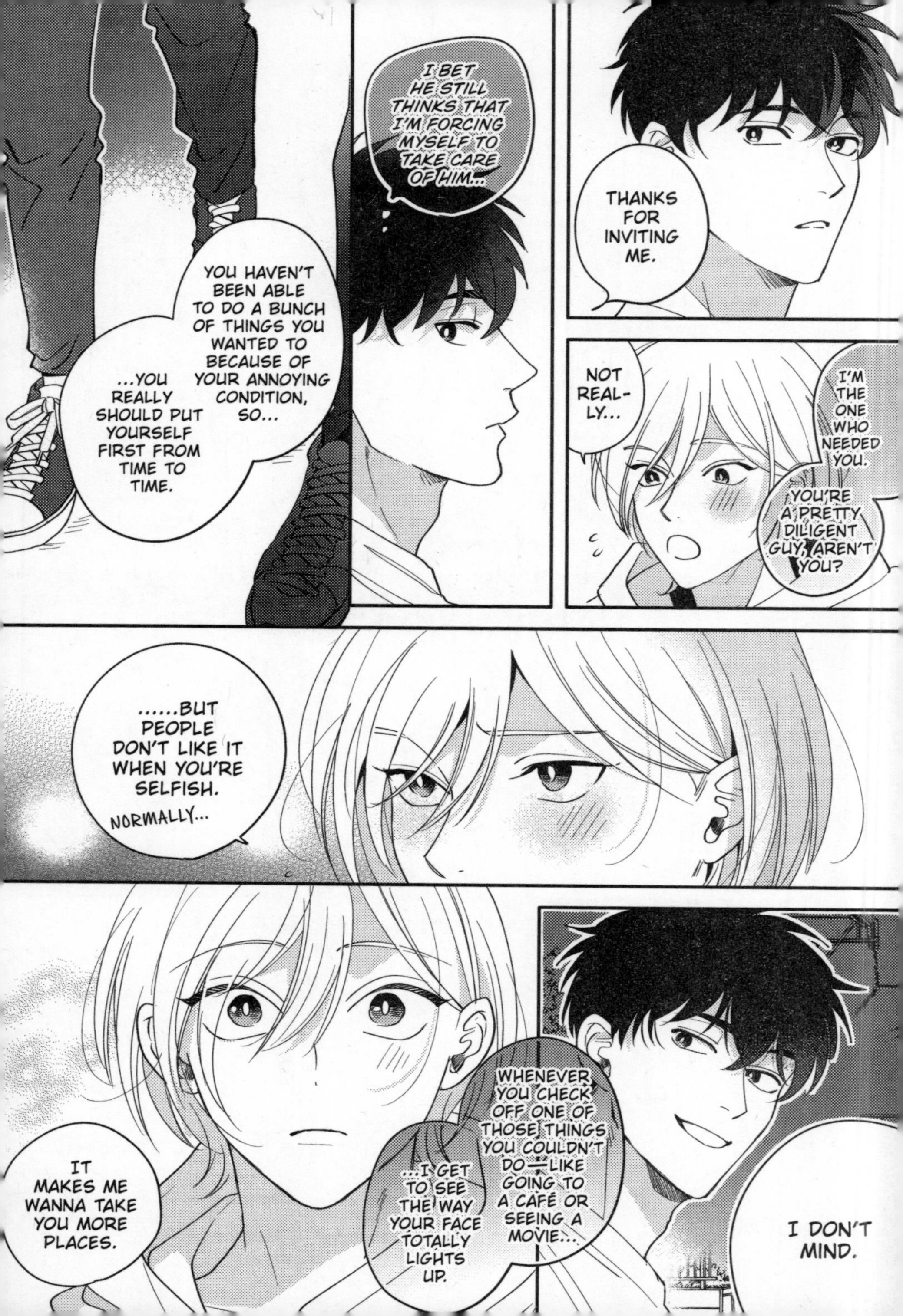
THANKS FOR INVITING ME.
NOT REALLY...
I'M THE ONE WHO NEEDED YOU.
YOU'RE A PRETTY DILIGENT GUY, AREN'T YOU?
I BET HE STILL THINKS THAT I'M FORCING MYSELF TO TAKE CARE OF HIM...
YOU HAVEN'T BEEN ABLE TO DO A BUNCH OF THINGS YOU WANTED TO BECAUSE OF YOUR ANNOYING CONDITION, SO...
...YOU REALLY SHOULD PUT YOURSELF FIRST FROM TIME TO TIME.
......BUT PEOPLE DON'T LIKE IT WHEN YOU'RE SELFISH.
NORMALLY...
I DON'T MIND.
WHENEVER YOU CHECK OFF ONE OF THOSE THINGS YOU COULDN'T DO—LIKE GOING TO A CAFÉ OR SEEING A MOVIE...
...I GET TO SEE THE WAY YOUR FACE TOTALLY LIGHTS UP.
IT MAKES ME WANNA TAKE YOU MORE PLACES.

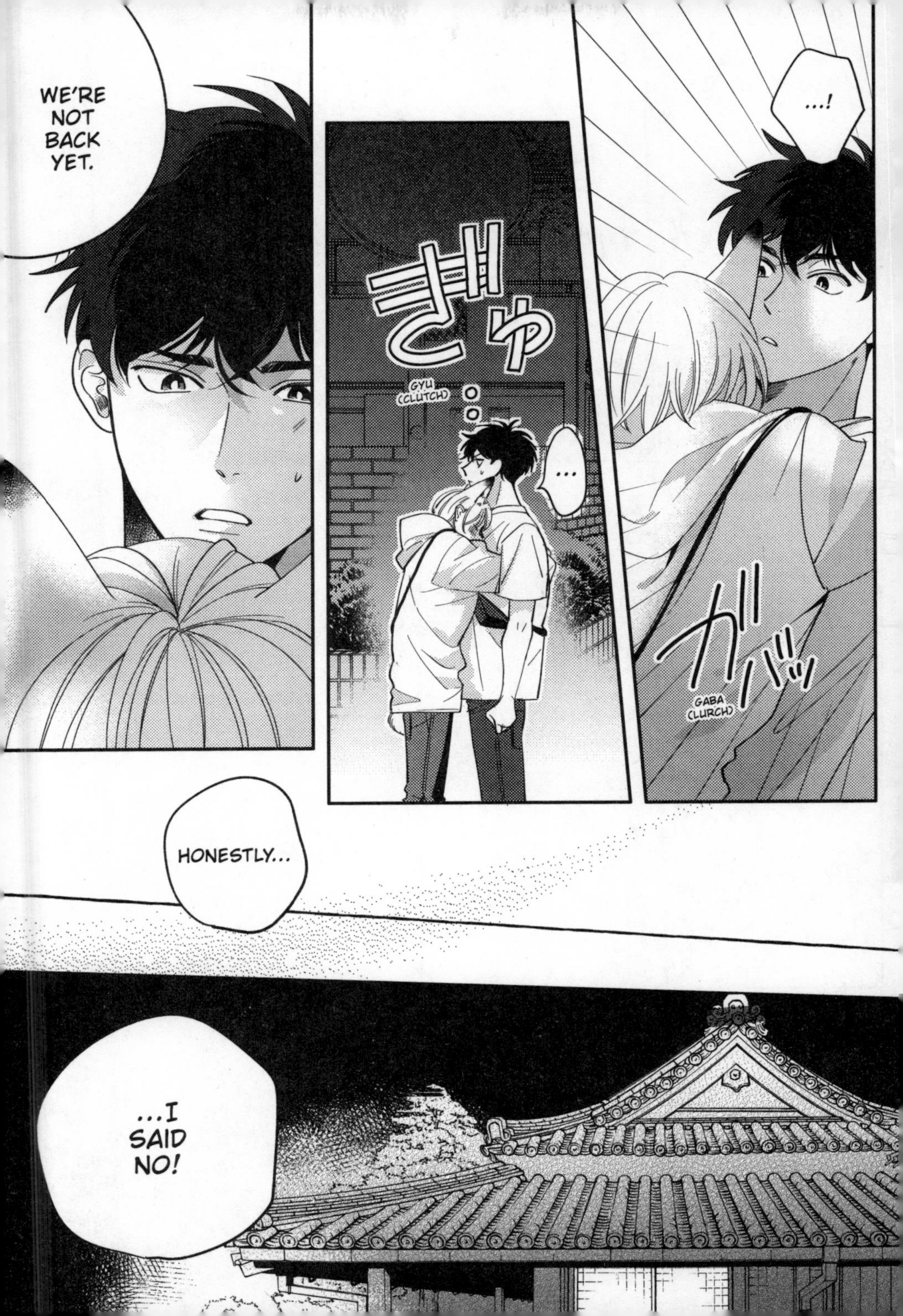
...!
ガバッ
GABA (LURCH)
ぎゅ
GYU (CLUTCH)
...
WE'RE NOT BACK YET.
HONESTLY...
...I SAID NO!

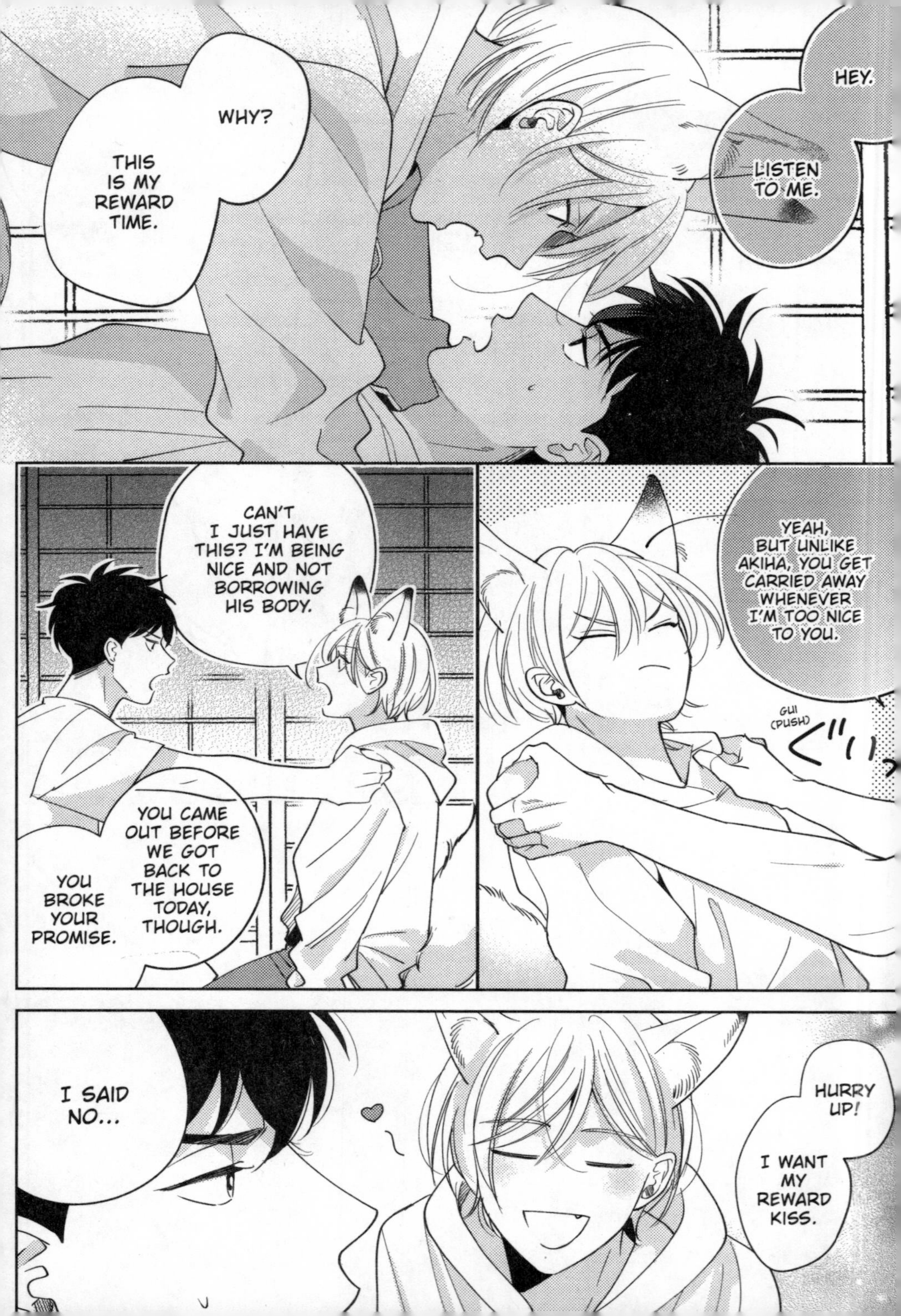
HEY.
LISTEN TO ME.
WHY?
THIS IS MY REWARD TIME.
YEAH, BUT UNLIKE AKIHA, YOU GET CARRIED AWAY WHENEVER I'M TOO NICE TO YOU.
GUI (PUSH)
ぐいっ
CAN'T I JUST HAVE THIS? I'M BEING NICE AND NOT BORROWING HIS BODY.
YOU CAME OUT BEFORE WE GOT BACK TO THE HOUSE TODAY, THOUGH.
YOU BROKE YOUR PROMISE.
HURRY UP!
I WANT MY REWARD KISS.
I SAID NO...

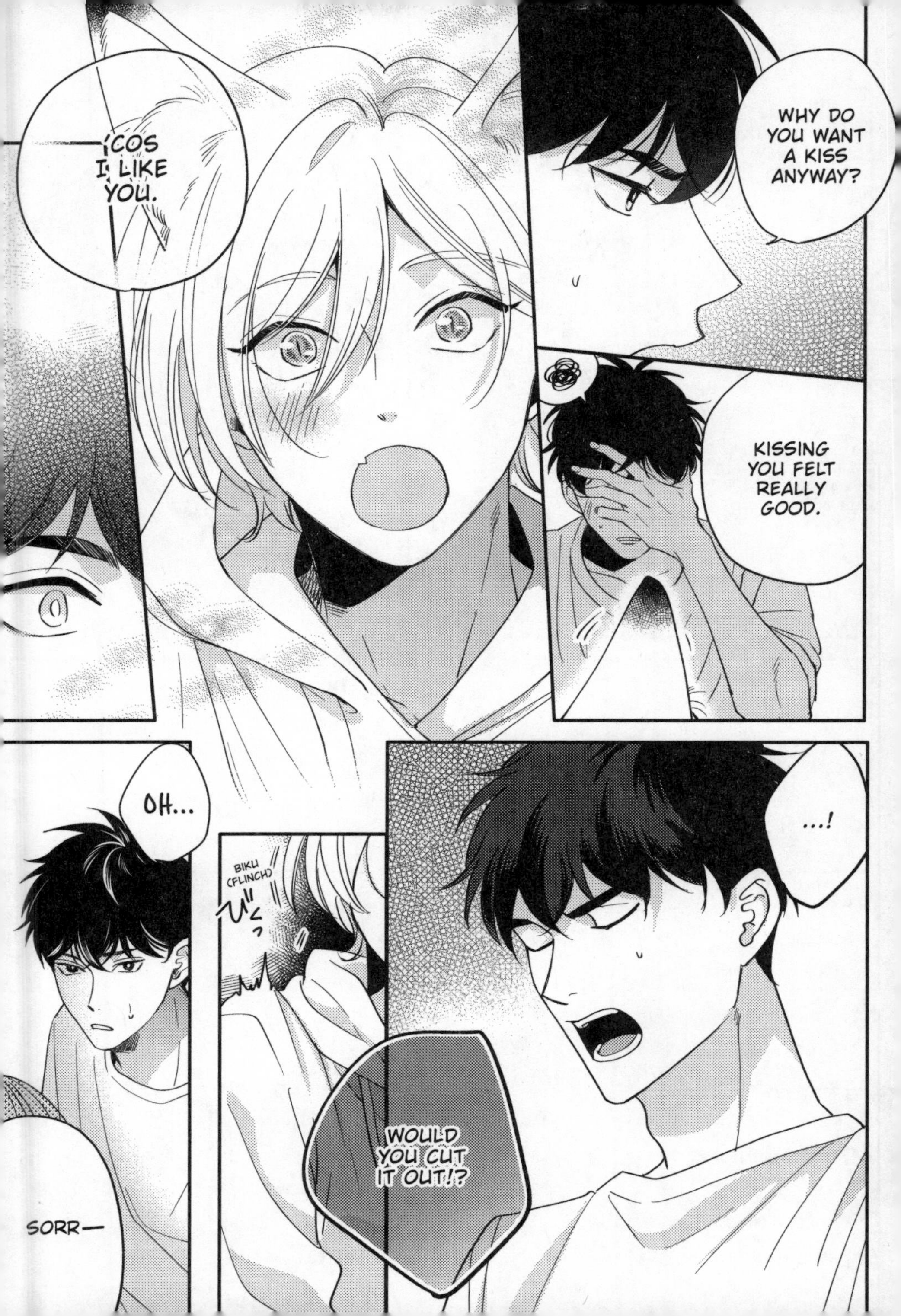
WHY DO YOU WANT A KISS ANYWAY?
KISSING YOU FELT REALLY GOOD.
'COS I LIKE YOU.
...!
WOULD YOU CUT IT OUT!?
BIKU (FLINCH)
OH...
SORR—

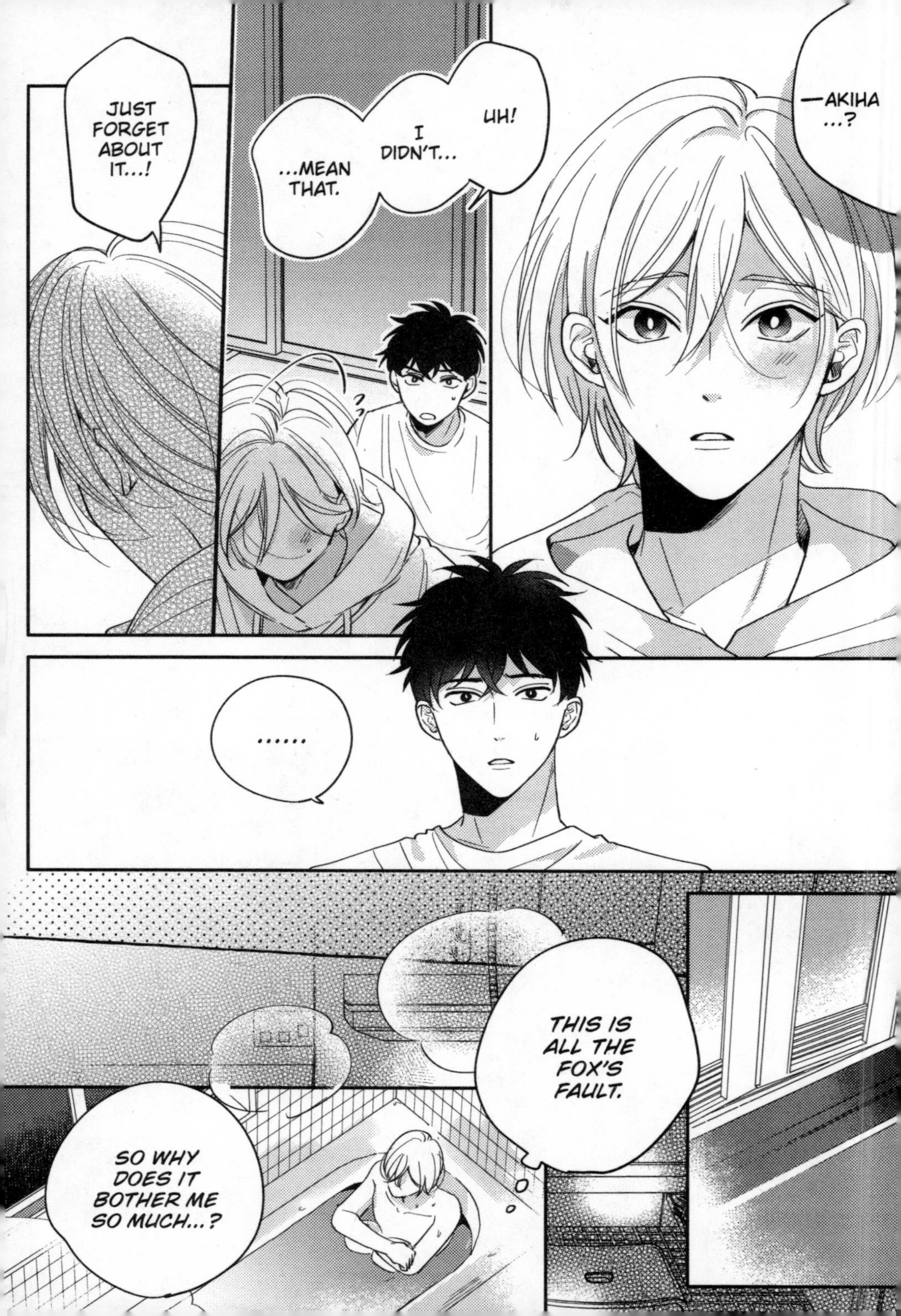
—AKIHA ...?
UH! I DIDN'T... ...MEAN THAT.
JUST FORGET ABOUT IT...!
......
THIS IS ALL THE FOX'S FAULT.
SO WHY DOES IT BOTHER ME SO MUCH...?

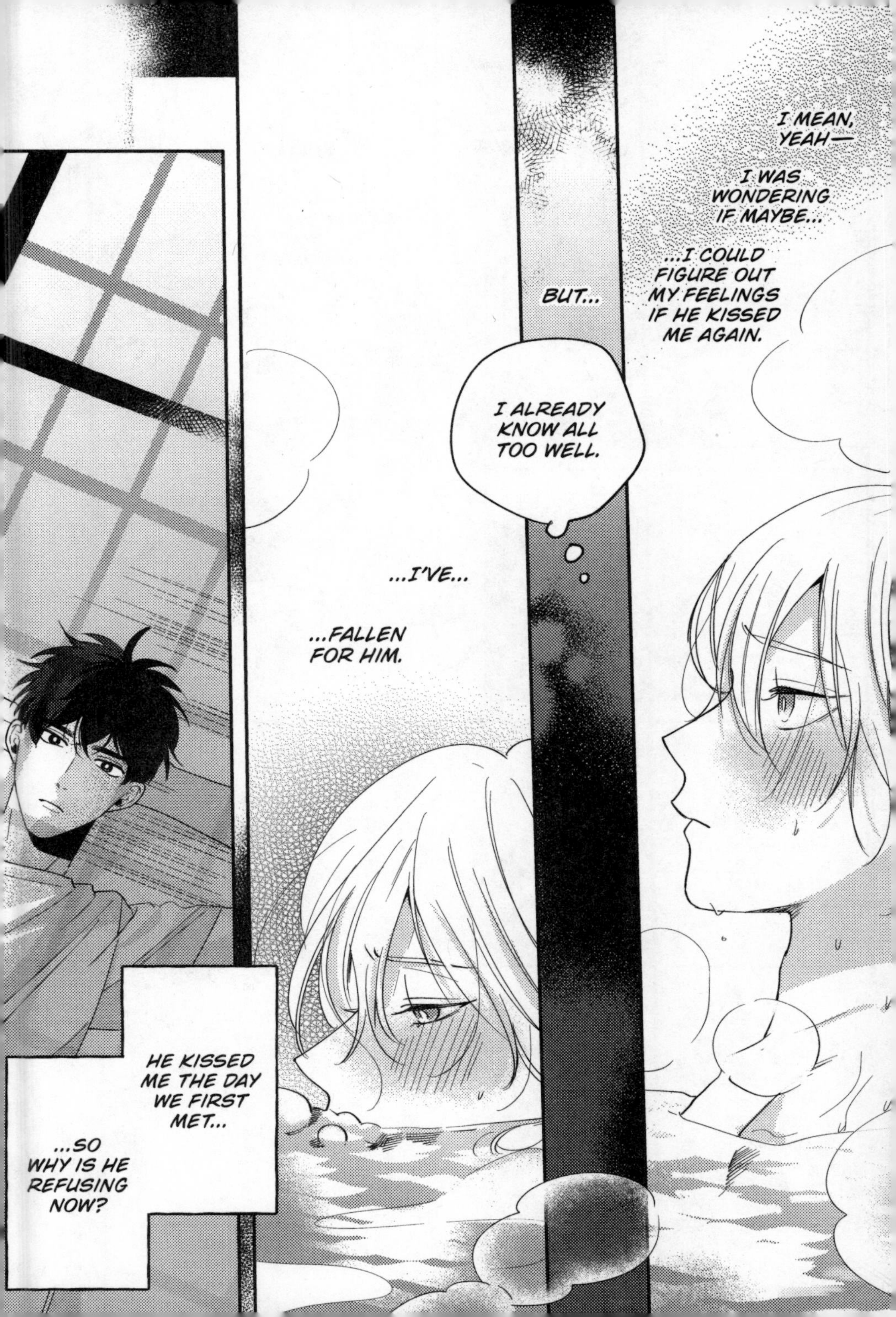
I MEAN, YEAH—
I WAS WONDERING IF MAYBE...
...I COULD FIGURE OUT MY FEELINGS IF HE KISSED ME AGAIN.
BUT...
I ALREADY KNOW ALL TOO WELL.
...I'VE...
...FALLEN FOR HIM.
HE KISSED ME THE DAY WE FIRST MET...
...SO WHY IS HE REFUSING NOW?

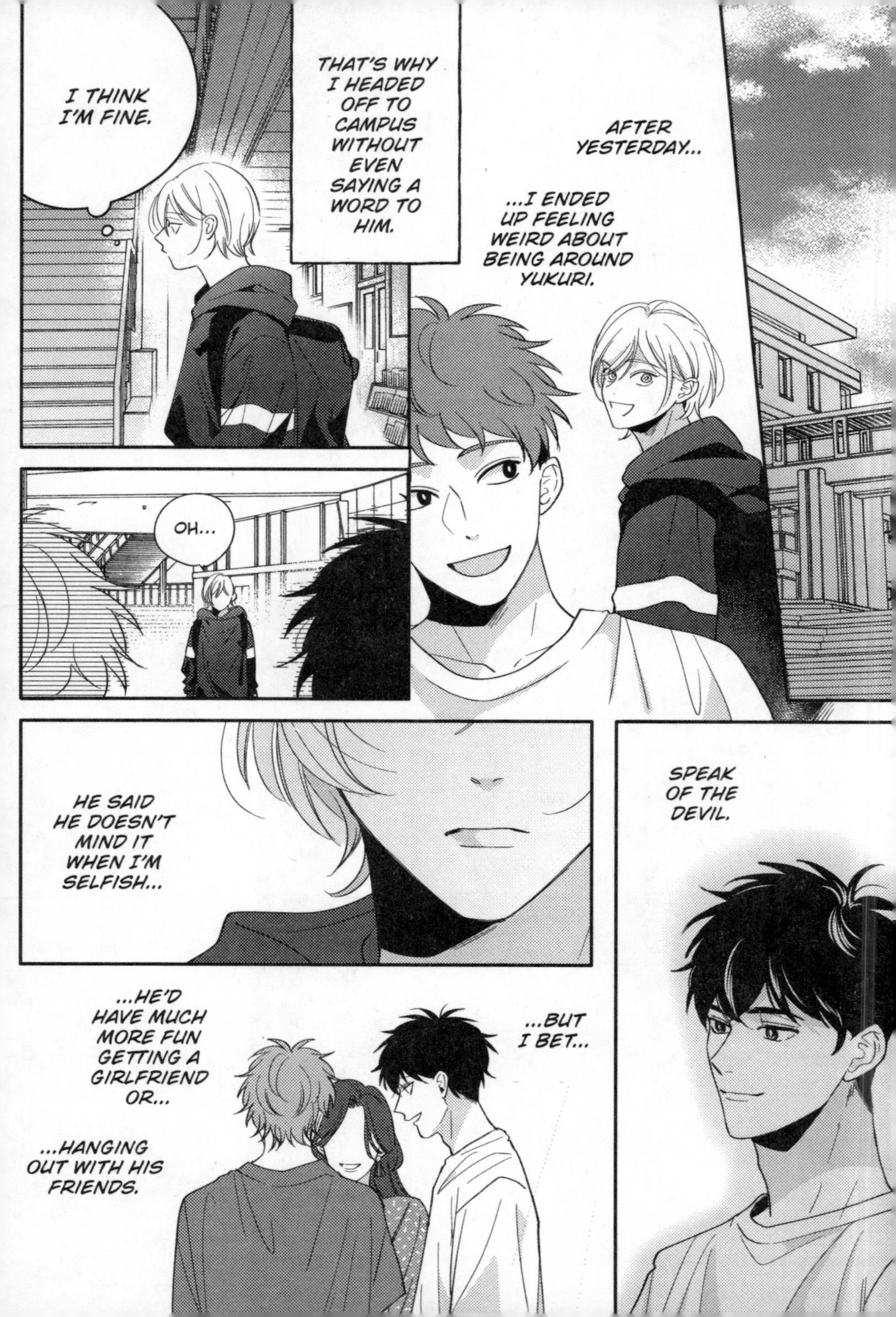
AFTER YESTERDAY...
...I ENDED UP FEELING WEIRD ABOUT BEING AROUND YUKURI.
THAT'S WHY I HEADED OFF TO CAMPUS WITHOUT EVEN SAYING A WORD TO HIM.
I THINK I'M FINE.
OH...
SPEAK OF THE DEVIL.
HE SAID HE DOESN'T MIND IT WHEN I'M SELFISH...
...BUT I BET...
...HE'D HAVE MUCH MORE FUN GETTING A GIRLFRIEND OR...
...HANGING OUT WITH HIS FRIENDS.

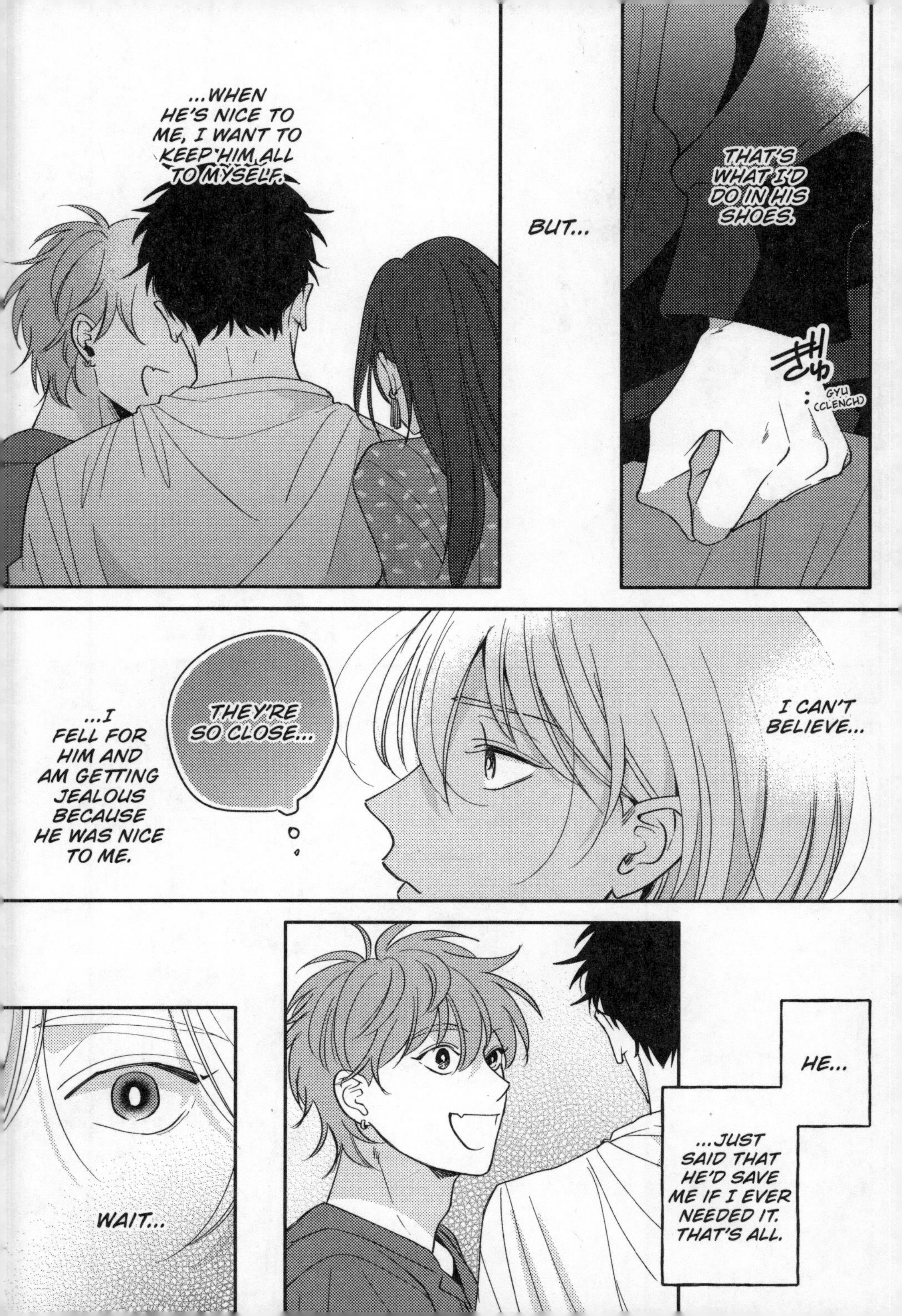
THAT'S WHAT I'D DO IN HIS SHOES.
ぎゅ
GYU (CLENCH)
BUT...
...WHEN HE'S NICE TO ME, I WANT TO KEEP HIM ALL TO MYSELF.
I CAN'T BELIEVE...
THEY'RE SO CLOSE...
...I FELL FOR HIM AND AM GETTING JEALOUS BECAUSE HE WAS NICE TO ME.
HE...
...JUST SAID THAT HE'D SAVE ME IF I EVER NEEDED IT. THAT'S ALL.
WAIT...

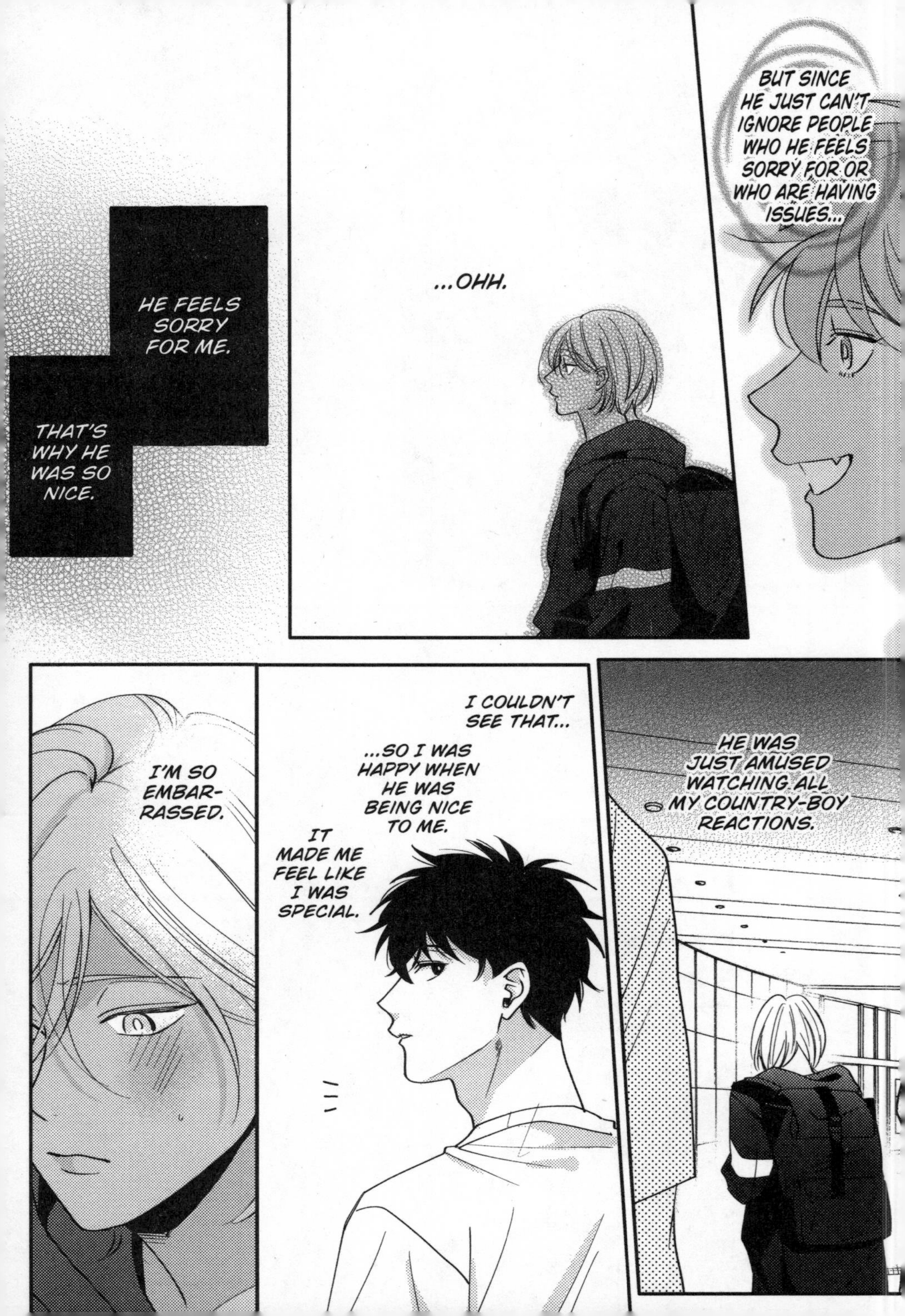
BUT SINCE HE JUST CAN'T IGNORE PEOPLE WHO HE FEELS SORRY FOR OR WHO ARE HAVING ISSUES...
...OHH.
HE FEELS SORRY FOR ME.
THAT'S WHY HE WAS SO NICE.
HE WAS JUST AMUSED WATCHING ALL MY COUNTRY-BOY REACTIONS.
I COULDN'T SEE THAT...
...SO I WAS HAPPY WHEN HE WAS BEING NICE TO ME.
IT MADE ME FEEL LIKE I WAS SPECIAL.
I'M SO EMBARRASSED.

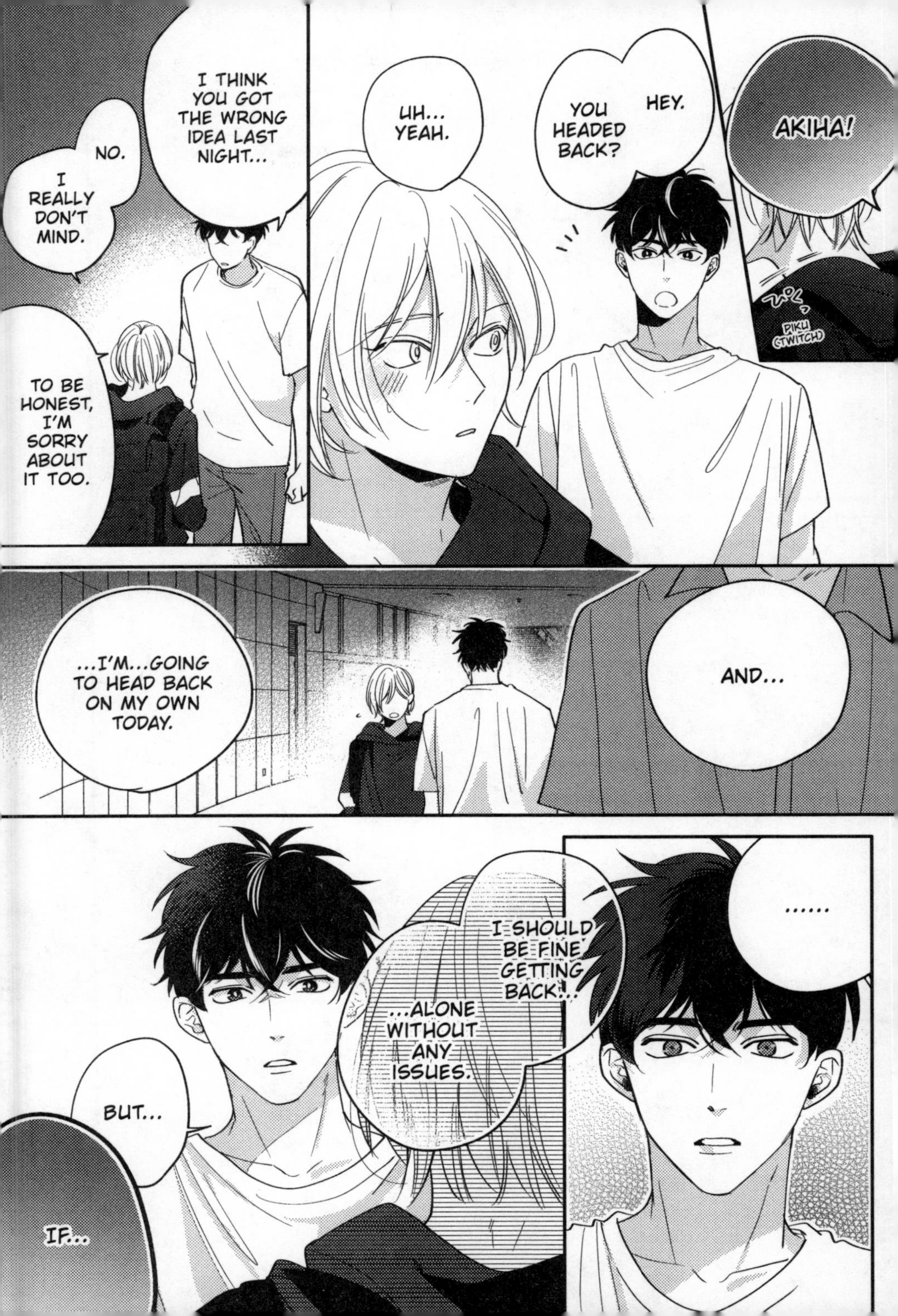
AKIHA!
ぴくっ
PIKU (TWITCH)
HEY.
YOU HEADED BACK?
UH... YEAH.
I THINK YOU GOT THE WRONG IDEA LAST NIGHT...
NO.
I REALLY DON'T MIND.
TO BE HONEST, I'M SORRY ABOUT IT TOO.
AND...
...I'M...GOING TO HEAD BACK ON MY OWN TODAY.
......
I SHOULD BE FINE GETTING BACK...
...ALONE WITHOUT ANY ISSUES.
BUT...
IF...

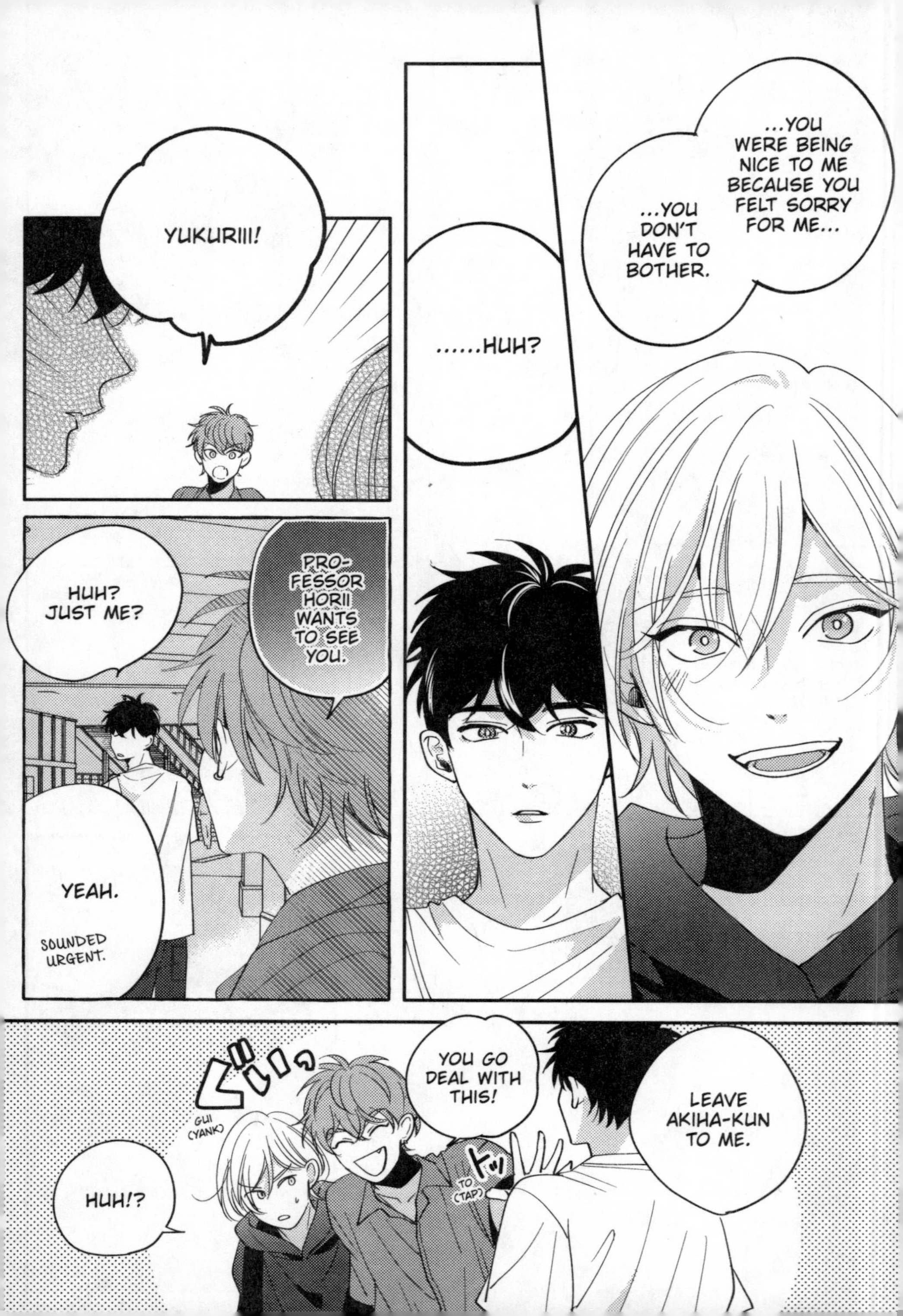
...YOU WERE BEING NICE TO ME BECAUSE YOU FELT SORRY FOR ME...
...YOU DON'T HAVE TO BOTHER.
......HUH?
YUKURIII!
PRO-FESSOR HORII WANTS TO SEE YOU.
HUH? JUST ME?
YEAH.
SOUNDED URGENT.
LEAVE AKIHA-KUN TO ME.
TO (TAP)
YOU GO DEAL WITH THIS!
GUI (YANK)
HUH!?

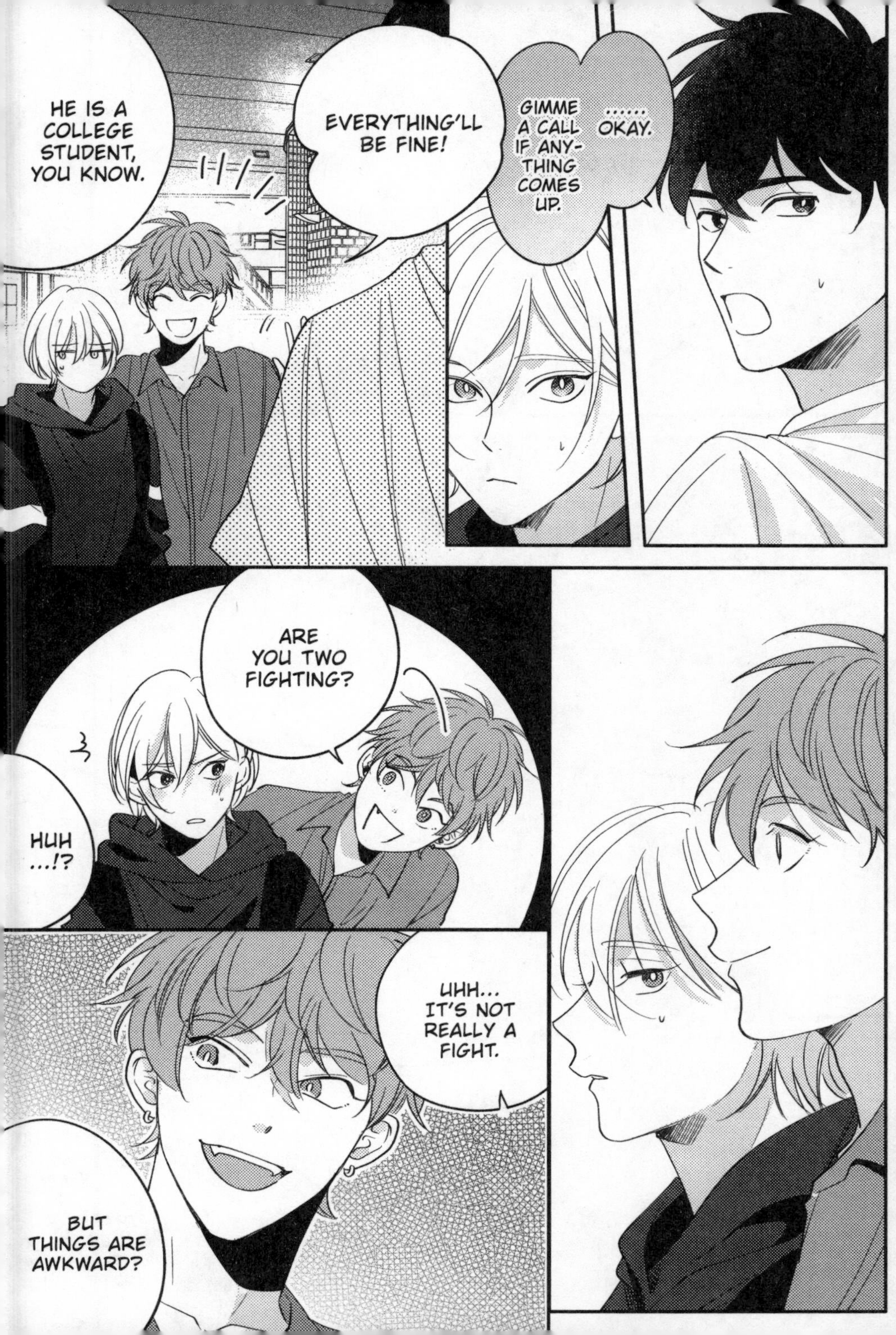
......OKAY.
GIMME A CALL IF ANY-THING COMES UP.
EVERYTHING'LL BE FINE!
HE IS A COLLEGE STUDENT, YOU KNOW.
ARE YOU TWO FIGHTING?
HUH ...!?
UHH... IT'S NOT REALLY A FIGHT.
BUT THINGS ARE AWKWARD?

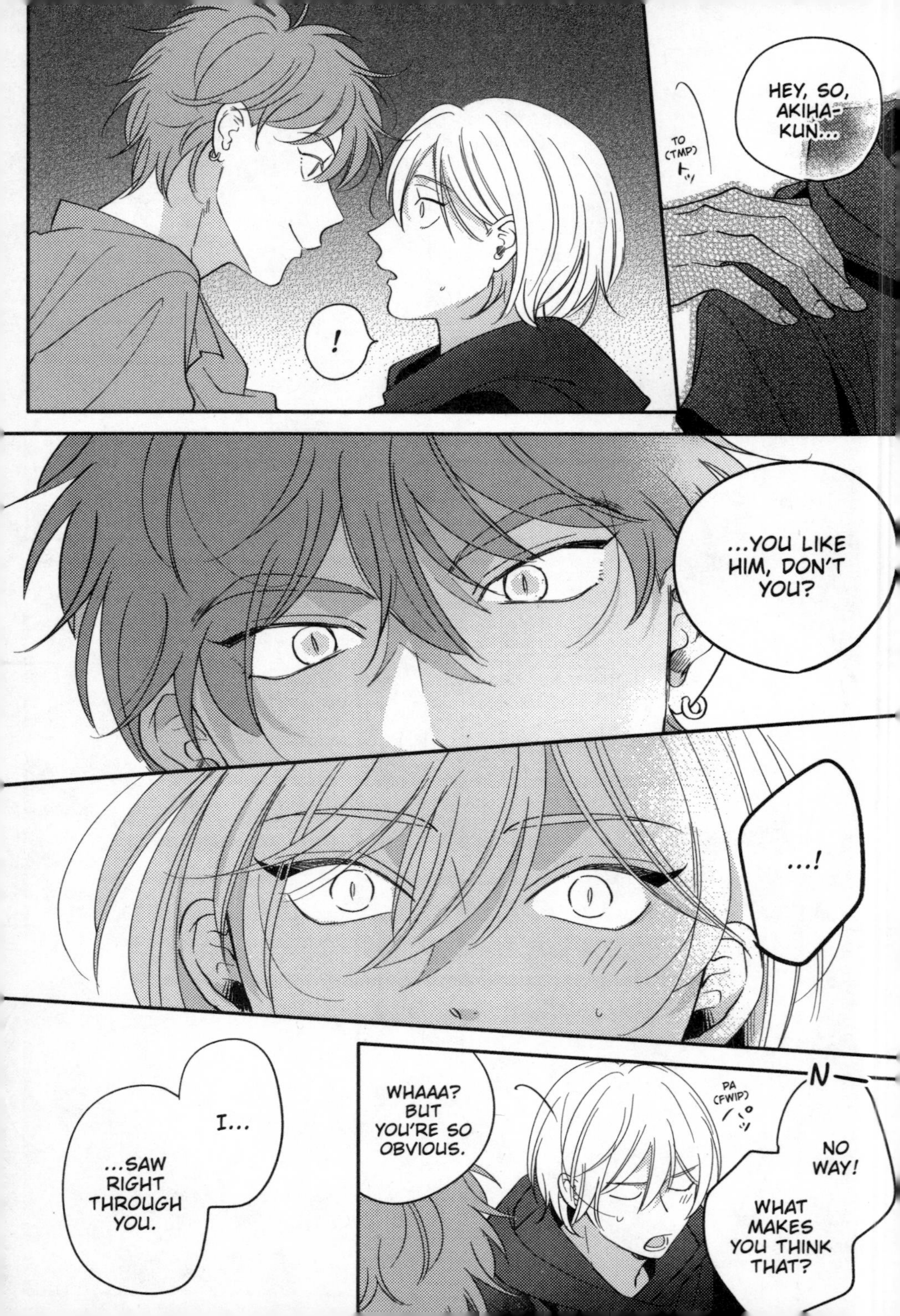
HEY, SO, AKIHA-KUN...
TO (TMP) トッ
!
...YOU LIKE HIM, DON'T YOU?
...!
N—
PA (FWIP) パッ
NO WAY!
WHAT MAKES YOU THINK THAT?
WHAAA? BUT YOU'RE SO OBVIOUS.
I...
...SAW RIGHT THROUGH YOU.

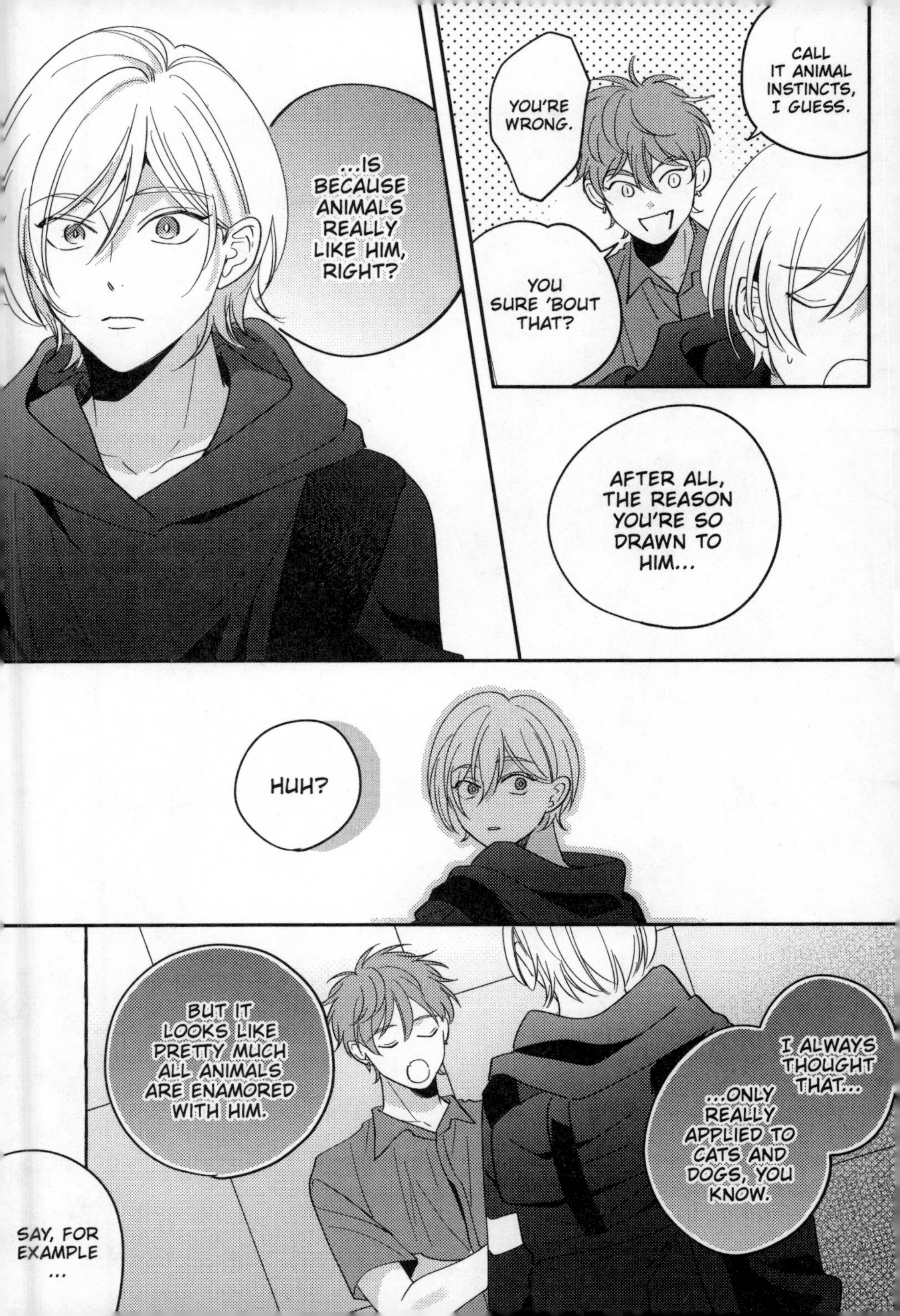
CALL IT ANIMAL INSTINCTS, I GUESS.
YOU'RE WRONG.
YOU SURE 'BOUT THAT?
AFTER ALL, THE REASON YOU'RE SO DRAWN TO HIM...
...IS BECAUSE ANIMALS REALLY LIKE HIM, RIGHT?
HUH?
I ALWAYS THOUGHT THAT...
...ONLY REALLY APPLIED TO CATS AND DOGS, YOU KNOW.
BUT IT LOOKS LIKE PRETTY MUCH ALL ANIMALS ARE ENAMORED WITH HIM.
SAY, FOR EXAMPLE ...

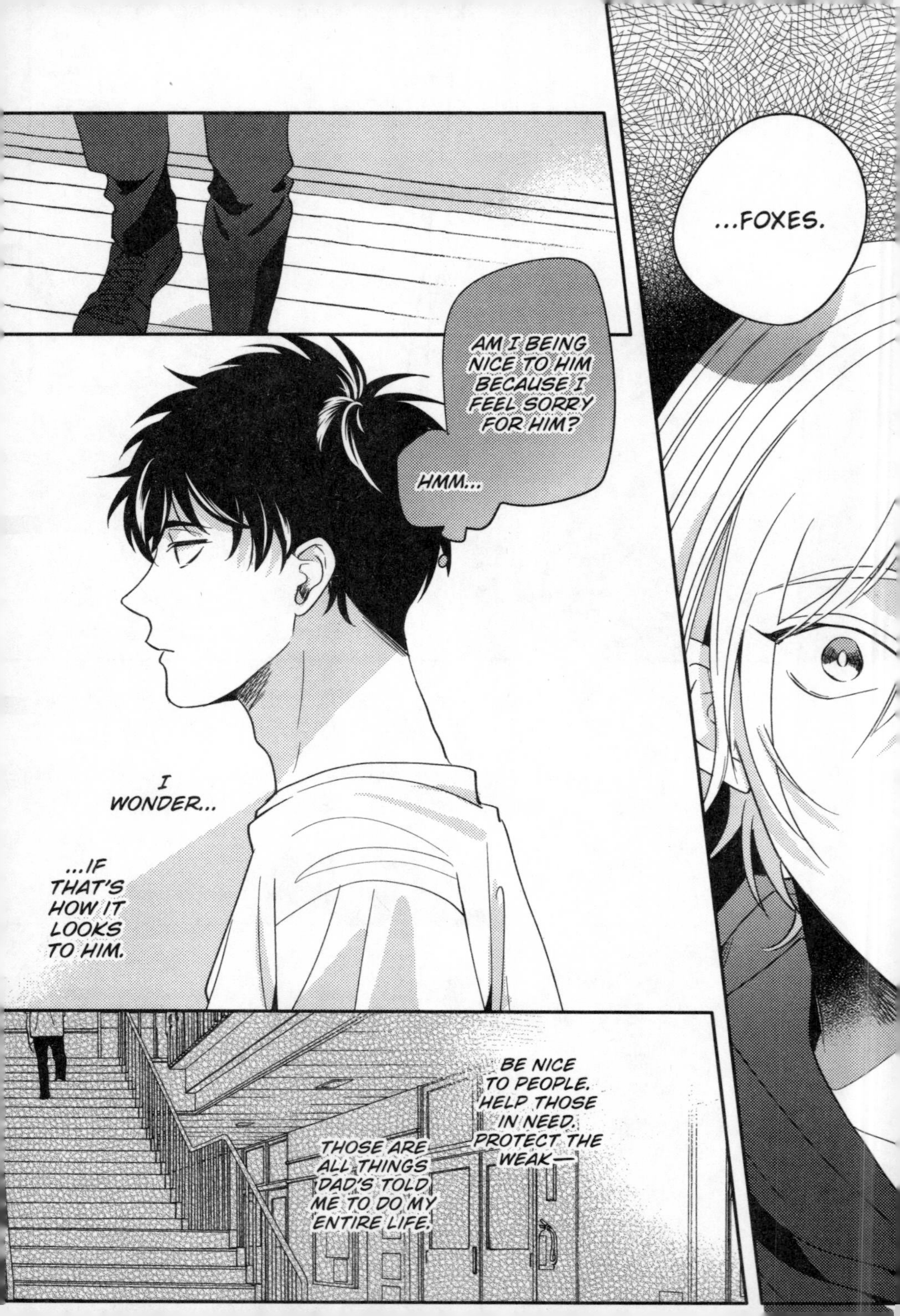
...FOXES.
AM I BEING NICE TO HIM BECAUSE I FEEL SORRY FOR HIM?
HMM...
I WONDER...
...IF THAT'S HOW IT LOOKS TO HIM.
BE NICE TO PEOPLE. HELP THOSE IN NEED. PROTECT THE WEAK—
THOSE ARE ALL THINGS DAD'S TOLD ME TO DO MY ENTIRE LIFE.

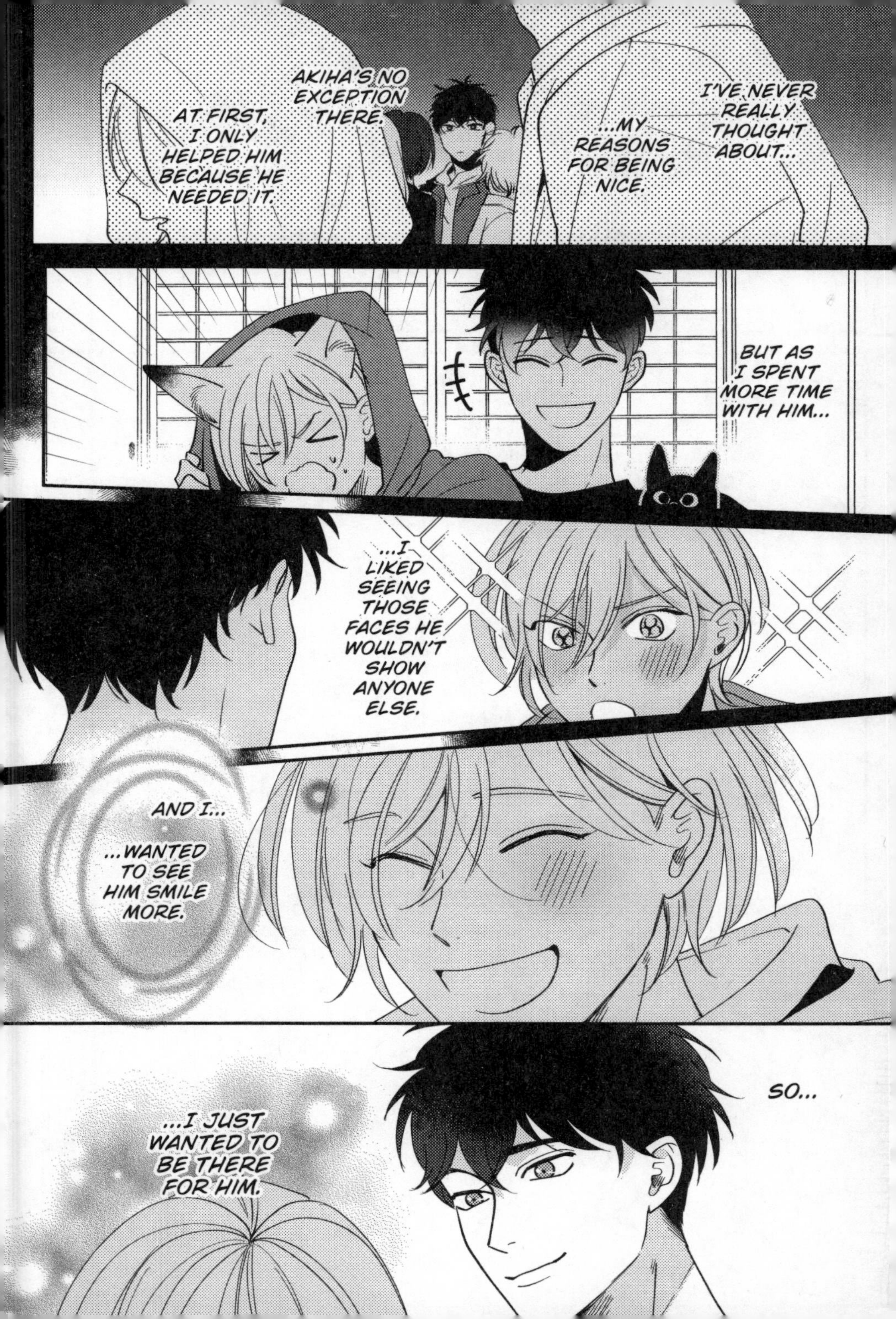

I'VE NEVER REALLY THOUGHT ABOUT...
...MY REASONS FOR BEING NICE.
AKIHA'S NO EXCEPTION THERE.
AT FIRST, I ONLY HELPED HIM BECAUSE HE NEEDED IT.
BUT AS I SPENT MORE TIME WITH HIM...
...I LIKED SEEING THOSE FACES HE WOULDN'T SHOW ANYONE ELSE.
AND I...
...WANTED TO SEE HIM SMILE MORE.
SO...
...I JUST WANTED TO BE THERE FOR HIM.

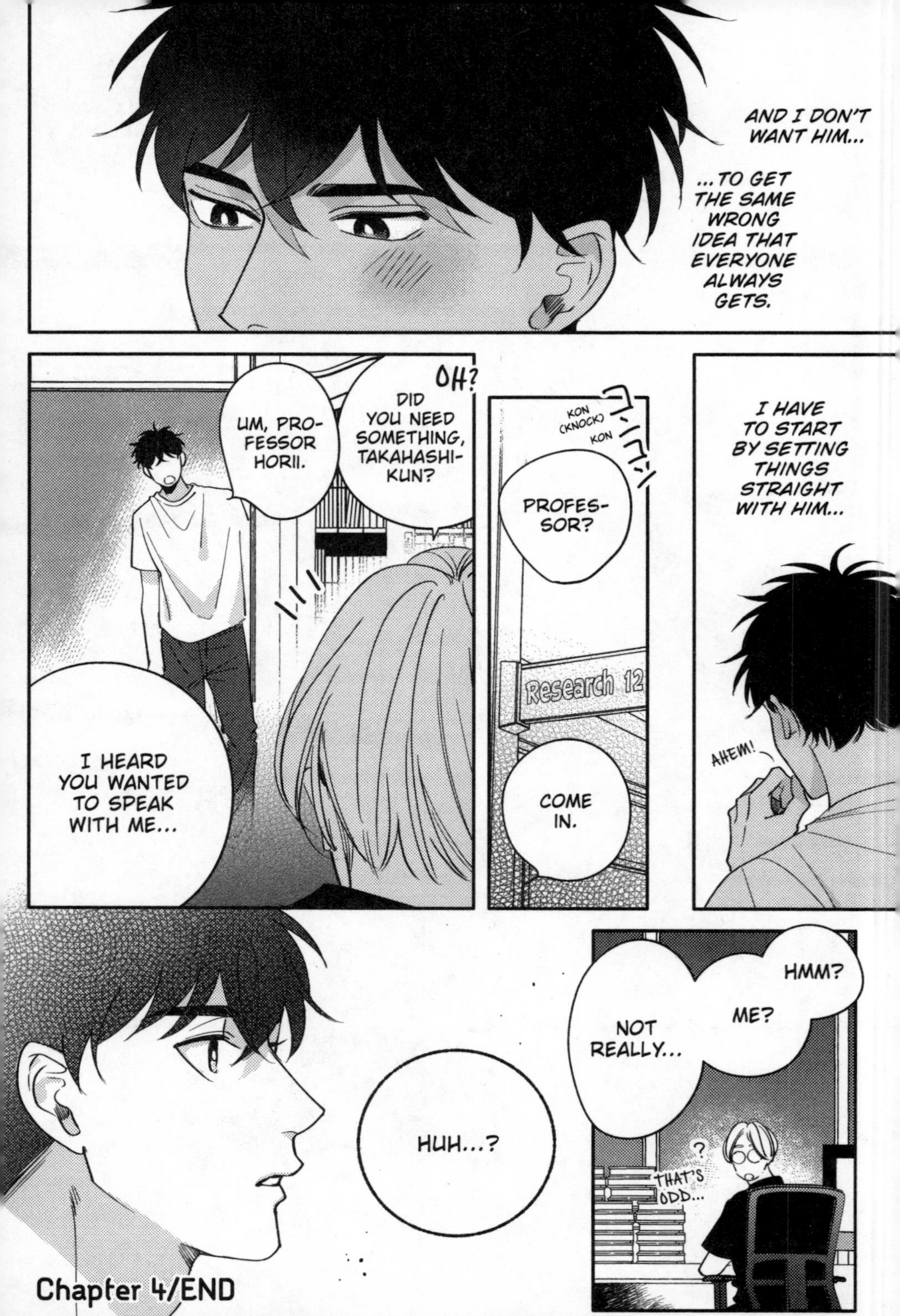
AND I DON'T WANT HIM...
...TO GET THE SAME WRONG IDEA THAT EVERYONE ALWAYS GETS.
I HAVE TO START BY SETTING THINGS STRAIGHT WITH HIM...
AHEM!
KON (KNOCK) KON
PROFESSOR?
Research 12
COME IN.
OH?
DID YOU NEED SOMETHING, TAKAHASHI-KUN?
UM, PROFESSOR HORII.
I HEARD YOU WANTED TO SPEAK WITH ME...
HMM?
ME?
NOT REALLY...
?
THAT'S ODD...
HUH...?

Chapter 4/END

Fox-Colored jealousy

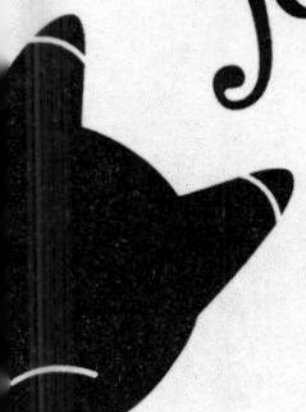

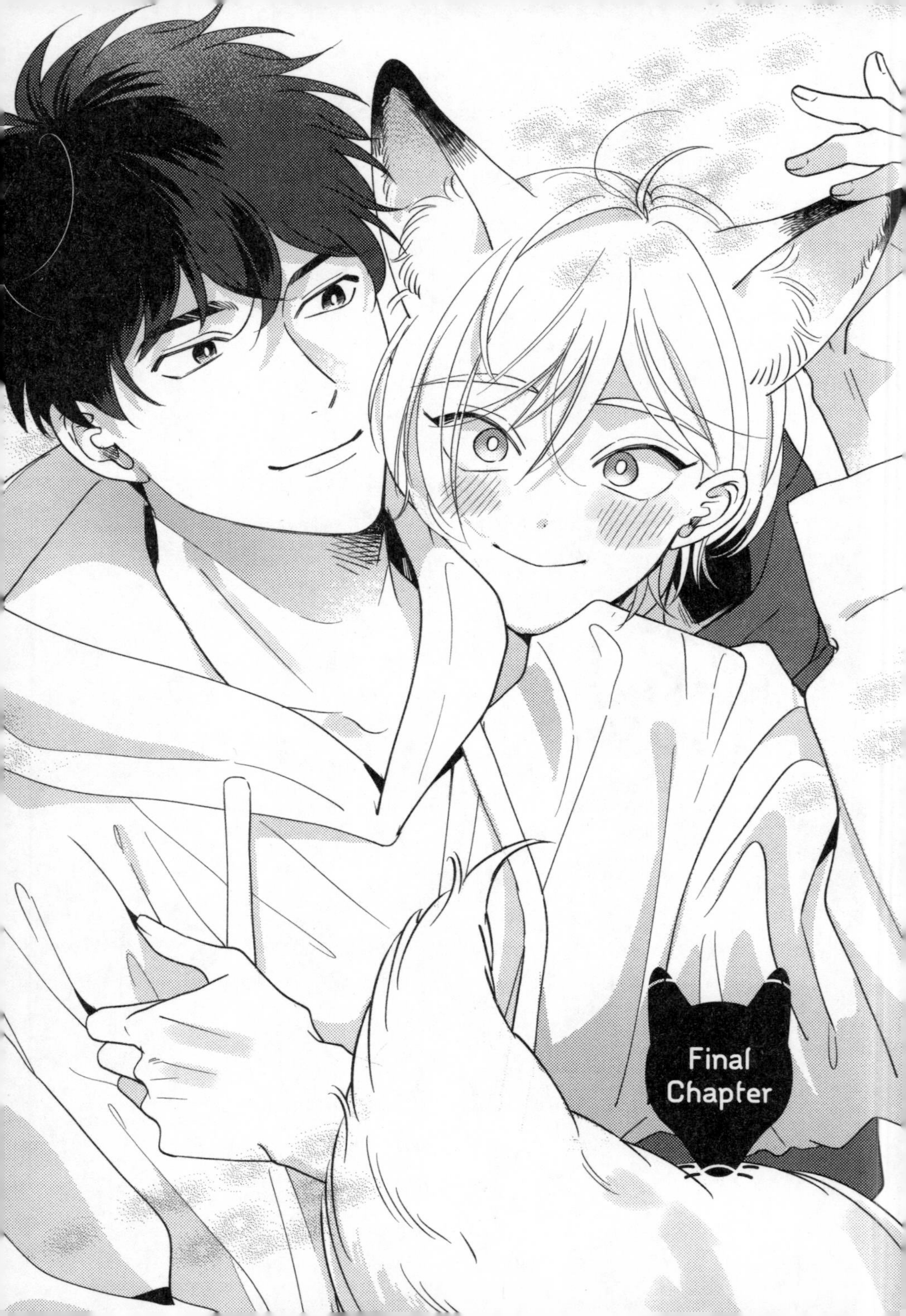
Final
Chapter

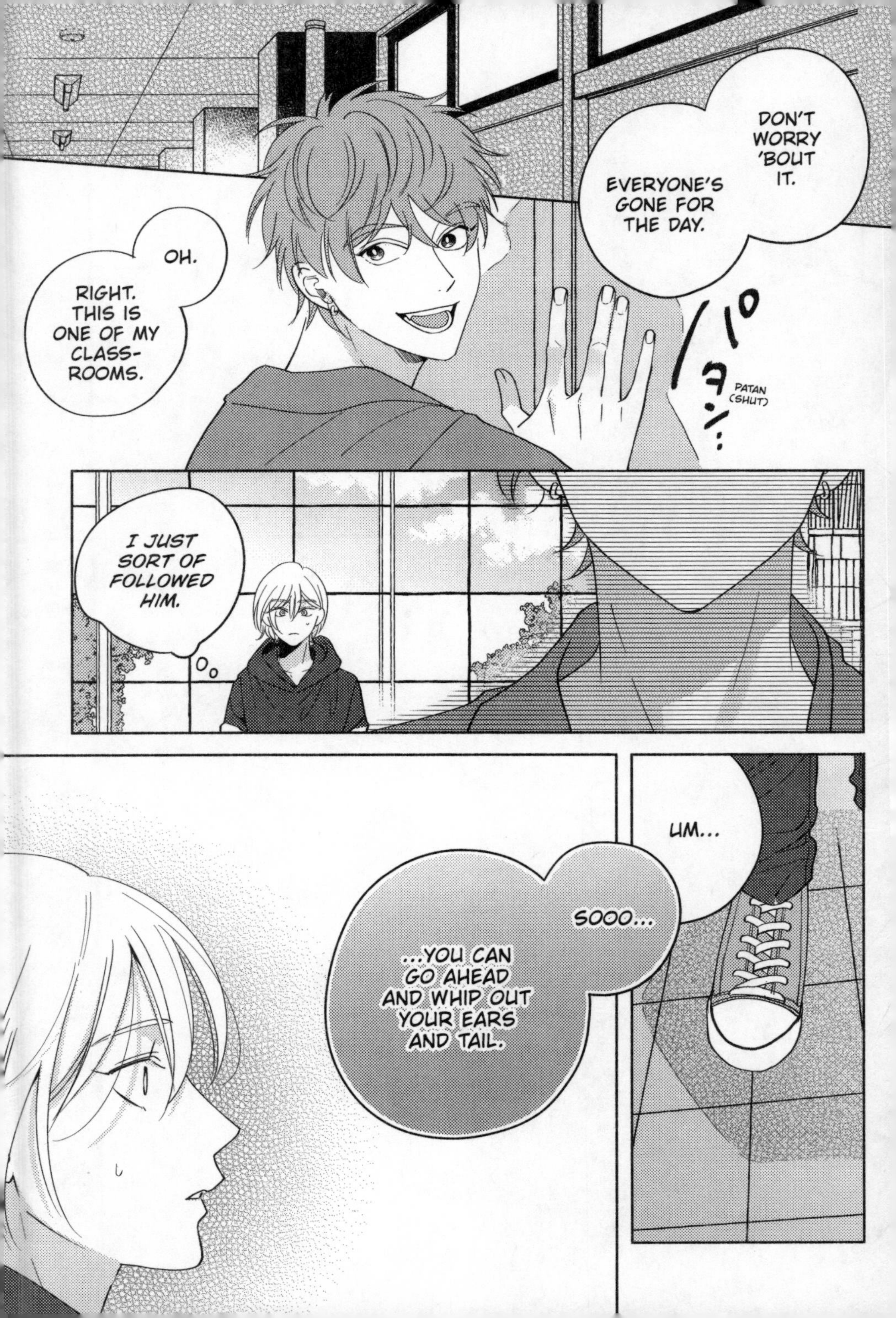
DON'T WORRY 'BOUT IT.
EVERYONE'S GONE FOR THE DAY.
パタン
PATAN (SHUT)
OH.
RIGHT. THIS IS ONE OF MY CLASS-ROOMS.
I JUST SORT OF FOLLOWED HIM.
UM...
SOOO...
...YOU CAN GO AHEAD AND WHIP OUT YOUR EARS AND TAIL.

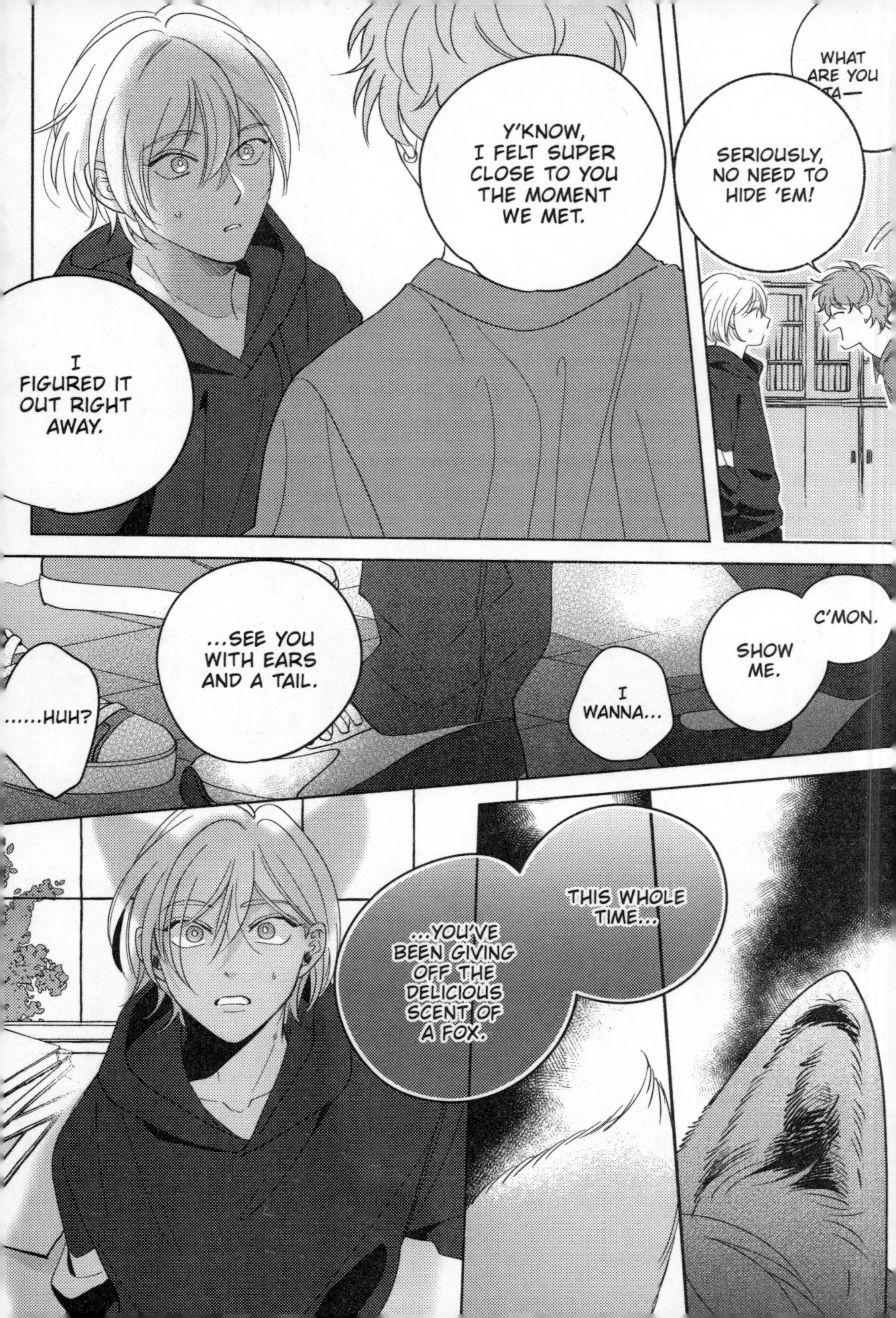
WHAT ARE YOU TA—
SERIOUSLY, NO NEED TO HIDE 'EM!
Y'KNOW, I FELT SUPER CLOSE TO YOU THE MOMENT WE MET.
I FIGURED IT OUT RIGHT AWAY.
C'MON.
SHOW ME.
I WANNA...
...SEE YOU WITH EARS AND A TAIL.
......HUH?
THIS WHOLE TIME...
...YOU'VE BEEN GIVING OFF THE DELICIOUS SCENT OF A FOX.

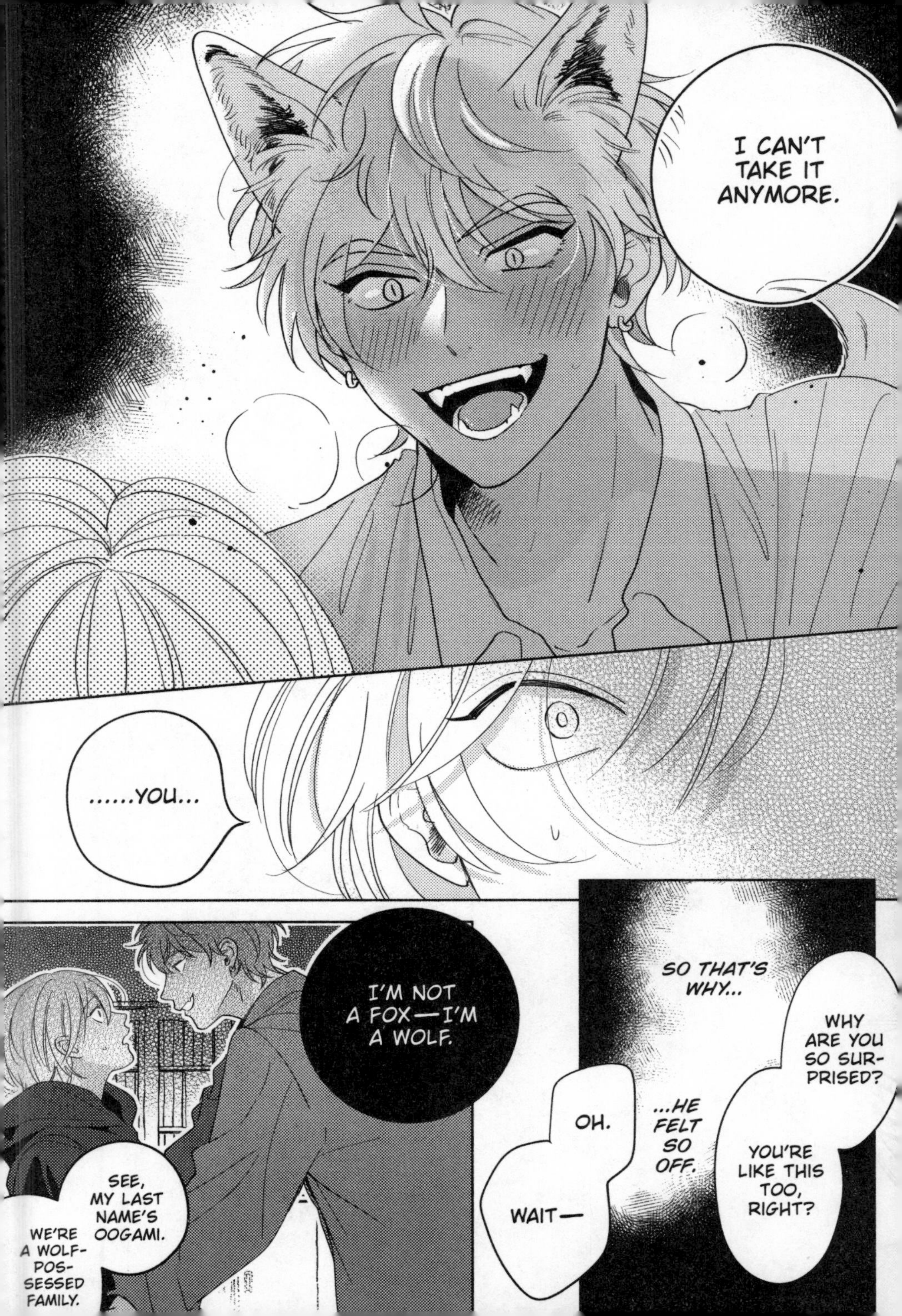
I CAN'T TAKE IT ANYMORE.
......YOU...
SO THAT'S WHY...
WHY ARE YOU SO SURPRISED?
YOU'RE LIKE THIS TOO, RIGHT?
...HE FELT SO OFF.
OH.
WAIT—
I'M NOT A FOX—I'M A WOLF.
SEE, MY LAST NAME'S OOGAMI.
WE'RE A WOLF-POSSESSED FAMILY.

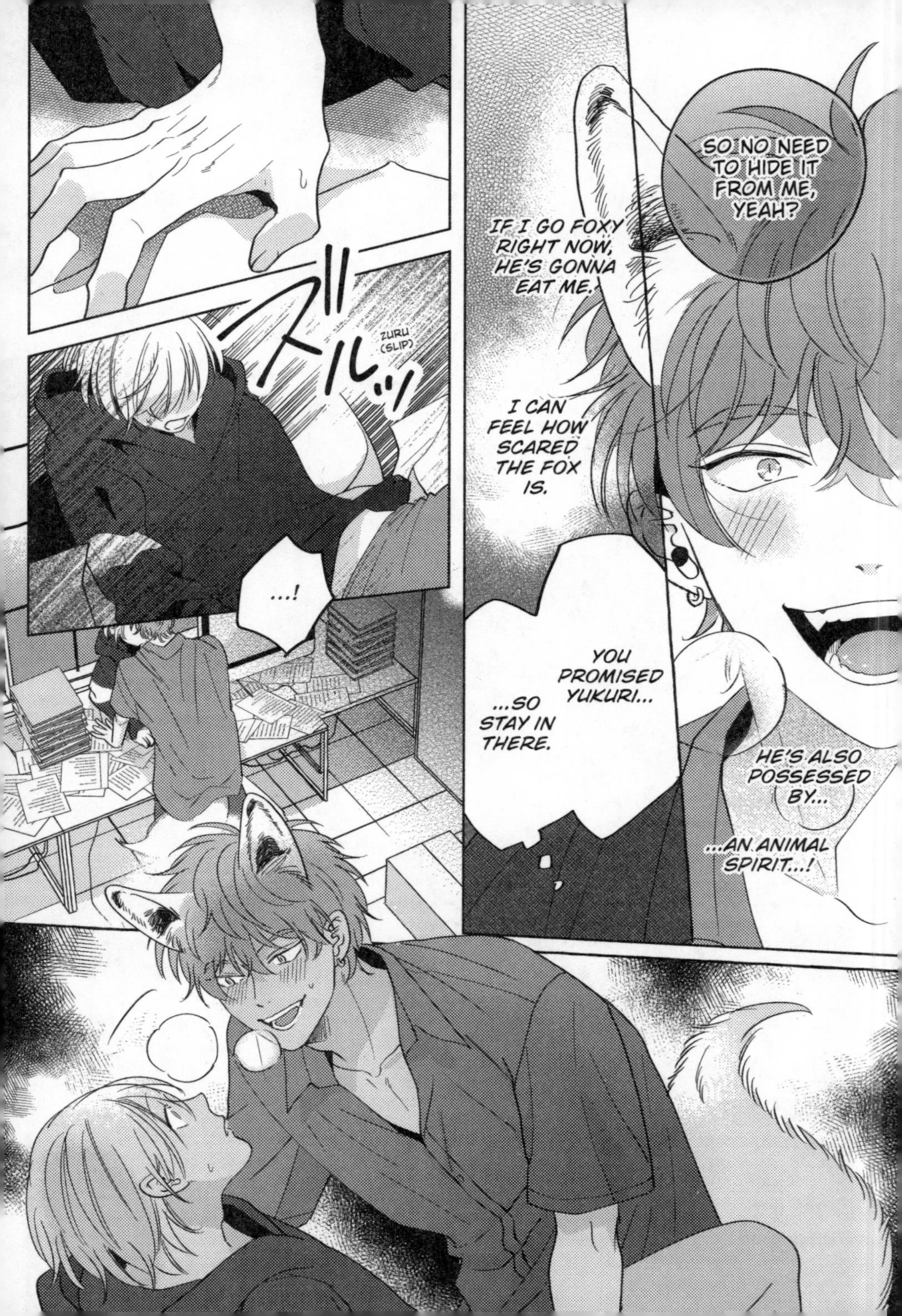
SO NO NEED TO HIDE IT FROM ME, YEAH?
IF I GO FOXY RIGHT NOW, HE'S GONNA EAT ME.
I CAN FEEL HOW SCARED THE FOX IS.
YOU PROMISED YUKURI...
...SO STAY IN THERE.
HE'S ALSO POSSESSED BY...
...AN ANIMAL SPIRIT...!
ZURU (SLIP)
...!

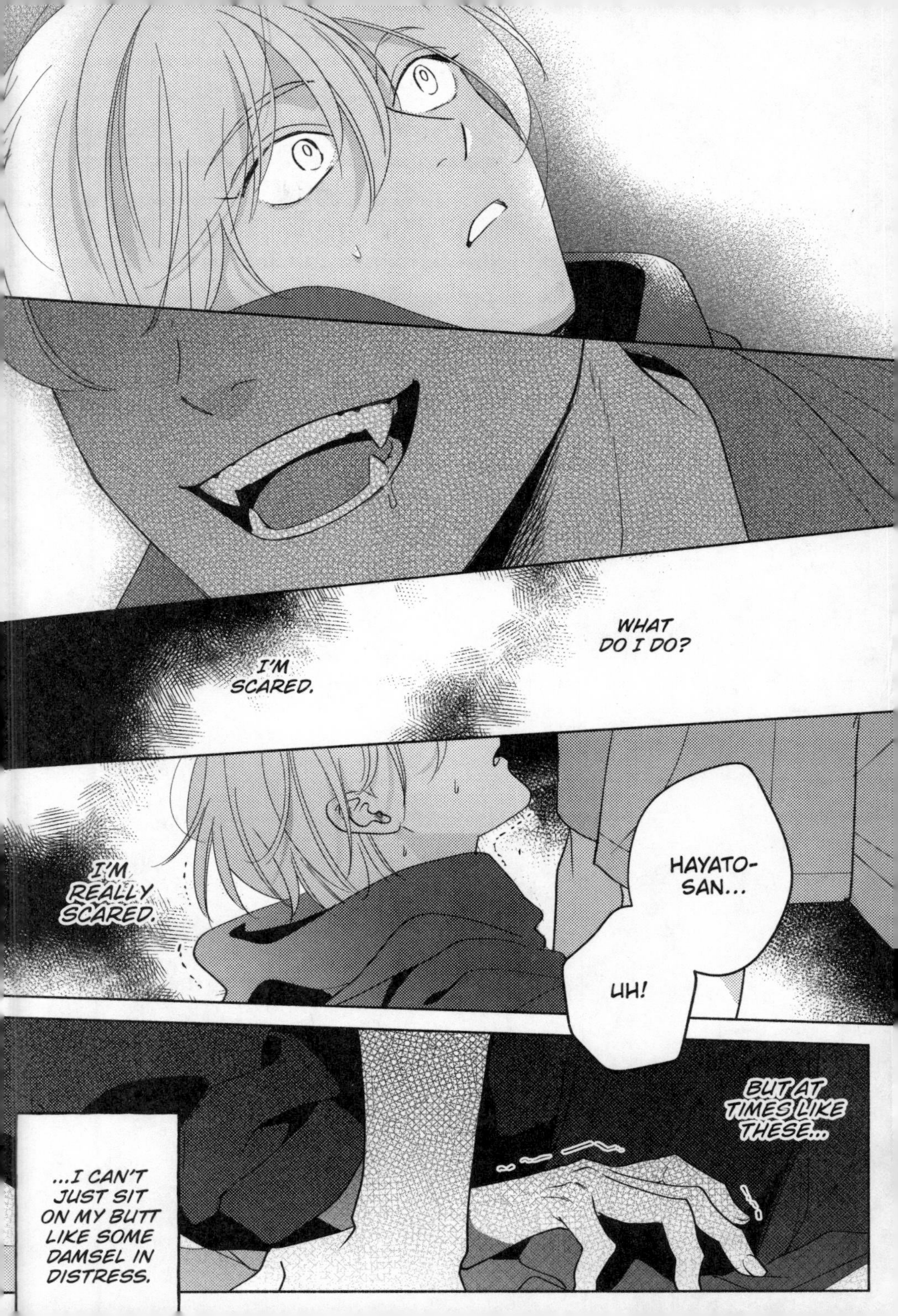
WHAT DO I DO?
I'M SCARED.
HAYATO-SAN...
I'M REALLY SCARED.
UH!
BUT AT TIMES LIKE THESE...
...I CAN'T JUST SIT ON MY BUTT LIKE SOME DAMSEL IN DISTRESS.

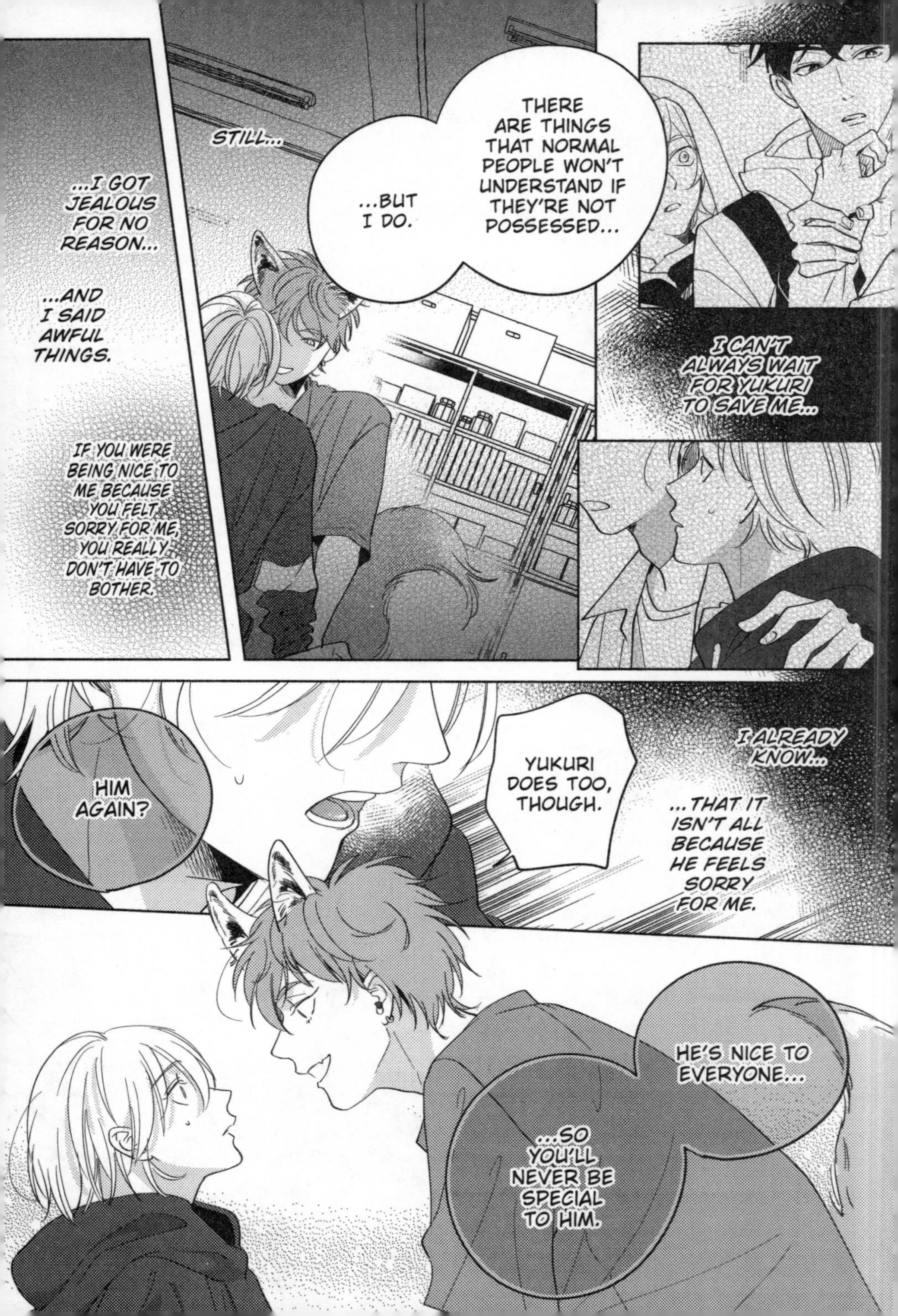
I CAN'T ALWAYS WAIT FOR YUKURI TO SAVE ME...
THERE ARE THINGS THAT NORMAL PEOPLE WON'T UNDERSTAND IF THEY'RE NOT POSSESSED...
...BUT I DO.
STILL...
...I GOT JEALOUS FOR NO REASON...
...AND I SAID AWFUL THINGS.
IF YOU WERE BEING NICE TO ME BECAUSE YOU FELT SORRY FOR ME, YOU REALLY DON'T HAVE TO BOTHER.
I ALREADY KNOW...
...THAT IT ISN'T ALL BECAUSE HE FEELS SORRY FOR ME.
YUKURI DOES TOO, THOUGH.
HIM AGAIN?
HE'S NICE TO EVERYONE...
...SO YOU'LL NEVER BE SPECIAL TO HIM.

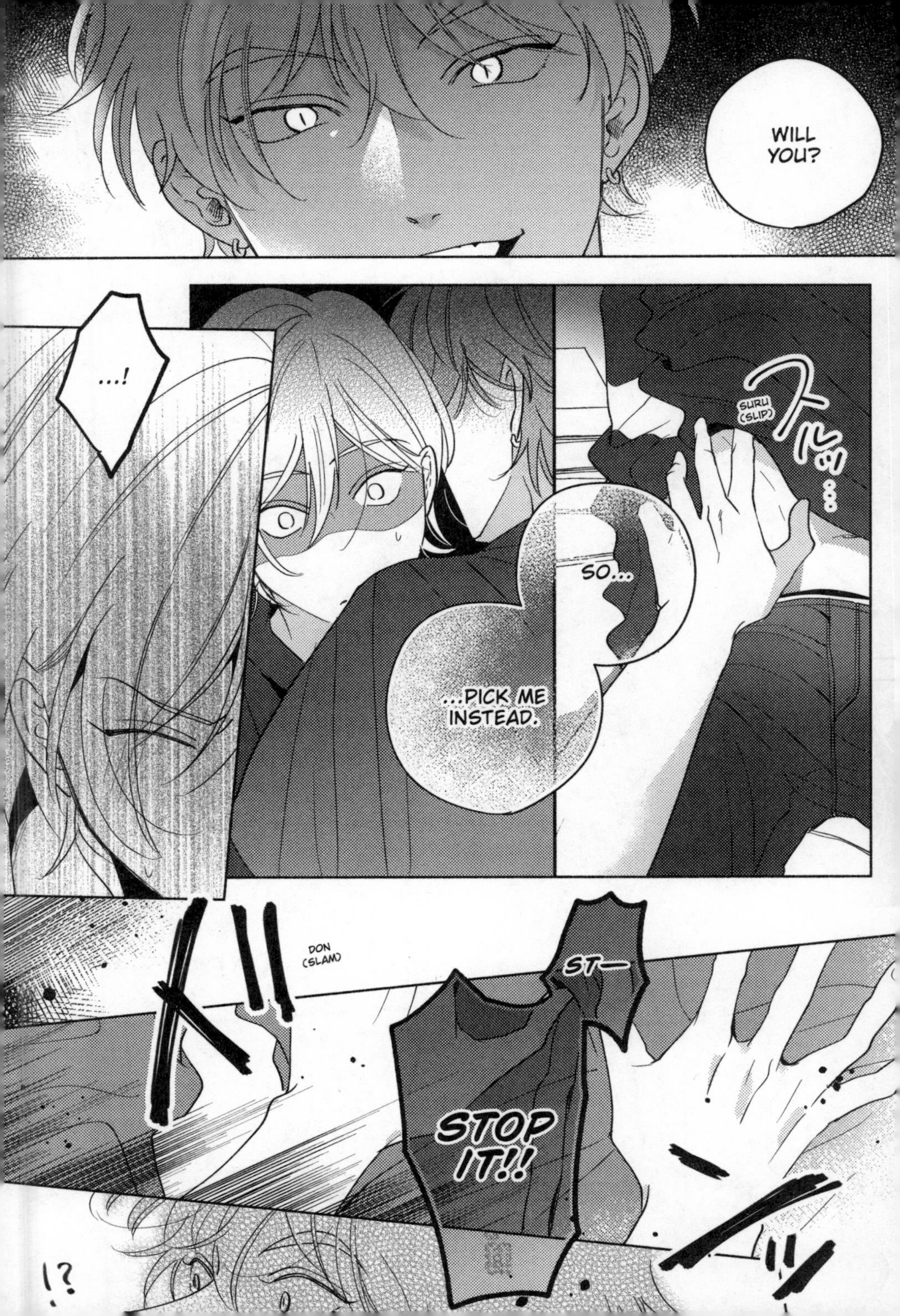
WILL YOU?
スルッ…
SURU (SLIP)
SO...
...PICK ME INSTEAD.
...!
ST—
STOP IT!!
DON (SLAM)
!?

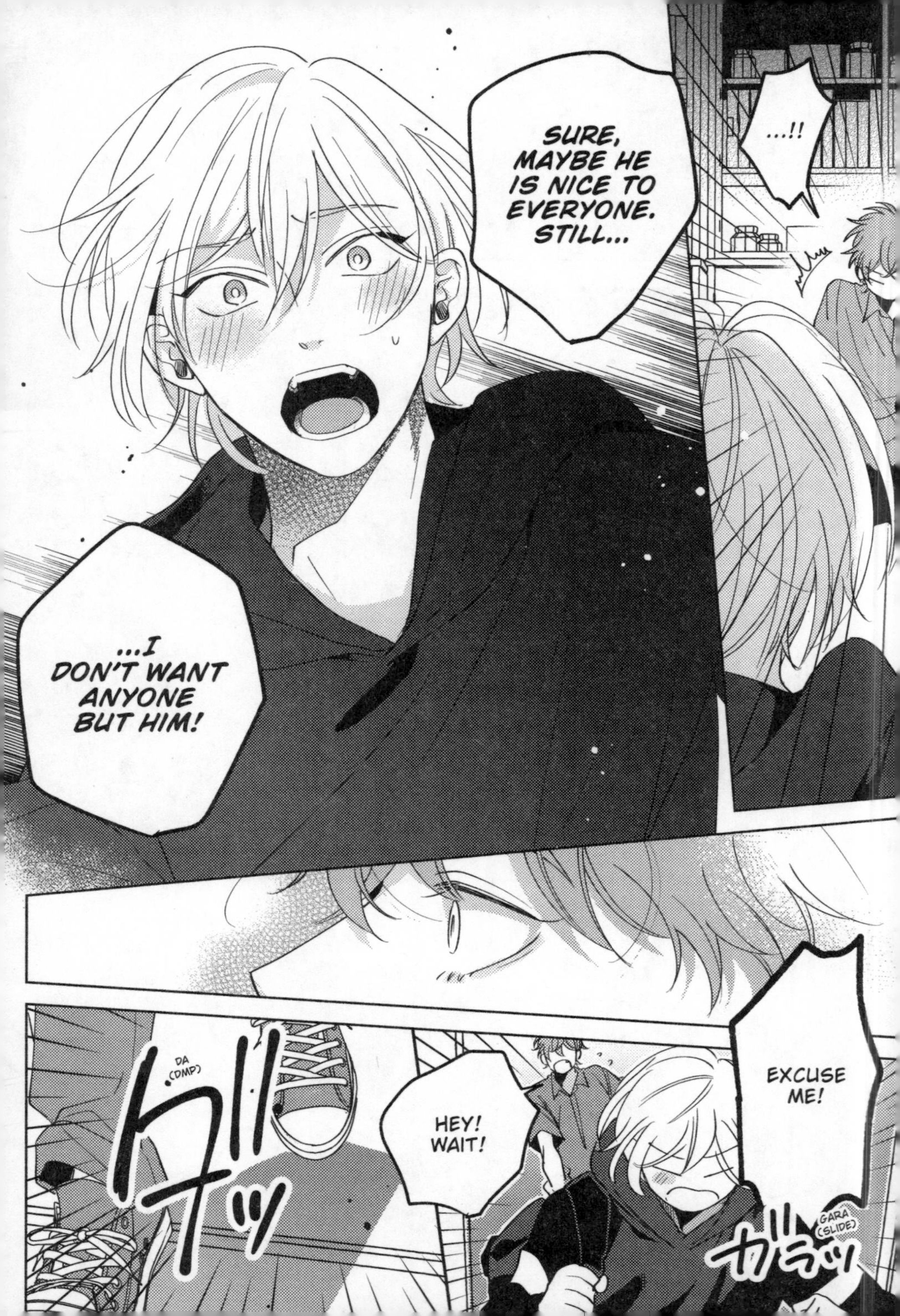
...!!
SURE, MAYBE HE IS NICE TO EVERYONE. STILL...
...I DON'T WANT ANYONE BUT HIM!
EXCUSE ME!
GARA (SLIDE)
HEY! WAIT!
DA (DMP)

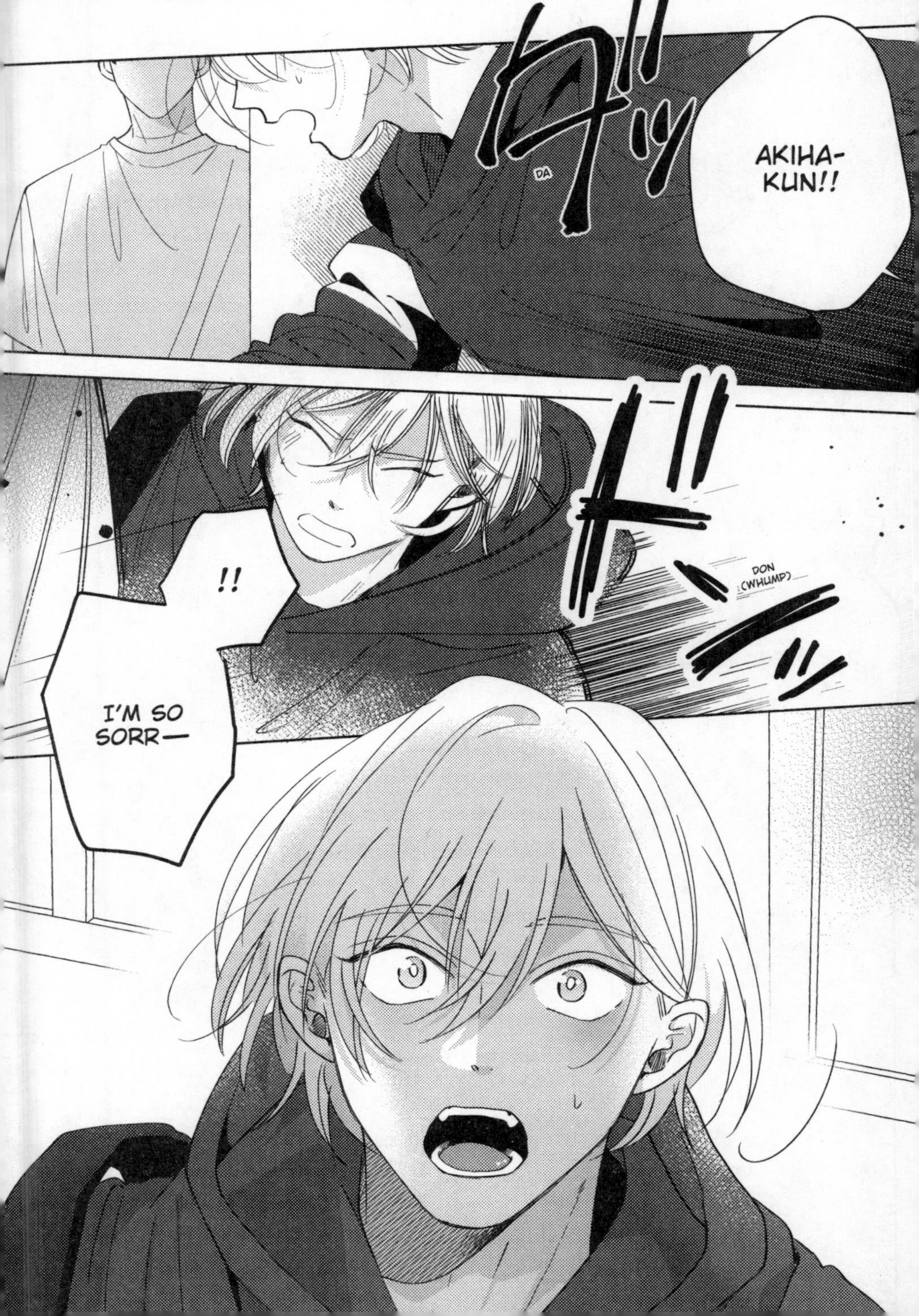
AKIHA-KUN!!
DA
DON (WHUMP)
!!
I'M SO SORR—

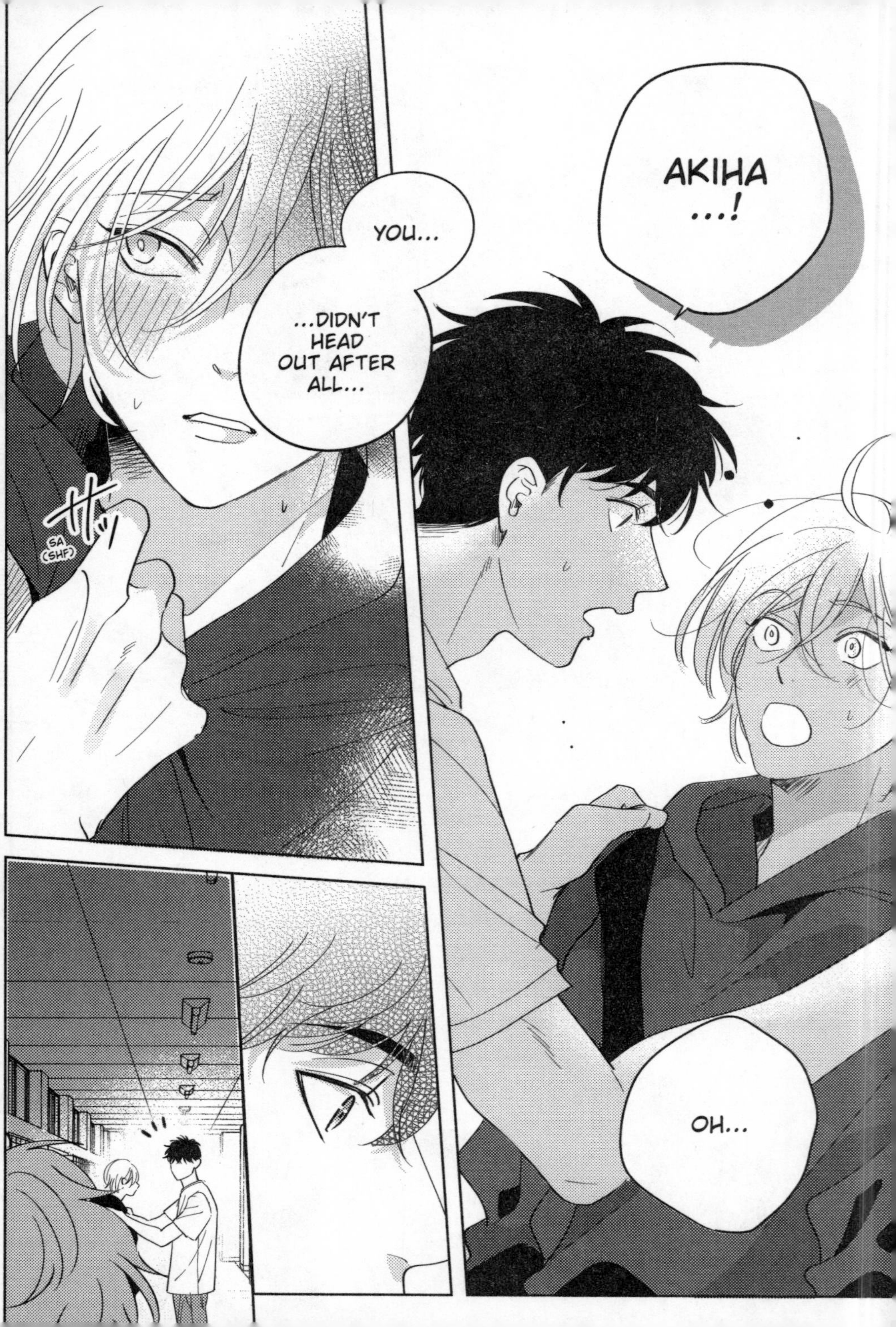
AKIHA ...!
OH...
YOU...
...DIDN'T HEAD OUT AFTER ALL...
SA (SHF)

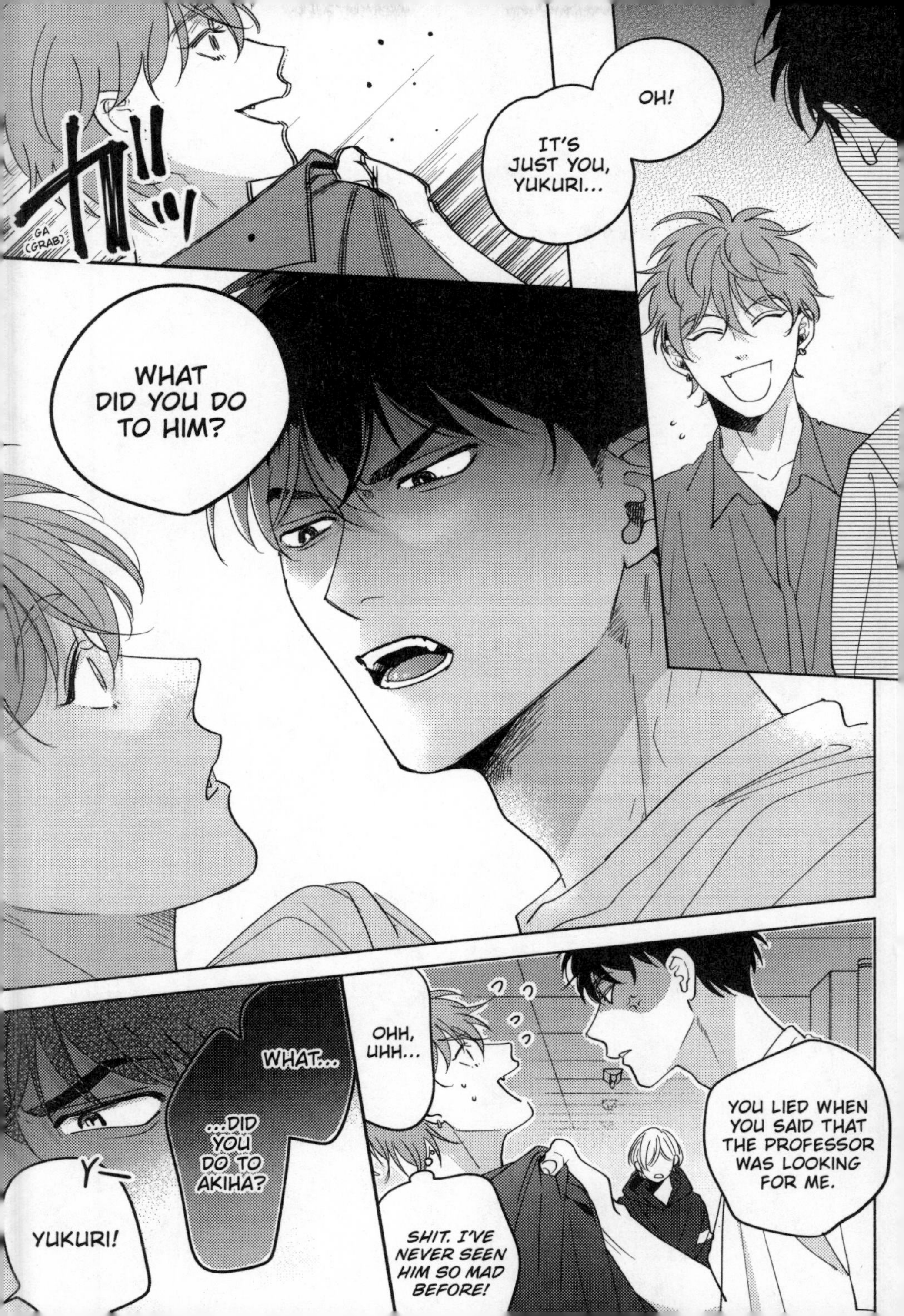
OH!
IT'S JUST YOU, YUKURI...
GA (GRAB)
WHAT DID YOU DO TO HIM?
YOU LIED WHEN YOU SAID THAT THE PROFESSOR WAS LOOKING FOR ME.
OHH, UHH...
SHIT. I'VE NEVER SEEN HIM SO MAD BEFORE!
WHAT...
...DID YOU DO TO AKIHA?
Y—
YUKURI!

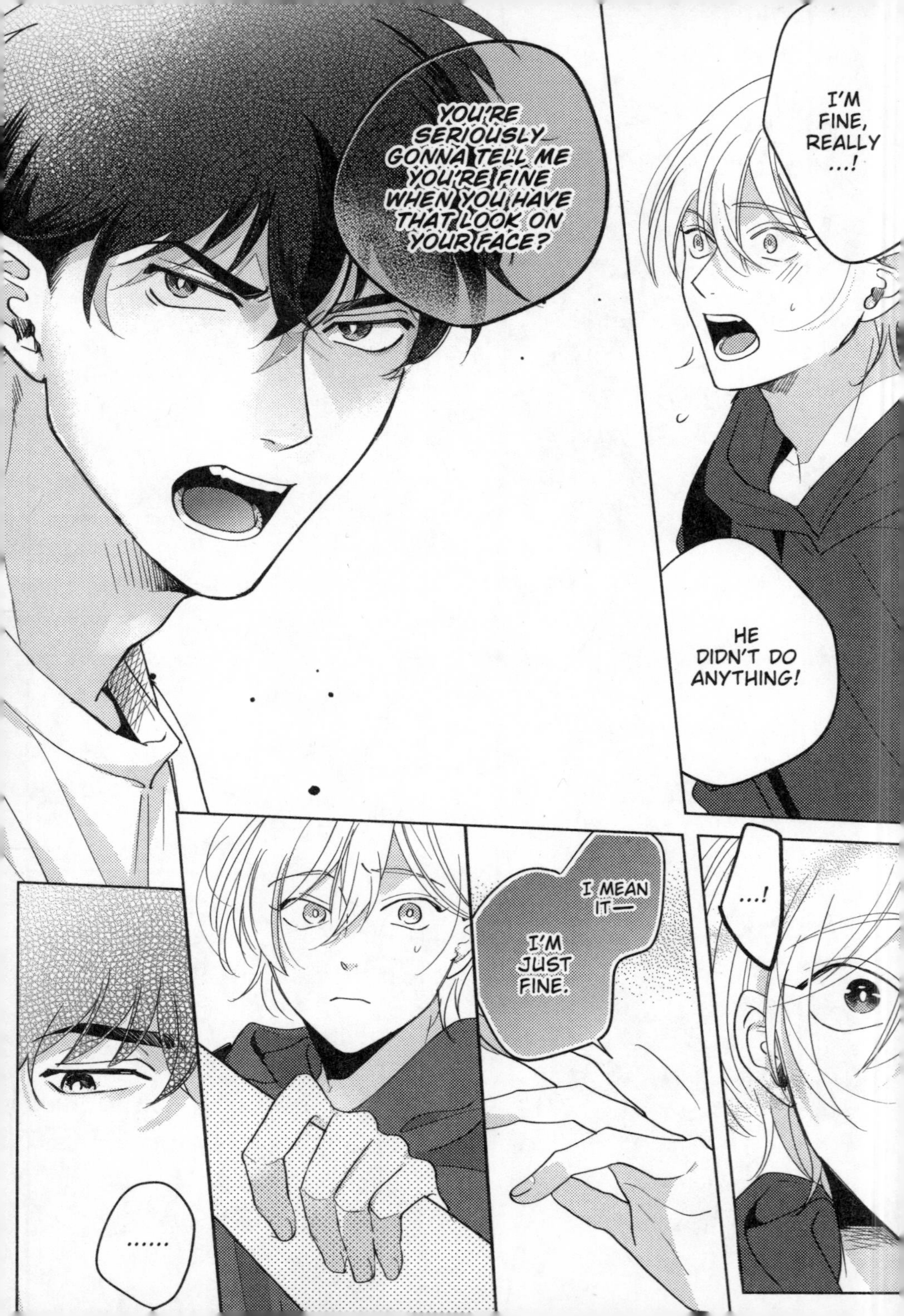
I'M FINE, REALLY ...!
HE DIDN'T DO ANYTHING!
YOU'RE SERIOUSLY GONNA TELL ME YOU'RE FINE WHEN YOU HAVE THAT LOOK ON YOUR FACE?
...!
I MEAN IT—
I'M JUST FINE.
......

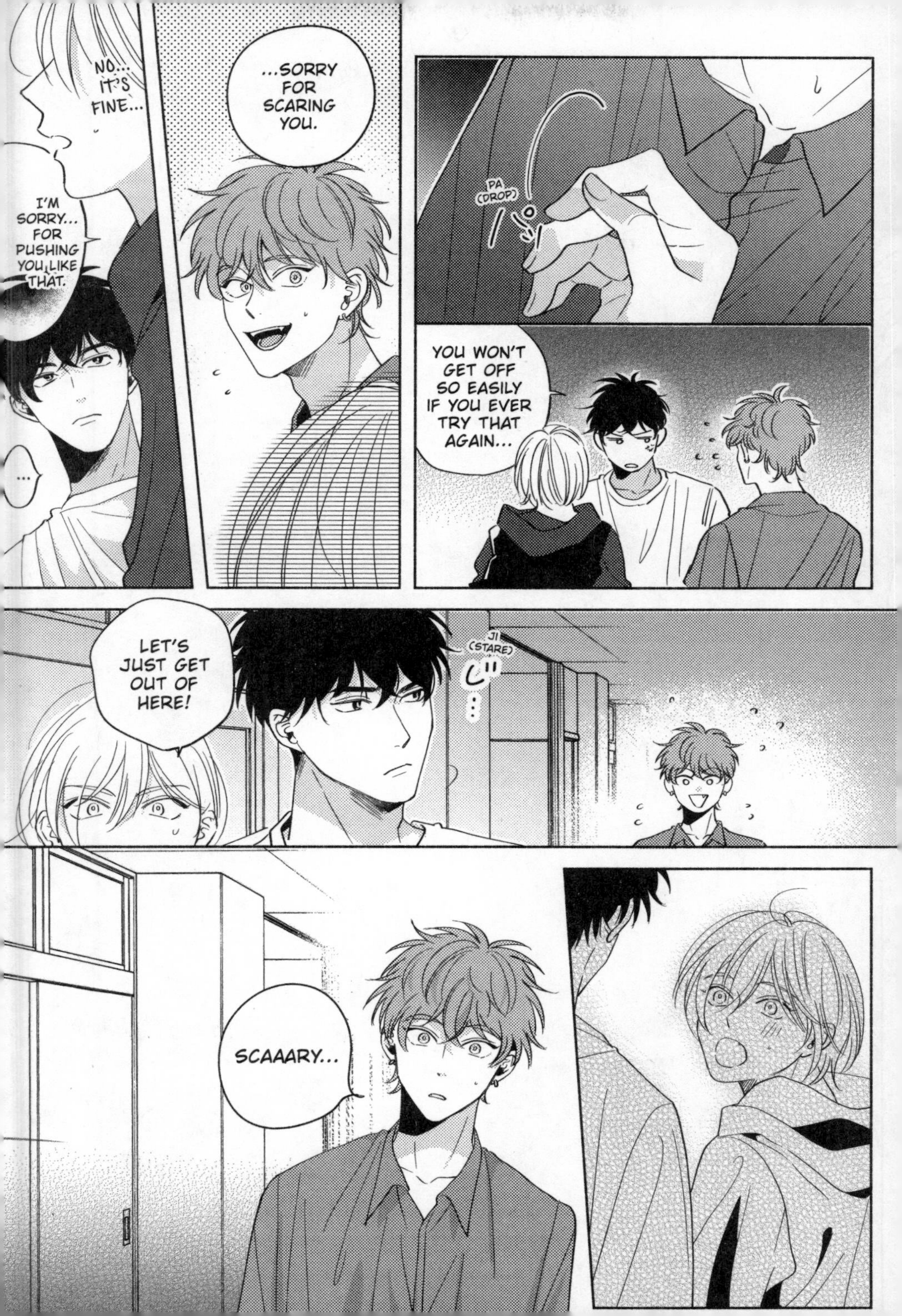
PA (DROP)
YOU WON'T GET OFF SO EASILY IF YOU EVER TRY THAT AGAIN...
...SORRY FOR SCARING YOU.
NO... IT'S FINE...
I'M SORRY... FOR PUSHING YOU LIKE THAT.
...
JI (STARE)
LET'S JUST GET OUT OF HERE!
SCAAARY...

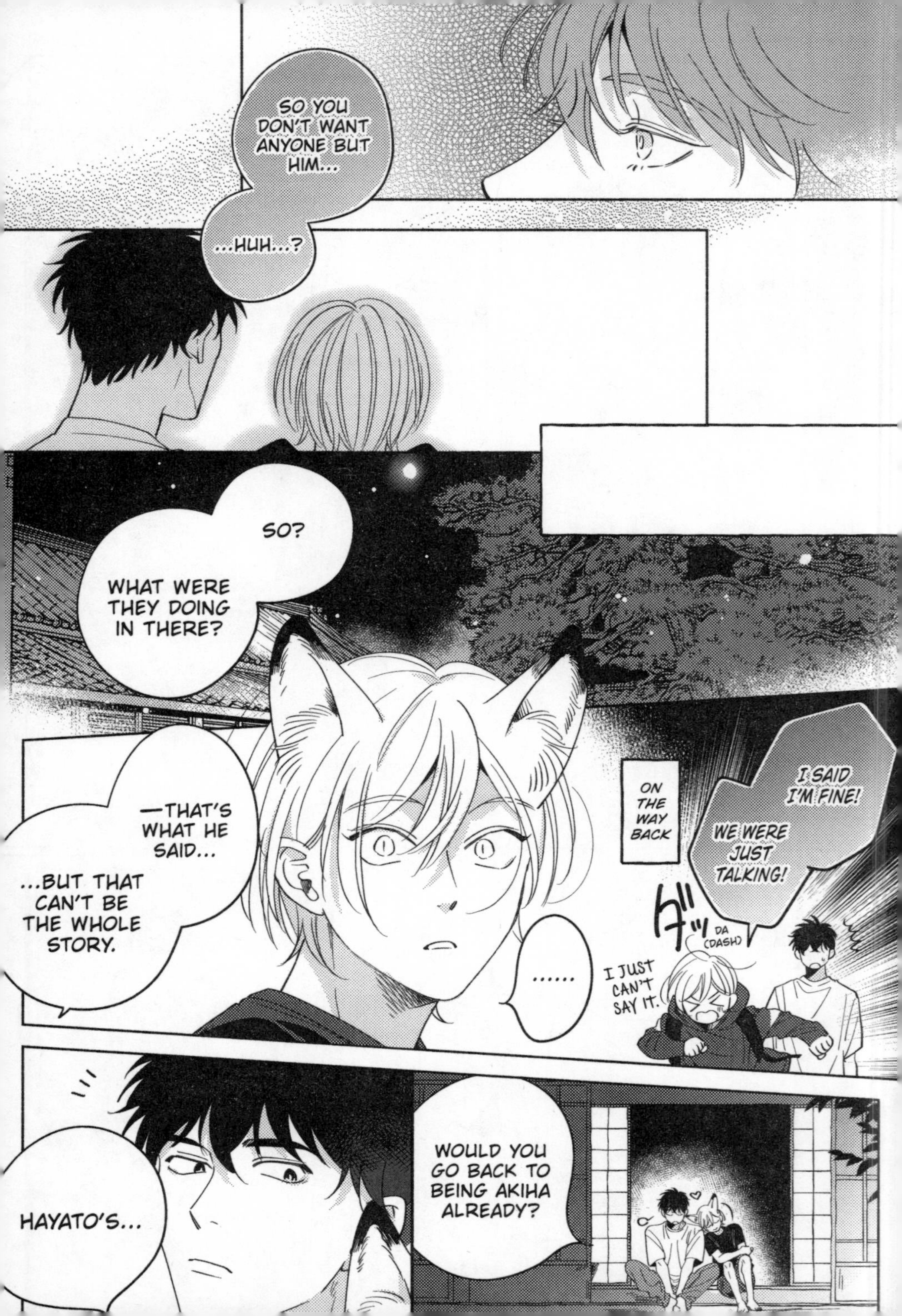
SO YOU DON'T WANT ANYONE BUT HIM...
...HUH...?
SO?
WHAT WERE THEY DOING IN THERE?
ON THE WAY BACK
I SAID I'M FINE!
WE WERE JUST TALKING!
ダッ DA (DASH)
I JUST CAN'T SAY IT.
—THAT'S WHAT HE SAID...
...BUT THAT CAN'T BE THE WHOLE STORY.
......
WOULD YOU GO BACK TO BEING AKIHA ALREADY?
HAYATO'S...

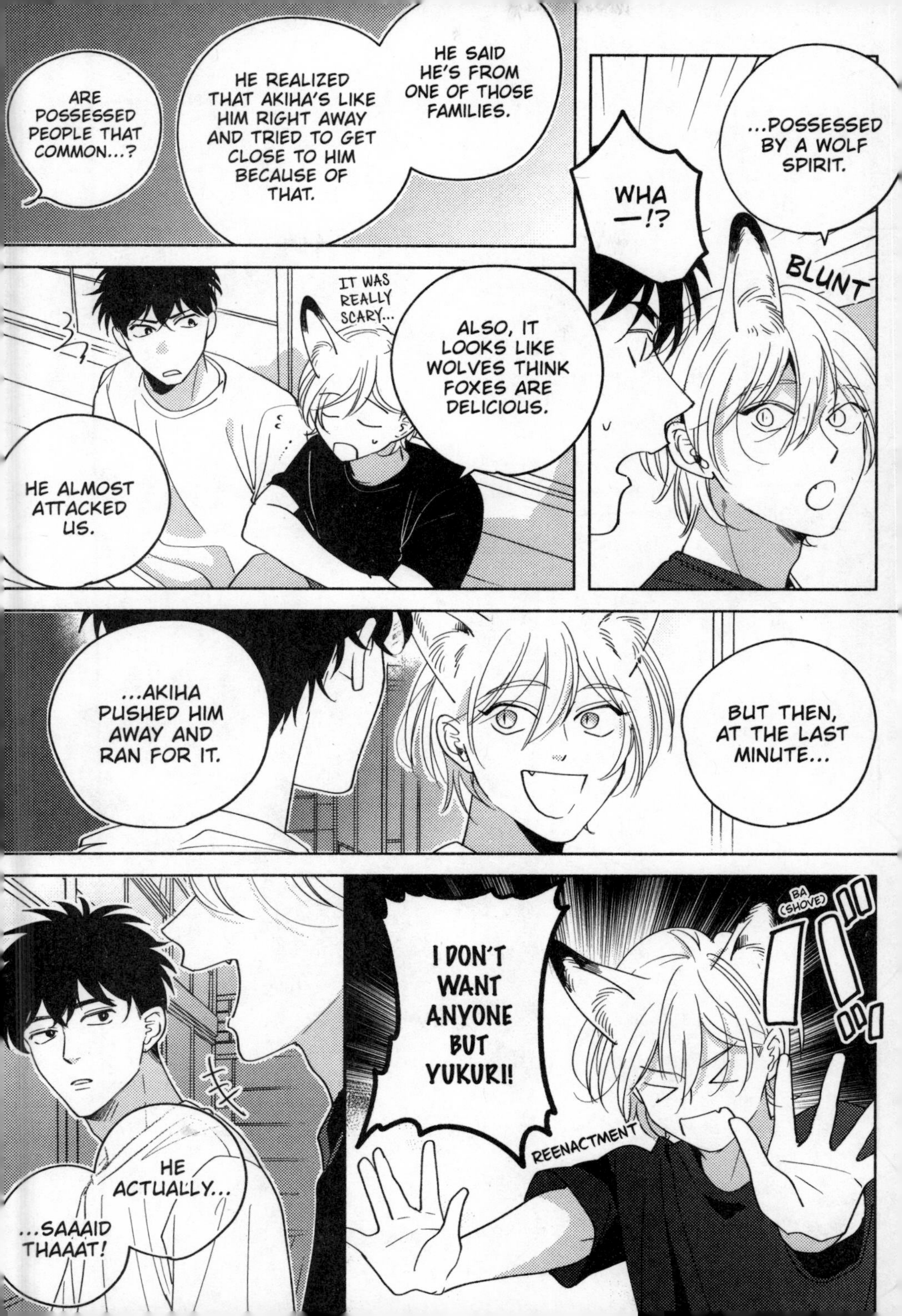
HE SAID HE'S FROM ONE OF THOSE FAMILIES.
HE REALIZED THAT AKIHA'S LIKE HIM RIGHT AWAY AND TRIED TO GET CLOSE TO HIM BECAUSE OF THAT.
ARE POSSESSED PEOPLE THAT COMMON...?
...POSSESSED BY A WOLF SPIRIT.
WHA—!?
BLUNT
ALSO, IT LOOKS LIKE WOLVES THINK FOXES ARE DELICIOUS.
IT WAS REALLY SCARY...
HE ALMOST ATTACKED US.
BUT THEN, AT THE LAST MINUTE...
...AKIHA PUSHED HIM AWAY AND RAN FOR IT.
BA (SHOVE)
I DON'T WANT ANYONE BUT YUKURI!
REENACTMENT
HE ACTUALLY...
...SAAAID THAAAT!

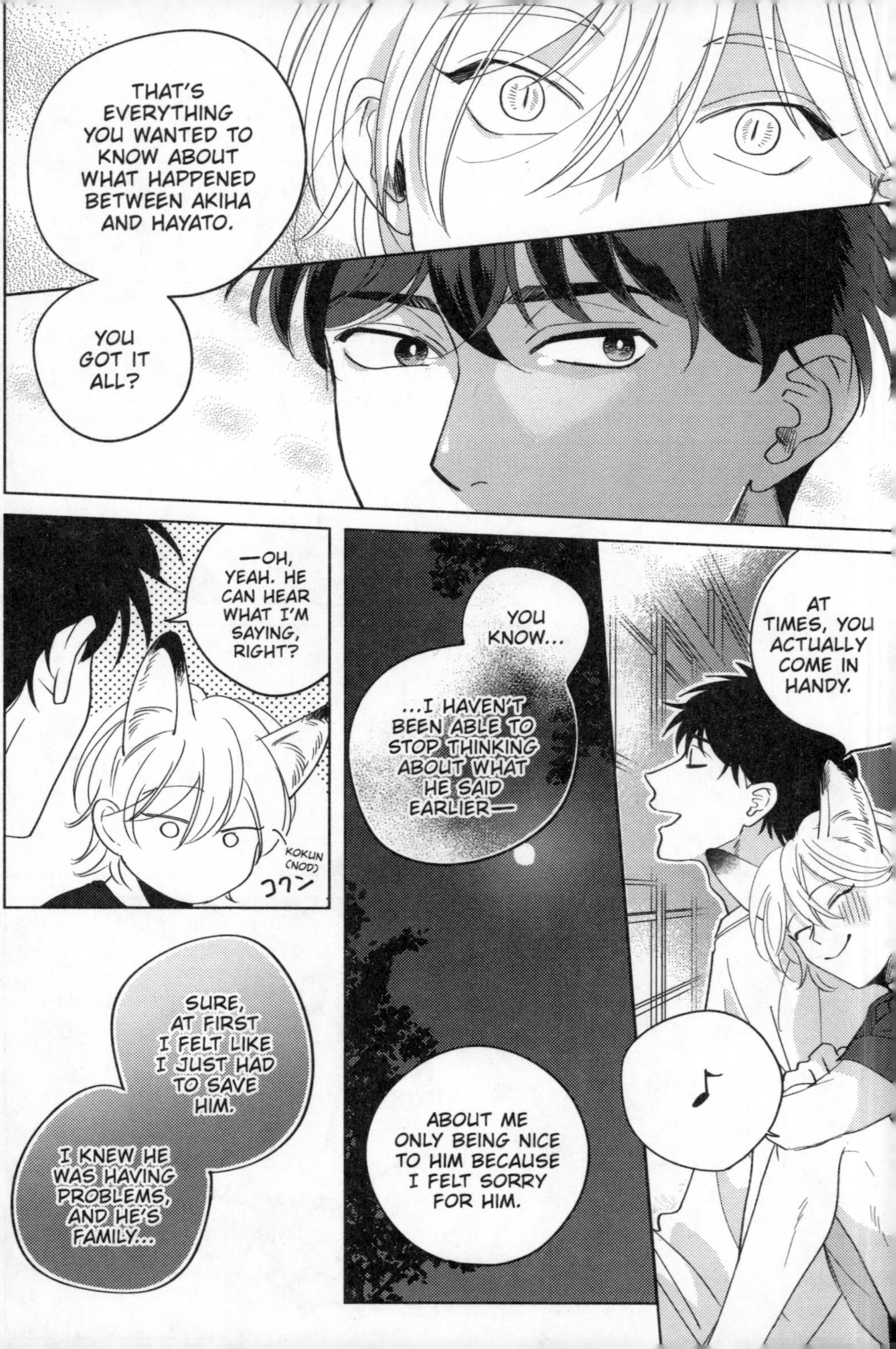
THAT'S EVERYTHING YOU WANTED TO KNOW ABOUT WHAT HAPPENED BETWEEN AKIHA AND HAYATO.
YOU GOT IT ALL?
AT TIMES, YOU ACTUALLY COME IN HANDY.
♪
—OH, YEAH. HE CAN HEAR WHAT I'M SAYING, RIGHT?
KOKUN (NOD)
コクン
YOU KNOW...
...I HAVEN'T BEEN ABLE TO STOP THINKING ABOUT WHAT HE SAID EARLIER—
ABOUT ME ONLY BEING NICE TO HIM BECAUSE I FELT SORRY FOR HIM.
SURE, AT FIRST I FELT LIKE I JUST HAD TO SAVE HIM.
I KNEW HE WAS HAVING PROBLEMS, AND HE'S FAMILY...

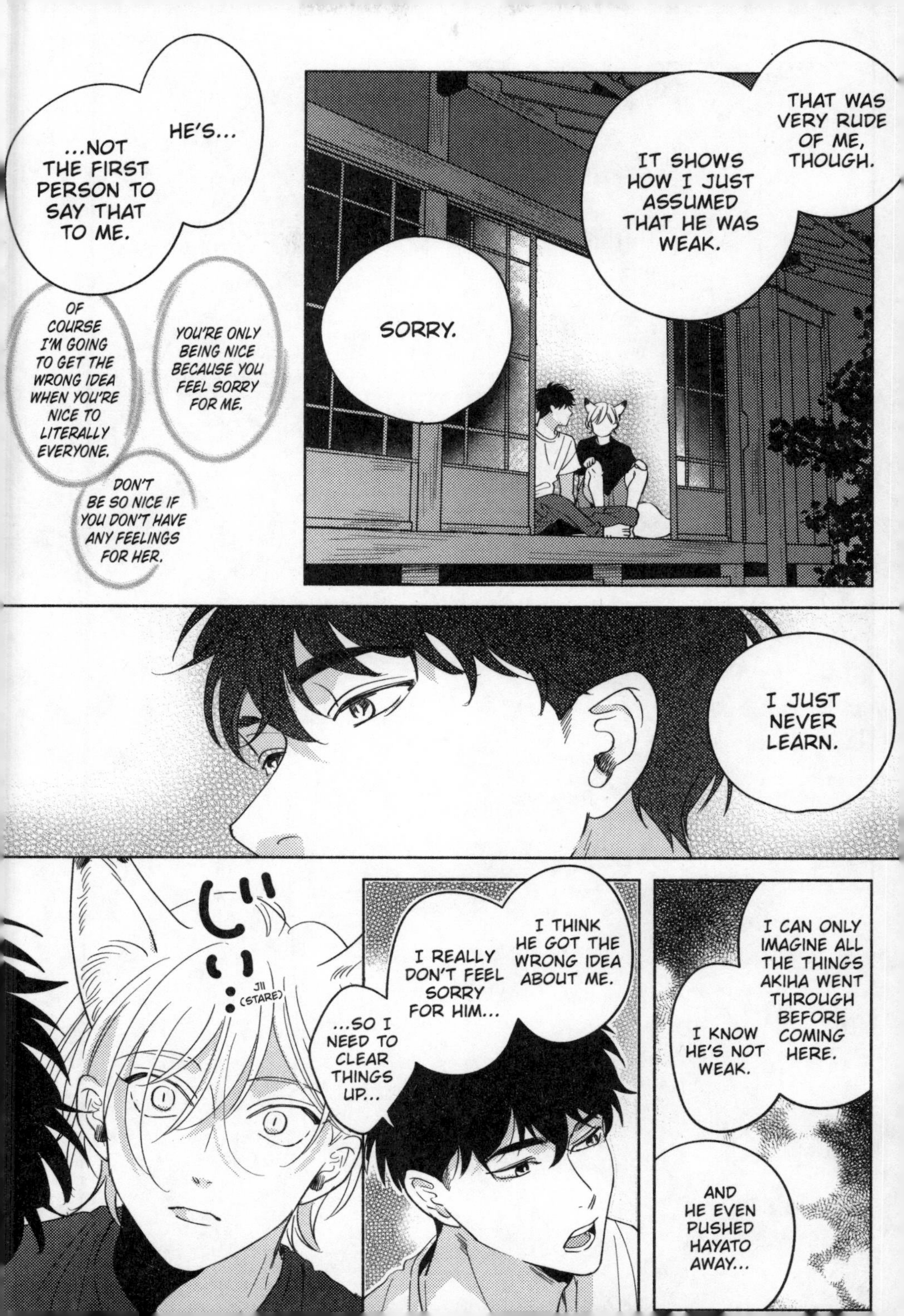
THAT WAS VERY RUDE OF ME, THOUGH.
IT SHOWS HOW I JUST ASSUMED THAT HE WAS WEAK.
SORRY.
HE'S...
...NOT THE FIRST PERSON TO SAY THAT TO ME.
YOU'RE ONLY BEING NICE BECAUSE YOU FEEL SORRY FOR ME.
OF COURSE I'M GOING TO GET THE WRONG IDEA WHEN YOU'RE NICE TO LITERALLY EVERYONE.
DON'T BE SO NICE IF YOU DON'T HAVE ANY FEELINGS FOR HER.
I JUST NEVER LEARN.
I CAN ONLY IMAGINE ALL THE THINGS AKIHA WENT THROUGH BEFORE COMING HERE.
I KNOW HE'S NOT WEAK.
AND HE EVEN PUSHED HAYATO AWAY...
I THINK HE GOT THE WRONG IDEA ABOUT ME.
I REALLY DON'T FEEL SORRY FOR HIM...
...SO I NEED TO CLEAR THINGS UP...
じ
JII (STARE)

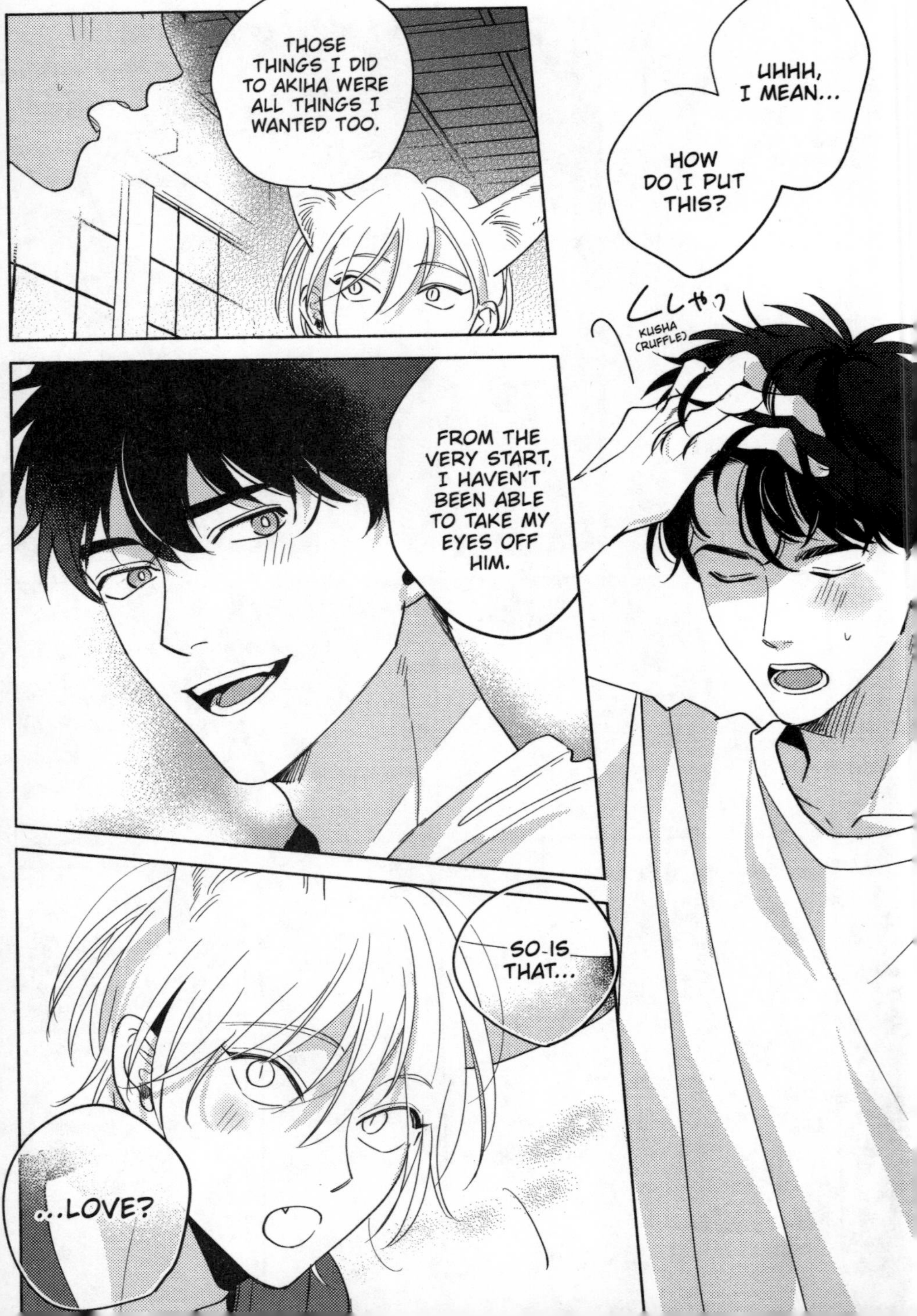
UHHH, I MEAN...
HOW DO I PUT THIS?
くしゃっ
KUSHA (RUFFLE)
THOSE THINGS I DID TO AKIHA WERE ALL THINGS I WANTED TOO.
FROM THE VERY START, I HAVEN'T BEEN ABLE TO TAKE MY EYES OFF HIM.
SO IS THAT...
...LOVE?

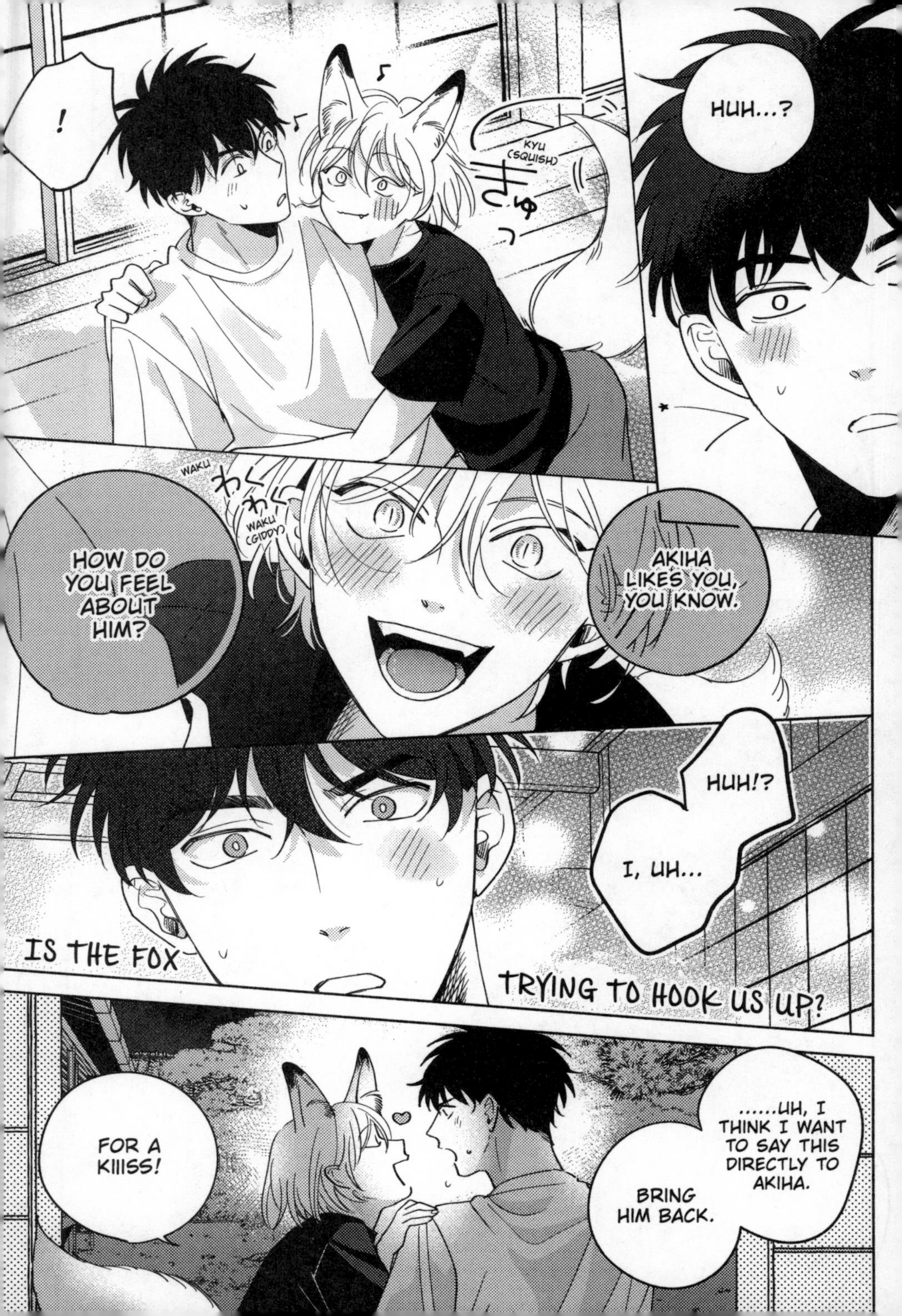
HUH...?
!
KYU (SQUISH)
きゅっ
AKIHA LIKES YOU, YOU KNOW.
WAKU WAKU (GIDDY)
わくわく
HOW DO YOU FEEL ABOUT HIM?
HUH!?
I, UH...
IS THE FOX TRYING TO HOOK US UP?
......UH, I THINK I WANT TO SAY THIS DIRECTLY TO AKIHA.
BRING HIM BACK.
FOR A KIIISS!

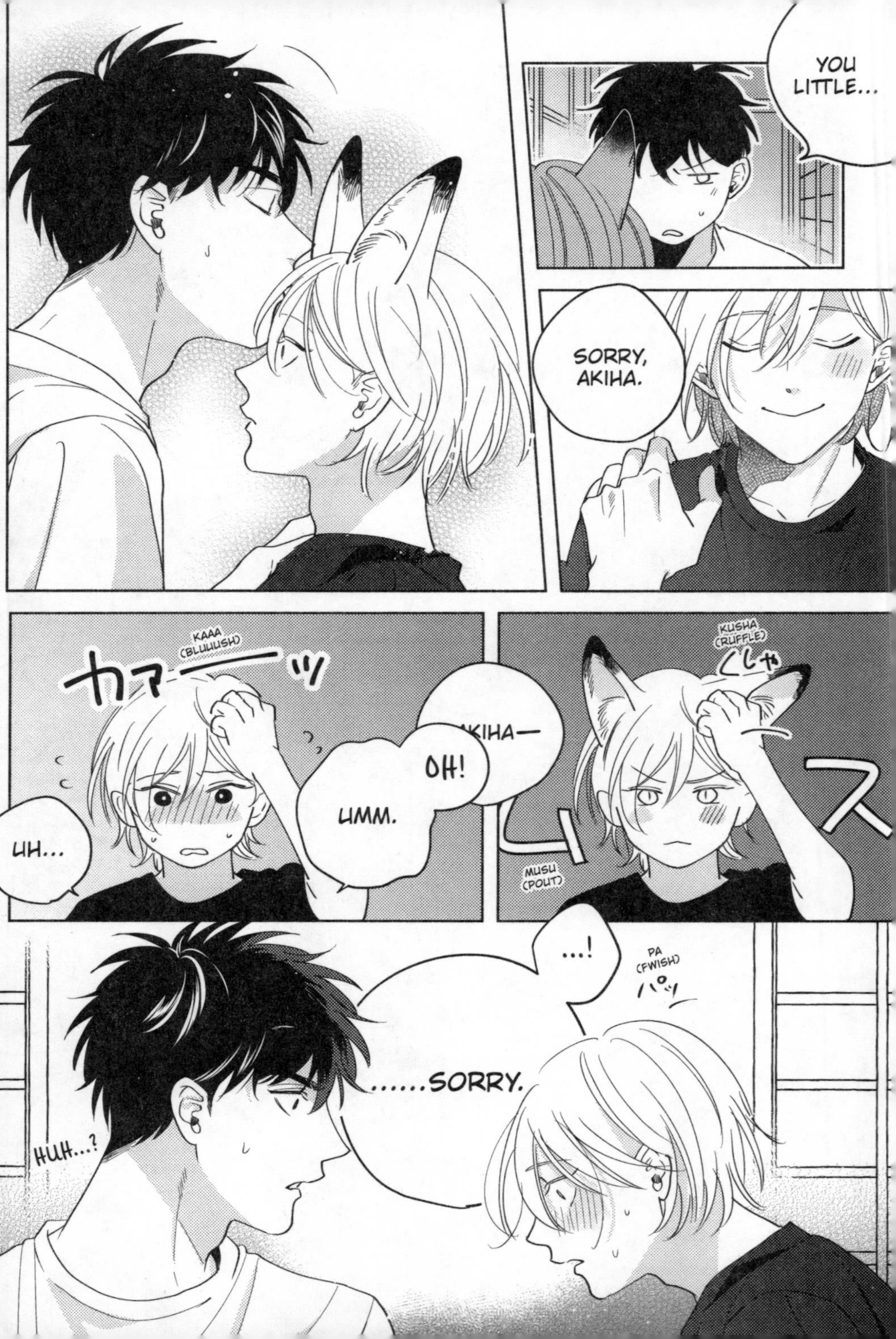

YOU LITTLE...
SORRY, AKIHA.
KUSHA (RUFFLE)
くしゃ
KIHA—
ムス
MUSU (POUT)
OH!
UMM.
カァーッ
KAAA (BLUUUSH)
UH...
...!
PA (FWISH)
パッ
......SORRY.
HUH...?

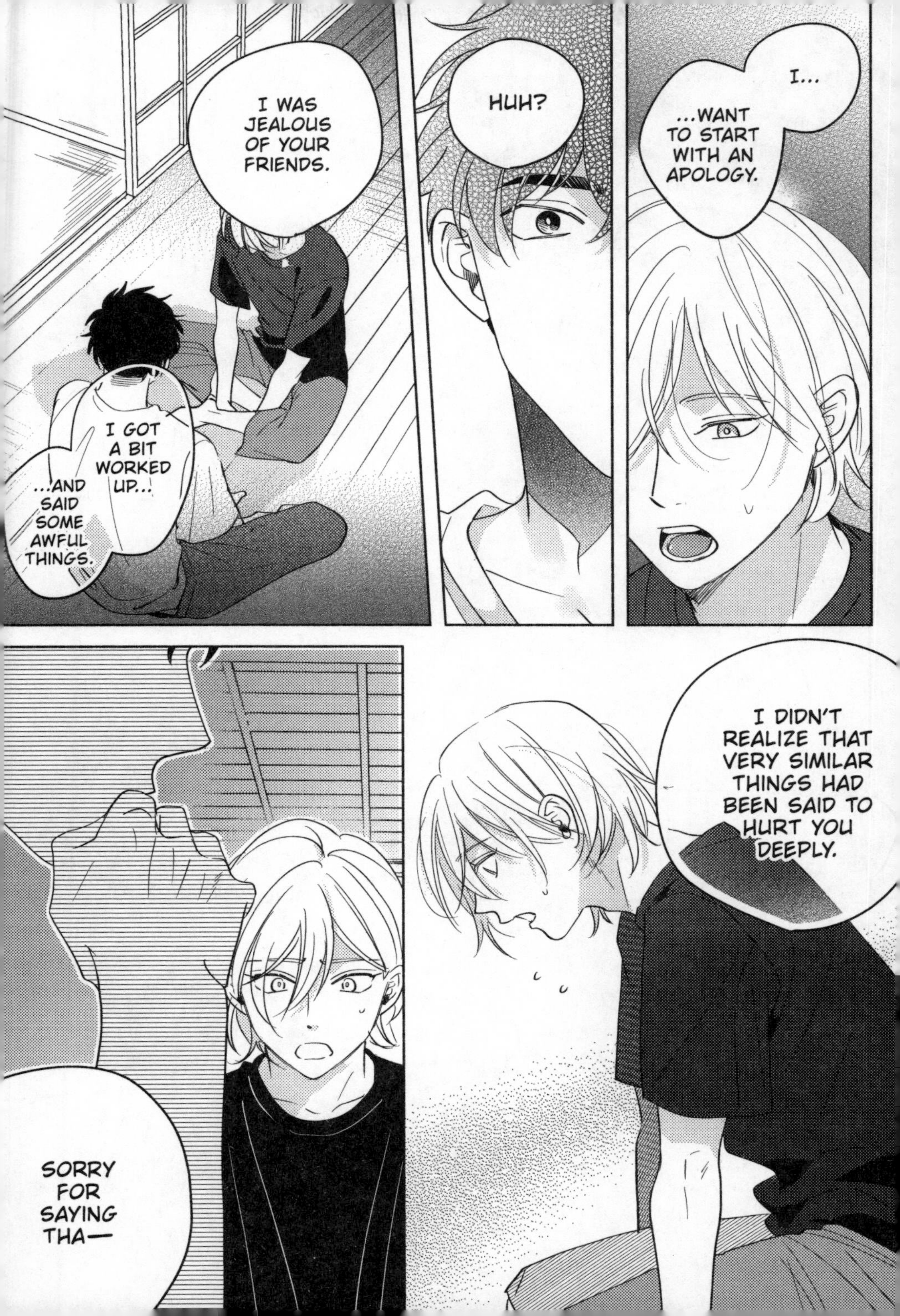
I...
...WANT TO START WITH AN APOLOGY.
HUH?
I WAS JEALOUS OF YOUR FRIENDS.
I GOT A BIT WORKED UP...
...AND SAID SOME AWFUL THINGS.
I DIDN'T REALIZE THAT VERY SIMILAR THINGS HAD BEEN SAID TO HURT YOU DEEPLY.
SORRY FOR SAYING THA—

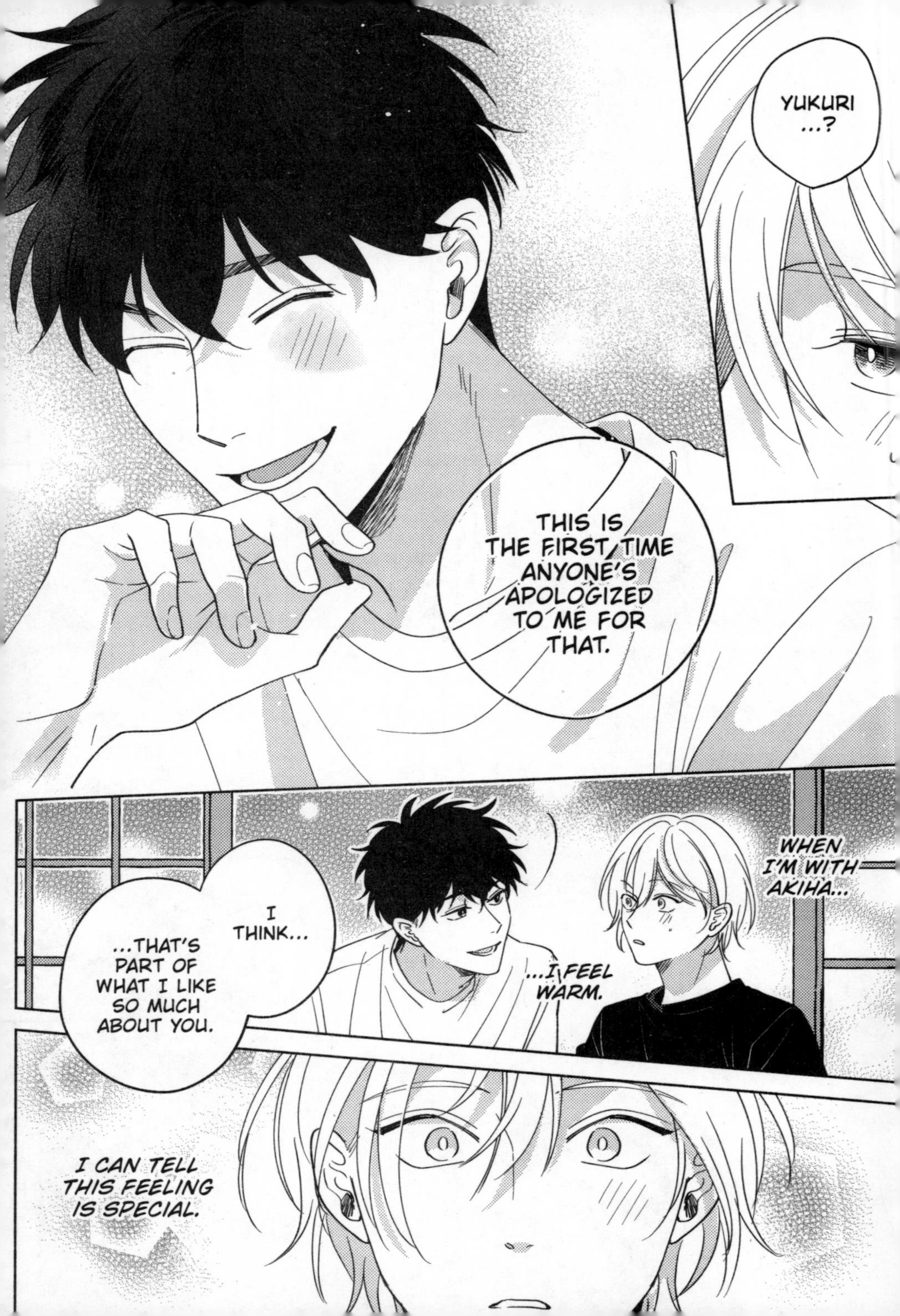
YUKURI ...?
THIS IS THE FIRST TIME ANYONE'S APOLOGIZED TO ME FOR THAT.
WHEN I'M WITH AKIHA...
...I FEEL WARM.
I THINK...
...THAT'S PART OF WHAT I LIKE SO MUCH ABOUT YOU.
I CAN TELL THIS FEELING IS SPECIAL.

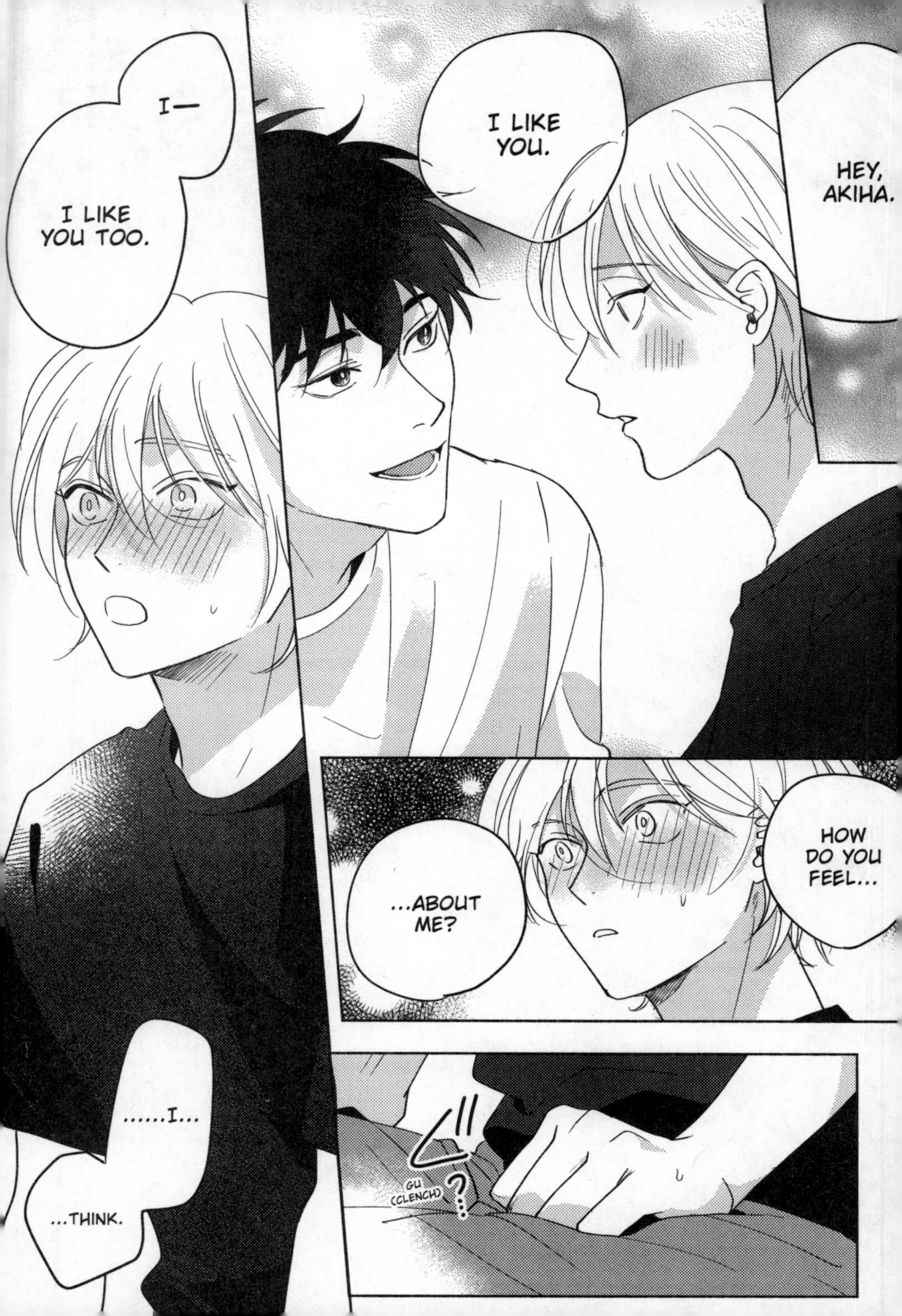
HEY, AKIHA.
I LIKE YOU.
HOW DO YOU FEEL...
...ABOUT ME?
GU (CLENCH)
I—
I LIKE YOU TOO.
......I...
...THINK.

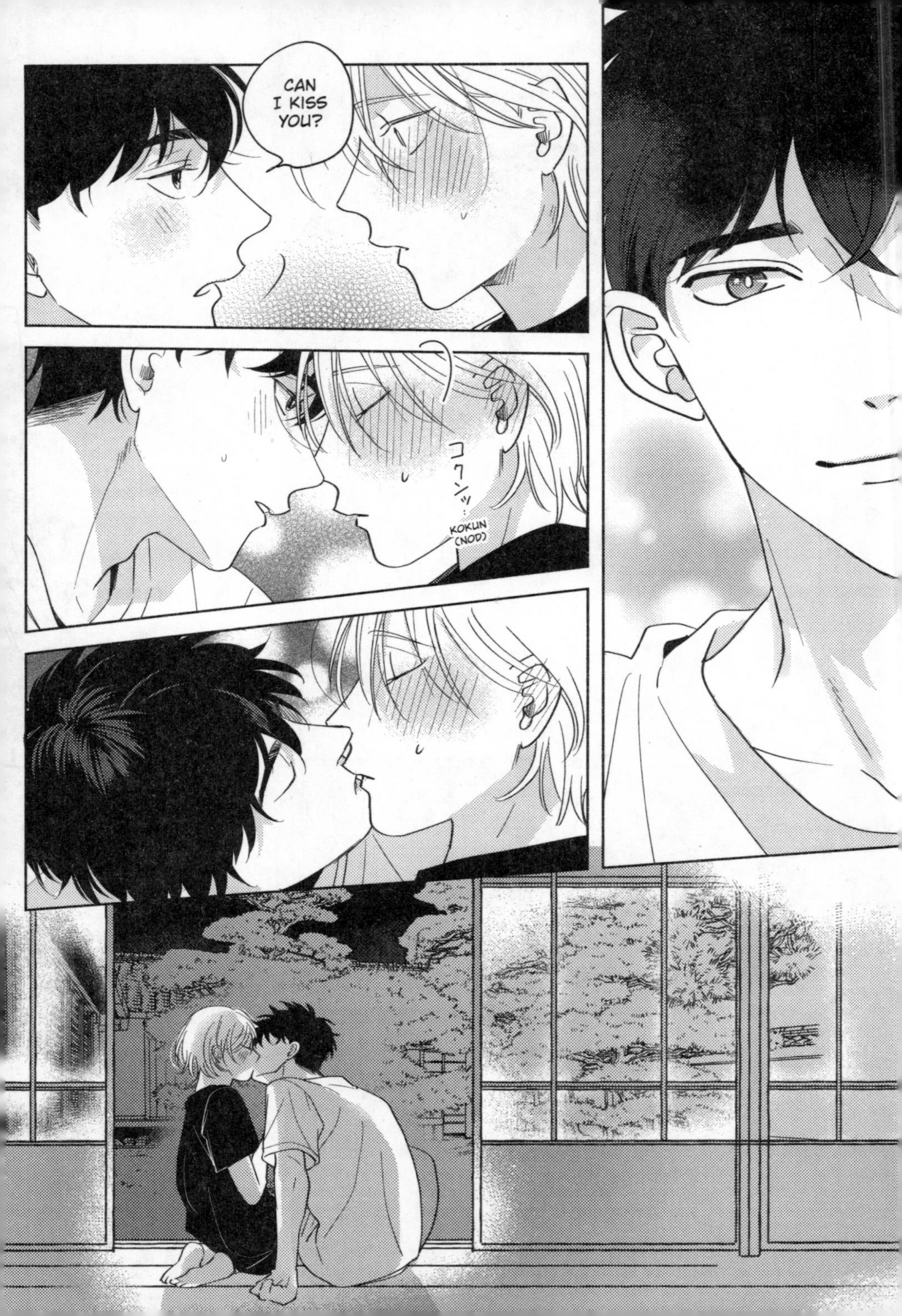
CAN I KISS YOU?
コクンッ
KOKUN (NOD)

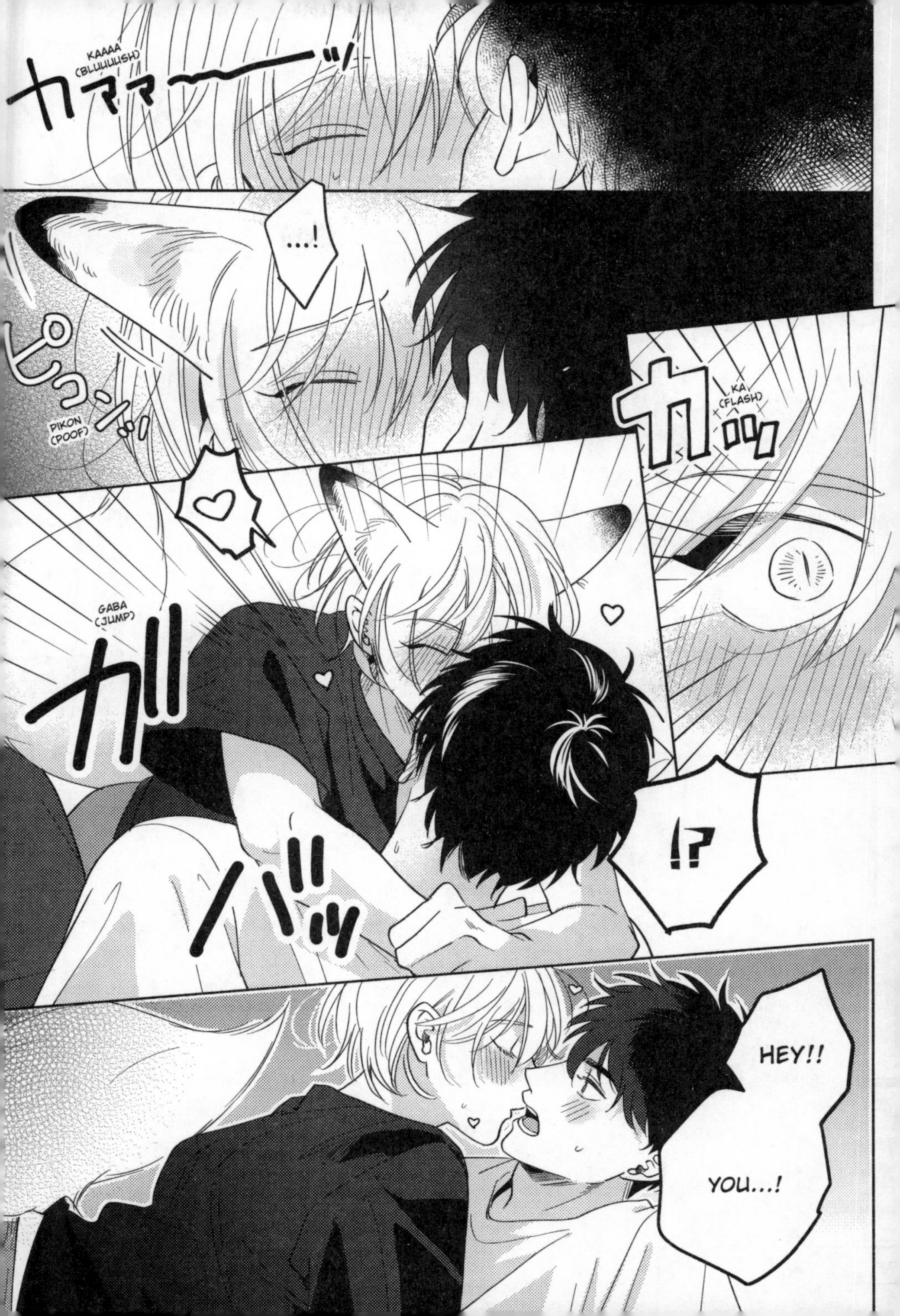
KAAAA (BLUUUUSH)
...!
PIKON (POOF)
KA (FLASH)
GABA (JUMP)
!?
HEY!!
YOU...!

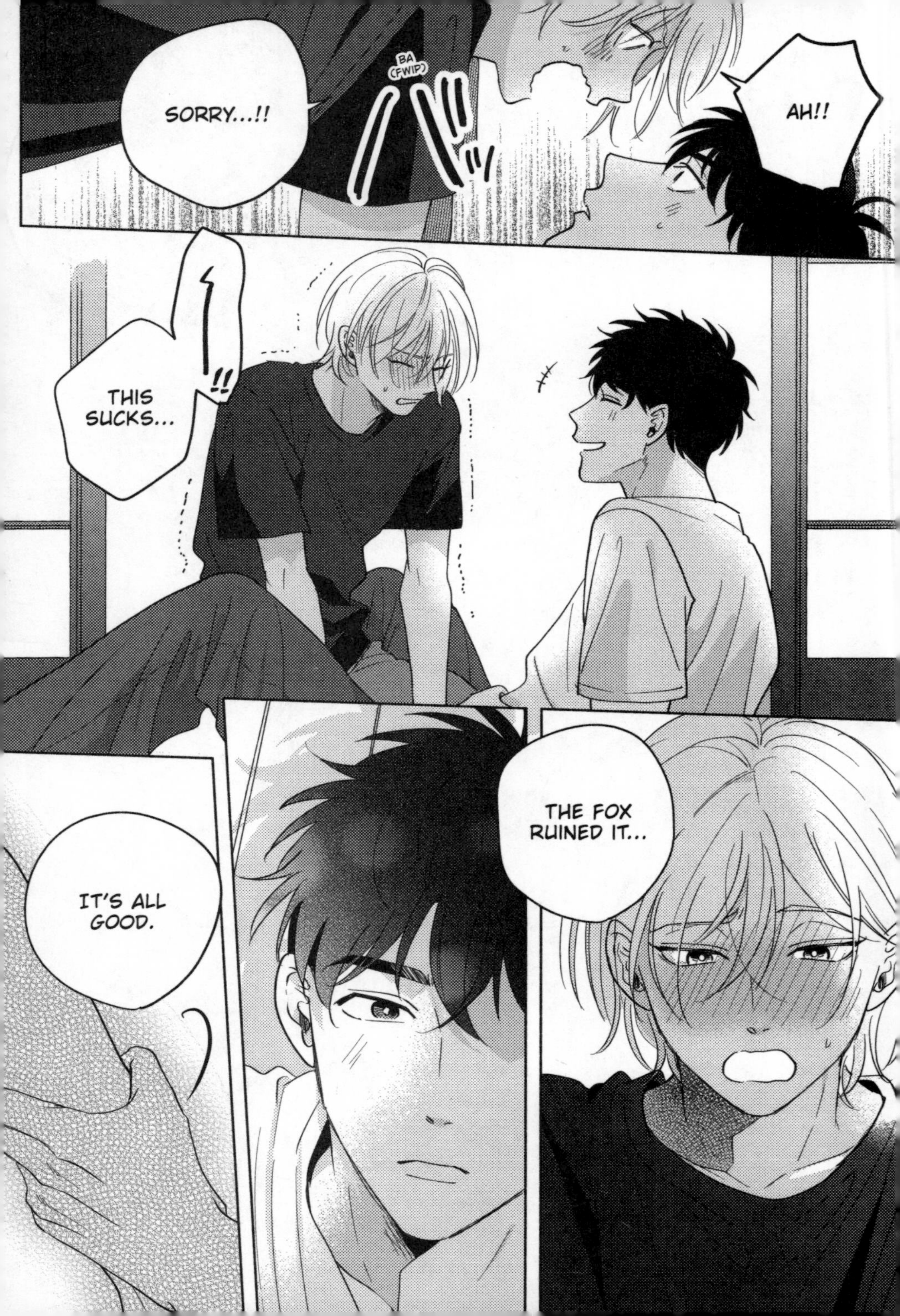
AH!!
BA (FWIP)
SORRY...!!
—!!
THIS SUCKS...
THE FOX RUINED IT...
IT'S ALL GOOD.

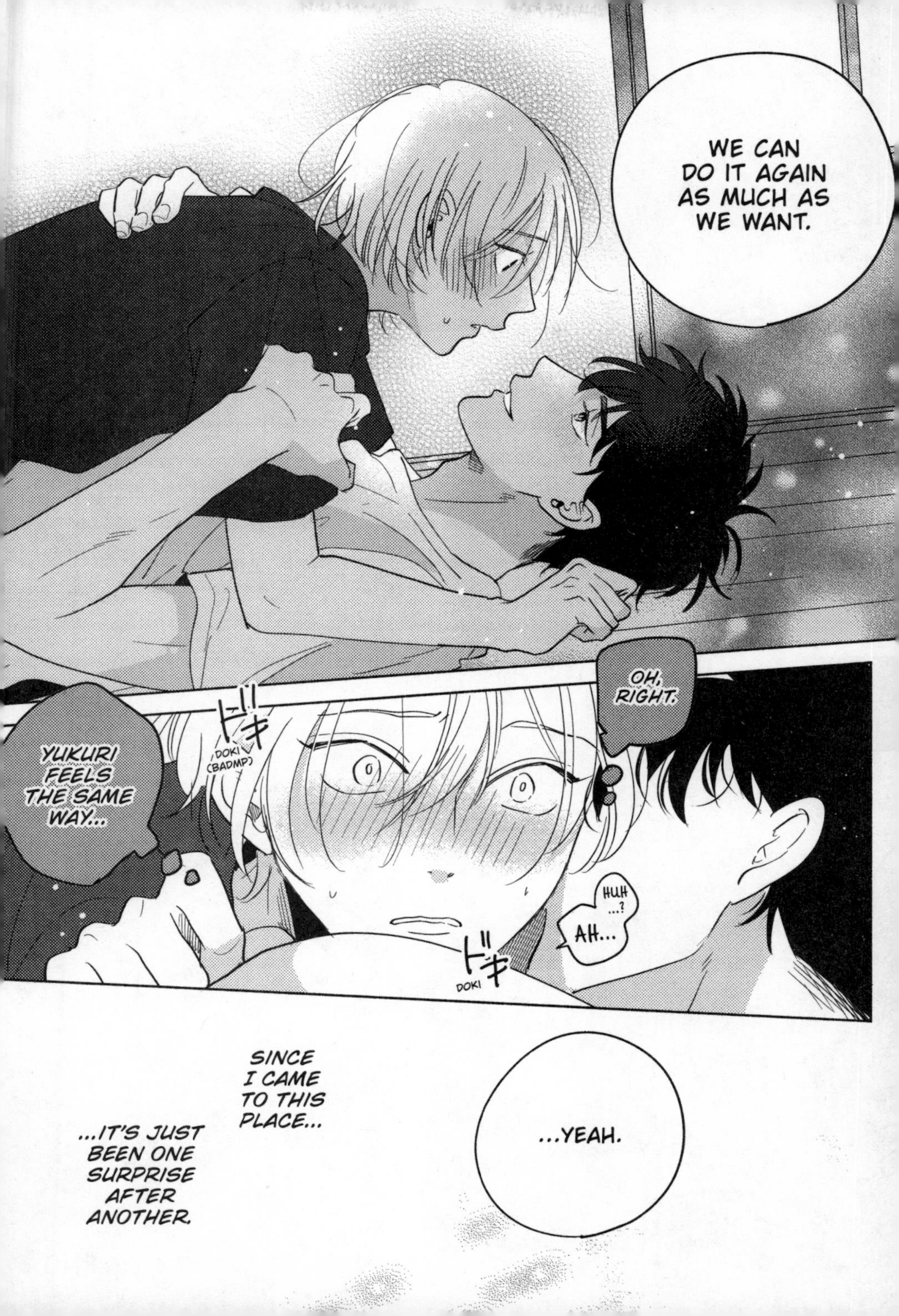
WE CAN DO IT AGAIN AS MUCH AS WE WANT.
OH, RIGHT.
DOKI (BADMP)
YUKURI FEELS THE SAME WAY...
HUH ...?
AH...
DOKI
...YEAH.
SINCE I CAME TO THIS PLACE...
...IT'S JUST BEEN ONE SURPRISE AFTER ANOTHER.

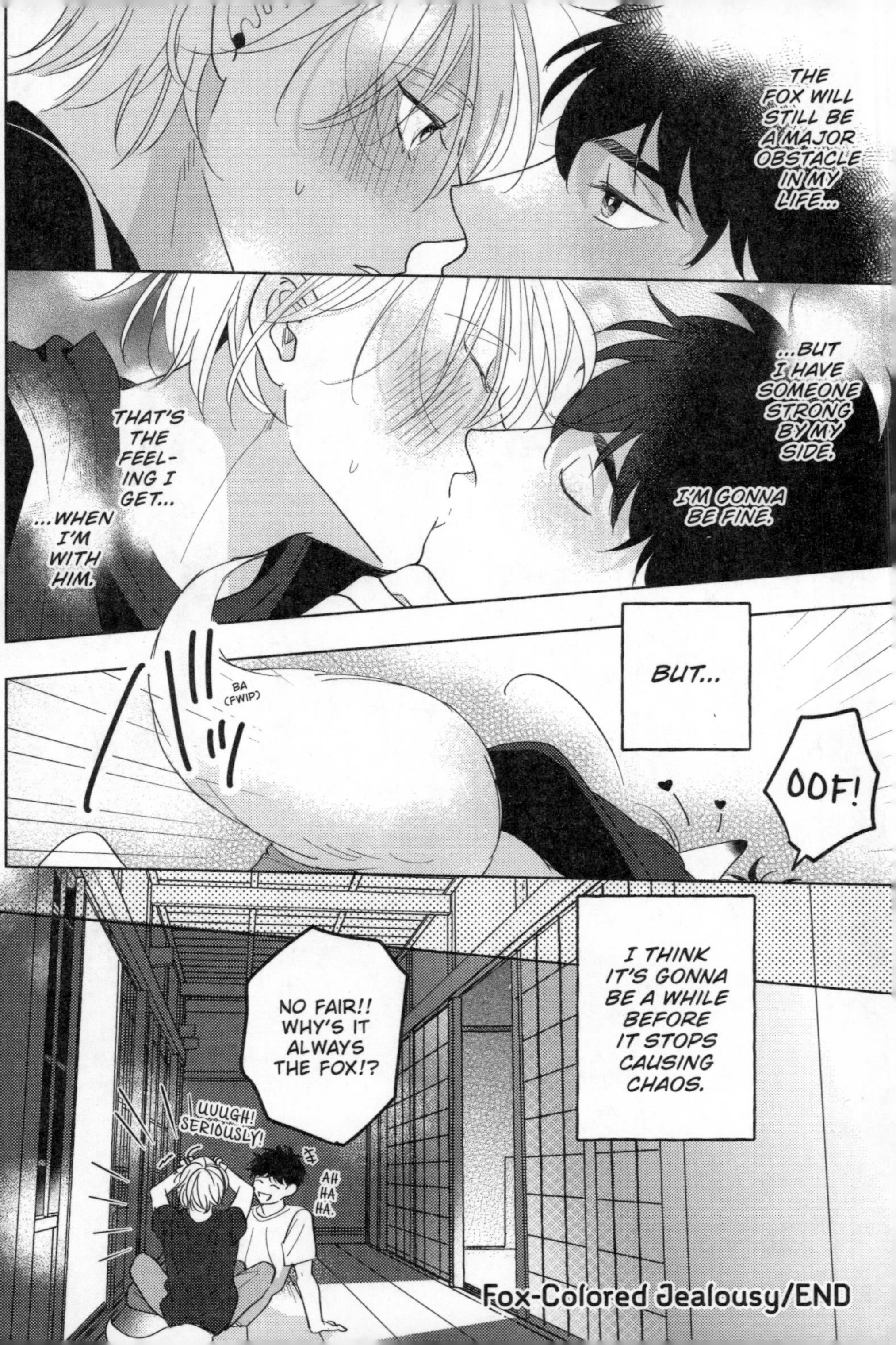
THE FOX WILL STILL BE A MAJOR OBSTACLE IN MY LIFE...
...BUT I HAVE SOMEONE STRONG BY MY SIDE.
I'M GONNA BE FINE.
THAT'S THE FEEL-ING I GET...
...WHEN I'M WITH HIM.
BUT...
OOF!
BA (FWIP)
I THINK IT'S GONNA BE A WHILE BEFORE IT STOPS CAUSING CHAOS.
NO FAIR!! WHY'S IT ALWAYS THE FOX!?
UUUGH! SERIOUSLY!
AH HA HA.
Fox-Colored Jealousy/END

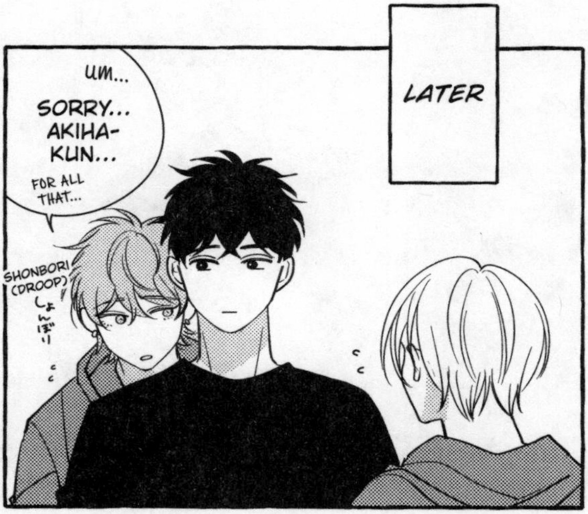
LATER
UM...
SORRY... AKIHA-KUN...
FOR ALL THAT...
SHONBORI (DROOP)
しょんぼり

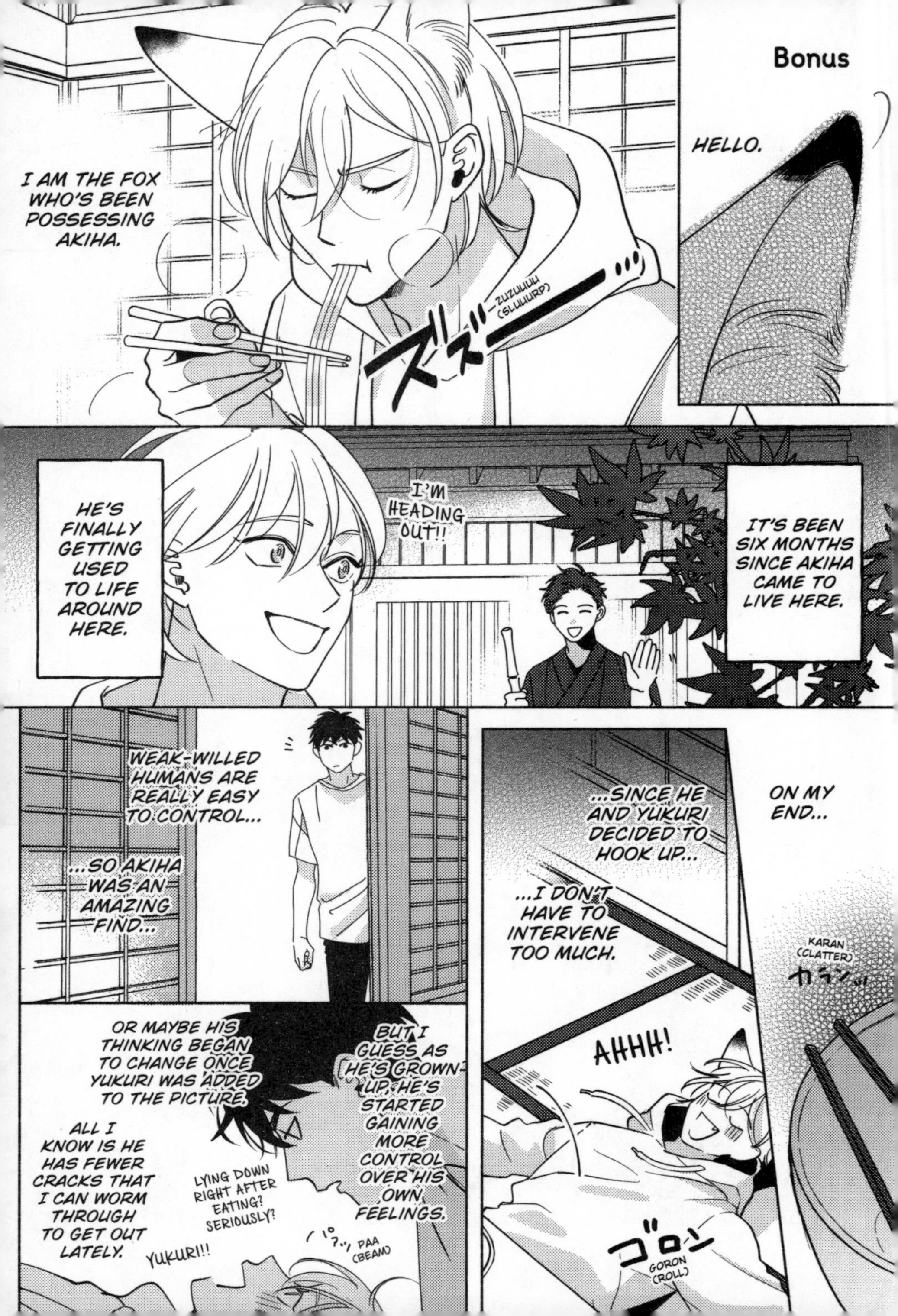
Bonus
HELLO.
I AM THE FOX WHO'S BEEN POSSESSING AKIHA.
ズズー
ZUZUUUU (SLUUURP)
IT'S BEEN SIX MONTHS SINCE AKIHA CAME TO LIVE HERE.
I'M HEADING OUT!!
HE'S FINALLY GETTING USED TO LIFE AROUND HERE.
ON MY END...
...SINCE HE AND YUKURI DECIDED TO HOOK UP...
...I DON'T HAVE TO INTERVENE TOO MUCH.
カラン
KARAN (CLATTER)
AHHH!
ゴロン
GORON (ROLL)
WEAK-WILLED HUMANS ARE REALLY EASY TO CONTROL...
...SO AKIHA WAS AN AMAZING FIND...
BUT I GUESS AS HE'S GROWN UP, HE'S STARTED GAINING MORE CONTROL OVER HIS OWN FEELINGS.
OR MAYBE HIS THINKING BEGAN TO CHANGE ONCE YUKURI WAS ADDED TO THE PICTURE.
ALL I KNOW IS HE HAS FEWER CRACKS THAT I CAN WORM THROUGH TO GET OUT LATELY.
LYING DOWN RIGHT AFTER EATING? SERIOUSLY?
パァッ
PAA (BEAM)
YUKURI!!

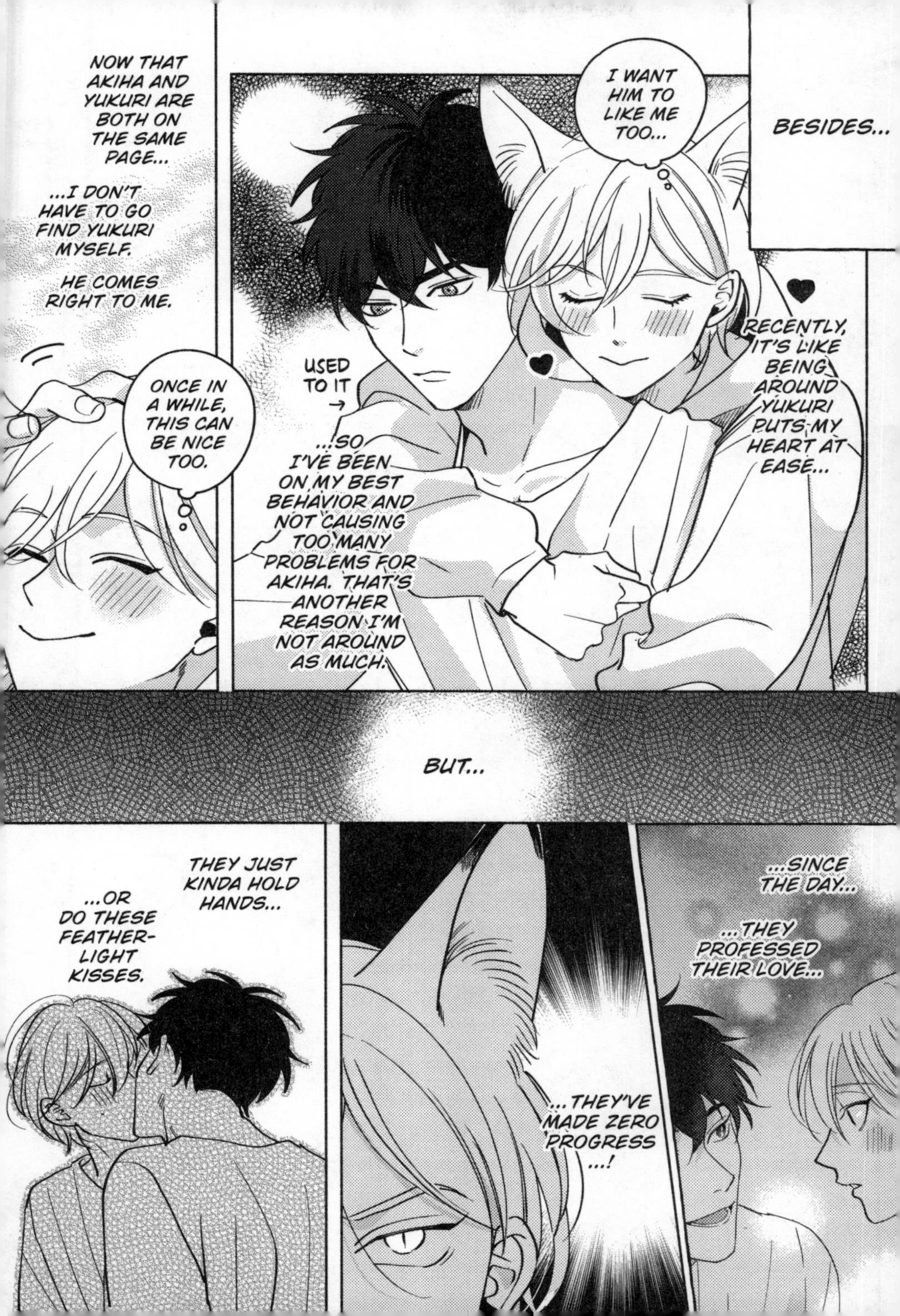
BESIDES...
I WANT HIM TO LIKE ME TOO...
RECENTLY, IT'S LIKE BEING AROUND YUKURI PUTS MY HEART AT EASE...
USED TO IT →
...SO I'VE BEEN ON MY BEST BEHAVIOR AND NOT CAUSING TOO MANY PROBLEMS FOR AKIHA. THAT'S ANOTHER REASON I'M NOT AROUND AS MUCH.
NOW THAT AKIHA AND YUKURI ARE BOTH ON THE SAME PAGE...
...I DON'T HAVE TO GO FIND YUKURI MYSELF.
HE COMES RIGHT TO ME.
ONCE IN A WHILE, THIS CAN BE NICE TOO.
BUT...
...SINCE THE DAY...
...THEY PROFESSED THEIR LOVE...
...THEY'VE MADE ZERO PROGRESS ...!
THEY JUST KINDA HOLD HANDS...
...OR DO THESE FEATHER-LIGHT KISSES.

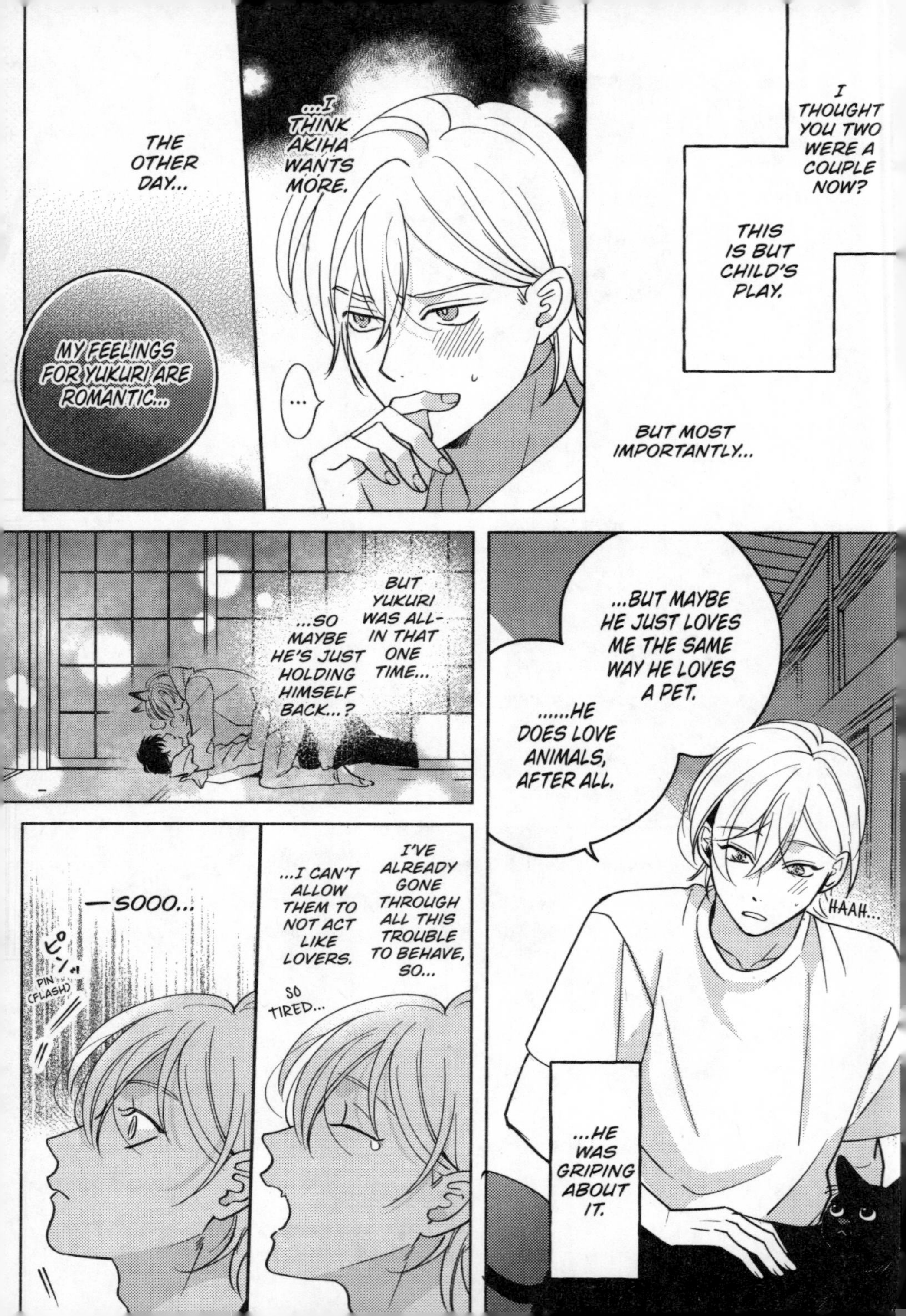
I THOUGHT YOU TWO WERE A COUPLE NOW?
THIS IS BUT CHILD'S PLAY.
BUT MOST IMPORTANTLY...
...I THINK AKIHA WANTS MORE.
...
THE OTHER DAY...
MY FEELINGS FOR YUKURI ARE ROMANTIC...
...BUT MAYBE HE JUST LOVES ME THE SAME WAY HE LOVES A PET.
......HE DOES LOVE ANIMALS, AFTER ALL.
HAAH...
...HE WAS GRIPING ABOUT IT.
BUT YUKURI WAS ALL-IN THAT ONE TIME...
...SO MAYBE HE'S JUST HOLDING HIMSELF BACK...?
I'VE ALREADY GONE THROUGH ALL THIS TROUBLE TO BEHAVE, SO...
...I CAN'T ALLOW THEM TO NOT ACT LIKE LOVERS.
SO TIRED...
—SOOO...
ピン
PIN (FLASH)

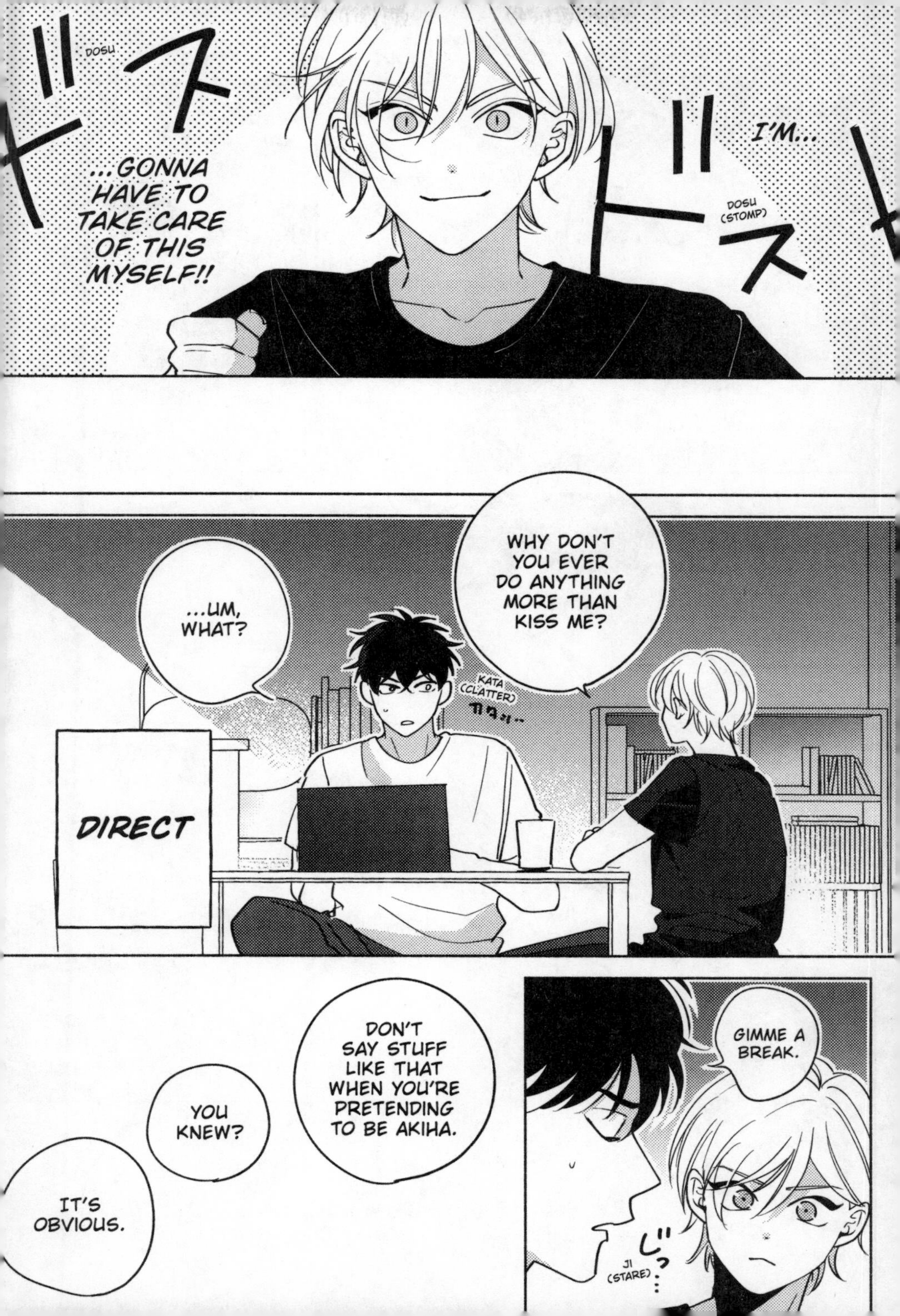
I'M...
DOSU (STOMP)
...GONNA HAVE TO TAKE CARE OF THIS MYSELF!!
DOSU
WHY DON'T YOU EVER DO ANYTHING MORE THAN KISS ME?
KATA (CLATTER)
...UM, WHAT?
DIRECT
GIMME A BREAK.
JI (STARE)
DON'T SAY STUFF LIKE THAT WHEN YOU'RE PRETENDING TO BE AKIHA.
YOU KNEW?
IT'S OBVIOUS.

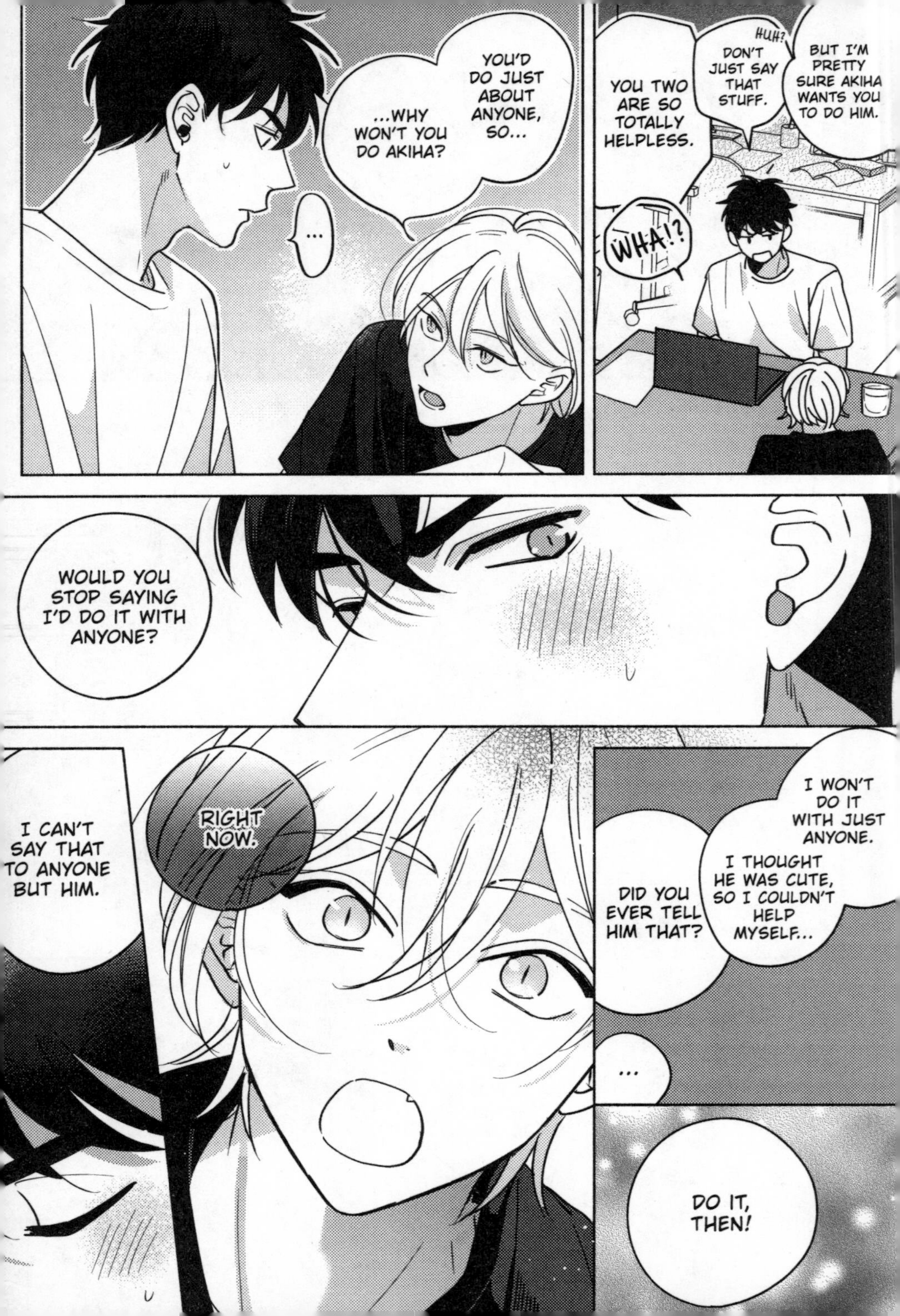
BUT I'M PRETTY SURE AKIHA WANTS YOU TO DO HIM.
HUH?
DON'T JUST SAY THAT STUFF.
YOU TWO ARE SO TOTALLY HELPLESS.
WHA!?
YOU'D DO JUST ABOUT ANYONE, SO...
...WHY WON'T YOU DO AKIHA?
...
WOULD YOU STOP SAYING I'D DO IT WITH ANYONE?
I WON'T DO IT WITH JUST ANYONE.
I THOUGHT HE WAS CUTE, SO I COULDN'T HELP MYSELF...
DID YOU EVER TELL HIM THAT?
...
DO IT, THEN!
RIGHT NOW.
I CAN'T SAY THAT TO ANYONE BUT HIM.

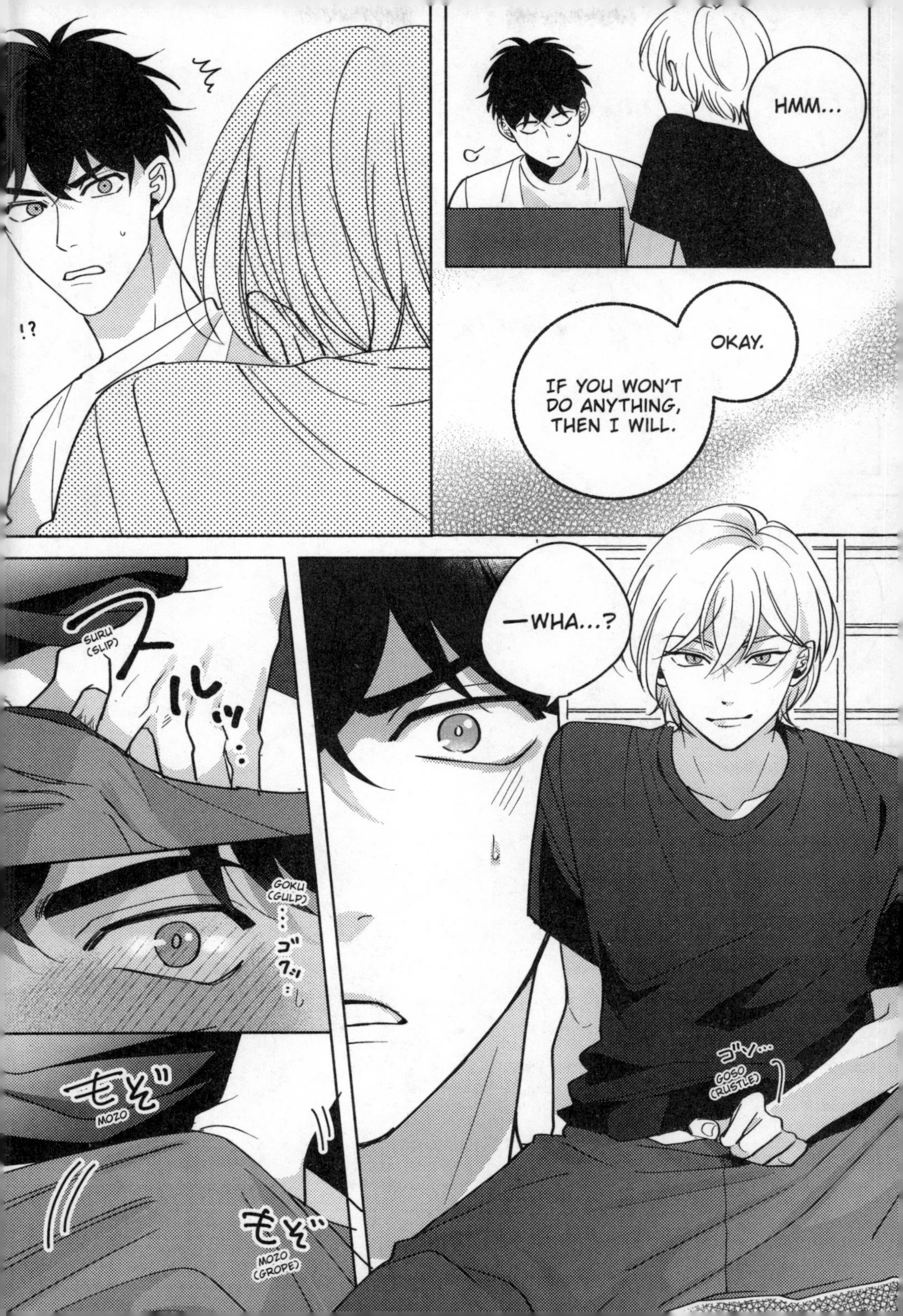
HMM...
OKAY.
IF YOU WON'T DO ANYTHING, THEN I WILL.
!?
—WHA...?
ゴソ…
GOSO (RUSTLE)
スルッ…
SURU (SLIP)
…ゴクッ…
GOKU (GULP)
もぞ
MOZO
もぞ
MOZO (GROPE)

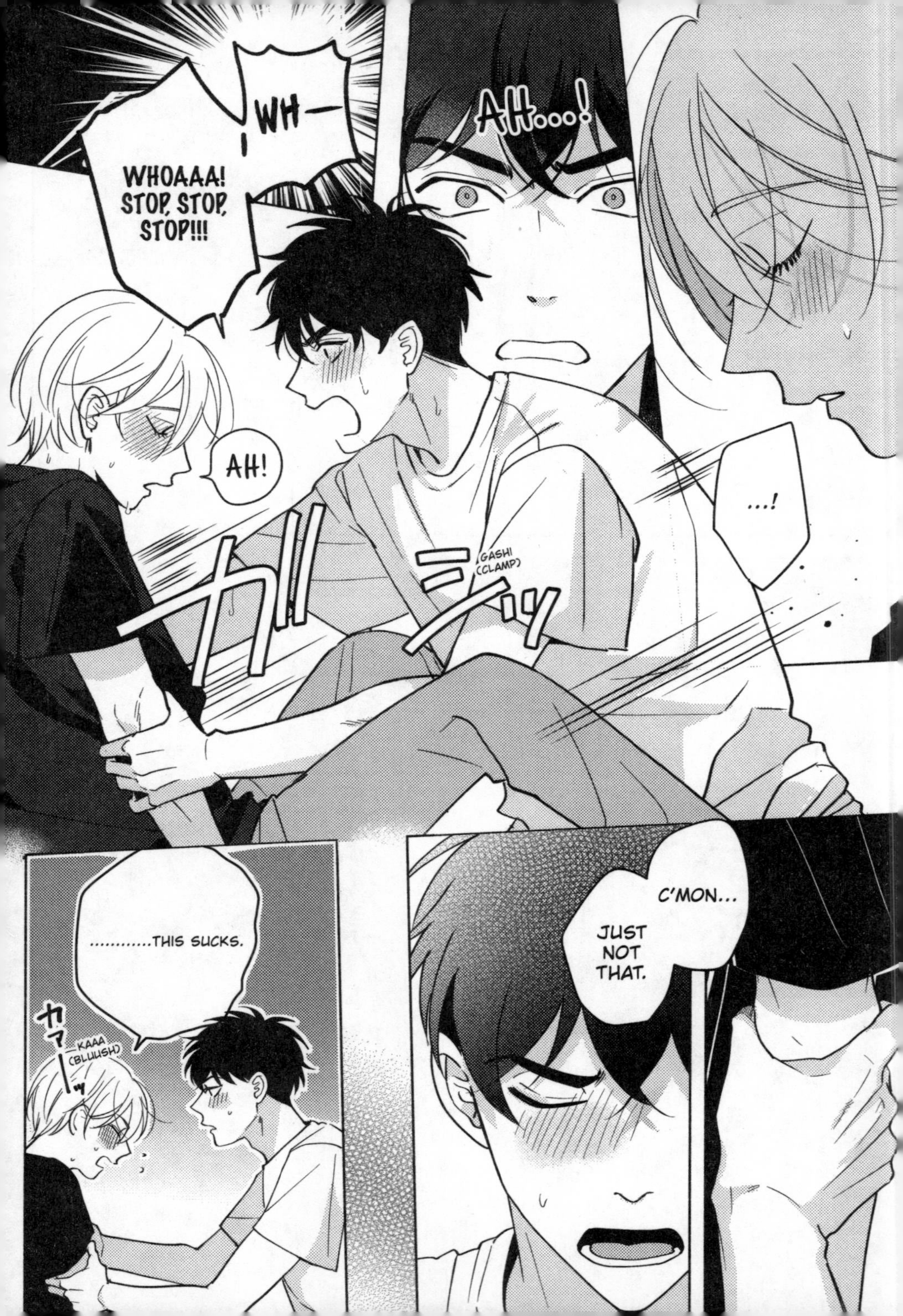
AH...!
...!
WH—
WHOAAA! STOP, STOP, STOP!!!
AH!
ガシッ
GASHI (CLAMP)
C'MON...
JUST NOT THAT.
............THIS SUCKS.
カァーッ
KAAA (BLUUSH)

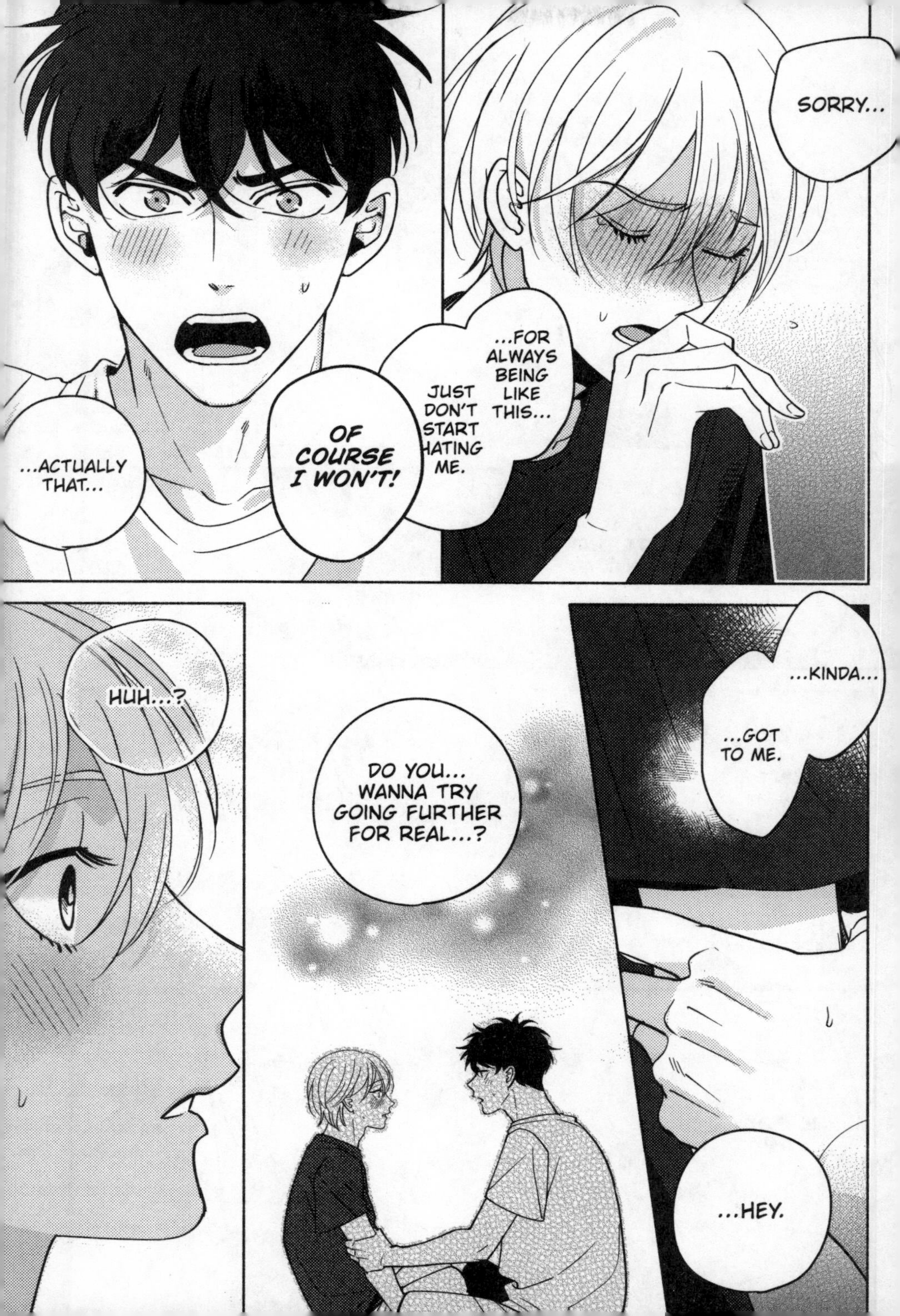
SORRY...
...FOR ALWAYS BEING LIKE THIS...
JUST DON'T START HATING ME.
OF COURSE I WON'T!
...ACTUALLY THAT...
...KINDA...
...GOT TO ME.
...HEY.
DO YOU... WANNA TRY GOING FURTHER FOR REAL...?
HUH...?

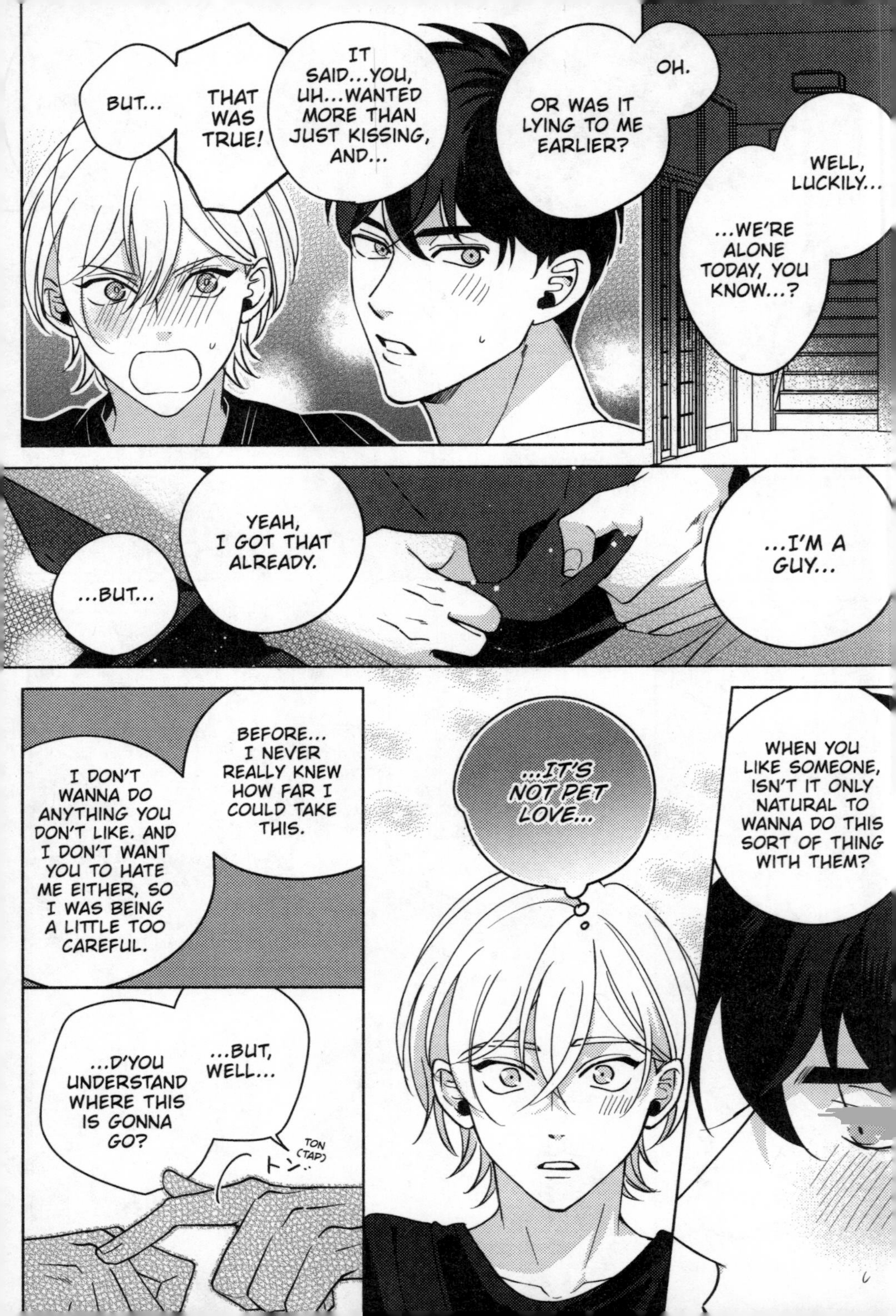
WELL, LUCKILY...
...WE'RE ALONE TODAY, YOU KNOW...?
OH.
OR WAS IT LYING TO ME EARLIER?
IT SAID...YOU, UH...WANTED MORE THAN JUST KISSING, AND...
THAT WAS TRUE!
BUT...
...I'M A GUY...
YEAH, I GOT THAT ALREADY.
...BUT...
WHEN YOU LIKE SOMEONE, ISN'T IT ONLY NATURAL TO WANNA DO THIS SORT OF THING WITH THEM?
...IT'S NOT PET LOVE...
BEFORE... I NEVER REALLY KNEW HOW FAR I COULD TAKE THIS.
I DON'T WANNA DO ANYTHING YOU DON'T LIKE. AND I DON'T WANT YOU TO HATE ME EITHER, SO I WAS BEING A LITTLE TOO CAREFUL.
...BUT, WELL...
...D'YOU UNDERSTAND WHERE THIS IS GONNA GO?
TON (TAP)

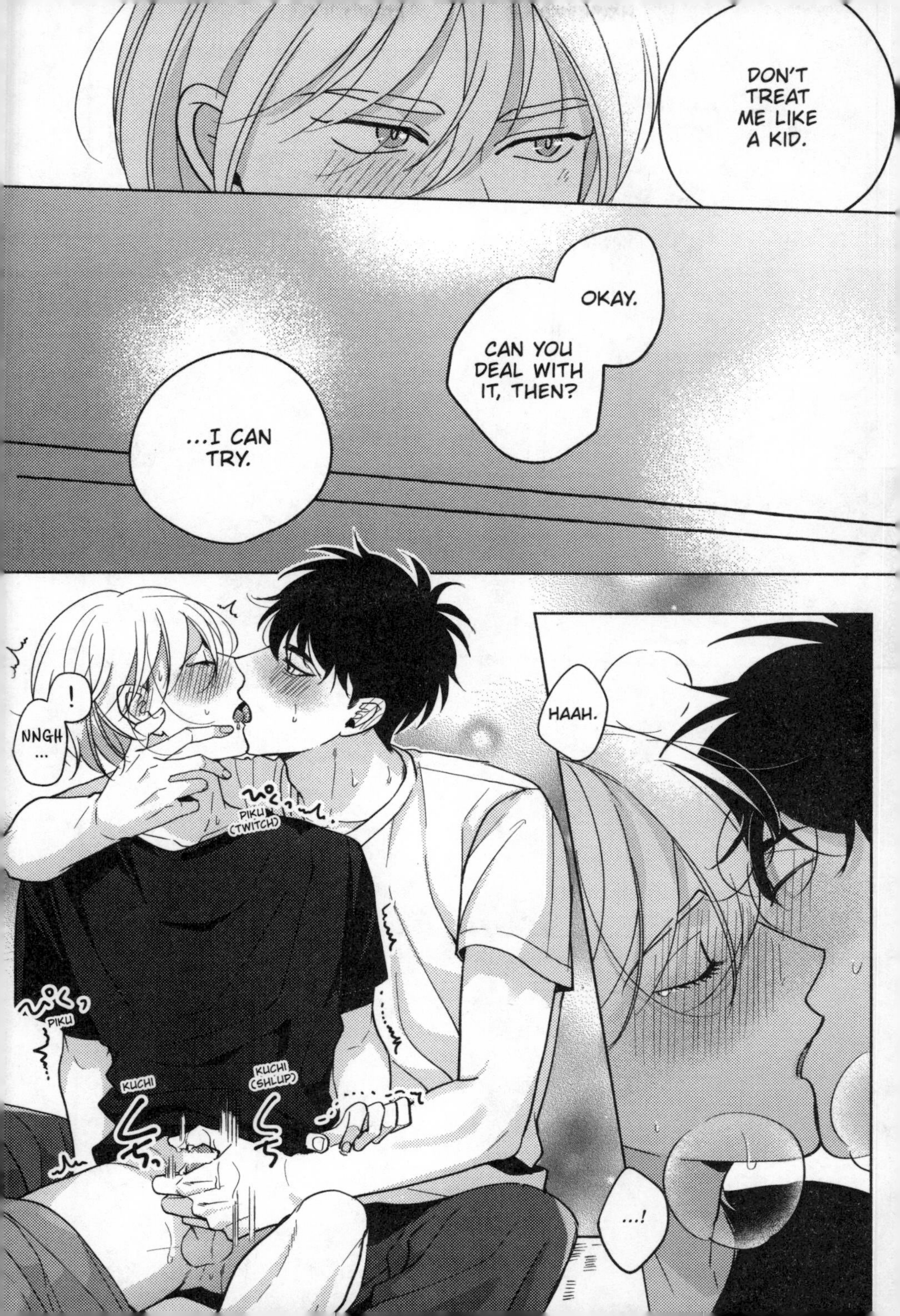
DON'T TREAT ME LIKE A KID.
OKAY.
CAN YOU DEAL WITH IT, THEN?
...I CAN TRY.
HAAH.
...!
!
NNGH ...
PIKU (TWITCH)
PIKU
KUCHI (SHLUP)
KUCHI

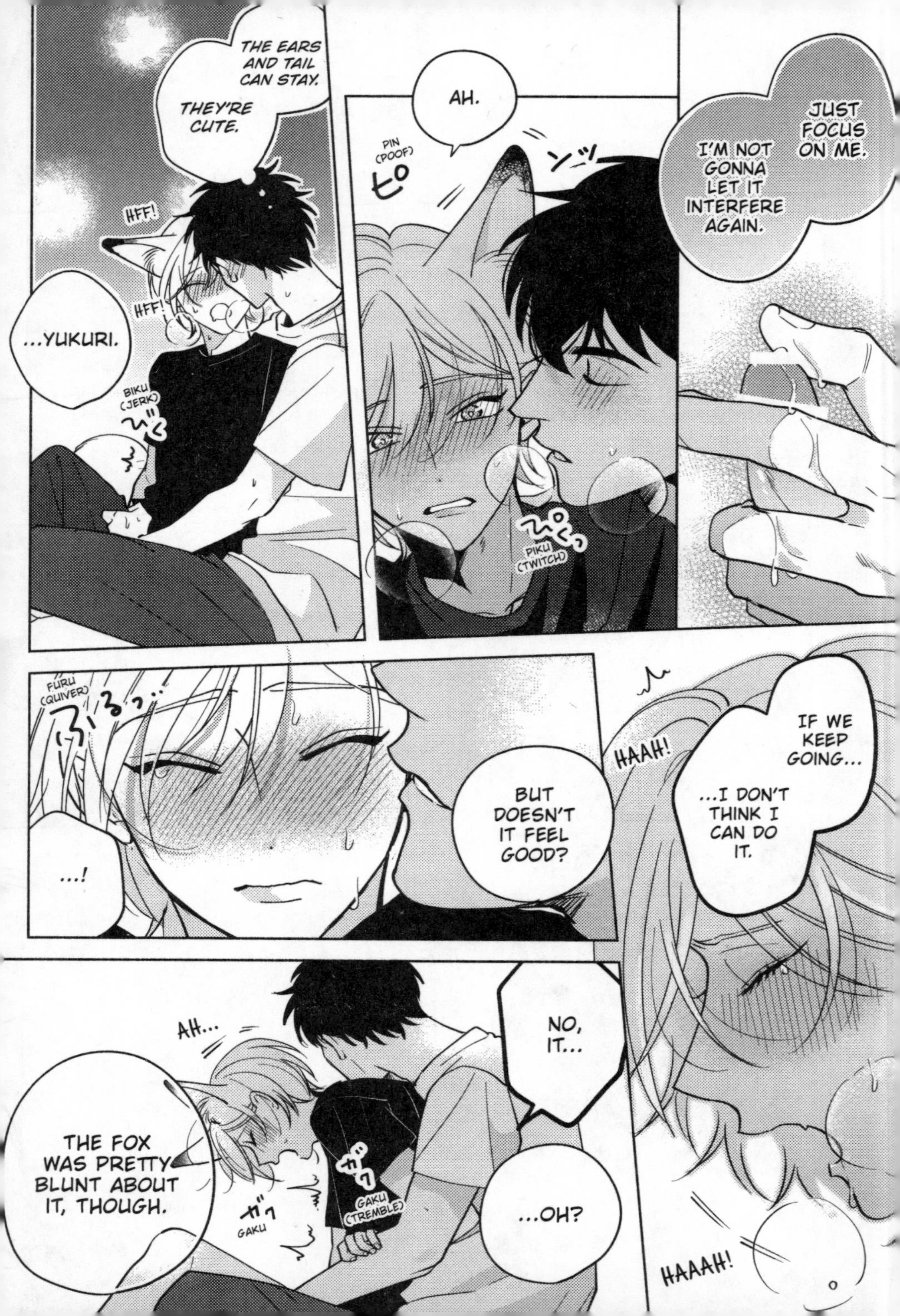
JUST FOCUS ON ME.
I'M NOT GONNA LET IT INTERFERE AGAIN.
AH.
PIN (POOF)
PIKU (TWITCH)
THE EARS AND TAIL CAN STAY.
THEY'RE CUTE.
HFF!
HFF!
...YUKURI.
BIKU (JERK)
IF WE KEEP GOING...
...I DON'T THINK I CAN DO IT.
HAAH!
HAAAH!
BUT DOESN'T IT FEEL GOOD?
FURU (QUIVER)
...!
NO, IT...
AH...
...OH?
GAKU (TREMBLE)
GAKU
THE FOX WAS PRETTY BLUNT ABOUT IT, THOUGH.

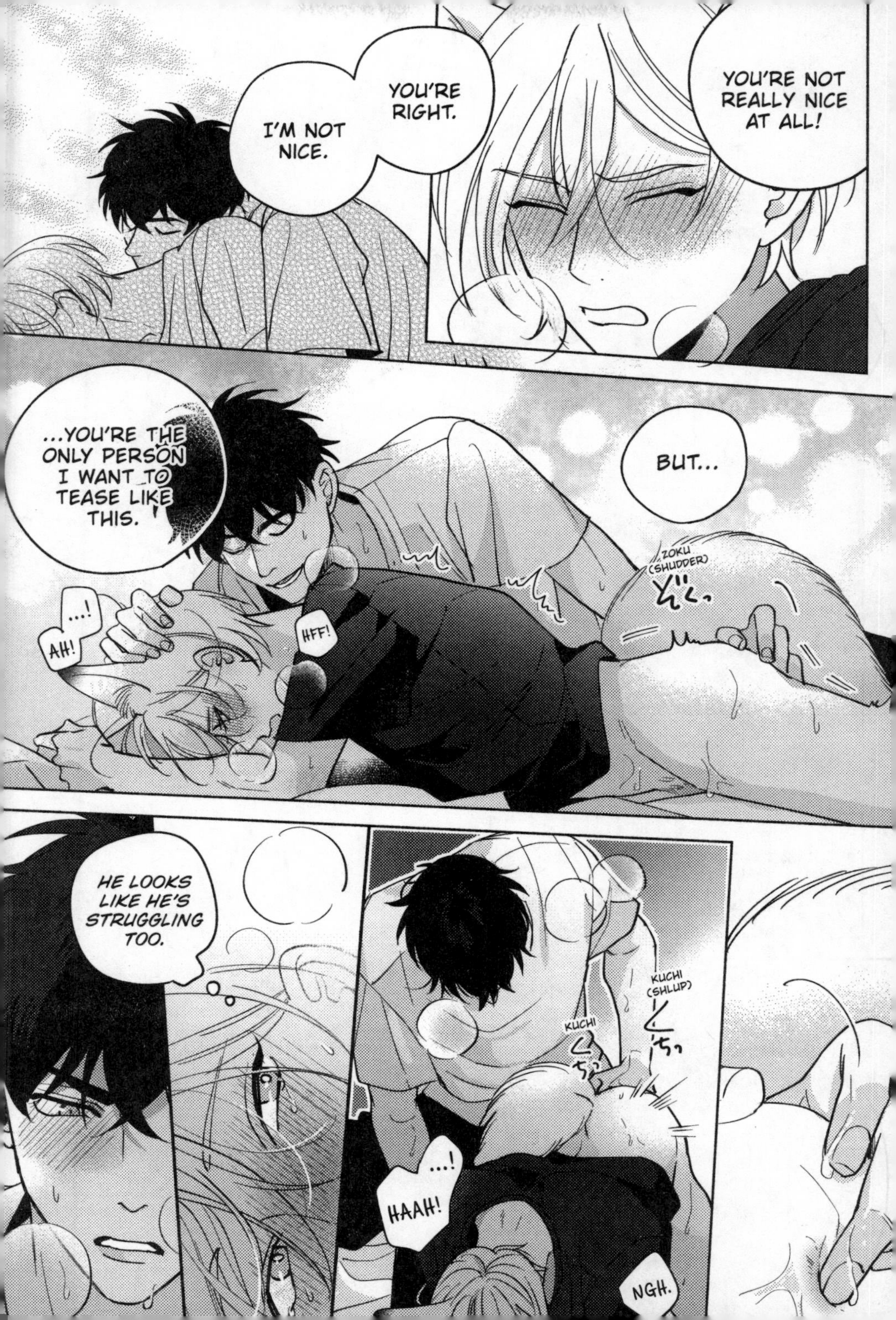
YOU'RE NOT REALLY NICE AT ALL!
YOU'RE RIGHT.
I'M NOT NICE.
BUT...
...YOU'RE THE ONLY PERSON I WANT TO TEASE LIKE THIS.
ZOKU (SHUDDER)
ぞくっ
HFF!
...!
AH!
KUCHI (SHLUP)
くちっ
KUCHI
くちっ
...!
HAAH!
NGH.
HE LOOKS LIKE HE'S STRUGGLING TOO.

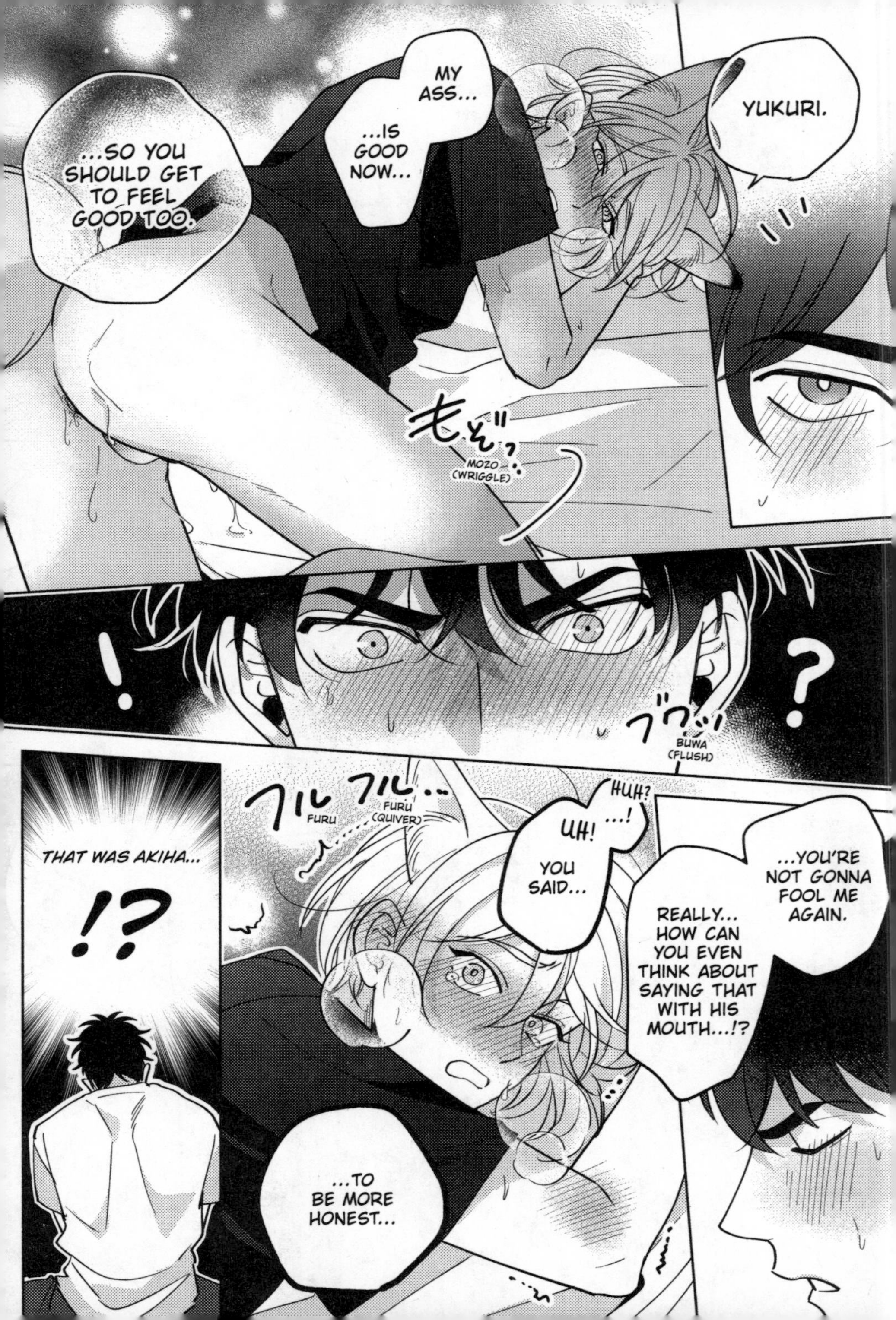
YUKURI.
MY ASS...
...IS GOOD NOW...
...SO YOU SHOULD GET TO FEEL GOOD TOO.
もぞっ
MOZO (WRIGGLE)
!
?
ブワッ
BUWA (FLUSH)
...YOU'RE NOT GONNA FOOL ME AGAIN.
REALLY... HOW CAN YOU EVEN THINK ABOUT SAYING THAT WITH HIS MOUTH...!?
HUH? ...!
UH!
YOU SAID...
...TO BE MORE HONEST...
フル フル...
FURU FURU (QUIVER)
THAT WAS AKIHA...
!?

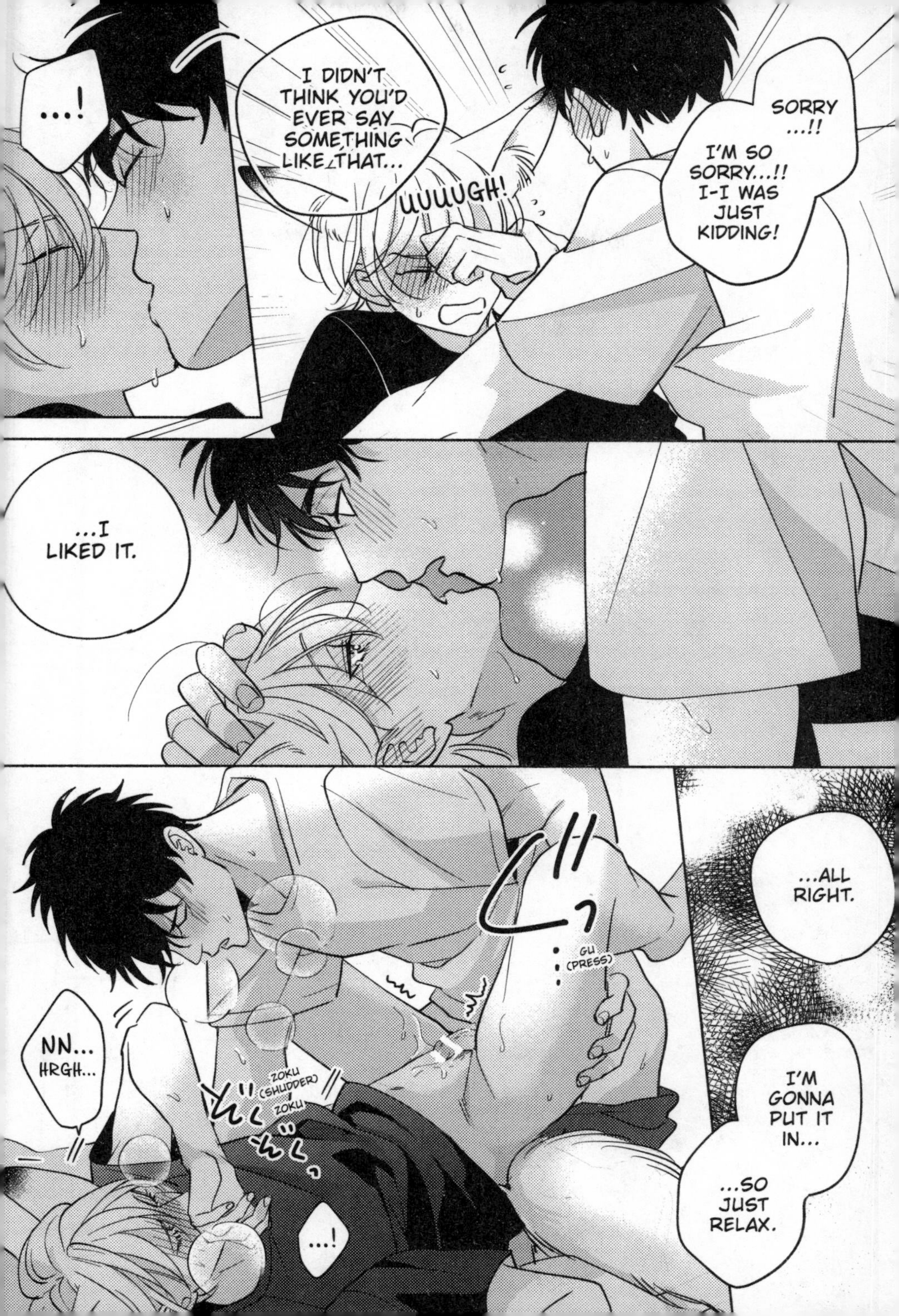
SORRY ...!!
I'M SO SORRY...!! I-I WAS JUST KIDDING!
I DIDN'T THINK YOU'D EVER SAY SOMETHING LIKE THAT...
UUUUGH!
...!
...I LIKED IT.
...ALL RIGHT.
I'M GONNA PUT IT IN...
...SO JUST RELAX.
GU (PRESS)
ZOKU (SHUDDER) ZOKU
NN... HRGH...
...!

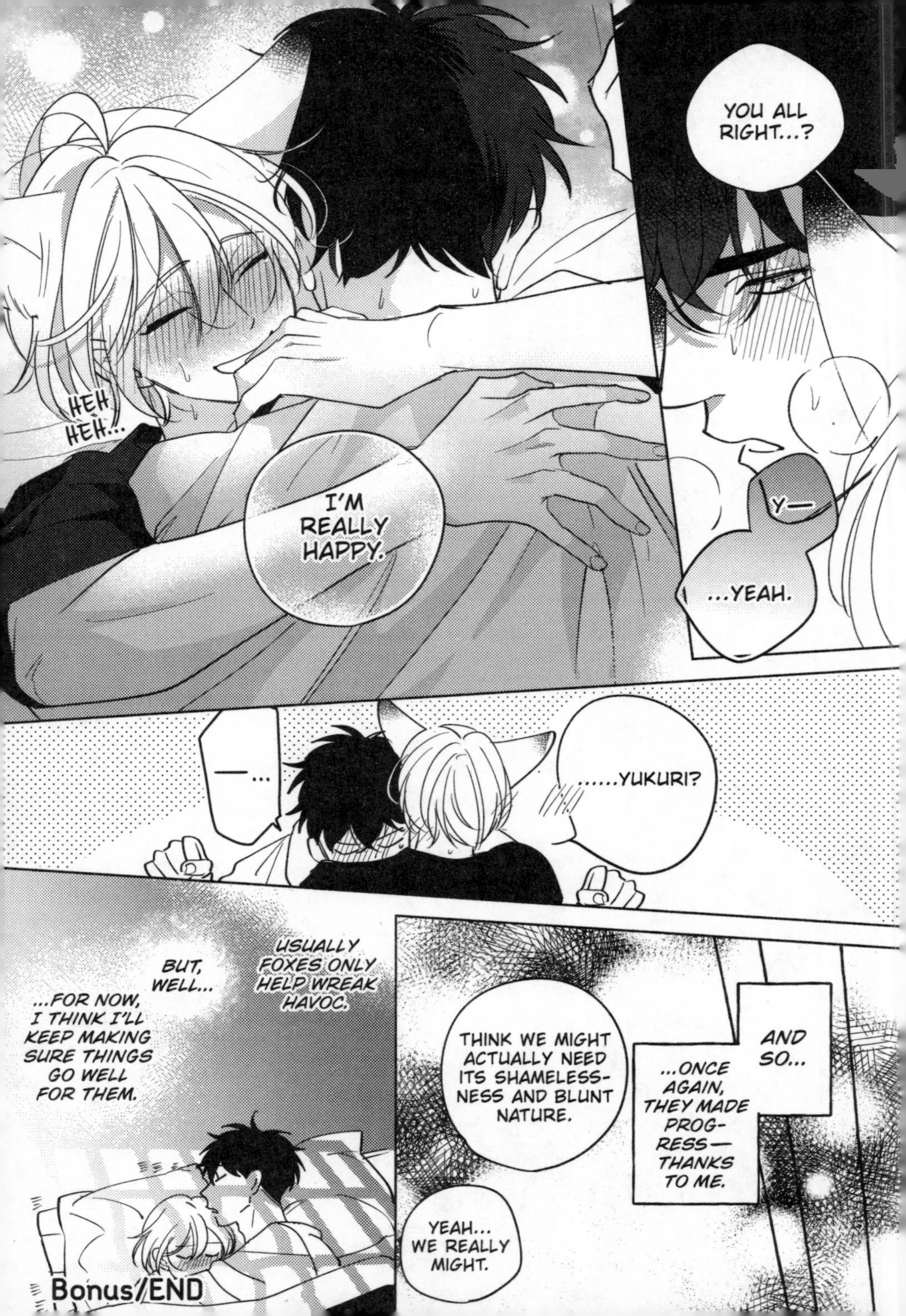
YOU ALL RIGHT...?
Y—
...YEAH.
HEH HEH...
I'M REALLY HAPPY.
......YUKURI?
—...
AND SO...
...ONCE AGAIN, THEY MADE PROGRESS—THANKS TO ME.
THINK WE MIGHT ACTUALLY NEED ITS SHAMELESSNESS AND BLUNT NATURE.
YEAH... WE REALLY MIGHT.
USUALLY FOXES ONLY HELP WREAK HAVOC.
BUT, WELL...
...FOR NOW, I THINK I'LL KEEP MAKING SURE THINGS GO WELL FOR THEM.
Bonus/END

Fox-Colored jealousy

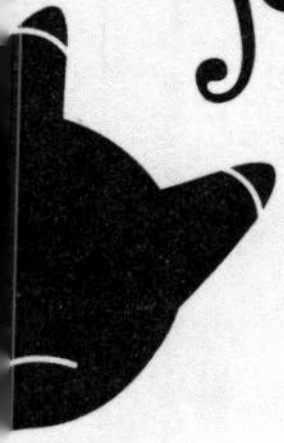

Fox-Colored Jealousy

Machi Suehiro

Translation: Leighann Harvey   Lettering: Dietrich Premier

YAKIMOCHI WA KITSUNE IRO
© 2020 by Machi Suehiro/HOME-SHA Inc.
All rights reserved. First published in Japan in
2020 by HOME-SHA Inc. English translation
rights arranged with SHUEISHA, Inc. through
Tuttle-Mori Agency, Inc., Tokyo.

English translation © 2024 by Yen Press, LLC

Yen Press
150 West 30th Street, 19th Floor
New York, NY 10001

Visit us at yenpress.com
facebook.com/yenpress
twitter.com/yenpress
yenpress.tumblr.com
instagram.com/yenpress

First Yen Press Edition: April 2024
Edited by Yen Press Editorial: Danielle Niederkorn
Designed by Yen Press Design: Lilliana Checo

Yen Press is an imprint of Yen Press, LLC.
The Yen Press name and logo are trademarks of
Yen Press, LLC.

Library of Congress Control Number:
2024930149

ISBNs: 978-1-9753-9058-7 (paperback)
       978-1-9753-9059-4 (ebook)

10 9 8 7 6 5 4 3 2 1

WOR

Printed in the United States of America